NORTH CAROLINA SLAVES
AND
FREE PERSONS OF COLOR

PASQUOTANK COUNTY

William L. Byrd, III

HERITAGE BOOKS
2006

HERITAGE BOOKS
AN IMPRINT OF HERITAGE BOOKS, INC.

Books, CDs, and more—Worldwide

For our listing of thousands of titles see our website
at
www.HeritageBooks.com

Published 2006 by
HERITAGE BOOKS, INC.
Publishing Division
65 East Main Street
Westminster, Maryland 21157-5026

International Standard Book Number: 978 -0-7884-3284-2

For David and Miguel

Contents

Introduction

The records in this book were transcribed from original papers located in the North Carolina State Archives. Most of these papers are listed under general headings such as "Slaves and Free Negroes," or "Slaves and Free Persons of Color." Occasionally they are listed under the heading of "Miscellaneous Records".[1]

This particular group of papers were selected from the North Carolina county of Pasquotank. Not a few of these records are torn and faded. In some cases, part of the original text is missing, and many of the names of individuals are almost indecipherable. Nevertheless, every attempt has been made to transcribe these papers as accurately as possible.

Included are many civil and criminal actions pertaining to slaves and free persons of color. The interactions between both Blacks and Whites are displayed on an antagonistic and intimate level, and are dramatically played out through crime and punishment. The criminal cases are filled with intrigue involving murder, felonies, trading with slaves and harboring slaves.

---

[1] Thornton W. Mitchell, "Preliminary Guide to Records Relating to Blacks in the North Carolina State Archives," ***Archives Information Circular*** 17(June 1980): 3-4.

The different sections are broken down into the following categories: Petitions to Sell or Divide Slaves, Civil Actions, Concealment of a Slave, Patrol Records, Insurrection Papers, Negroes Taken Up, Criminal Actions, Bills of Sale, and Miscellaneous.

Pasquotank was created in 1670 as a precinct of Albemarle County. It was named after the Pasquotank Indians, who lived in that part of the State.

Pasquotank was bounded by Albemarle Sound and Perquimans, Gates, and Camden counties. The date of the first courthouse has not been ascertained. However, from 1737 to 1757, the courthouse was located at Brook Field. Some years later it was moved to Relfe's Point. From 1765 until 1785 the courthouse was located at Winfield. Soon after, the Assembly decided to move it to Nixonton. In 1800, Elizabeth City was named as the county seat, and remained as the county seat to the present day.[2]

---

[2] David Leroy Corbitt, ***The Formation of the North Carolina Counties: 1663 - 1943*** (Raleigh: Division of Archives and History, 1950) 65-66

Acknowledgements

All acknowledgements regarding this book belong to the staff of the North Carolina State Archives. Without their help, it would not have been possible.

Chapter One

Pasquotank County

Petitions to Sell or Divide Slaves

North Carolina State Archives
Pasquotank County Records
Records of Slaves and Free Persons of Color
C.R.075.928.10

Watsons Petition
[No Date]

North Carolina }
Pasquotank County }

To the Worshipful the Justices of Pasquotank County
The Petition of Alexander Watson Sheweth that your Petitioner in Right of his Wife was Intituled to one third part of a Negro Fellow named Jupiter and that he hath since purchased one other of Stephan Briant[?], and that the remaining Third belongs to Rebecca Williams your Petitioner therefore

Prays an Order for the Sale of the afsd Negroe in Order to pay to the said Rebecca her third part of the Money arising by the Sale.
Alexr. Watson

****

[No Date]

John L Trotman, Admr., to the Court
Petition to Sell Slaves
Order Made, Sale Made
Issue Ex. For Costs
Jordan, Solicitor

Two Orders with Seals & & Postage made on this Petition
Direct Letters to Mintonville, Gates Co.

To the Worshipful Court

Your Petitioner Zachariah Nixon represents that he is the Administrater of John L Trotman - that is necessary to Sell two Slaves, Adeline & Balinda, & Joanna and [?] to pay the debts of the Intestate and prays the Court herewith to Sell the same and as in duty bound &c
Jordan, Solicitor

On hearing this Petition the Court being Satisfied of the allegations in the bill orders that the Administrator to Sell the Slaves Mentioned in this Petition To Wit & Joanna to the highest bidder for Cash or Credit of 6 Months and make due return of the Same to the next Court.

****

Richd Pool et al
To Sell a Negroe
The Court
Court of Pleas & Quarter Sessions Sept. Term 1818

To the Worshipful, the Parties now Sitting
Your Petitioner Richard Pool, Joshua Raper & Ann Raper infants under 21 years of age by their guardian Richd. Pool, Show to your Worships that

your Petr. Are tenants in Common of a certain Negroe man named Jim, aged about fifty years, & that they are desirous of making a division of said negroe, they therefore pray your Worships to decree a sale of said negroe at such place & on such credit as to your Worships shall deem proper so that a division may be affected, And as in duty bound.
Tho. D. Martin
Atto for Pltf

Court of Pleas & Quarter Sessions, Sept. Term 1818
To the Worshipful the Justices now Setting

Your Petitioner Richard Pool, Joshua Raper & Ann Raper infants under 21 Years of age, by their Guardian Richard Pool, Show to your Worships that your Petitioners are tenants in common of a certain Negro Man named Jim, aged about fifty years, & that they therefore are desirous of making a Division of said Negro, they therefore pray your Worships to decree a Sale of said Negro at such place and on such Credit as your Worships Shall deem Proper, so that a division so that a division may be effected, and as in duty bound &c.
Thos. D. Martin, Atto for Petr.
Copy Test
Will: T. Muse, Clk

State of North Carolina }
Pasquotank County }
On Petition of Richard Pool & others, Ordered that he have leave to Sell negro man Jim on a Credit of Six Months before the Court House door in Elizabeth City, he Advertising the said negro as the law directs, & taking Bond with approved Security from the purchaser, & Make a Report of his Proceedings thereon to the next Term of this Court.
Test, Will: T. Muse, Clk

Richard Pool & Als, Copy of the Peto. & to Order for Sale of a Negro
The Court
Recorded in Book C Page 168.
Pasquotank, December Term 1818

Returned Dec Term 1818, & ordered to be [?]

Pasquotank County
Petitions to sell or Divide Slaves

Will: T. Muse, Clk

Account of Sale of the Negroe within mentioned, Sold the 28 August 1818, 2 thirds of Jim To Richard Pool $205.33
John Pool

****

Will T. Muse, Bill of Costs
Jno. Curran et al
William T. , Bill of Costs
John Curran et al

State Tax	2.00
3 Subpoenas at 10/p	3.00
3 Copies of Bill, 18 Copy sheets at 2/ pr copy Sheet	3.60
2 Continuances at 1/3 each	0.25
Dismission	0.20
Sheriff of Perquimans for Service of Subpoenas	
Shf Pasquotank for service two Subpoenas	
James Iredell Comptt Solicitor	
	20.00

This Indenture Tripartite, made this 18th day of January in the year of our Lord one thousand eight hundred an nineteen between John Carran of Pasquotank County of the first part, William T. Muse of the said County of the second part, & Thomas D. Martin who is mutually chosen trustee by the aforesaid parties of the other part -
And State of North Carolina; Witnesseth, that Whereas the said John Corran stands justly indebted to the said William T. Muse in the sum of nine hundred eighty & eight dollars 98/100 due by bond bearing date even date with these presents which he the said John Corran honestly desires to secure and pay. In consideration thereof, and in, and in further consideration of the sum of fifty cents, to him in hand paid by the said Thomas D. Martin trustee aforesaid before the signing, sealing and delivery of these presents, the receipt whereof the said John Corran doth hereby acknowledge, the said John Curran doth for himself, his Heirs and Assigns, give grant, bargain, Sell and Deliver, and by these presents hath

given, granted, bargained, sold and delivered to the said Thomas D. Martin his Heirs and Assigns forever, for the purposes herein after mentioned, The following negroe slaves, to wit, negroe man Luke, Eden, and Quilla, and negroe women Sylvia and Lydia and their increase., to have and to hold, The above described negroe Slaves and every part thereof, with all the rights and privileges thereunto belonging, free and clear from the lawful claim or claims or incumbrances of any person whatever, unto him the said Thomas D. Martin, his Heirs and Assigns forever: In Trust Nevertheless, that he the said Thomas D. Martin or his Heirs shall and may at any time after the first day of June next, ensuing sell the said negroe Slaves to the highest bidder for ready money at such time and place as he the said Thomas D. Martin or his Heirs shall think proper, first giving Ten days notice by public advertisement of the time and place of sale, and the money arising from such Sale to apply to the discharge of the aforesaid debt of John Corran aforesaid due and owing to the said William T. Muse or so much thereof as may then remain due and unpaid, and also the interest thereon, together with the costs of advertising, recording this instrument, and all other costs accruing by reasons of these presents, and to make and execute Bills of Sale to the purchaser thereof, and the balance of the money, if any, to be paid to the said John Corran his Heirs or Assigns It is expressly understood by all the parties to these presents, that the aforesaid negroes, shall remain in the possession of the said John Corran untill the first day of June next, ensuing the date of these presents. In witness whereof we the above named have hereunto set our hands and seals the day and the year first above written

Signed, Sealed, and delivered in the presence of John C Ehringhaus

John Corran (Seal)
Will: T. Muse (Seal)
Tho D. Martin (Seal)

John Corran, Deed of Trust
William T. Muse
Registerd

State of North Carolina }
Pasquotank County }

Pasquotank County
Petitions to sell or Divide Slaves

This Deed in Trust from John Carren to Thomas D Martin for the use of William T. Muse was entitled and prooved in open Court by the oath of John C. Ehringhaus Ordered to be registered
Test, Will T. Muse, Clk
Registered May the 12th 1819 in Book & Page 225.
By John C Ehringhaus

****

William Banks et al
To Pto. Sale negroe
The Court, Prayer granted

Court of Pleas and Quarter Sessions March Term 1819

To the worshipful the Justices now sitting:

Humbly complaining shew unto your worships your petitioners William Banks, Patsey Banks, Thaddeus Banks and Jonathan Banks infants under 21 years of age by Abraham Fletcher their guardian, that they are the joint owner of a negroe man of the name of Ben who is confined in the jail of Pasquotank under a feloneous charge, and should he be convicted thereof, an entire loss of his value in money will accrue to your petitioner; They therefore pray your worships to pass an order authorising their said guardian to Sell said negroe Ben, to some speculator in human flesh that he may be carried beyond the limits of this State, So that the good citizens of this State may be relieved from all apprehensions of the Commissioner of future crimes by said negroe, and his value in money be secured to your Petitioners, and as in duty bound your petitioners, shall ever pray &c.
Tho. D. Martin, Atto for the petitioners.

****

Division Between Benj. & Thomas Harvey
June 5th 1819
Retd June Seven 1819 and ordered to be recorded
Test, Will: T. Muse
Recorded in Book G, Page 14

Persuant to the requested of Benjn and Thomas Harvey, we the Subscribers have proceeded to Value and divide the Negroes belonging Jointly between them in the following manner this 5th day of June 1819

Pasquotank County
Petitions to sell or Divide Slaves

Thomas Harveys Negroes	
Bill	$650
Edmund	625
Abraham	375
Joe	600
Frank	600
Sampsam	325
Polepus	300
Patience & 3 Children	816.66
Mariah	500
Pleasant	400
	$5191. [?]

To Balance due from Benjn to Thomas Harvey 58-34
Thomas Halfe for Keeping Pheabe 50

	5306 [?]

Benjn Harveys

Emanuel	650
Jack a Black Smith	1000
Tom	650
Atlas	650
Pampe	300
Suckey	275
Betty & 2 Children	525
Hannah	500
Mariah	300
Old Sam	000
Old Pheabe for keeping	50
Stephen	400
	$5300

R H Smith, Jno. McDonald & John Mullen

****

Wm. T. Muse, Bill
John Corran & al
Pasquotank, Spring Term 1822

Pasquotank County
Petitions to sell or Divide Slaves

Iredell, 6 Copy sheets
State of North Carolina}In Equity
Pasquotank County}Spring Term 1822

To the Honorable the Judge of the Court of Equity for the said County, the Bill of Complaint of William T. Muse humbly Sheweth.
That sometime in the month of January One Thousand Eight Hundred and Nineteen John Corran of the said County being indebted to your Orator in the sum of Nine Hundred and Eighty Eight dollars 98/100 due by Bond bearing date the 18th of January 1919 and being desirous of securing the payment of the same, did with the consent of your Orator convey by Bill of Sale to Thomas D. Martin the following negroes to wit, Luke, Eden, Quilla, Silvia, Lydia & their increase in Trust that the said Thomas D. Martin should & might at any time after the first day of June next ensuing Sell the said negro Slaves to the highest bidder for ready money after giving proper notice & apply the money arising from such Sale to the discharge of the said Debt & the interest accruing thereon together with the costs of executing the Trust & the balance of the money if any to be paid to the said John Corran - all which will more fully appear, reference being had to the said Bill of Sale or conveyance in Trust bearing date 18th January 1819 & duly proved & recorded which your Orator has ready to produce - Your Orator further Shewith that the said Debt has never been discharged nor any part of it and and that the said Negro Slaves have never been Sold but have remained & still are in the possession of the said John - - Your Orator further Showeth that the said Thomas D. Martin died sometime in the month of **[Blank]** in the year 1820 having first duly made his last Will & Testament, which has since been duly proved & recorded - And that he appointed Benjamin Sutton & William Wood Executors thereof, who have accordingly qualified & taken upon Themselves the burthen & execution thereof - that the said executors are unwilling to **[Torn]** with the execution of the said Trust and are desirous that some other Trustee should be appointed -- Your Orator further sheweth that the said John Corran tho applied to both refused to pay the said Debt or to deliver up the said negroes to be sold pursuant to the said conveyance in Trust - In tender consideration whereof and forasmuch as your Orator is altogether remediless in the premises by the strict rules of the Common law & can only have relief in a Court of Equity where matters of this sort are properly cognizable to the end therefore that the said John Corran & the said Benjamin Sutton & William Wood Executors as aforesaid may true & perfect **[?]** make to the premises and that the said negroes may be decreed

Ja. Iredell, Solr. For Compltt.

****

Appraisment & valuation & Division of the negroes belonging to the Estates of Mary Brosher and Nancy Pendleton
Return'd Jany Term
Probate Court 1824 & ordered to be recorded
Teste, Charles Grice, Clk
Recorded in Book G, Page 279

State of North Carolina } Novr. Prob: Court 1823
Pasquotank County }

Ordered that William Wilson, Thomas L Shannenhaus, Thomas Jordan, Thomas Barnard, and John McDonald be appointed to divide the negroes belonging to the Estate of Mary Brasher and Nancy Pendleton Dec'd and make report to this Court
Teste, Charles Grice, Clk

Apraise and Valuation of the Negroes belonging to the Estates of Nancy Pendleton and Mary Broshier Dec'd and also a division of the same as follows

Old woman Polly for Keeping	62.50
Man Davis	300
James	300
Jupiter	400
Miles	400
Boy Osborn	300
Caleb	275
Jefferson	125
Woman Comfort	100
Woman Crissey	245
Woman Cherry	300
	$2775

Divided between Edmond H. Perkins in Right of his wife Betsey Nancy Pendleton and Maranda Pendleton to say 3 Heirs $925

$2775

Divided between Edmond H. Perkins in Right of his wife Betsey Nancy Pendleton and Maranda Pendleton to say 3 Heirs $925

No 1 has Man Davis	$300	Nancy Pendleton
Jupiter	$400	
Boy Jefferson	125	
Woman Comfort	100	
	$925	
To pay No. 3 for Keeping old Molly 20 - 83/		
$904.16/1/2		

No 2 has James	$300
Osborn	300
Crissey	275
To receive from No. 3	50
	925
To pay for Keeping Old Molly to	No. 3
	20. 83/1/2
	$904.16/1/2

No 3 Miles$400 To Edmd H Perkins in right of his wife	
Caleb	275
Cherry	300
To Pay to No 2	975
	925
his part for Keeping Old Molly	20.83/1/2
	$904. 16 1/2

In Obedience to an Order of Court to us directed we have together proceeded to appraise and Value the Negroes and also divided them belonging to the Estates of Nancy Pendleton & Mary Broshier among the Lawfull Representatives of which the above is a Statement.
Given from under our hands the 18th Decr. 1823.

Wm. Wilson, Thos E Shannonhaus, Thomas Jordan, John McDonald & Thos Barnard

Pasquotank County
Petitions to sell or Divide Slaves

****

Order for Division of Negroes
Mark Taylor & Wife
Report made at
March Term 1824

State of North Carolina } Decemr Term
Pasquotank County } 1823

On Petition of Mark Taylor and Wife to the Court of Pleas and Quarter Sessions for the County aforesaid; it is Ordered That Benjamin Sutton, Lemuel C Moore, William Martin, Stephen Chally and Abner Williams, be appointed to divide, Negroes, Say Frances, Betsey, Stephen & Bob, between Mark Taylor in right of his Wife and Elizabeth Nicholson and make report thereof.
Teste, Charles Grice, Clk

Agreeable to the annexed order of Court to us directed we the undersigned Commissioners have met at Court House on Elizabeth City on Thursday the first day of January 1824 to Divide the Negroes between Mark Taylor in right of wife Mary and Elizabeth Nicholson, which we done as follows.

Valuations of Negroes

1st Negro woman Franky Valued at	$175
2nd Negro Boy Bob	375
3rd Negro man Stephen	325
4th Negro Woman Betsey	275
Whole and Valuations is	1150
Mark Taylors in right of his wifes part is	575
Elizabeth Nicholsons part is	575
	1150
1st Mark Taylors Share as follows	
Negro Woman Franky	175
Boy Bob	375
To Rec'd from Elizabeth Nicholson	25

	575
2nd Elizabeth Nicholsons share as follows	
Negro Woman Betsey	275
Negro Man Stephen	325
	600
To pay to Mark Taylor	25
	575

Given under our hands the day & date above written
Benj. Sutton, Stephen Charles, Leml. C Moore & Abner Williams

****

Wm. Albertson et al
Petition to Sell Negroes
The Court
Pasquotank, March Term 1826
Granted

To the Worshipfull The Court of Pasquotank County

To March Term of the Worshipfull Court of Pleas and Quarter Sessions held for the County of Pasquotank.

The Petition of the undersigned Petitioners respectfully sheweth That whereas in the Division of the Estate of the late Ashbury Sutton Dec'd the four Children of William Albertson, To Wit -- Ann R.Relfe wife of James S. Relfe, Benjamin Albertson, and Penelope and Emeline Albertson; Three Negroes To Wit -- Woman Rose, and Woman Sarah and her Girl Child Mary, were apportioned and set apart, as part of their proportion of said Deceased Estate in right of their Mother -- And whereas it is impossible, with property so Circumstanced, that an Equitable division can be made amongst the said heirs, without exposing the same to sale. And further more two of the said heirs -- Ann the wife of James S. Relfe and Benjamin Albertson, having arrived to mature age, which Entitle them to receive their proportions of said property separate and distinct from the other heirs, now Minors.

We the undersigned Petitioners William Albertson in right of his two Children, Penelope & Emeline Albertson as their Guardian, and James S. Relfe in right of his wife Ann, and Benjamin Albertson for himself, pray the aid & interference of the Worshipfull Court in their behalf, by passing an order of your said Court Authorising your Petitioners to expose to public Sale the above named Negroes at a credit of six months, for notes with approved Securities, and that an equal distribution of the amount arising from such sale, be made amongst the said Respective heirs.

And your Petitioners as in duty bound will ever pray &c &c

Elizabeth City Pasquotank County March Term 1826
Wm Albertson
The Prayer of the Petitioners Granted By the Court

****

Elisha Dresser Dupree[?]
Petition to Sell Negroes, The Court
Copy & order Issued
Pasquotank, March Term 1826

State of N. Carolina } January Term 1836
Pasquotank County } Court of Probate

To the Worshipful Court now Setting
The Petition of Elisha Dupree Admr. on the Estate of Hugh Pritchard, Humbly Sheweth, that one of the of said Hugh, an infant named Elisha is dead and that the said Hugh, in his Will gave a negro Dave to the said Elicha, and your petitioners is desirous of making division of the said Negro Dave among the surviving heirs, pray your Worships, to grant an order for said negro to be divided among the legal heirs, and your petitioner
Charles Grice
Granted
His
Elisha X Dupree
Mark

****

Daniel Simpson & others
Petition to Sell Negroes
The Court

Pasquotank County
Petitions to sell or Divide Slaves

Copy & order issued, fees paid, $2.95

State of North Carolina }
Pasquotank County } March Term 1830

To the Worshipfull the Justices of the Court of Pleas & Quarter Sessions for the County of Pasq. Aforesaid

The Petition of Daniel Simpson, Will D Whetney, Miles Richardson & George Ferebee of lawfull age & Benj. Richardson by George ferebee his Guardian.

Your Petitioners humbly sheweth unto this Worshipfull Court that they are joint owners of three Negroes (to wit Old Woman Hannah & Girls Patsey & Thamer) and that a Division of said Negroes cannot be made without an injury to your Petitioner -- therefore your Petitioner prays this worshipfull Court to Grant an Order to Sell said Negroes upon such credit as to them shall be deemed right -- in order that a fair & equitable division may be made.

Your Petitioners as in duty bound will ever pray &c.

Granted & Month credit

Daniel Simpson, Wm D. Whitney, Geo Ferebee.

His
Miles X Richardson
Mark

****

Jno. B. Mansard's Admr.
Pet. To Sell Negroes
The Court
To Decr. Term 1832
Prayer Granted

State of North Carolina } Court of Pleas & Quarter Sessions
Pasquotank County } December Term 1832

To the worshipful the Justices of the Court of Pleas & Quarter Sessions of the County aforesaid the Petition of John L. Bailey Administrator of John B. Mansard sheweth your worships that he as Administrator as aforesaid has not in his possession assets sufficient to pay off all the debts due by the Estate of said Mansard, Your Petitioner

therefore pray your worships to order and decree that he shall sell at public auction a negro man called Bob Mullen belonging to the Estate of said Mansard for the purpose of paying debts due by said Estate and as in duty bound your Petitioner will ever pray &c
Hoskins, Solr.

****

Jos. Relfe & als
Petition for a Sale of Negroes for a Division
The Court
December Term 1832
Pasq County Court
Granted

State of North Carolina }
Pasquotank County } December Term 1832

To the Worshipfull Justices of the Court of Pleas and Quarter Sessions.

The Petition of Jos. Relfe, Malachi Relfe and Josiah Relfe per his Guardian Joseph Relfe humbly complaining respectfully sheweth unto your Worships that they are entitled as tenants in common on the following negroes to Wit - Negro man Mathias -- Negro woman Matilda & Child Mary -- that a division of the said negroes cannot be made without a sale of the said negroes -- Your Petitioner humbly requests your Worship to Grant an order directing the sale of the said negroes upon a Credit of six months and that after all expenses are paid the Balance to be paid over & your Petitioners Equally and as in duty bound your Petitioners will Ever Pray.
W. C. Ehringhaus
Sol. For Pet.

****

Abner Williams for himself
As Guardian to A Thornton
Petition to Sell Negroes
Petition Granted by the Court, Filed 1834
Sept T. 35

Pasquotank County
Petitions to sell or Divide Slaves

State of North Carolina } Court of Pleas & Quarter Sessions
Pasquotank County } December Term 1834

To the Worshipfull the Justices presiding
The Petition of Abner Williams, and of Abner Thornton an infant under age by his Guardian Abner Williams, shew to your Worships that they are joint Owners of a negro Slave named Mary, that for the purpose of a Division to each of your Petitioners of their share, they pray Your Worships for an order, authorizing & directing Your Petitioner Abner Williams to Sell the said Negro Slave on a Credit of six months, with such other order as your Worships may seem necessary, and as in duty bound &c
Abner Williams

Abner Williams
Petition to Sell Negro, The Court
Coppy of a Petition & order
Returnable to March Term 1834
Pasquotank County Court

State of North Carolina } Court of Pleas & Quarter Sessions
Pasquotank County } December Term 1834

To the worshipful the Justices presiding.
The Petition of Abner Williams and of Abner Thornton an infant under age by his Guardian Abner Williams show to worships that they are joint owners of a negro Slave named Mary - that for the purpose of a Division to each of your Petitioners [?] slave they pray your Worships for an order authorizing & directing Your Petitioner Abner Williams to Sell the said negro slave on a Credit of Six Months with such other order as your Worships may seem necessary and as in duty Bound &c
(Signum) Abner Williams

State of North Carolina }
Pasquotank County } December Term 1834

Ordered by the Court that the Petitioner Abner Williams have leave to Sell the negro mentioned in the Petition upon a Credit of Six Months & that he make due Report to the next Term of this Court to be

held for said County at the Court House in Elizabeth City on the first Monday in March next.
Issued 15 decr 1834 } Teste, Stephen Charles, Clk

****

Charles White
Petition to Divide Negroes, The Court
Filed Sept. T. 1837

State of North Carolina } Court of Pleas & Quarter Sessions
Pasquotank County } September Term 1837

To the Worshipfull the Justices now presiding.
The Petition of Charles White of the County of Perquimans, respectfully sheweth to your Worships, that he lately intermarried with a certain Sarah Elizabeth Winslow, daughter ans Orphan of John Winslow of Pasquotank County dec'd, that there are some negroes & other property belonging to your Petitioner, and some other of the children of the said John Winslow, and your Petitioner is desirous to have his part therein recorded & allotted to him. Your Petitioner further sheweth that Sarah Winslow the mother & Guardian to your Petitioner's wife Sarah Elizabeth & the other Orphans [?] of the said John Winslow, has removed to the County of Perquimans where she now resides, and has the property in her possession Your Petitioner therefore prays your Worships to appoint three or more Commissioners, residing in the County of Perquimans, to divide among the Orphans of the said John Winslow, the negroes and other property, now in the possession of their Guardian the said Sarah Winslow, agreable to the last Will and Testament of the said John Dec'd, so as to enable your Petitioner to obtain possession for his share thereof, and that the said Commissioners may make a Report in writing of their proceedings to the next term of this Worshipfull Court & your Petitioners &c.
Commissioners: David White, Jonathan White, Robert Newby and Henry White
Charles White
Her
Sarah X Winslow, Guardian
Mark

Pasquotank County
Petitions to sell or Divide Slaves

Charles White's Petition to Divide Negroes &c
The Court, Copy & order
Recd Book A, Page 2
Perquimans

State of North Carolina } Court of Pleas & Quarter Sessions
Pasquotank County } September Term 1837

To the Worshipfull the Justices now presiding.
The Petition of Charles White of the County of Perquimans Respectfully Sheweth to your Worships, that he lately intermarried with a certain Sarah Elisabeth Winslow daughter & orphan of John Winslow of Pasquotank County Dec'd that there are some negroes & other property belonging to your Petitioner & some other of the children of the said John Winslow & your Petitioner is desirous to have his part divided & allotted to him - Your Petitioner further sheweth that Sarah Winslow the mother & Guardian to your Petitioners wife Sarah Elisabeth & the other orphans interested of the said John Winslow has removed to the County of Perquimans where she now resides & has the property in her possession - Your Petitioner therefor prays Your Worships appoint three or more Commissioners residing in the County of Perquimans to divide among the orphans of the said John Winslow the negroes & other property now in the possession of their Guardian the said Sarah Winslow agreeable to the Last Will & Testament of the said John Dec'd so as to enable your Petitioner to obtain possession of his share thereof & that the Commissioners may make a Report in writing of the proceedings & next Term of this Worshipful Court & Your Petitioner &c
A True Copy
Teste, Stephen Charles, Clk
Signed, Charles White
Her
Sarah X Winslow, Guard.
Mark

Pasquotank County- Court of Pleas & Quarter Sessions, September 1837.

Ordered that David White, Jonathan White, Robert Newby and Henry White be appointed Commissioners to divide the property Mentioned in the above Petition among the Petitioners & make Report of their proceedings to the next term of this Court to be held on the first Monday in

December next - Witness Stephen Charles, Clerk of the said Court with the Seal of the said Court This Septr 1837 at Elizabeth City.
Stephen Charles, Clk

In Obedience to the annexed Order we the undersigned have proceeded to Value and divided the Negroes agreable to the Last Will and Testament of John Winslow Dec'd between his Daughter Patsy Winslow and Charles White who intermarried with his other daughter Sarah Elizabeth Winslow as follows Viz Negro woman Peggy, Valued at four hundred dollars, set apart to Charles White and he the said Charles is to pay Patsy Winslow by her Guardian fifty dollars -- Negro boy Jerry Valued at three hundred dollars set apart to Patsy Winslow, and she is to receive from Charles White fifty dollars, which makes the Value of each ones lot three hundred and fifty dollars -- which we submit to the Court.

Given under our hands and seals the 18th day of November 1837.

The Commissioners duly qualified before Jordan Winslow
Henry White (Seal)
Jonathan White (Seal)
Robert Newby (Seal)

****

Wm S. Markham & Others
Petition to Sell
The Court, Dec Term 1837

Pasquotank } Court of Pleas & Quarter Sessions, Dec Term 1837.

To the Worshipfull the Justices of the Court aforesaid the Petition of Wm. S. Markham & Wife Susan Martha Pendleton an Infant by her Guardian Benj. Charles Elizabeth Pendleton by her Guardian Abraham White respectfully shew that they are tenants in Common of four negroes and that division cannot be made without a [?] pray Your Worships that the Clerk of this Court be directed to sell [?] for division.
C.R. Kenn[?], Solr.

W.S. Markham & Wife Susan Pendleton Pr B H Charles Guard. & Eliza Pendleton Pr Guardian To the Court.
Pasquotank County Court

Pasquotank County
Petitions to sell or Divide Slaves

March Term 1838
Petitions Docket

1837 Dec T. Docketing, Petition, & order	$100
1838 March T. Judgment	15
Allowance to Clk for Sale	15.00
CRK Atto for Pltff	4.00
	20.75

SW Markham & Wife Susan Martha Pendleton pr B. H. Charles guard. Eliz Pendleton pr Abr: White
To the Court, Petition to Sell Negroes for Division.

An order having been made at last Court directing the undersigned to sell the negroes on a Credit of Six Months - In pursuance to said order & after due notice of the time & place of sale I did on the 30th Dec 1837 offer the negroes here mentioned at public sale when they produced the following sum, viz
Negro Aaron **[Faded]** To Saml. Madling**[?]** who gave his note with D B Pendleton his Security
Robin 506 To DB Pendleton who gave his note with Thad Freshwater his Security.
Easter 615 To A Whedbee who gave his note with Jas. Mullen & W.W. Davies his Security
Hannah 41 To H. White with J.H. Morris & Ruben White his Security.$1263
All of which is Respectfully Submitted.
Stephen Charles, Clk
March T. 1838

Rept made & [ ] Clk allow $15 for sale & Report & pay [ ] to parties & take the receipts therefore.

****

Job Gray & Others To the Court
Report of Sale
Dec. Term 1838

Gray and others To the Court

Pasquotank County
Petitions to sell or Divide Slaves

Pasquotank County Court
Petition to Sell Negroes for a Division

An order having been passed at the September Term 38 of this Worshipfull Court directing the Clerk of the said Court to sell the Negroes Mentioned in the Petition on a Credit of Six Months.

In accordance with the said order I proceeded on the Twentieth day of October 1838 due notice of the time and place of said sale haven been given by public advertisement in different public places in said County to sell the said negroes when Daniel Sawyer appeared & bid for Negro Man Caleb $699.50 who appeared & gave note with Joseph Pritchard & JD Stokely his securites. Elliott Whithurst appd & bid for Negro Joseph 800.75 & appd & gave his note with A. McPhinn his Security & Newton Edney appd & bid for negro Girl Fronny 610.50 & appd & gave his note with Mark Spencer & Job Carver his securities
Total Sales $2110.75
All of which is respectfully Submitted

****

N. Hollowell et als
To the Court
Div. of Negroes
Filed March 1840, Order Recorded
Rec'd Division Book, Page 7

State of North Carolina } Court of Pleas & Quarter Sessions
Pasquotank County } Dec Term 1839

To the Worshipfull of Noah Hollowell in right of his wife Mariann -- Albert Trueblood & Ann Trueblood & William Trueblood infants by their Guardian Noah Hollowell -- Priscilla Trueblood -- Exum Trueblood -- Stephen Pendleton in right of his wife Mary -- Nixon Trueblood, Mary Elizabeth & Patience Markham infants by their Guardians William Markham -- Respectfully shew unto your Worships that they are the owners of the following negroes -- Viz Mathias, Maricha, Thomas, Lewis, Nancy, Georg, Stephen, Damon, Harriett & John, And your Petitioners Respectfully pray your Worships to appoint

Commissioners to divide the same negroes between your Petitioners according to law, and as in duty bound &c

Ordered by the Court that Jesse L. Pool, Addison Whedbee, F. Fletcher and Alfred White be appointed Commissioners -- to allot and divide the above negroes as prayed for in the Petition

N. Hollowell et als
Petition & Order To
The Court for Div. Of Negroes
Prayer Granted
Return Pasq C.C.
March Term 1840
Elliot

State of North Carolina } Court of Pleas and Quarter Sessions
Pasquotank County } Decr. Term 1839

To the Worshipful the Justices of the Court aforesaid
The Petition of Noah Hollowell, in Right of his wife Mariam Trueblood, Ann Trueblood, & William Trueblood infants by their guardian Noah Hollowell, Pricilla Trueblood, Exum Trueblood, Mary, Stephen Pendleton in right of his wife Mary, Nixon Trueblood, Mary Elizabeth & Patience Markham infants by their Guardian William Markham -- Respectfully shew unto your Worships that they are the owners of the following negroes viz Mathias, Maricha, Thomas, Lewis, Nancy, George, Stephen, Damon, Harriett & John, and your Petitioners Respectfully pray Your Worships to appoint Commissioners to divide the said negroes between your Petitioners according to Law -- and as in duly bound &c.
Gilbert Elliott
A True Copy Teste Stephen Charles, Clk.

Ordered by the Court that J L Pool Esq., Addam Whedbee, Francis Fletcher and Alfred White be appointed Commissioners to divide the above negroes as prayer for -- and make Report.
Teste Stephen Charles, Clk.

In Pursuance to an order of Court to us directed we the Commissioners therein Named, have proceeded to Divide the Negroes Belonging to the

Pasquotank County
Petitions to sell or Divide Slaves

Estate of **[Faded]** Trueblood Decd. Between his heirs and make this Return of the same

To Pricilla Trueblood the Widow of the Decd. Man Mathias vallued at Seven Hundred Dollars, Girl Nancy valued at Four Hundred, Boy Stephen valued at Five Hundred, she is to pay to Noah Hollowell one Hundred Dols. -- To William Markham Guardian to Mary E Markham & Patience Markham, Woman Maricha valued at Four Hundred Dollars, Boy Daimon valued at Three Hundred Dolls. and child John valued at one Hundred Dols. Wm. Markham is to pay unto Noah Hollowell Fifty Dollars -- Unto Exum Trueblood, Boy Thos. Valued at nine Hundred Dollars, and is to pay unto Noah Hollowell Guardian to the Heirs of Wm. Trueblood one Hundred and fifty Dollars -- Unto Noah Hollowell Boy Lewis valued at Six Hundred Dollars, and is to receive from Priscilla Trueblood One Hundred Dollars and from Wm. Markham Guardians fifty Dollars -- Unto the Heirs of Wm Trueblood by Noah Hollowell their Guardian, Boy George valued at Four Hundred Dols. And Girl Harriett valued at Two Hundred Dollars and is to receive from Exum Trueblood One Hundred and fifty Dollars -- Given under our hands and Seals This the 27th Decr 1837. Addison Whedbee, Francis Fletcher & Jesse Pool. **[Poor].**

****

Wilson Williams
Petition to the Court
To Divide Negroes

State of North Carolina } Court of Pleas & Quarter Sessions
Pasquotank County } Sessions, March Term 1840

To the Justices of the Court aforesaid.

The Petition of Wilson Williams in right of his wife, Respectfully shows unto your worships that, he is a tenant in common with Joseph Shaw, Lucy Shaw, Benj Lowry & Sarah Shaw, in the following negroes viz negro woman Cloe, woman Marianne, Boy Edmond, Girl Clarinda & Tina, Your Petitioner being intitled to one fifth part of said Negroes, and being anxious to have a division of the same, therefore prays your worships to order that a Copy of this Petition be served upon his Co Tenants and farther to appoint three free holders to divide said negroes, and as in duty bound and etc

G Elliot Sol.

Wilson Williams Petr to divide negroes
To the Court

Returnable Pasq C.C., June Term 1840
Executed by delivering a Coppy of the
Within to B B Lowrey
Joshua A Pool, Shff
By Jos. S. Keeling, DShff
A Copy of the within left with Sarah Shaw & left
At residence of B. L. [?] Shaw this 25th May 1840
G. Elliot

State of North Carolina } Court of Pleas and Quarter Sessions
Pasquotank County } March Term 1840

To The Justices of the Court aforesaid

The Petition of Wilson Williams in Right of his Wife Respectfully shews unto your Worships that he is a tenant in common with Joseph Shaw, Lucy Shaw, Benj Lowry and Sarah Shaw, in the following negroes Viz negro woman Cloe, woman Mariam, Boy Edmund, girl Clarinda & Tina.

Your petitioner being entitled one fifth part of said negroes, and being anxious to have a division of the same therefore prays your Worships to order that a copy of this petition be served upon his cotenants and further to appoint three freeholders to divide said negroes.

And as in duty bound and &c.
G. Elliott, Solr.
A True copy, teste Stephen Charles, Clk. For Petr.

Ordered by the Court that James Mullen, James Mullen Jr. and Joseph Mullen be appointed Commissioners to divide the within name negroes, a copy of this petition being first served upon the cotenants of the Petitioner
Test, Stephen Charles, Clk.

****

Charles Harriss & als by Guardian Martin Harriss

Pasquotank County
Petitions to sell or Divide Slaves

Pet to sell slaves
The Court
Filed at Fall Term 1841
Ct. of Equity

Charles Harriss & als
Guardian to the Court
Petition to sell a Slave
Filed at Fall Term 1841

The Clerk and Master in [?] Decree of this Honorable Court, after having given due legal notice by advertisements of the time and place of Sale -- Sold on the 8th day of November 1841 before the Court House door the negro Slave Phillip named in the said Petition, to the highest bidder, When William [?]tora became the purchaser, for the sum of five hundred Dollars, who gave his note with Stephen Charles as his surety for that amount. All of which is respectfully submitted by.
John C Ehringhaus.

Charles Harris & als Guardian } Court of Equity Spring Term 1842
The Court } Petition to Sell Negro

The Report of sale of the Negro made at this term is conformed -- Ordered that the Clerk & Master collect the money when [?] pay it over to the Guardian

Negro Man Phillip to William Glover	$500
Charges costs of Petition &c	$1.25
Attorneys fee	10
Allowance to Clk Master	20
Paid [?]	4.50
	35.75
	$464.25
Interest received from William Glover	6.14
	$470.35

1842 May paid [?]	$150
1842 Aug 13 [?]	100
1842 Sept 8 amount of your note	

1842 with 4 Mo. Int.	45.70
	295.70
	$174.65

Received September the 13th 1842 from John C. Ehringhaus Clark and Master of the Court of Equity one hundred & seventy four 45/100 the balance as per Statement above
Witness, William C. Butler
Martin Harris as Guardian.

E. City November 8th 1841
Phillip the property of John Harriss [?] Jaile fees as sold by the Clk & Master of Equity of Pasquotank County $4.50
Recevd. Payment in full of the Clk.
Jos. S. Keeling, Jailor

State of North Carolina } Sept Court of Equity
Pasquotank County } Fall Term 1841

This Petition of Charles Harriss, Wilson Harriss, Emily Harriss, Jordan Harriss, Henry Harriss and Lucy Harriss, infants by this Guardian Martin Harriss respectfully shew unto your Honors; that as heirs at law of John Harriss their father; they are tenants in Common of a certain negro slave named Philip -- Your Petitioners further shew your Honors, that Sd. Slave is of such bad & suspicious Character, that he is at all times liable to be apprehended or [?] of the commission of some office -- and that on account of his bad character -- the neighbors have threatened to [?] the sd. slave, some great bodily harm -- whereby your Petitioners might at least be greatly damaged --if not lose the negro entirely -- That at this time, the [?] of your Petitioners, have incarcerated the sd Slave, without any legal process, and without that if he, the sd slave, makes his appearance at large again they will do him some injury - That may it please your Honors; your Petitioners are not only at great expence, in amount sd slaves bad conduct but are in continual danger of loosing him, on account [**Torn**] They therefore pray your Honors that you make a sale of the said slave, by act of Assembly in such cases made and provided - and that your Honor, will make such other & further orders in the premises, as to your Honors may seem meet & proper, and your Petitioners &.

Pasquotank County
Petitions to sell or Divide Slaves

Davis Whitehurst, William Cox, & CB. Eheringhaus **[Smudged]** Grandy Harris, James Wood, G.W. Smithson make oath that they know the slave Philip mentioned in this Petition and that they [?] set forth then [?] to the Infants, that the should be sold
Sworn to before me this 29th Oct 1840
Stephen Charles, Clk
Davis Whitehurst, Grandy Harris,
His
William X Cox
Mark
His
James X Wood
Mark

****

T. Jordan's Petition to the Court
Sell Negroes
Ex to J. T., 43
Septr Term, 1841

Pasquotank } County Court
} Septr Term 1841

To the Worshipful the Justices of this Court aforesaid the Petition of Joshua A. Pool, Admtr of Thos. Jordon [?] that the estate of his Testator is so much indebted as to make a sale of his negroes necessary and he prays an order of your Worships for the sale of the same on a credit of six months & Your Petr &
C. R. [?], Sol.

****

C.R. Kearny[?], Admrs of Brooks
Petition to the Court
Sell of Negroes
March Term 1841

Pasquotank } County Court
} March Term 1841

Pasquotank County
Petitions to sell or Divide Slaves

To the Worshipfull the Justices of the Court aforesaid the Petition of C.R. Kearny Admrs. of Wm. C. Brooks respectively show that the Estate of his [?] is so much indebted to make a Sale of his Negroes necessary and he Prays an order of sale on a credit of six months &
Your Petr &c
C. R, Kearny[?]

Acct Sales of B. Charles negroes, July 5th 1842 at 6 Mos, ints from date.
Boy Jerome to Mr. Morris $350.

****

J. A. Pool's Pet. To the Court
Ex. To [?] T., 43J
June Term

County Court } Pasquotank
1841 }

To the Worshipfull the Justices of the Court aforesaid the Petition of Joshua A. Pool Admr. of Thomas Jordan shows that the Estate of Thos. Jordan is so much indebted as to make a Sale of all his Negroes & prays an order to sell them on a credit of six months.
C.R. Kearny[?]

****

Joseph Jones and Wife
Petition to the Court
To sell Negroes

In pursuance of an order of the Court of Pleas and Quarter Sessions held for the County of Pasquotank on the first Monday in March last, made in the above Case, I shall sell at public auction before the Court House door in Elizabeth City on the 27th of April next the following Negroes: Viz; Negro Woman Hannah and her Child Penelope; Terms made known on the day of the Sale, March 22nd 1842
Stephen Charles, Clk.

Pasquotank County
Petitions to sell or Divide Slaves

A Coppy of the Within set up at Newbegun Creek on the 31st of March 1842
One at Nixenton on the 1st day of April 1842, one at New South Church on the 22nd of March 1842, And One at the Court House
The Above notices set up by Daniel Richardson was sworn to by him before me the 23rd April 1842
Jn. Pool SS

Joseph Jones & Wife Emily
Petition to Sell Negroes Pr [?]
Service [?]
Philip Pritchard as Gargend **[Guardian]**
Granted, Ehringhaus Sol for Plt

Rec'd from Stephen Charles, one note Stephen Stafford for ninety three Dollars with int. from 27th April 1842, it being for negro woman named in within Petition.
Philip Pritchard

September 14th 1842 Rec'd from Stephen Charles Clerk of County Court of Pleas & Quarter Sessions two notes to the amount of Two hundred & Seventy five Dollars with interest from 27th April 1842 - it being in full satisfaction to each of us in this Case
Joseph Jones & Philip Pritchard
Witness, Wm. [?]

State of North Carolina } Court of Pleas and Quarter Sessions
Pasquotank County } March Term 1842

The Petition of Joseph Jones and his wife Emily Jones, late Emily [?] Respectfully show unto your Worships that they, with one Margaret Jennings[?] are tenants in Common of two negro slaves to Wit - negro woman Hannah, and her child Penelope which slaves they hired from Betty Jennings dec'd - Your Petitioners you that actual partition of sd slaves cannot be made without [?] value, the therefore pray you, that you order a sale of sd slaves for a division, and that the Clerk of this Court be appointed to make the sale and report to the next term - and that a copy of

this petition be [?] Philip Pritchard the guardian of Margaret Jennings the Infant and your Petitioners &c
Jno CB Ehringhaus
Sol for Plt

Jos. Jones & Wife to Sell Negroes for Division
M Term 1842

Account of Sales of Negroes sold on Wednesday the 27th of April 1842 agreeable to above Petition
Woman Hannah aged about 45 years

To Stephen Stafford	$93.00
Girl Penny to Jos. Jones	$182.00
	$275.00

Stephen Charles, Clk.

****

S. Charles, Admr & B. H. Charles
Petition to Sell Negroes
March Term 1842

To the Worshipfull the Justices of the Court aforesaid the Petition of Stephen Charles, Admr. of Benjn H. Charles respectfully shows that the debts of this Estate of his [?] are so large as to order a Sale of his Negroes necessary and he prays an order of your Worships to sell all the Negroes of his Interest on a Credit of Six Months & Yr Petr in duty bound &c
C. R. [?] Sol

****

State of North Carolina } Court of Pleas & Quarter Sessions
Pasquotank County } Decr. Term 1843

To the worshipful the Justices of said Court, humbly Complaining respectfully shows to your worships, your Petitioner John Bray, Admr of Charity Hariss, that the said Charity hath left a negro slave named Caroline, and that it is necessary to sell the said slave for the purpose of satisfying certain Executions against the said Charity's Estate and that there

is no other property belonging to said Estate; To the [?] that the said slave may be sold, the Petitioner John Bray aforesaid, prays your worships give an order of sale upon such Tenus as to your worships may seem meet and proper and as in duty bound your petitioner will ever pray.
J. N. Tettell, Sol.
Which petition was granted by the court aforesaid.
Test W.W. Griffin, Clk

John Bray
Pet. To Sell Negro
The Court, Petition Granted

State of North Carolina } Court of Pleas
Pasquotank County } Quarter Sessions

To the worshipful, the Justices of the Court of Pleas and Quarter Sessions for the County of Pasquotank, humbly Complaining, respectfully show unto your worships, your petitioner, John Bray administrator of Charity Harriss, that the said Charity hath left a negro slave named Caroline, and that it is necessary to sell the said Slave for the purpose of satisfying certain executions against the said Charity's estate; and that there is no other property belonging to said estate. To the end, therefore, that the said slave may be sold, The Petitioner, John Bray, aforesaid, prays your worships for an order of sale upon such terms as to your worships may seem meet and proper - and as in duty bound your petitioner will ever pray.
J.N. Tettel[?]

Receiv'd of John Bray my fees in the case of Petitioner to Sell negro girl Caroline, made at December Court 1843
Jany. 1st 1844

Estate of Charity Harris
In as with John Bray, Administrator, 1844 January 22 - Cr By Sale of Negro Slave Caroline as per order of Pasquotank County Court December Term 1843 $256.00
Witness J Perkins[?]
His

John X Bray
Mark

****

Albertson White & others
Petition to the Court
To Sell Slave for Division
Ehringhaus, Sol.

State of North Carolina } Court of Pleas & Quarter Sessions
Pasquotank County } June Term 1844

To the Worshipfull the Justices of the Court afsd the Petition of Albertson White, Daniel White, Seth White, Henry White - of full age -- and Penelope White, Axey White, Meriam White - Infants by their Guardian Acenath White & Margaret White infant by the Clerk of this Court, Guardian ad litem respectfully show that they are tenants in Common of a certain negro slave named Frank late the property of Benjamin White and that actual partition cannot be made without sale of sd slave, they therefore pray that the sd slave may be sold for a division according to Act of Assembly in such case made and provided - And that Alfred, a [?] Esq be appointed to make sd sale.
Jno CB Ehringhaus, Sol.

****

Wilson Williams Pet. To the Court
To divide Negroes
Ret June Term 1845
A Copy of the Within Left with Benja B Lowry
& a Copy left at the house of B B Lowry for Lucy Shaw
2nd Day April 1845

State of North Carolina } In Obedience to
Pasquotank County } to the Annexed Writ

We the under sined on the 24th July 1845 met at the House of Wilson Williams for the Purpos of dividing the Negros belonging to the heirs at Law of Adam Shaw and did [?] them in manner & form as follows, as pr agreement by the the heirs to Wit Negro Man Edmon to B B Lowry to Wilson W. Williams Woman Clarandy to Lucy Shaw woman Clary & girl Tener and said Henry Shaw is to pay to B.B. Lowry Twenty five Dollars and all cost to be Paid by Benj B Lowry & Wilson W Williams Given under our Hand & Seals the day & date above written.

Mordecai Morriss (Seal)
Jno C Barnes (Seal)
James W. [?] (Seal)
Joshua Pool, Shff (Seal)

Wilson Williams Petr. To the Court
To Divide Negroes
Ret Sept Term 1845
Executed & Report filed Within
Joshua Pool, Shff

State of North Carolina } Court of Pleas & Quarter Sessions
Pasquotank County } March Term 1845

To the Worshipful, the Justices of the Court aforesaid:

Your Petitioners Wilson Williams respectfully shew unto your Worships that he is tenant in Common with B.B. Lowry & Lucy Shaw in the following negroes to wit, Boy Edmund, woman Chloe & Claranda & girl Tena late belonging to late belonging to **[Blank]** and your Petitioners further shew that he is desirous of a Partition of said Slaves and humbly pray your Worships to appoint Five Freeholders to partition said negroes between your Petitioners & B. B. Lowry & Lucy Shaw, And your petitioners, as in duty bound will ever pray.

C. Elliott, Solicitor

On the hearing of this petition it was ordered that a Copy be sent to B.B. Lowry & Lucy Shaw & that they be summoned to stand [?] at the next Term of this Court, why the said negroes shall not be divided between the said tenants in Common.

This is therefore to Command you Joshua A. Pool, Shff of said County, to Summon B.B. Lowry & Lucy Shaw to appear at our next term of Court & Show Cause if any [?] division shall not be made in the [?] named in the above petition.

Test, W.W. Griffin, Clk.

Wilson Williams Petr to the Court
For Div of Negros
Granted
Issued Copy
3 Copies & 3 Subpoenas
Elliott

State of North Carolina } Court of Pleas & Quarter Sessions
Pasquotank County } June Term 1845

To the Worshipful, the Justices of the Court Aforesaid:

Your Petitioners Wilson Williams respectfully shew unto your Worships that he is Tenant in Common with B.B. Lowry & Wife & Lucy Shaw in the following negroes to wit, Boy Edmund, woman Chloe & Clarinda & girl Tenar late belonging to **[Blank]** and your Petitioners further shew that he is desirous of a Partition of said negro slaves and humbly pray your Worships to appoint Five Freeholders to partition said negros between himself, B.B. Lowry & Lucy Shaw, And your petitioners, as in duty bound, will ever pray.
G. Elliott, Solicitor

It appearing to the satisfaction of the Court that notice has been given to the defendant in this petition - it is ordered, adjudged & decreed that James W. Mullen Esq - Joseph Mullen, John S. Commander, John C. Barnes & Mordacai Morris Senr., be appointed Commissioners to make division in said negros mentioned in the above petition, between the Petitioner & B.B. Lowry & Lucy Shaw as prayed for.
Test, W.W. Griffin, Clk

State of North Carolina } Court of Pleas & Quarter Sessions
Pasquotank County } March Term 1845

To the worshipful the Justices of the Court aforesaid. The petition of Wilson Williams Respectfully shew your worships that, he is a tenant in Common with Benj B Lowry, Lucy Shaw, in the following negro slaves

viz, Boy Edmond, woman Cloe & Woman Clarenda, and girl Tena. And your petitioner respectfully prays that you will order that a copy of this petition be served on the said B.B. Lowry & Lucy Shaw & that they be summoned to show cause at the next term of this Court Why the said negroes shall not be divided between the said tenants in Common, and in duty bound &c
Gilbert Elliott, Sol. For petitioner.

****

W G Cook, Admr. et als
Petition for Sale of Slave
To the Court
Filed Sept Term 1846
Brooks

State of North Carolina } Court of Pleas & Quarter Sessions
Pasquotank County } September Term

To the worshipful the Justices of the Court Afsd. The Petition of William G Cook as the administrator of John A Shaw Dec'd William W Griffin admr of Emma Griffey Dec'd and said Griffin as Gaurdian to William, Adaline & Sarah Griffey humbly complaining respectfully showeth to your worships that they are tenants in Common of a negro slave Betty & child formerly belonging to Felix Griffey Dec'd & they further show that they are unable to settle the Estate of their **[?]** & make a just & careful division & distribution of this property without a sale of said girl Betty & child and therefore prays that your Worships may appoint a Commissioner who shall be required to advertise the said Girl Betty for **[Blank]** days at two or more publick places in this county & expose to publick sale the said Girl Betty on a credit of six months & make report to the next Term of this Court and your Petitioner will ever pray.
G.W. Brooks, Sol. For Plt.

To J. A. Shaw Admr	74.84
To Emma Griffey, Admr	74.84
To Wm Griffin Guardian } William - Adaline & } Sarah Griffey ea 74.84 }	224.52
	$374.20

nett Amt Sales 374.20
W.W. Griffin, Clk

****

Nixon A. Lane & Wife
& T.R. Cobb Grd
Petition to Sell Slave for Division
To the Court
Filed at June Term 1850
Ehringhaus, Sol.

State of North Carolina } Court of Pleas & Quarter Sessions
Pasquotank County } June Term 1850

The Petition of Nixon A. Lane & Wife Nancy formerly Nancy Trueblood - and Clarky Trueblood infant by her Guardian Thomas R. Cobb shew unto your worships, that they are tenants in Common of and in a certain negroe slave named Sidney - They shew that said negro slave Sidney - is now leased out until January 1st 1851 - They therefore pray that your worships decree & order a Sale of said slave Sidney - for the purpose of a division between your Petitioners - & as in duty &c
Ehringhaus, Sol.

This case being heard - It is ordered by the Court, that the Clerk of this Court; proceed to sell the sd. slave Sidney - for the interest of Petitioners in said slave - after giving Thirty days notice at three publick places in this County - according to Act of Assembly - & Report to the next Term of this Court.
Ehringhaus, Sol.

****

Susan & Jesse S. Trivine[?] **[Ervine]** et als of full age
And P White et als inft per Guardians
Petition to Divide Slaves to the Court
Filed December Term 1850
Brooks

Pasquotank County
Petitions to sell or Divide Slaves

State of North Carolina } Court of Pleas & Quarter Sessions
Pasquotank County } December Term 1850

To the Worshipful the Justices of the Court aforesaid.

The pettition of Susan Trivine, Jesse Trivine, Wm. T. White, Farribee White, Wilson Winslow and wife Mary Elizabeth - and [?] White of full age and Joseph P. White, Sarah Ann White & Wesley White infants by their Guardian Jonathan White humbly complaining, sheweth unto your Worships that they are entitled as tenants in Common to certain Negro Slaves to Wit Harry, Bytha, Jim, Charles, Henry, Axey, & George, your prtitioners show your worships that said Slaves were the property of Wm H. Trivine and are now subject to division between your petitioner his distributers & next of kin as follows To the Petitioner Susan Widow of the said WH Trivine dec'd one third in value to Jesse S. Trivine a brother of the said W.H. Trivine one third of the remaining two thirds to Wm T. White, Wilson Winslow and wife Mary Elizabeth, Ferribee White, Joseph P White, Sarah Ann White & Wesley White, children of Nancy Deceased sister of said WH Trivine, one third of said remaining - two thirds in value in Common, and to Danas White, Addison White and Caleb White children of Mary White a sister of said WH Trivine, the remaining third of said two thirds, in value in Common - Your Petitioners pray your worships to appoint a Justice of the Peace and three freeholders honest men Commissioners to devide said slaves between your Petitioners as aforesaid and that your worships will from time to time make such other and further orders and decrees in the premises and Justices appertain - And as in duty bound your Petitioners will ever pray &c
G.W. Brooks, Sol. Pro Petitioners.

Upon the hearing of the foregoing Petition it is ordered that partition of slaves mentioned in this Petition be made and it is adjudged by this Court that the Petitioners are entitled as follows in said slaves. The petitioner Jesse S Trivine to one third of the remaining two thirds, in value of the same, the petitioner Wm T. White, Ferribee White, Wilson Winslow & wife Elizabeth, Joseph P. White, Sarah Ann White and Wesley White to one third of two thirds in value of same as tenant in Common, and the Petitioners Danas White, Addison White & Caleb White to the one third of two thirds in value of said slaves as tenants in Common, And it is ordered by the Court that Thomas Miller Esqr, Hezekiah Jackson, Daniel White &

Jos B. Reed be appointed Commissioners to make Partition of said Slaves & make report to the next Term of this Court.

Susan Twine et als
Order to Divide negroes
The Court
Ret. M. T. 51

	2.25
Shff	3.20
Atty	4.00
	9.45

Executed & the Report Filed Within
Joshua Pool, Shff

State of North Carolina } Court of Pleas & Quarter Sessions
Pasquotank County } Decr. Term 1850

Upon the hearing of the Petition of Susan & Jesse A. Twine of full age & others infants by their Guardian for division of the negroes of the Estate of [?] Turine Dec'd - prayer of the Petition granted and ordered by the Court that Thomas Miller Esqr, Hezekiah Jackson, Danl White & Jos B. Reed be appointed Commissioners to make division of the negroes, as follows to wit, to To Petitioner Susan Twine the one third in value of the said Slaves - the Petitioner Jesse Twine, one third of remaining two thirds in value of the same, the Petitioners Wm T. White - Ferribee White, Wilson Winslow & wife Elizabeth, Jos P. White, Sarah Ann White & Wesley White to one third of two thirds in value of the same as tenants in Common & the Petitioner Danas White, Addison White & Caleb White, to one third of Two thirds value of the said slaves as tenants in Common and make report of the same to the next Term of this Court.
Test, W.W. Griffie, Clk
Decr 18th 1850

State of North Carolina Pasquotank County in obedience to the annext order of Court to me directed I Joshua A Pool Sheriff of the County aforesaid on the 27th Day of Dec 1850 met at the Residence of Wm. H.

Twine for the purpose of dividing the negroes between the heirs at Law of said Twine Dec'd accompanied by Thomas Miller Esqr, Hezekiah Jackson, Daniel White & Jos. B. Reed Good and Lawful men, appointed by the Court of Pleas & Quarter Sessions and the Commissioners being duly sworn and required to divide the negroes did proceed to set off to the heirs in name & form as follows to wit to Susan Quin widow of said Wm. H. Quin Woman Betha Valued at four hundred Dollars, Boy Jim Valued at five hundred Dollars, Lot No. 1 to the heirs at law of Nancy White, Boy Charles Valued at five hundred Dollars & Boy George Valued at one hundred & twenty five Dollars, Lot No. 2 to Jesse Twine, Boy Henry Valued at five hundred Dollars & Girl Axey Valued at two hundred Dollars, Lot No. 3 to the heir at Law of Mary White Dec'd, Man Harry Valued at five hundred & seventy five Dollars. And we further say Lot No. 1 the heir of Nancy White shall pay over to Susan Twine two Dollars & Eighty nine Cents & Lot No. 2 Jesse Twine shall pay over to Susan Twine, Thirty Dollars & Seventy Eight Cents & allso Jesse Quin shall pay over to the heir at Law of Mary White forty Seven Dollars & Eleven Cents, Given under our hands and Seals.

Joshua Pool, Shff

Thos Miller	(Seal)
Hezekiah Jackson	(Seal)
Daniel White	(Seal)
Jos. B. Reed	(Seal)

****

Mrs. Elisa Pritchard et als
Petition to the Court to Sell Negro
Rec'd my Fee, Wm F. Martin

Eliza Pritchard et als } Pasquotank County
Petition To Sell Negro } In Equity, Spring Term/51

State of North Carolina } In Equity, Special Superior Court
Pasquotank County } December 1850

To the Honorable the Judge of the Court aforesaid,

Humbly complaining respectfully showeth unto your Honor Your Petitioners Mrs Elisa Pritchard of full age in her own right and Richard Griffin, Mary Evan, Simon, Joseph, and Martha Ellen Pritchard - infants by their Guardian Mrs Elisa Pritchard - that they are tenants in Common of a certain negro Man by Name Oliver - that said negro is exceedingly insubordinate, disobedient and impudent, that it almost impossible to control him - Your Petitioners further show your Honor that the said negro has made two attempts to run away and was detected first in time to prevent his escape - that the last attempt was made but a few days ago at which time in endeavouring to escape he knocked your petitioner Mrs Pritchard down and hurt her considerable - they further show your Honor that at the same time he made an attack upon Griffin Pritchard another of your Petitioners and was with difficulty arrested by him - Your Petitioners further show your Honor that the said negro is becoming worthless by reason of his constant neglect of duty and by leaving home almost every night and strolling about in the neighbourhood

They further show your Honor that the said negro is strongly suspected of stealing and further that the said negro is now in jail and they pray your Honor for an order of sale of said negro upon such terms as to your Honor may seem Meet.
Wm. F.Martin, Sol for Petr

Griffin Pritchard one of the Petitioners makes oath that the facts set forth in the foregoing Petition are true to the best of his knowledge and belief.
Sworn to & Subscribed before me this 13th of December 1850
Griffin Pritchard
S. Davis [?] JP

This Case coming on to be heard upon Petition evidence & Report of Master and it appearing to the satisfaction of the Court that a Sale of the negro mentioned is necessary and advisable it is orderd and decreed by the Court the prayer of the Petitioners is granted and it is ordered and decreed by the Court that the Petitioner Mrs Elisa Pritchard sell the negro mentioned within at private or public sale for Cash, or upon a credit of six months with interest from date if upon a credit that she take bond with approved security from the purchaser, and that she make report of her sale to the next term of this Court

---

The Petitioner Elisa Pritchard having been directed by this Honl. Court to sell the negro named in the Petition above referred to begs leave to Report that she offered said Negro for Sale at public Auction before the Court House Door in Elisabeth City on Saturday the 21st of December 1850 for cash - when Griffin Jennings appeared & bid the sum of $906.00 which was the highest and best bid, and the negro was knocked off to him -

Sale of Negro Oliver for Cash }
To Griffin Jennings } $906.00

All which is respectfully submitted

Her
Elisa X Pritchard
Mark
Griffin Pritchard

****

J. Edney Guard
Order to Sell Slave
The Court

Decr. Term 1850

Upon hearing the petition of Jonathan Edney, Guardian &c et als for sale of negro slave Fanny for division - the prayer of petitioners granted by the Court, and it was ordered that Jonathan Edney sell the negro upon a credit of six months with Interest from date and make report of the same.

Test, W.W, Griffn, Clk
Issued Decr 20th 1850

Account Sales of negro Fanny sold in pursuance to the above order of the Court on the 2nd day of January 1851
Fanny to Cartrite Edney for $ 580.00

****

William Coppersmith
Guardian
Petition to the Court Sell Slave
Petr Filed March Term 1851
Brooks

State of North Carolina } Court of Pleas & Quarter Sessions

Pasquotank County
Petitions to sell or Divide Slaves

Pasquotank County } March Term 1851

To the worshipful, the Justices of the Court of Pleas & Quarter Sessions of the County of Pasquotank, The petition of William Coppersmith infant by his Guardian Elisha S. Nash humbly complaining respectfully showeth unto your worships, that your petitioner is the owner of a certain Negro slave named Nanny about twenty four years old, That said slave has been for several years past and still continues to be of very bad Character and unmanageable, that she ran away while under the control of this Admr of your Petitioners father without reasonable provocation, and although a suitable reward was by him offered for the apprehension of said slave for a considerable length of time she [?] her hire to the Estate of your petitioners father and could not be arrested, That the said Administrator was compelled to hire her out for a very small sum to such persons as the said slave preferred or she would immediately run away, That for this reason much sacrifice has been born by your petitioner, That the said slave has a husband who lives very near (& as your petitioner believes) is well acquainted in much of the great Dismal Swamp and aided by her said husband as your petitioner believes she is, an easy opportunity is afforded her of escape from any who may and may hire her and her arrest much more difficult, That your Petitioner was unable to obtain more than twenty dollars for the year 1850 for said girl whereas she would have commanded (had she been of good Character), much more than that sum, Your petitioner shows that every proper exertion has been made to control said slave without success, that said slave refused to go into the possession of employment of any person; but insisted upon remaining with her husband in the vicinity of the Dismal Swamp, Your Petitioner has had said slave arrested & believes that if she is released she will escape and become an [?] to your petitioner or will remain obstinate and unmanageable and remain of little profit to your petitioner, Your petitioner prays your worships to order a sale of said slave on such terms and at such place as to your Worships may seem meet and proper as by a sale of said slave, your petitioner believes that his interests would be very greatly promoted, And as in duty bound your petitioner will ever pray.
G.W. Brooks, Solr. For Petitioner.

Court of Pleas & Quarter Sessions }
March Term 1851 }

Upon the hearing of this petition and evidence, it is ordered and adjudged by the Court that the prayer of the petitioner be granted, the Court being satisfied that the interest of the petitioner would be greatly promoted by a sale of the slave named in this petition and it is ordered by the Court that the Guardian Elisha S. Nash sell said slave on a credit of six months after advertising sale & make report to the next Term of this Court

---

State of North Carolina }
Pasquotank County }

To the Worshipful the Justices of the Court of Pleas & Quarter Sessions of Pasquotank County.

In Obedience to the annexed order of Court to me directed I proceeded to offer according to Notice Negro Naney for sale to the highest bidder on a credit of six months When and Where William J Nash appeared and bid for the said slave the sum of Seven hundred and Eighty Seven dollars and fifty Eight Cents - was the best and highest bid Rec'd for said slave and the said Wm. J Nash was duly declared the purchaser of said slave at the aforesaid sum, all of which is respectfully submitted.
Elisha Nash

****

James E. Weeks & wife et als
Order to divide Slaves to the Court
Ret to D.T. 51
Executed and a Report Filed within
Wm Newbould, Shff

Clk	2.25
Atty	4.00
Shff	3.10
	$9.35

State of North Carolina
Pasquotank County

Met at the home of James E. Weeks on the 4th of October 1851 accompanied by the following Commissioners to wit Ira Small, Joseph B. Shaw, Joseph B. Reed & D Draper duly sworn and by me in pursuance of the annext order to divide and allot between James E. Weeks & Wife and Stephen Mullen the following Negroes to wit, Anthony, Suckey, old Jess, Cherry, Isam, Willis Jamaca, Solomon, Mose Boy Jess, Lovey, Betty & Julia, Lea & Manda & Harriet, Caroline, Tim & Bill, Harriet, Joe & Eliza, Jefferson. Who being first duly sworn did set appart and allot to Each his or her share to wit to Stephen C. Mullen, they allot the following Negroes valued as follows, Anthony & Suckey $250, Solomon $775, Isam $600, Jess $600, Betty $550, Julia $550, Harriet & child Jefferson $600, Boy Joe $375, & Girl Eliza $200 and to James E Weeks & Wife Mary Man Jess & Cherry $50, Mose $800, Willis $750, Jamaca $600, Lovey $600, Caroline $550, Lea & 2 children Manda & Harriet $900, Boy Bill $250, Boy Tom $200 and they further say that James E. Weeks shall pay Stephen C Mullen one Hundred Dollars the excess in value, and that each shall Enjoy his or her Share as set appart and alloted of by the above named Commissioners, given under our hands and Seals this 4th of October 1851.

Witness
Wm Newbould, Shff
Jos B. Reed (Seal)
Jos B. Shaw (Seal)
D.D. Raper (Seal)
Ira Small (Seal)

Jas E Weeks & Wife et al
Petition to the Court to Divide Slaves
Executed
Brooks, Solr.

Pet of Jas E Weeks & Wife Mary L Formerly Mary L Mullen & Stephen C. Mullen infant by his Guardian George Reed for division of Slaves held in Common by the Petitioners being the shares set apart in Common to said Mary L & S C, in Division of their Fathers Slaves.
Commissioners, Jos B. Reed Esqr, Ira Small, D.D. Raper, Jos B. Shaw & Thos Brooks, Jr.

Sept. Term 1851

Upon the hearing of the petition of James E Weeks and wife Mary L. and Stephen O. Mullen by his guardian Geo. Reed for division of negroes, It was ordered by the Court Jos. B. Reed Esqr., Ira Small, D.D.

Raper, Jos B. Shaw and Tho.[?] be appointed commissioners to partition and divide the negroes as prayed for in the petition and make report to the next term of this Court.
Test, W.W. Griffin, Clk
Issued 8th Sept 1851.

State of North Carolina } Court of Pleas & Quarter Sessions
Pasquotank County } September Term 1851

To the Worshipful the Justices of the Court aforesaid.
Humbly complaining respectfully showeth unto your Worships your Petitioners Jas E. Weeks & wife Mary L. formerly Mary L. Mullen and and Stephen C. Mullen infant by his Guardian George Reed that they are tenants in common of the following negroes to wit being the negroes set apart in Common to Your Petitioners in the division of their Fathers Slaves - and they pray your Worships that you will appoint three freeholders unconnected with Your Petitioners either by consanguinity or affinity who shall devide said Negroes between Your Petitioners and allot to each their their share in severalty, according to the Statute in such case made & provided - and as in duty bound will ever pray.
G.W. Brooks Sol for Petrs.
Wm. F. Martin

The above case coming on to be heard upon Petition & the prayer of the Petitioners is granted and it is ordered that Joseph B. Reed Esqr, Ira Small, D.D. Raper, Jos B. Shaw & Tho. Banks Jr. be appointed Commissioners to divide the negroes named and that they allot to each of the Petitioners their share in Severalty and make report of their proceedings to the next Term of this Court.

****

North Carolina } County Court
Pasquotank County } June Term 1851

To the Worshipful Justices of the Court aforesaid
The Petition of William G. Pool, Solomon Pool, by his guardian George D. Pool, humbly Complaining respectfully show to your Worships that they

are Tenants in Common of certain negroes to wit: Harriet, Eliza, Jane, Charlotte, Nancy, Clarissa, Mary, Joe, Dave, Jordan & Joe (Child of Clarissa) all of which [?] to by the death of Solomon Pool, Dec'd.

They therefore pray your Worships to appoint three freeholders not connected with the parties by consanguinity or affinity, to make a division of said property between your Petitioners, that each may enjoy his part in severalty according to their rights & such other & further according to the Statute in such case made & provided -- & as in duty bound they will ever pray &c
John Pool, Solr.

Wm G. Pool et al
Order to divide Negroes
To the Court
Ret Sept 1851
Augt. 30th 1851

Met at the house of Geo. D. Pool Esqr and the negros not being it was thought best by the Commissioners & parties to post pone action
J.A. Pool, Shff
S. D. Pool, DShff

State of North Carolina }
Pasquotank County }

Met at the house of George D Pool the 10th of October 1851 accompanied By the following Commissioners to wit, James W. Hinton, Pritchard Jordan, George Bratties duly sworn by me in pursuance of the annext order to divide and allot between Wm G. Pool and Solomon Pool the following Negroes to wit. Jordan, Jo (Clarissa's child) Dave, Clarissa, Harriet and child Rose, Mary, Eliza, Jane, Charlotte, and Nancy who being first duly sworn did set apart and allot to Each his Share to Wit to Wm G. Pool they allot the following Negroes valued as follows, Dave valued at $700 & (Clarissa's Child) $400, Mary $400, Eliza $300 and Jane $250 and to Solomon Pool, Jordan valued at $50, Jo $700, Clarissa $400, Harriet & Child Rose $600, Charlotte $200 and Nancy $150 and they further say that Solomon Pool shall pay William G. Pool twenty five dollars the excess in value and that Each shale enjoy his Share as set apart and allotted of by the

above named and undersigned Commissioners, given under our hands and Seals this 10th of October 1851.
Witness, Wm Newbould, Shff
Pritchard Jordan (Seal)
George Bratties (Seal)
James W Hinton (Seal)

Wm G. Pool et al
Petition to divide Negroes
To the Court
Ret to D.T. 51
Execute and and a Report filed within
Wm NewBould, Shff

June Term 1851

Upon hearing the Petition of W. G. Pool & Solomon Pool infant by his Guard. , George D. Pool, for division of negroes, Prayer of the Petitioners was Granted by the Court and it was ordered that James W Hinton Esqr - Pritchard Jordan and Geo. W. Bratties be appointed to make division in negroes as prayed and report the same to the next term of this Court.
Test, W.W. Griffie, Clk
Issued June 12th 1851

Wm. G. Pool et al
Pet. To Divide Slaves
The Court

Upon hearing it is ordered & adjudged by the Court that this Petition be granted & that James W. Hinton, Pritchard Jordan & George W. Brothers[?] be appointed the Commissioners to make the division of the property herein named between the Petitioners, & make report to the next Term of this Court.

Septr Term 1851

Upon hearing of the petition of W G Pool & Sol Pool infant by his Guardian George D. Pool, for division of negroes - the prayer of the

Petitioners was granted by the Court and it was orderd that James W. Hinton Esqr, Pritchard Jordan, George W. Brothers be appointed to make division in the negroes as prayed for and report to the next term of this Court.
Test W.W. Griffin, Clk
Issued Sept 13th 1851.

****

Clarky Etheridge et als Pr Guardn.
Petition to the Court to Sell negro
Granted

State of North Carolina } Court of Pleas & Quarter Sessions
Pasquotank County } June Term 1852

To the Worshipful the Justices of the Court aforesaid.
Humbly complaining respectfully showeth unto your Worships your Petitioners Clarky Etheridge of full age and Henry Etheridge and Thomas Etheridge per Guardn. That they are tenants in common of a negro man named **[Blank]** that said negro has recently been guilty of gross misconduct and offences against the criminal Law of the State, being charged and justly so with the crime of Larceny and your Petitioners pray your Worships for an order to Sell said Negro on account of his bad conduct and for the purposes of division among your Petitioners, upon such Terms and at such time as to Your Worships may seem meet - And as in duty bound &c.
Wm. F. Martin Sol. For Plts

The foregoing Petition coming on to be heard and the Court being Satisfied of the truth of the matter set forth in the same, the prayer of the Petitioners is granted and it is ordered adjudged and decreed by the Court the Petitioner, Clarkey Etheridge sell the negro named within at public or Private sale upon a credit of six months with interest from day of sale, taking bond with approved Security from the purchaser and that she report to the next Term of this Court.

Report of the Commissioners

Pasquotank County
Petitions to sell or Divide Slaves

Account Sales of Negro man Hardy sold by order of the Court June 20th 1852 for cash - upon Petition of Clarky Etheridge et als, for misconduct. Man Hardy to Wm Glover $800

****

Major Everton & Wife
Petition for Partition of Slaves
M.L. Culpepper et als pr Guardn.
Service Accepted
G. W. Brooks Guardian
Martin - Solr.

State of North Carolina } Court of Pleas & Quarter Sessions
Pasquotank County } September Term 1853

To the Worshipful the Justices of the Court aforesaid.
Humbly complaining respectfully showeth unto Your Worships, Your Petitioners Major Everton and Matilda his wife, that they are tenants in Common with Mary Louisa Culpepper, M. Bertrand, Culpepper - Carter Culpepper, & Zion Culpepper - of the following negroes to wit - man Jacob - Woman Maria and her two children, and girl Lovy - that they are desirous of enjoying their share in said negroes in severalty - that the other tenants in Common are infants and that one GW Brooks is their Guardian - Your Petitioners therefore pray your Worships that the said Mary Louisa, M. Bertrand, Carter & Zion Culpepper may by their Guardn. - Your Petitioners therefore pray your Worships that the said Mary Louisa, M. Bertrand, Carter & Zion Culpepper may by their Guardn. G.W Brooks be made party Defendants to this petition according to the course of the Court and that Your Worships will decree a Partition of said negroes according to the Statute in Such case made and provided - that Your Petitioners may have their share in severalty - That Your Worships will make such other & further orders in the premises as to Your Worships may seem meet and as in duty bound &c
Wm. F. Martin - Sol for Plts

The foregoing Petition coming on to be heard, it is ordered adjudged and decreed by the Court, that partition of the negroes named, be made, as prayed for by Petitioners, and that W Mep[?], James Whidbee, W W Griffey & James Hinton be and they are hereby appointed Commissioners to make said partition and that they report to the next term of the Court.

Major Everton
Petition to divide Slaves
M L Culpepper et als pr Guardn.

In obedience to an order of the Worshipful Court of Pasquotank County directing us to divide the negroes named in this Petition and to allot to the Petitioner his share in Severalty - the undersigned being first duly sworn, did proceed to value the negroes named as follows.

Woman Maria valued at	$850.00
Girl Lovy valued at	700.00
Woman Maria's two children valued at	400.00

The undersigned do further report that the Petition being entitled to one fifth interest in said Negroes which amounts to $390.00 in valuation - they have allotted and set off to him in Severalty the two children of Maria valued by the undersigned at $400.00 and do direct that the Petition Major Everton, pay to the Defendants, the other tenants in common the Sum of $10.00 being the excess of the value of the slaves allotted to him over his share - All which is respectfully Submitted witness our hands & seals.
James W Hinton (Seal)
W.W. Griffin (Seal)
Jas. M. Whedbee (Seal)

****

Malachi White et al
Petition to Divide Negroes
The Court
Granted
Martin - Sol.

State of North Carolina } Court of Pleas & Quarter Sessions
Pasquotank County } December Term 1852

To the Worshipful the Justices of the Court aforesaid.

Pasquotank County
Petitions to sell or Divide Slaves

Humbly complaining respectfully showeth unto Your Worships Your Petitioners, Malachi White of full age and Robert White an infant pr Guardn. George W.Smithson that they are tenants in common of the following negroes to wit Woman Clarisa, Boy Jim, Tom, Sam, & Lea[?], that they are desirous of enjoying their shares in said Negroes in severalty, and they therefore pray Your Worships that you will appoint Commissioners to divide said Negroes, allotting and setting off to each of your Petitioners his share in severalty, according to the Statute in such case made & provided, that Your Worships will make such other & further orders in the premises as to your Worships may seem meet & as in duty bound &c

---

The above Petition coming on to be heard, the prayer of the Petitioner is granted, and it is ordered adjudged and decreed by the Court, that D.D. Raper, John B. Thompson, and Jos B. Read Esqr, be, and they are hereby appointed Commissioners to divide the negroes named in the Petition, allotting & setting off to each Petition his share in severalty & that they make report to the next Court.

December Term 1853 } Ordered by the Court that D.D. Raper, Jno Thompson, Jos. B. Reed Esqr be appointed Commissioners to divide the Negroes belonging to Malachi White & Robert White, allotting & setting off to Each his Share in Severalty & that they make report to the next Court
Dec 1853
Test, Jas W. Hinton

We the undersigned having been appointed Commissioners to divide & allot the negroes belonging to Malachi & Robert White, in obedience to an order of Court was issued, beg leave to submit the following report.

We have valued the negroes as follows - Woman Clarisa Seven hundred & Twenty five Dollars; Boy Jim at Eight hundred Dollars, boy Tom at Eight hundred Dollars & Boy Lead at six Hundred Dollars.

We have allotted to Malachi White Woman Clarissa & Boy Sam & to Robert White Boy Jim, Tom & Lead, and as in the division of Sd Negroes we have allotted a larger share to Robert than to Malachi White, we have furthermore ordered that Robert White pay over to Malachi the

sum of Four hundred & twelve 50/100 Dollars which being done makes their shares Equal according to the valuation & Division above stated, all of which is respectfully submitted
January 3rd 1853
Sworn to before me
Jos Pool, JP
Jas. B. Reed JP (Seal)
John Thompson (Seal)
D.D. Raper (Seal)

****

John H. Perry & als
Division of Slaves
The Court, June Term 1855
Pool

North Carolina } County Court
Pasquotank County } June Term 1855

The Petition of John H. Perry, Andrew J. Perry & James D. Perry & Wm. F. Hasket (by his Guardn. A.J. Perry) shew the Court that they are tenants in common of certain slaves to wit: Tom, Nelson, Tom Hollowell, Job, Jacob, Aaron, Rachael, Clarky & Harriet - which they wish divided between them, that each heir enjoy his share in severalty.

They pray the Court to appoint three freeholders unconnected with the parties, to set apart & allot to each his share in said slaves in severalty - according to law & report to the next Term of this Court - & as in duty bound &c
John Pool, Solr.

County Court, To wit:

Upon hearing the above petition it is considered by the Court that the prayer of the petitioners be in all aspects granted & that Wilson Winslow, Wm. T. White & John Thompson be appointed Commissioners to make said Partition & make report to the next Term of this Court, according to law.

Pasquotank County
Petitions to sell or Divide Slaves

Jno H. Perry & als
Order for Sale of Slaves
The Court
Ret Septr Term
Execution & Report
Filed within
Wm. Newbould, Shff
Rec'd my Fee, John Pool

State of North Carolina } Court of Pleas & Quarter Sessions
Pasquotank County } June Term 1855

The Petition of Jno H Perry, AJ Perry, Jas D Perry & W.F. Hasket by his Guardn. A J Perry shows the Court - that they are tenants in common of certain Slaves towit: Tom, Nelson, Tom Hollowell, Job, Jacob, Aaron, Rachel, Clarky, Charity & Harriet that they wish divided between them that Each may Enjoy his share in Severalty, They Pray the Court to appoint three free holders unconnected with the parties to set apart & allot to each his share in sd. slaves in severalty according to law & report to the next Term of this Court & as in duty bound &c
John Pool, Solr.

To the Sheriff of Pasquotank County

You are hereby commanded to summon Wilson Winslow, W.T. White & John Thompson Commissioners to make the partition set forth in the foregoing Petition & make due returns of the report of Sd. Commissioners at the next term of this Court

Witness Jas W Hinton, Clk of our Court this the 1st Monday of June 1855.
Issued June 1st 1855.
Test, James W Hinton, Clk

State of North Carolina }
Pasquotank County }

We the undersigned Commissioners appointed by the Court of Pleas & Quarter Sessions of said County met at the House of Andrew J

Perry on the 10th of June 1855 in obedience to the annext order to divide & allot between the respective Claimants the following negros value as follows; Old Tom valued at $500, Tom Nixon valued at $1000, Job valued at $1000, Jacob valued at $900, Aaron valued at $500, Rachael valued at $300, Clark valued at $800, Charity & Child Sarah Jane valued $1000, Harriet valued at $400 -- who being duly Sworn did set apart to John H Perry the following Negroes valued as follows, Jacob valued $900, Charity & Child Sarah Jane valued at $1000 they allott to Andrew J Perry, Job valued at $1000, Clark valued at $800 they allott to James Perry, Old Tom valued at $500, Harriett valued at $400, Aaron valued at $500 they allot to Wm. F. Hasket, Tom Nixon valued at $1000, Harriet valued at $300 they farther say that John H Perry shall pay to Wm F. Hasket three hundred Dollars difference in valuation, they also say that Andrew J Perry shall pay to James Perry two hundred Dollars difference in valuation, given under our hands & Seals this the 10th 1855.
W.S. Winslow (Seal)
John Thompson (Seal)
William T.White (Seal)
Test, Wm. Newbould, Shff

North Carolina }County Court
Pasquotank County } June Term 1855

The Petition of John H. Perry, Andrew J Perry, Andrew Perry & James D. Perry & Wm F. Hasket (by his Guardn. A.J. Perry) shew the Court that they are tenants in common of certain slaves to wit: Tom, Tom Hollowell, Job, Jacob, Aaron, Rachael, Clarky, Charity & Harriett - which they wish divided between them, that each may enjoy his share in severalty.

They pray the Court to appoint three freeholders unconnected with the parties, to set apart & allott to each his share in said slaves in severalty according to law & report to the next Term of this Court, & as in duty bound &c.
John Pool, Solr.

County Court, to wit;

Upon hearing the above petition, it is considered by the Court that the prayer of the Petitioners be in all respects granted & that Wilson

Winslow, Wm. T. White & John Thompson be appointed Commissioners to make said Partition & make report to the next Term of this Court according to law.

****

Sarah Whitehurst & Wm. Wood & Wife
Petition to Divide Slaves
Filed to Decr Term 1855

North Carolina } Court of Pleas & Quarter Sessions
Pasquotank County } December Term 1855

To the Worshipful the Justices of the Court aforesaid
The Petition of Sarah Whitehurst and William Wood and wife Elizabeth humbly complaining respectfully sheweth unto your Worships that they are tenants in Common of the following named negro slaves to Wit; Densen, Phillis, Jane, Elizabeth & Lydia.

That said Slaves belonged to Sarah Whitehurst a daughter of Your Petitioner Sarah and a sister of the petitioner Elizabeth Wood -- And at the death of said Sarah Whitehurst which took place in the year 1854 all her personal property descended to the Petitioner Sarah & William Wood & wife Elizabeth in right of his said wife Elizabeth.

Your Petitioners are desirous that partition shall be made of said Slaves, that Each the said petitioner Sarah & Wood & wife Elizabeth may have and enjoy their respective moities in severalty.

To the end therefore that partition may be made accordingly they pray your Worships to order and decree such partition to be made and that you will appoint suitable and discreet Commissioners to examine Value & make partition of said Slaves, And that you will from time to time grant such other and further orders and decrees in the premises as the nature of your petitioners may require, And as in duty bound &c.
G W Brooks, Sol.

Sarah Whitehurst et al
Order to value Negroes
Report 1856
Executed & Report
Filed within, Wm Newbould, Shff

Pasquotank County
Petitions to sell or Divide Slaves

State of North Carolina
Pasquotank County

We the undersigned Commissioners appointed by the Court pf Pleas & Quarter Sessions met at the House of Mrs Sarah Whitehurst on the 28th day of December 1855 in obedience to the annext order to divide & allot between Wm. Wood & Wife Elizabeth & Mrs Sarah Whitehurst heirs of Sarah Whitehurst Daughter of Keeling[?] Whitehurst Dec'd the following Negroes valued as follows, Denson $950, Phillis $250, Elizabeth $350, Lydia $250, Jane $600 who being duly sworn according to law did set apart & Allott to William Wood & Wife Elizabeth the following Negroes valued as follows, man Denson valued at $950, girl Lydia valued at $250 be allotted to Sarah Whitehurst, Woman Phillis valued at $250, Girl Elizabeth valued at $350, Girl Jane valued at $600 all of which is respectfully submitted to your Worships, given under our hands & Seals this the 28th of December 1855.
Signed in presence of William Newbould, Shff.
Samuel F. Overman (Seal)
Joseph Jennings (Seal)
Seth Morgan (Seal)

State of North Carolina } Court of Pleas and Quarter Sessions
Pasquotank County } December Term 1855

To the Worshipful the Justices of said Court, The Petition of Sarah Whitehurst and William Wood & wife Elizabeth respectfully sheweth unto your Worships that they are tenants in common of the following slaves, to wit: Denson, Phillis, Jane, Elizabeth & Lydia.

Your petitioners further show, that they desire to hold their shares of said slaves in severalty, and to that end they pray your Worships to appoint four free holders unconnected with them by consanguinity or affinity to devide the said Slaves into two equal shares and to allot and set apart to each of your petitioners one of said shares in severalty, and to report their proceedings in due form of Law to the next Term of this Court. And your petitioners as in duty bound will ever pray.
Geo. W Brooks
Attorney for Petitioners.

Pasquotank County
Petitions to sell or Divide Slaves

State of North Carolina } Court of Pleas & Quarter Sessions
Pasquotank County } December Term, 1855

To the Sheriff of Pasquotank, Greetings:
You are hereby commanded to summon Joseph Jennings, M[?] Jackson, Seth Morgan & Samuel Overman., Commissioners to divide the slaves named in the petition into two equal shares and to allot to each of the petitioners one share thereof in severalty and to report proceedings thereof in due form of Law to the next Term of this Court.

Witness, James W. Hinton, Clerk of our said Court this the first Monday of Decr. In the year of our Independence, A.D. 1855.
Issued the 28th day of Decr 1855.
James W Hinton, Clk.

North Carolina } Court of Pleas & Quarter Sessions
Pasquotank County } December Term 1855

This cause coming on to be heard upon the petition and evidence in the cause upon consideration thereof, The Court doth declare that the petitioners are entitled to partition of the said slaves into two Equal parts, or shares, one to be set apart to the petitioner Sarah & the other to the said Wm. Wood & wife, and the Court doth order and decree such Partition to be made accordingly, and the Court doth appoint Joseph Jennings Esquire, Macy Jackson, Seth Morgan & Samuel Overman freeholders Commissioners to examine value & make partition of said Slaves accordingly & make their report to the next Term of this Court.

****

Catharine Eheringhaus et als
Petition to Sell Negroe
The Court
Granted, Decree within
Bill of Sale made
Timothy Pendleton
1856, John Eringhause

State of North Carolina } in Equity

Pasquotank County
Petitions to sell or Divide Slaves

Pasquotank County } Spring Term 1856

To the Honorable the Judge of the Court aforesaid Humbly complaining respectfully show unto your Honor your Petitioner Catherine Eheringhaus of full age, Matilda G Eheringhaus, Wm. Eheringhaus, William F. **[Editor's Note: Most of this document is faded]** infant by their next friend John C. Eringhaus, that they are tenants in common of a negro woman named Ann and her child that said negro woman hard to manage it being next to impossible for your Petitioners to control her, that her morals are very bad and that to your Petitioners as a house servant she is almost valueles , Your Petitioners therefore pray your Honor for a decree of sale of said negro woman & her child to be made by the clerk & Master of this Court, and that the proceeds of said sale may be invested by him in the purchase of another negro woman to be held by your Petitioners in the same way as tenants in common as they Ann & her Child - That Your Honor will make such other & further orders in the premises as to your Honor may seem meet and as in duty bound &c
Wm. F. Martin, Sol for Plts

This cause coming on to be heard it is ordered & adjudged & decreed by the Court that the Clerk & Master sell the negro woman & child in the Petition names within at public or private sale for the best price that can be obtained, that the money arising from the sale be invested by the master in the purchase of another negro to be conveyed to & held by the Petitioner in the same way they own & held the said negro woman & child ordered to be sold.

Catherine Eringhaus } Petition to sell Negro Woman & Child
The Court }

In pursuance to the order & of this Court made on this case, the Clerk & Master sold the Negro Woman Anna & her Infant child to Timothy Pendleton of the County of Pasquotank, for the sum of Eight hundred & fifty Dollars and **[?]** for the same money, purchased of R E Hiott of the County of Norfolk & State of Virginia a Negro Girl named **[?]** and took a Bill of Sale for the same in his **[?]** the said negro Girl
All which is Submitted
C Ehringhaus **[?]**

Pasquotank County
Petitions to sell or Divide Slaves

****

State of North Carolina } Court of Pleas & Quarter Sessions
Pasquotank County } December Term 1857

To the Worshipful the Justices of the Court aforesaid
Humbly complaining respectfully showeth unto your Worships Your Petitioners, Sarah P. Casey of full age, Margaret E. Thomas, and Wm Carter Casey infants by their next friend Wm. C. Davis, that they are tenants in common of a negro woman named Courtney, that they are desirous of owning their shares in said negro in severalty - that actual partition cannot be made, and they prey your worships to appoint to appoint some suitable person as a commissioner by whom said negro may be sold under decree of this Worshipful Court, at such time & place & upon such terms as to your worships may seem meet for the purpose of partition among your Petitioners - that your Worships will make such other & further orders as to your Worships may seem meet and as in duty bound &c
Wm. F. Martin, Sol for Plt

This case coming on to be heard and it appearing to the Court that the matters set forth in the petition are true, it is ordered & adjudged & decreed by the Court that the Clerk of this Court sell the negro in the pleadings named at public sale before the Court House door in Eliz City upon a credit of six months interest from day of sale, having first advertised said sale for fifteen days, that bond with approved security from the purchaser & make report to the next term of this Court.

Sarah P. Casey
Order for sale of slave
And Report to the Court
To March Term 1858

North Carolina } Court of Pleas & Quarter Sessions
Pasquotank County } Decr. Term 1857

Pasquotank County
Petitions to sell or Divide Slaves

The petition of Sarah Casey of full age, Margaret E. Thomas, and Wm. Carter Casey infants by their next friend Wm. C. Davis to sell a Certain negro Slave named Courtney & coming on to be heard and it appearing to the Court that the matters set forth in the said petition are true - it is ordered, adjudged & decreed by the Court that the Clerk of this Court sell the negro in the pleadings named at public Sale before the Court House door in Eliz City upon a credit of six months interest from day of sale, having first advertised said sale for fifteen days that he take bond with approved security from the purchaser & make report to the next term of this Court.
Test, James W. Hinton, Clk
By Chas G. Elliott, DC

North Carolina }
Pasquotank County }

The undersigned in pursuance to the annexed Order of Court -- did proceed to sell the Negro Slave named in said Order after having duly advertised the same - before the Court House Door in E City - and then and there appeared Thos. M. Newby Jr., and bid the sum of One hundred dollars for said Slave - which being the highest and best bid, the said Thos. M. Newby Jr was duly declared the purchaser of the said Slave.
J W Hinton, Clk

****

Robt. P. Small, Admrs
Petition to Sell Negroes
To the Court, 1857
Granted - Decree within

State of North Carolina } Court of Pleas & Quarter Sessions
Pasquotank County } December Term 1857

To the Worshipful the Justices of the Court aforesaid
Humbly Complaining respectfully showeth unto your Worships Your Petitioner, Robt. P. Small that he is the Admr. duly qualified of one N.B. Small - that his Intestate owned at his death two Negroes to wit -- Addison and Alfred - that he left five next of kin entitled to distribution in his Estate

- That actual partition of said negroes cannot be made among the next of kin - Your Petitioner therefore prays Your Worships for a decree of sale of said Negroes to be made by Your Petitioner for the purpose of Division among the next of kin of his Intestate - & the Paymt of debts if required for that purpose that your Worships will make such other & further orders as to your Worships may seem meet and as in duty bound &c.
Wm. F. Martin Solr for Petr.

The above cause coming to be heard & it appearing to the Court that the matters set forth in the Petition are true - it is ordered adjudged & decreed by the Court, that the Petitioner sell the Negroes in the pleading, named before the Court House door in Elizabeth City, upon a credit of six months interest from day of Sale, at public auction having first advertised said Sale for twenty days - that he take bond with approved security from the purchaser & make report to the next Term of this Court.

Account of Sales of Negroes of the late N B Small sold by R P Small his Admr. by order of the Court of Pleas & Quarter Sessions of Pasquotank County sold at public auction before the Court House Door in Elizabeth City, Jany 1st 1858 upon a credit of six months interest from day of Sale.

Negro boy Addison to Edwin Small for	805.00
Negro boy Alfred to Julia Small for	805.00
	$1610.00

Robt P Small

****

Richard Henry, Joshua & Morris
Snowden pr Guardian
Petition to sell Negro
Negro sold to Nathan [?] for $1000
July 6th 1857 and Amt paid, receits within
Rec"d Sol fee of $20.00 of Clerk and Master
Wm. Martin Solr.

State of North Carolina } In Equity
Pasquotank County } Spring Term 1857

Pasquotank County
Petitions to sell or Divide Slaves

To the Honorable the Judge of the Court aforesaid,
Humbly complaining respectfully showeth unto Your Honor Your Petitioners Richard Henry Snowden, Morris Snowden & Joshua Snowden infants by their Guardian Richard H. Lister that they are tenants in common of a negro man named Jessy **[Jerry]**, that said negro has at this Term of the Superior Court of Law been tried for Murder, convicted of Manslaughter and is now in prison - that in the neighborhood there is some excitement against the negro and a general desire expressed that he should be sold out of the State - Your Petitioners further show that they are desirous he should be sold out of the State, that actual partition cannot be made except by a sale, and they pray Your Honor that you will order a Sale to be made of said negro for the purpose of partition by some Suitable person and further will decree that he be sold out of the State - That Your Honor will make such other & further orders as to Your Honors may seem meet and as in duty bound &c.
Wm. F. Martin, Sol for Petrs.

The undersigned make oath that they know the negro named in above Petition and believe that it would be to the interest of the Wards to sell him out of the State.
Sworn to & subscribed before me this April 1857
James W Hinton Clk
W.W. Griffie & Wm. Newbould

The within Cause coming on to be heard upon Petition evidence &c the Court doth declare that a sale of the negro named in the Petition is advisable, and it is ordered adjudged & decreed by the Court that the Clk & Master sell the negro in the pleading named, either at public or private sale, conditioned to be taken & carried out of the State of North Carolina & not to be brought again to the State - It is further ordered & decreed by the Court that Clk & Master after making Sale of the proceeds of said sale, less the Costs incurred in this behalf and make report to the next Court.

****

James W. Shannonhouse et al
Order for division of Slaves

Pasquotank County
Petitions to sell or Divide Slaves

To the Court
Report & Return 1858
Execution & Report Filed within
Wm. Newbould, Shff

Hinton	2.25
Newbould	3.10
Granby	4.00
	$9.35

State of North Carolina } Court of Pleas and Quarter Sessions
Pasquotank County } December Term 1857

To the Worshipful the Justices of said Court,
The Petition of James W. Shannonhouse of full age and William Shannonhouse & Mary A. Shannonhouse infants by their guardian Benj. I Shannonhouse respectfully sheweth unto your worships that they are tenants in common of the following slaves to wit: Harry, Joshua, Alfred, Evan, Nelson, John, Henry, Rose, Penny & three small children, Hulda & three children.

Your Petitioners further show, that they desire to hold their shares of said slaves in severalty, and to that end they pray your Worships to appoint three free holders unconnected with them by consanguinity or affinity to divide the said slaves into three equal shares and to allot and set apart to each of your Petitioners one of the said shares in severalty, and to report their proceedings in due for of Law to the next Term of this Court. And your petitioners as in duty bound will ever pray.
W. G. Granbery, Attorney for Petitioners.

State of North Carolina } Court of Pleas and Quarter Sessions
Pasquotank County } December Term 1857

To the Sheriff of Pasquotank, Greeting:
You are hereby commanded to summon Mark S. Sawyer, Ephraim M. Staunton, Jos. B. Shaw & Benoni Cartwright, Commissioners to divide the slaves named in the petition into three equal shares and to allot to each of

the petitioners one share thereof in severalty and to report proceedings thereof in due form of Law to the next Term of this Court.

Witness, James W. Hinton, Clerk of our said Court this the first Monday of December in the 82nd year of our Independence, A.D. 1857.
Issued the 29th day of December 1857.
J.W. Hinton, Clerk
By Charles G. Elliott, D.C.

On motion the following free holders, to wit, Benoni Cartwright, Ephraim M. Staunton, and Jos B Shaw & Benoni are appointed Commissioners to divide the Slaves named in the petition into three equal Shares and to allot to each of the petitioners one share there of in severalty, and to report their proceedings in due form of law to the next term of this Court.

Jas. W. Shannonhouse
Report of the Commissioners
To the Court, March Term, 1858

State of North Carolina
Pasquotank County

We the undersigned Commissioners appointed by the Court of Pleas & Quarter Sessions for the County aforesaid to divide the slaves belonging to Jas W Shannonhouse of full age, Wm. R. Shannonhouse & Mary A Shannonhouse infants by their guardian B. Shannonhouse, in obedience to the annext order to us directed & being duly sworn upon the Holy Evangelist of almight God did meet examine & value the said slaves

Lot No. 1

Nelson	1000
Rose	600
Joshua	300
Rhody	400
Asbery	500
	2800
Harry deducted	50
	2750

Lot No. 2

Alfred	950
Henry	700
Margaret	650
Penny & Simon	450
	2750

Lot No. 3	
Evan	950
Jno [?]	750
Thos Jefferson	450
Sarah	400
Hulda	200
	2750

Which Three lots with their valuation were placed in a hat & Each drawn out for the Petitioners according to their respective age where lot No. 3 fell to Jas W Shannonhouse, Lot No. 3 fell to William R. Shannonhouse and Lot No. 2 to Mary A. Shannonhouse which division we set apart to each of the Petitioners in severalty & respectfully submit the same to your Worships, Given under our hands & Seals this December 30th 1857.

Mark S. Sawyer (Seal)
E.M. Staunton (Seal)
Jos B. Shaw (Seal)

****

Rachael & Emily Harvey's Petr. For Partition of Slaves
To the Court
Petr. Filed Decr Term, 1857
Brooks

North Carolina } Court of Pleas & Quarter Sessions
Pasquotank County } December Term 1857

To the Worshipful the Justices of the Court aforesaid.
The petition of Rachael Harvey of full age and Emily Harvey by her Guardian Thomas Harvey humbly complaining respectfully showeth unto your worships that they are tenants in Common of a number of slaves (a list of the names of said slaves appended Marked "A") which they derived

from the Estate of their Dec'd Father Thomas Harvey, they show that they can be divided fairly and Equally in value between your petitioners and your petitioners are desirous that Partition of said slaves shall be made so that Each may have [?] & enjoy his share in severalty.

Your petitioners pray your worships that you will order & decree that partition of said slaves be made into two equal parts or lots in value or as equal in value it may be and that you will appoint a Justice of the Peace & three free holders good & lawful men commissioners to examine & value said slaves & make partition of same between your petitioners accordingly

And that you will from time to time make all such other and further orders and decrees in the premises as the nature of your petitioners Case may require and as in duty bound your petitioners will ever pray.
G W Brooks, Solr, for Petitioners

Rachael & Emily Harvey
Petition to divide Slaves
Return March Term 1858
Brooks

Hinton	2.25
Newbould	3.10
Brooks	4.00
	$9.35

Satisfied in full & money paid in office
Wm. Newbould, Shff

State of North Carolina } Court of Pleas and Quarter Sessions
Pasquotank County } Term 1858

To the worshipful the Justices of said Court,
The Petition of Rachel Harvey of full age, and Emily Harvey by her Guardian Thomas Harvey respectfully sheweth unto your worships that they are tenants in common of the following slaves, to wit: Nathan, Daniel, Washington, Edmond, Bill, Tony, Amy, Mary, Louisa, Hester & two Children, Pleasant & one child, Abbey & four children, Nancy & three children, and old Man Tom.

Your petitioners further show, that they desire to hold their shares of said slaves in severalty, and to that end they pray your Worships to appoint a Justice of the Peace & three free holders unconnected with them by consanguinity or affinity to divide the said slaves into two equal shares and to allot and set apart to each of your petitioners one of said shares in severalty, and to report their proceedings in due form of Law to the next Term of this Court. And your petitioners as in duty bound will ever pray.
G.W. Brooks Attorney for Petitioners.

State of North Carolina } Court of Pleas and Quarter Sessions.
Pasquotank County } December Term, 1857

To the Sheriff of Pasquotank, Greeting:
You are hereby commanded to summon Geo. D. Pool Esqr., Jos. B. Shaw, TD Pendleton & Elisha Eason Commissioners to divide the slaves named in the Petition into two equal shares and to allot to each of the petitioners one share thereof in severalty and to report proceedings thereof in due form of Law to the next Term of this Court.

Witness, James W. Hinton, Clerk of our said Court this the first Monday of December in the 82nd year of our Independence, S.D. 1857.
Issued the 23rd day of December 1857
Jas. W. Hinton, Clk
By Chas G. Elliott, D.C.

Court of Pleas & Quarter Sessions }
December Term 1857 }

This Cause Coming on to be heard and being heard upon the petition & evidence in the cause the Court doth declare that the Petitioners Rachel & Emily are tenants in common of the slaves mentioned of equal shares or [?] in value and that they are entitled to partition of said slaves and the Court doth order & decree that partition of said slaves be made accordingly and the Court doth appoint GD Pool Esqr, Jos. B. Shaw & T.D. Pendleton & Elisha Eason Commissioners to make such partition and make report to the next Term of this Court.

(A) Names of the slaves belonging to Rachael & Emily Harvey.

Pasquotank County
Petitions to sell or Divide Slaves

Nathan, Daniel, Washington, Edmond, Bill, Tony, Amy, Mary, Louisa, Hester & two children, Pleasant & one child, Abbey & four Children & old Man Tom.

North Carolina }
Pasquotank County } March Term 1858

To the Worshipful the Justices of the Court of Pleas & Quarter Sessions of Pasquotank County

We the undersigned Commissioners appointed for that purpose hereunto the annexed order to us directed did assemble at the residence of Thos Harvey on the 24th day of Decr 1857 and having brought before us the slaves belonging to the Petitioners named in said order and being first duly sworn to do equal justice to the parties in the division of said slaves between the Petitioners did proceed to examine and value said Slaves as follows, to wit:
Man Nathan $1300, Daniel 900, Washington 950, Edmond 250, Boy Bill 1000, Tony 800, Woman Mary 850, Louisa, Willis & Adaline1200, Amy & 2 children 1300, Hester & 2 children 1300, Nancy & 3 children, Penny, Ellen, Manual 1500, Abbey & 2 children, John & Martha 1000, Girl Francis, 700. Total $12, 600.

We then proceeded to assess the damages of two Negroes. First Old Tom, we assess damages $150 which we assign and set apart to Rachael Harvey - Owner of Lot No. 1 - We Assess damages of Negro Woman Pleasant & child (Woman Seriously afflicted with fits $150 Which we assign & set apart to Emily Harvey owner of lot No. 2. We then proceeded to make partition of the said Slaves as follows to Wit
Lot No. 1 composed of the following named slaves, Man Nathan 1300, Edmond 250, Tony 800, Woman Hester 2 children, Abbey & Jerry 1300, Girl Francis 700, Woman Louisa 850, Woman Amy 2 children, Willis & Adeline 1200. Total $6400

Lot No. 2 Woman Nancy & 3 Children, Penny, Ellen, Manual 1500, Boy Bill 1000, Washington 950, Woman Mary 850, Boy Daniel 900, Woman Abby & 2 children, John & Martha 1000. Total $6200.

Lot No. 1 of which we do assign & set apart to the Petitioner Rachael Harvey - And we further direct that the petitioner Rachael Harvey and owner of Lot No. 1 shall pay over to Emily Harvey the Owner of Lot No. 2 $100 to make said lots of equal value $6300. All of which is respectfully submitted.

Jos B. Shaw (Seal)
Elisha Eason (Seal)
T.D. Pendleton (Seal)

****

Wm Jackson & Wife
Petition for Sale of Slaves for Division
Martha Pendleton
Petr to Sept Term 1858
Service accepted
Brooks

Petr of Wm Jackson & Wife Fanny & Martha Pendleton for Sale of Negro Woman Violet for Division - Martha is under age & without a Guardian.

North Carolina } Court of Pleas & Quarter Sessions
Pasquotank County } Sept Term 1858

To the Worshipful the Justices of the said Court, The Petition of Wm. Jackson and Wife Fanny humbly complaining respectfully showeth unto your Worships that Your Petitioners in right of the Petitioner Fanny are tenants in Common with Martha Pendleton of a certain Slave named Violet. That said Slave is the only Slave owned in Common by the Petitioners & the said Martha, That the said Martha is an infant and without a Guardian to protect her rights & interest, Your Petitioners desire that partition of said Slave be made by sale of said slave under the direction of this Court -- And to the end that a Sale of said Slave may be rightfully made for the purposes aforesaid, and that the rights & interest of the said Martha Pendleton may be fully protected in this proceeding, Your Petitioners pray your Worships to appoint some suitable person Guardian Ad Litem to the said Martha that capias & Subpoena issue to be served upon the said Martha that she may by her said Guardian come into Court & see proceedings & that you will order and decree a sale of said slave to be made for the purposes aforesaid on such terms as to your Worships may

seem meet & proper and that you will from time to time make all such other and further Orders and Decrees in the premises as to law and justice appertain, And as in duty bound &c
G W Brooks, Solr.

In pursuance of an order of the Court made at March Term 1859 appointing me commissioners to sell an old negro woman named Violet belonging to me, my wife & Martha Pendleton, I did after having advertised her according to Law, proceed to sell her on the 2nd day of April 1859 at the Court House door when & where J. Wilcox appeared & bid for her the sum of Twenty dollars which was the last & best bid obtained & she was struck off to said Wilcox at said bid, Given under my Hand & Seal the 2nd of April 1859.
Wm. Jackson (Seal)

****

Jno. H. Kenyon & Wife et al
Order for Division of slaves
Report & Return to March Term 1858
Execution & Report filed
Wm. Newbould, Shff
Satisfied in full & money paid in office
Rec'd my fee, John Pool

Hinton	2.25
Newbould	3.10
Pool	4.00
	$9.35

State of North Carolina } Court of Pleas and Quarter Sessions
Pasquotank County } December Term 1857

To the Worshipful the Justices of said Court,
The Petition of John H. Kenyon & Wife Elizabeth Frances & George D. Pool, Guardian to Lemuel Fletcher, respectfully sheweth unto your worships that they are tenants in common of the following slaves to wit: Rachael & Serena & Children Jim, & Martha & Charles & Jane.

Your Petitioners further show, that they desire to hold their shares of said slaves in severalty, and to that end they pray your Worships to appoint four free holders unconnected with them by consanguinity or affinity to divide the said slaves into two equal shares and to allot and set apart to each of your petitioners one of said shares in severalty, and to report their proceedings in due form of law to the next Term of this Court. And your petitioners as in duty bound will ever pray.
Pool, Attorney for Petitioners.

State of North Carolina } Court of Pleas and Quarter Sessions
Pasquotank County } December Term, 1857

To the Sheriff of Pasquotank, Greeting
You are hereby commanded to summon D.D. Raper, J. B. Reid, Ro. Pendleton & Mager Bell Commissioners to divide the slaves named in the petition into two equal shares and to allot to each of the petitioners one share thereof in severalty and to report proceedings thereof in due form of Law to the next Court.

Witness, James W. Hinton, Clerk of our said Court this the first Monday of December in the 82nd year of our Independence, A.D. 1857.
Issued the 16th day of December 1857.
James W. Hinton, Clerk
By Chas. G. Elliott, D.C.

Thos Murden & Wife et al
Order for division of Slaves
To the Court
Report & Return to March Term 1858
Execution & Report filed within
Wm. Newbould, Shff
Satisfied in full & money paid in office
Wm Newbould, Shff
Rec'd my Fee, John Pool

Hinton	2.25
Newbould	3.10
Pool	4.00

Pasquotank County
Petitions to sell or Divide Slaves

$9.35

Thomas Murden & Wife et al
To Divide Slaves
The Court, December Term 1857

North Carolina } County Court
Pasquotank County } Decr. Term 1857

The Petition of John H Kenyon & Thomas Murden & Wife Jane, shows the Court that they are tenants in Common of Slaves Nancy, Sarah, Nelly, Lucy & Miles. They pray the Court to appoint commissioners to set off to each his share in said slaves in severalty according to law & as in duty bound &c.
Pool, Solr.

Decr. Term, 1857 S.S.

Ordered by the Court that the petition be granted, & that D.D. Raper, Jos. B. Reid, Robert Pendleton & Major Bell be appointed Commissioners to divide said Slaves, & make report to the next Term of this Court.

State of North Carolina } Court of Pleas and Quarter Sessions
Pasquotank County } December Term 1857

To the Worshipful the Justices of said Court,
The petition of John H. Kenyon, & Thomas Murden & Wife Jane respectfully sheweth unto your worships that they are tenants in common of the following slaves to wit: Nancy, Sarah, Nelly, Lucy, and Miles.

Your petitioners further show, that they desire to hold their shares of said slaves in severalty, and to that end they pray your Worships to appoint four free holders unconnected with them by consanguinity or affinity to divide the said slaves into two equal shares and to allot and set apart to each of your petitioners one of said shares in severalty, and to report their proceedings in due for of Law to the next Term of this Court. And your petitioners as in duty bound will ever pray.

Pool, Attorney for Petitioners

State of North Carolina } Court of Pleas and Quarter Sessions
Pasquotank County } December Term 1857

To the Sheriff of Pasquotank County. Greeting:
You are hereby commanded to summon D.D. Raper, Jos. B Reid, Robert Pendleton & Mager Bell Commissioners to divide the Slaves named in the petition into two equal shares and to allot to each of the petitioners one share thereof in severalty and to report proceedings thereof in due form of Law to the next Court

Witness James W. Hinton, Clerk of our said Court this the first Monday of December in the 82nd year of our Independence, A.D. 1857.
Issued the 16th day of December 1857,
James W. Hinton, Clerk
By Chas. G. Elliot, D.C.

State of North Carolina }
Pasquotank County }

We the undersigned Commissioners appointed by the Court of Pleas and Quarter Sessions met at the House of John H. Kenyon on the 21st of December 1857 in obedience to the annext order to divide & allot between the respective Claimants in severalty the following negroes valued as follows: Woman Rachel valued at $500, Woman Serena & Child Augustus valued at $650, Girl Martha valued at $300, Boy Charles valued at $100, and Girl Jane valued at $800 who after being duly sworn have proceeded to allot and divide the same between the parties named in the Petition, in manner and Form as follows, to wit: Lot No. 1 Consisting of Woman Rachel valued at $500, and Woman Serena and child Augustus valued at $650 to Leml. S. Fletcher. Lot No. 2 Consisting of Girl Martha valued at $300, Boy Charles valued at $100 and Girl Jane valued at $800 to Jno. H. Kenyon in right of his wife. The said Jno. H. Kenyon is to pay over to Leml. S. Fletcher the sum of twenty five excess in valuation of his lot.
Given under our hands and Seals the day and year above written
Jos B. Reid (Seal)
Major Bell (Seal)

Edmund Chancey (Seal)
D.D. Raper (Seal)

State of North Carolina }
Pasquotank County }

We the undersigned Commissioners appointed by the Court of Pleas & Quarter Sessions met at the House of John H Kenyan on the 21st of December 1857 in obedience to the annext order to divide & allot between the respective Claimants in Severalty the following negros value as follows, Nancy & Child valued at $600, Sarah valued at $900, Nelly valued at $800, Lucy valued at $500 who being duly sworn according to Law did set off & allot to John H kenyon woman Nancy & child Miles valued at $600 & girl Nelly valued at $800 and to Thos J Murden & wife Jane we allot & set off Girl Sarah valued at $900 and girl Lucy valued at $500 and we further say that John H. Kenyan shall pay to Thos J Murden & wife Jane one hundred Dollars being the excess in value of the two lots, All of which is most respectfully submitted to Your Worships, given under our hands & Seals this the 21st of December 1857.
Jos B Reid (Seal)
Major Bell (Seal)
Edmund Chancy**[Cherry]** (Seal)
D.D. Raper (Seal)

****

Joel Hollowell & Wife
Petr for Division of Slaves
Jno Anderson White & Caleb White by Guardian
Petr Filed to Decr Term 1858
Service Accepted, Joseph White
Brooks

North Carolina } Court of Pleas & Quarter Sessions
Pasquotank County } November Term 1858

To the Worshipful the justices of the Court aforesaid.
The Petition of Joel Hollowell and wife Elizabeth humbly complaining respectfully sheweth that Your Petitioners in Right of the Petitioner

Elizabeth are tenants in Common with John Anderson White and Caleb White of three Slaves (Viz) Simon, Mary & Harriett, that the said John Anderson and Caleb are infants and that Joseph White has been regularly appointed their guardian. Your Petitioners show that the said Slaves may be divided without [?] to the interest of any of the parties interested. Your Petitioners are entitled to one third part in value of said Slaves and they are desirous that partition shall be made so that their share in the said Slaves may be set apart to them in Severalty, And to that end they pray Your Worships to order that Copy of this Petition be issued to be served upon said Jno. Anderson & Caleb by their said Guardian: And that you will order and decree that partition be made accordingly to the rights of the parties Entitled, and that you will from time to time make such other and further decrees in the premises as the nature of your Petitioners case may require and as in duty bound &c.
G.W. Brooks, Solr.

State of North Carolina } Court of Pleas & Quarter Sessions
Pasquotank County } December Term, 1858

To the Worshipful the Justices of said Court,
The Petition of Joel Hollowell & Wife Elizabeth with Jno & Caleb White respectfully sheweth unto your worships that they are tenants in common of the following slaves, to wit: Simon, Mary & Harriett. Your Petitioners further show, that they desire to hold their shares of said slaves in severalty, and to that end they pray your Worships to appoint three free holders unconnected with them by consanguinity or affinity to divide the said slaves into three equal shares and to allot and set apart to your petitioners one of said shares in severalty, and to report their proceedings in due form of Law to the next Term of this Court. And your petitioners as in duty bound will ever pray.
Attorney for Petitioners.

State of North Carolina } Court of Pleas and Quarter Sessions
Pasquotank County } Decr. Term 1858

To the Sheriff of Pasquotank, Greeting:
You are hereby commanded to summon A.J. Perry Esqr, Jno. H. Perry, Simon Munden & Stephen Harris, Commissioners to divide the slaves

named in the petition into three equal shares and to allot the petitioners one share thereof in severalty and to report proceedings thereof in due form of Law to the next term of this Court.

Witness, James W. Hinton, Clerk of our said Court this the first Monday of December in the 83rd year of our Independence, A. D. 1858.
Issued the 20th day of December 1858.
J. W. Hinton, Clerk
By Chas G. Elliott D C

Joel Hollowell & Wife } Court of Pleas & Quarter Sessions
John Anderson & Caleb White } Decr. Term 1858

This Cause Coming on to be heard upon the Petitioner answers & Evidence, The Court doth declare that the Petitioner Joel Hollowell & Wife are Entitled to one third part in value of the Slaves named in the Petition, that the petitioners are Entitled to partition of said slaves, it is therefore ordered adjudged and decreed by the Court that partition be made of said slaves by setting apart to the petitioners in right of the said Elizabeth one third part in value of same, and the Court doth appoint AJ Perry Esqr, Jno A Perry, Simon Munden & Stephen Harris commissioners to make said partition accordingly & make their report.

Joel Hollowell & Wife
Order for Division of Slaves
Jno. A. & C. White
Report & Return to March Term 1859
Execution & Report within
W.E. Man[?] by J Wilcox

In obedience to an order of Court we the undersigned Freeholders did after being duly sworn proceed to make partition or division of slaves named in said order as follows to Wit, To Joel Hollowell & Wife Elizabeth we allot & set over girl Mary, valued at Nine hundred dollars, the Guardian to Jno A. & Caleb White agreeing thereto.

In testimony whereof we have hereunto set our hands & Seals the 31st day of December AD 1858 in presence of J Wilcox DS
Andrew J Perry (Seal)
John H Perry (Seal)

Simon Munden (Seal)
Stephen Harris (Seal)

****

F. M. Godfrey, Admr. of Thos J. Etheridge
Petition to sell negro, The Court
Granted - decree within
Martin, Solr.

State of North Carolina } Court of Pleas & Quarter Sessions
Pasquotank County } December Term 1858

Humbly complaining respectfully showeth unto your Worships, your Petitioner F.M. Godfrey that he is the Admr. duly qualified upon the Estate of Thos J. Etheridge, that as such there is in his hands a negro by the name of Ned, that it is necessary to Sell said negro for the purpose of paying debts of his Intestate & for the purpose of partition among the next of kin - Your Petitioner further shows that said negro has recently been charged with the crime of stealing, that the next of kin are all of age, and have requested that the negro be sold at private Sale so as to be carried out of the State - that he has an offer for him of nine hundred dollars which he regards as his full value - Your Petitioner prays Your Worships for a decree of Sale of said negro as prayed for, that Your Worships will make such other & further orders as to Your Worships may deem meet and as in duty bound &c
Wm. F. Martin, Sol. For Petr.

This cause coming on to be heard upon Petition evidence and it appearing to the Court that the matters set forth in the Petition are true, it is ordered adjudged & decreed by the Court, that the Petitioner sell the negro Ned in the pleadings named at public Sale before the Court House Door in Eliz. City having first advertised said Sale for twenty days upon a credit of six months, that he take bond with approved security from the purchaser and make report to next Court.

F.M. Godfrey, Admr.
Order to Sell Slave, The Court

Rep't & Ret. To Sept Term 1858

Hinton	2.25
Martin	4.00
	6.25

Costs Paid, Martin

State of North Carolina } Court of Pleas & Quarter Sessions
Pasquotank County } September Term 1858

F.M. Godfrey, Admr.
Petition for Sale of Slave

The above cause coming on to be heard upon the Petition, Evidence & and it appearing to the Court that the matters set forth in the Petition are true, it is Ordered Adjudged, and Decreed by the Court that the Petitioner sell the negro Ned in the pleading named at public sale before the Court House door in Eliz. City having first advertised said sale for twenty days upon a credit of six months, that he take bond with approved security from the purchaser and make report to the next Term of this Court.
Test, Issued Sept 21st 1858
James W. Hinton, Clk
By Chas. G. Elliott, D.C.

Acct of Sale of Negro Man Ned belonging to the Estate of Thos J. Etheridge by Order of Pasquotank County Court by F.M. Godfrey, Admr. Sept 28th 1858 upon a credit of six Months with Int. from date of Sale to F.F. Banks for $950 (an Inventory of said note returned)
F.M. Godfrey.

****

Franklin W. Stokely & Wife
Order to Divide Slaves
The Court & Alfred Albertson als pr Gdn.
Rept & Ret. To D.J. 1858

Executed this precept by duly summoning the within named persons, who proceeded on the 4th day of Dec. 1858 to divide the negroes for their action and doings, see report filed within.
Wm. [?] Shff
Costs $13.35 to Commissioners and the remainder in office} Wm E Mann, shff

Hinton	2.25
Mann	3.10
Martin	4.09
Commissioners	4.00
	$13.35

North Carolina }
Pasquotank County }

Pasquotank County Court Sept Term 1858
To the Worshipful the Justices of said Court - The Petition of Franklin W. Stokely & Wife Sally Ann humbly complaining respectfully shews the Court that they are Tenants in Common with Alfred Albertson & Elsbery Albertson of the following negroes to wit: Rose & her children, Hariett, Clarinda, Miles, Joseph, Martha, Eliza, Luke, & Man Dave - the Petitioners being entitled to one third of said negroes - Alfred & Elsbery are infants represented by Elias Garner **[Carner]** their guardian &c, they pray the Court to appoint Commissioners to Allott and set off to the Petitioners their share in severalty in said negroes &c &c
Martin, Solr.

North Carolina } Court of Pleas & Quarter Sessions
Pasquotank County } Sept. Term 1858

To the Sheriff of said County Greeting:
You are hereby commanded to summon Wilson Spence Esqr, James M. White, Wm. Williams Jr. & Wilson Williams to divide the slaves named in the above petition and to allott and set apart to the Petitioners One third part thereof in severalty and to report proceedings thereof in due form of Law to the next term of this Court.

Test James W. Hinton, Clerk of said Court the first Monday of September & in the 83rd year of our Independence AD 1858.

Issued Oct 2nd 1858.
James W. Hinton, Clk
By Chas. G. Elliott, D.C.

F. W. Stokely & Wife
Rt to divide Slave
Alfred Albertson et al pr Guard.
Service Accepted
Elias Carver, Martin, Sol.

State of North Carolina } Court of Pleas & Quarter Sessions
Pasquotank County } September Term 1858

To the Worshipful the Justices of the Court aforesaid.

Humbly complaining respectfully showeth unto Your Worships, Your Petitioners Franklin W. Stokely & Wife Sally Ann, that they are tenants in common with Alfred Albertson & Elsbery Albertson of the following negroes to wit: Rose and her children, Harriett & Clarandy & Miles & Joseph, Luke and a negro Man Dave - Your Petitioners being entitled to one third of said negroes - that sd. Alfred & Elsbery are infants represented by one Elias Carver as their Guardian, and Your Petitioners pray that said infants may be made parties defendants by copy & subpoena & show cause if any they have why Your Petitioners should not have partition of said slaves, having their share set off to them in severalty and your Petitioners pray Your Worships that you will appoint Commissioners to allot & set off to Your Petitioners their shares in severalty in said negroes - that Your Worships will make such other & further orders as to Your Worships may seem meet and as in duty bound &c.
Wm F. Martin, Solr. For Petrs

Granted W. Spence Esqr, Wm. Williams Sr., J.M. White, Wilson Williams appointed Commissioners.

To the Worshipful the Justices of the Court of Pleas and Quarter Sessions} December Term 1858.

We the undersigned Freeholders appointed by the Court of Pleas and Quarter Sessions of the County of Pasquotank having been duly sworn proceeded the 4th day of December to divide and make partition between and among Franklin W. Stokely & Wife Sally, Alfred Albertson & Elsbery

Albertson, that they are heirs and tenants in common of certain negroes (Viz) man Dave, Rose, Harriet, Claranda, Martha, Eliza, Mary, Joe, Miles and Luke and allot and assign to each his and her share in severalty as follows that is to say Lot No. 1 Rose, Mary, Eliza & Dave to Alfred Albertson, Lot No. 2, Joe, Clarenda, & Martha to Elsbery Albertson and to pay over to Lots No. 1 and 3 each Lot Thirty three 33/100 dollars and Lot No. 3, Miles, Harriett, & Luke to Franklin W. Stokely & Wife Sally all of which is respectfully submitted under our hands and Seals this 4th day of December 1858.

Signed in Presence of Wm E Mann, Shff
Wilson Spence JP (Seal)
Wm W. Williams (Seal)
Jas M White (Seal)
His
Wilson X Williams
Mark

Susan Perry & Kedar Perry et als
Petr for Division of Slaves
The Court
Pet filed to Decr Term 1858
Brooks

North Carolina } Court of Pleas & Quarter Sessions
Pasquotank County } December Term 1858

To the Worshipful the Justices of the Court aforesaid.
The Petition of Susan Perry, Kedar Perry, Joseph Perry & Jos. P. White and Wife Eliza Ann of full age and D W Morgan infant by Kedar Perry his Guardian humbly complaining respectfully showeth unto your Worships that they are tenants in Common of the following slaves to wit: old Woman Bertha, Jim, Harriett, Jane, Sarah or Sally and Harry, Your Petitioners interest and shares are not equal parts & shares, but your Petitioners derived their title in the following manner to Wit: that the said slaves were the property of Israel Perry dec'd, and the said Israel died intestate and without issue leaving your Petitioners Susan his Widow and the other Petitioners his brothers and sisters, his next of kin & distributed - That your Petitioner Susan thereupon became entitled to one half in value of the slaves whose names are mentioned & the other half of said slaves Equally.

Pasquotank County
Petitions to sell or Divide Slaves

Your Petitioners are desirous that Partition shall be made of the said slaves so that each may have and enjoy their shares in severalty, and to that end pray Your Worships to order and decree that partition be made of said slaves & that you will appoint Commissioners to make such Partition accordingly and that you will from time to time make all such other and further orders and decrees in the premises as the nature of your Petitioner's case may require, and as in duty bound &c
GW Brooks, Solr.

North Carolina } Court of Pleas & Quarter Sessions
Pasquotank County } December Term 1858

The Petition of Susan Perry, Cader Perry, Jos. Perry, & Jos. P. White & Wife Eliza Ann of full age and D. W. Morgan infant by C. Perry his Guardian, showing the Court that they are tenants in Common of the following Slaves viz: Old Woman Bertha, Jim, Harriett, Jane, Sarah or Sally & Harry and that their interests are as follows viz: Your Petitioner Susan is entitled to one half, and the other Petitioners to the other half in value of said Slaves equally - and praying that they may enjoy their shares of said Slaves in Severalty, Coming on to be heard, upon the Petition & evidence in the Cause it is ordered, Adjudged & Decreed by the Court that the said Petition be granted and the Court doth therefore appoint Jos B Reed Esqr, B.F. Mullen, Wilson S. Winslow, Caleb Sanderlin Commissioners to examine value and make Partition of said Slaves & make their report under their hands and Seals to the next term of this Court.
Test, J.W. Hinton, Clk
By Chas G. Elliott, D.C.

Susan Perry & als
Order to divide Slaves, The Court
Rept & Ret to March Term 1859
Served this Order, see report within
Costs paid in office
Wm. E. Mann, Shff

Hinton	2.25
Mann	3.10

Brooks	4.00
	9.35

State of North Carolina } Court of Pleas & Quarter Sessions
Pasquotank County } December Term 1858

To the Sheriff of Pasquotank County, Greeting:

You are hereby summon Jos. B. Reed Esqr, B.F. Mullen, W.S. Winslow, Caleb Sanderlin Commissioners to divide the Slaves named in the Petition as therein stated and to allot to each of the Petitioners his or her thereof accordingly and to report proceedings thereof in due form of Law to the next Court this the first Monday of December in the 83rd year of our Independence, A.D. 1858.
Issued the 18th day of December 1858.
J W. Hinton, Clk
By Chas. G. Elliott

Susan Perry & Kedar Perry et als } Petition for Division of Slaves
To the Court } Court of Pleas & Quarter Sessions
} December Term 1858

This Cause coming on to be heard and it appearing to the satisfaction of the Court that the allegations in the Petition in the Court are true. The Court doth declare that the Petitioners are entitled to the said Slaves mentioned in the shares and Interests as stated in the said Petition, And that the Petitioners are Entitled to Partition. The Court doth therefore appoint Jos B Reed Esqr, B.F. Mullen, Wilson Winslow and Caleb Sanderlin Commissioners to Examine Value and make Partition of said Slaves accordingly and make their Report.

In pursuance to the above proceedings we the Commissioners met at the house of Susan Perry on the 17th day of December 1858, and after being duly qualified, proceeded to value the said Slaves and allot and set apart to each Claimant the share in the same that each was entitled to, Viz To the Widow (Susan Perry) were given the following Slaves, Jim valued at nine hundred & fifty dollars, Boy Harry , valued at two hundred dollars, and woman Bertha valued at four hundred and fifty Dollars - making total amount, sixteen hundred dollars, being one half of the total amount of all the Slaves. To Cader Perry was given the girl Jane, valued at four hundred Dollars. To Joseph Perry was given the girl Sarah, valued at three hundred Dollars, and one hundred Dollars in money to be paid by Cader Perry, as Guardian out of the amount that the girl Harriett was valued at. To Joseph P. White was awarded the sum of four hundred dollars, in money to be paid by Cader Perry, as Guardian to Daniel Morgan, to come out of the amount that the girl Harriett was valued at. Making all told, sixteen hundred Dollars that amount being one half of the value of the said shares, the widow having received the other half all of which is most respectfully Submitted

Benj F. Mullen (Seal)
Jos B. Reed (Seal)
Caleb S. Sanderlin (Seal)

****

Emily Harvey by Thos Harvey, Guard.
Petition for Sale of Slave
The Court
Filed to Term 1858
Dismissed at March Term

North Carolina } Court of Pleas & Quarter Sessions
Pasquotank County } Sept Term 1858

To the Worshipful the Justices of the Court aforsaid.
The Petition of Emily Harvey by her Guardian Thomas Harvey Humbly Complaining respectfully showeth unto Your Worships that she is the owner of a negro slave Named Daniel, that the said Slave within the last few years become greatly adicted to running away and cannot be managed or made to remain in the services of such persons as hire him, That said Slave has absented himself from the services of his Master during the present year for several Months and as Your Petitioner believes has become resolute in his determination to remain obstinate and unmanagable, That said Slave did not voluntarily return the services of his Master, but was caught in the County of Perquimans but a short distance from the Dismal swamp and after many unsuccessful attempts had been made to find him, Your Petitioner believes that her interest require that said Slave be sold, otherwise Your Petitioner believes that his value in a short time

will be very greatly [?] from his vicious habits or will become an entire loss to her.

Your Petitioner therefore prays Your Worships to order and decree a sale to be made of said slave Daniel on such times as to Your Worships may seem meet & proper and that you will from time to time make such other and further orders & Decrees in the premises as the nature of Your Petitioners case may require, and as in duty bound &c.
G W Brooks, Sol.

****

A.J. Glover, Wm. Glover and
Florence Glover by her Guardn.
Petition to divide Slaves
To the Court, Martin, Solr.

State of North Carolina } Court of Pleas & Quarter Sessions
Pasquotank County } December Term AD 1858

To the Worshipful the Justices of said Court;
The Petition of A.J. Glover, Wm. Glover and Florence Glover are infants under twenty one years of age by her Guardian Wm. F. Martin, respectfully showeth unto Your Worships that they are tenants in Common of the following Slaves to Wit: negro man Jim, William, Frank, Harry, Bush, Nero, Luke, Primus, Jerry, John Yellow, John the Barber, George Butler, Isaac, Stephen, Lamb, Jess, Solomon, George Skinner, Old George, Stephen Norcum, Stephen Arrington, negro Boy Ben, Jim, Cat, Negro woman Rachael and two Children Sambo and Edmund, Martha and one child William, Josephine and one child Charles, Candis and two Children one named Ellen, the other a baby, negro woman Nancy Hinton, Nancy Cook, Rose, Little Nancy, Delilah, Abigail, Nelly, Patsey, negro girls Mary, Sabrey, Harriett, Mary - Jane, Sarah, Janet, Cherry, Kate, and Louisa, Your Petitioners further show, that they desire to hold their shares of said Slaves in Severalty, and to that end they pray Your Worships, to appoint three freeholders unconnected with them by consanguinity or affinity to divide the said Slaves into three equal shares and to allot and set apart to each of your Petitioners one of said shares in severalty, and to report their proceedings in due form of Law to the next term of this Court, And Your Petitioners as in duty bound will ever pray.
Wm. F. Martin, Attorney for the Petitioners.

Pasquotank County
Petitions to sell or Divide Slaves

AJ Glover & als
Order to divide Slaves
The Court
Report & Return to March Term 1859

Hinton	2.25
Mann	3.10
Martin	4.00
	$9.35

State of North Carolina } Court of Pleas and Quarter Sessions
Pasquotank County } December Term 1858

To the Worshipful the Justices of said Court.
The Petition of AJ Glover, Wm. Glover and of Florence L. Glover by her Guardian W. F. Martin respectfully sheweth unto your worships that they are tenants in common of the following slaves to wit: Jim Williams, Frank, Harry, Bush, Nero, Luke, Primus, Jerry, John Yellow, John the Barber, George Butler, Isaac, Stephen, Lamb, Jess, Solomon, George Skinner, Old George, Stephen Norcum, Stephen Arrington, Negro Boy Ben, Jim, Cat, negro woman Rachel & two children Sambo and Edmund, Martha & one child William, Josephine & one child Charles, (See paper filed for residue. Your Petitioners further show, that they desire to hold their shares of said slaves in severalty, and to that end they pray your Worships to appoint three free holders unconnected with them by consanguinity or affinity to divide the said slaves into three equal shares and to allot and set apart to each of your petitioners one of said shares in severalty, and to report their proceedings in due form of Law to the next Term of this Court. And your petitioners as in duty bound will ever pray.
W.F. Martin, Attorney for Petitioners.

State of North Carolina } Court of Pleas and Quarter Sessions
Pasquotank County } December Term 1858

To the Sheriff of Pasquotank , Greeting:

Pasquotank County
Petitions to sell or Divide Slaves

You are hereby commanded to summon W.W. Williams Esqr, George W. Brooks, D.D. Raper, J.W. Hinton, W.W. Kennedy, J.M. Whedbee Commissioners to divide the Slaves named in the Petition into three equal shares and to allot to each of the Petitioners one share in severalty and to report proceedings thereof in due form of Law to the next Term of this Court.

Witness, James W. Hinton, Clerk of our said Court this the first Monday of December in the 83rd year of our Independence, A.D. 1858.
Issued the 21st day of December 1858.
James W. Hinton, Clk
By Chas. G. Elliott, D.C.

G W. Brooks, D.D. Raper, J.W. Hinton, W.W. Kenneday, J.M. Whedbee, W.W. Williams, JP, On Decr. 27th 1858.

We the undersigned having been appointed by the Court of Pleas & Quarter Sessions held for the County of Pasquotank at December Term 1858 to make Partition of the slaves belonging to the Estate of Wm. Glover and between A.J. Glover, Wm. Glover & Florence Glover the distributees & heirs at law of the Sd W. Glover beg leave to submit the following report, We have placed the following valuation upon the said Slaves To Wit: Old George $600, Jesse $700, Geo. Skinner $800, Sam 1200, Stephen Norcom 1000, Nero 1000, Stephen Arrington 850, Jim 1000, Geo. Butler 1000, Frank 1000, Isaac 650, Harry 1050, Bush 1200, Little Stephen 800, Solomon 1000, Luke 1200, Jerry 1225, Primus 1100, Yellow John 1000, Jno. Butler 1050, Boy Ben 600, Jim 750, Cat 650, Rose 50.00, Rachel, Sambo & Edmn 1200, Nancy Cook 500, Martha & William 1000, Candis Ellen & Maria, 1100, Old Nance 50.00, Josephine & Child 1050, Little Nancy 900, Delilah 50.00, Abygail 900, Nelly 150, Patty 200, Harriett 750, Mary 750, Sabre 500, Mary Jane 600, Sarah 750, Janet 650, Serena 600, Cherry 450, Cate 300. The Entire Valuation being $33.925.00. We have divided said Slaves among the Petitioners as follows To Wit: To A.J. Glover we have set apart the following Slaves Viz. Geo Skinner $800, Nancy Cook $500.00, Harriett $750. Stephen Norcum $1000.00, Candis & 2 Children $1100.00, Louisa $600, Stephen Arrington $850, Isaac $650, Little Nancy $900, Bush $1200, Delilah $50.00, Old George $600, Ben $600, Abygail $900, Mary $750, Amounting in all to $11, 250.00, To William Glover we have set apart the following Slaves Viz. John the Barber $1050, Josephine & Child $1050, Mary Jane $600, Sam $1200,

Pasquotank County
Petitions to sell or Divide Slaves

Frank $1000, Sarah $750, Jerry 1225, Solomon $100, Cherry $450, Rose $50.00, Yellow John $1000, Cat $650, Primus $1100, Nelly $150, Amounting in all to $11, 275. To Florence Glover we have set apart the following Slaves Viz. Jim Williams $1000, Rachel & Children $1200, Geo Butler $1000, Jennet $650, Sabra $500, Jim $700, Harry $1050, Luke $1200, Nero $1000, Nanci $50, Little Stephen $800, Big Jim $750, Martha & 2 Children $1000, Cate $300, Patsy $200 amount in all id $11,400.

Memorandum, Total valuation of negroes $33.925.00
Set Apart as follows

To A.J. Glover	$11,250.00
To Wm Glover	11, 275.00
Florence Glover	11, 400.00
	$33, 925.00

The Valuation of each share say one third of $33, 925.00
$11,308.33

Value of A.J. Glovers Share of Negroes say one third of $33.925.00 is 11, 308.33

Value of A. J. Glovers share of Negroes say one third	$11, 308.33.
Amount Allotted to A.J. Glover in division as above	$11, 250.00.
Amount to be paid to A.J. Glover by Florence Glover	$58.33.
Value of Wm. Glovers share of Negroes say one third	$11, 308.33
Amt. allotted to W. Glover in division as above	$11, 275.00
Amt to be paid to W.Glover by Florence Glover	$33.33
To Florence Glovers share of Negroes Say one third	$11, 308.33
Amt Allotted to Florence Glover in division	$11,400.00
Amy to be paid by Florence to A.J. Glover	$58.33 &

1/3
W. Glover $33.33 1/3

****

A.H. Lindsay & Wife als
Order to Divide Slaves
The Court
Report & Return
March Term 1859

Hinton 2.25

Mann	3.10
Martin	4.00
	$9.35

Executed, Cost not paid
Wm. E. Morgan, Shff

A.H. Lindsay & Wife Adaline
And Georgiana Charles by her Guardian
Wm. F. Martin
Petition to Divide Slaves To the Court

State of North Carolina } Court of Pleas & Quarter Sessions
Pasquotank County } December Term AD 1858

To the Worshipful the Justices of said Court, The Petition of A.H. Lindsay & Wife Adaline and Georgiana Charles by her Guardian Wm. F. Martin respectfully showeth unto your Worships that they are tenants in Common of the following Slaves to Wit, John, Frank, Lindsay, Charles, Rose, Harriett, Sally and Betsey and her Child Jane, Your Petitioners further show, that they desire to hold their shares of said Slaves in Severalty and to that end they pray your Worships to Appoint three freeholders, unconnected with them by consanguinity or affinity, to divide the said Slaves in two equal shares and to allot and set apart to Each of your Petitioners, one of said shares in severalty, and to report their Proceedings in due form of Law to the next Term of this Court. And Your Petitioners as in duty bound, will ever pray.
W.F. Martin Atty for Petitioner

On Motion the following freeholders to Wit, D.D. Raper, M.S. Dance, [?] C. Blount, and Nathan Overman are appointed Commissioners to divide the Slaves named in the Petition into two equal Shares, and to allot to each of the Petitioners one Share thereof, in Severalty and to report their proceedings in due form of Law to the next Term of this Court.

State of North Carolina } Court of Pleas and Quarter Sessions
Pasquotank County } december Term 1858

Pasquotank County
Petitions to sell or Divide Slaves

To the Worshipful the Justices of said Court, The Petition of A.H. Lindsay & Wife Adeline & Georgiana Charles by her Guardian W.F. Martin respectfully sheweth unto your worships that they are tenants in common of the following slaves to wit: John, Frank, Lindsay, Charles, Rose Harriett, Sally & Betsey & her child Jane. Your Petitioners further show, that they desire to hold their shares of said Slaves in severalty, and to that end they pray your Worships to appoint four free holders unconnected with them by consanguinity or affinity to divide the said slaves into two equal shares and to allot and set apart to each of your petitioners one of said shares in severalty, and to report their proceedings in due form of Law to the next Term of this Court. And your Petitioners as in duty bound will ever pray..
W.F. Martin, Attorney for Petitioners.

State of North Carolina } Court of Pleas and Quarter Sessions
Pasquotank County } December Term 1858

To the Sheriff of Pasquotank County, greeting:
You are hereby commanded to summon D.D. Raper, M.S.Daud[?], Wm. C. Blount & Nathan Overman Commissioners to divide the slaves named in the Petition into two equal shares and to allot to each of the Petitioners one share thereof in Severalty and to report proceedings thereof in due form of Law to the next Term of this Court.

Witness, James W. Hinton, Clerk of our said Court this the first Monday of December in the 83rd year of our Independence, A.D. 1858.
Issued the 21st day of December 1858.
James W. Hinton, Clk
By Charles G. Elliott, D.C.

A.H. Lindsay & Wife Adaline
And Georgiana Charles by her Guardian
Wm. F. Martin
Pet. To divide Slaves
The Court

State of North Carolina }
Pasquotank County }

Pasquotank County
Petitions to sell or Divide Slaves

The undersigned having been appointed by the Worshipful Court of Pasquotank County to divide the Negroes held in Common between A.H. Lindsay and Wife Adeline, of full age and Georgiana Charles infant by her Guard. Wm. F. Martin, and having first been duly sworn upon the Holy Evangelist of Almighty God proceeded to inspect the negroes named in the Petition of said tenants in Common, assessing their value and dividing them as follows, to A.H. Lindsay & Wife they assign negroes Frank, Charles, Sally & Rose valued at $2966.00 -- To Georgiana Charles negroes John, Lindsay, Betsey & child & Harriett valued at $3025.00 and the said Georgiana by her Guardian is to pay over to A.H. Lindsay & Wife the sum of $59.00.

All of which is respectfully submitted this the 17th of December AD 1858 in the Presence of Geo Charles, JP

M.S. Dance (Seal)
Thos W. Newby (Seal)
Nathan Overman (Seal)

****

C. B. Brothers & W A. Bassett
Petition for Partition of Slaves
The Court
Filed to Decr Term 1859
Johnson & Brooks

North Carolina } Court of Pleas & Quarter Sessions
Pasquotank County } Decr. Term 1859

To the Worshipful the Justices of the said Court.
The Petition of Charles B. Brothers and Wm. A. Bassett humbly Complaining respectfully showeth unto your Worships that they are tenants in Common of Equal interest of three Negro Slaves to Wit, Woman Jane & her two children, John Wesley & George Holly that they derived their title to the said slaves in the following manner -- that the said Slaves belonged to one John Clarey a brother of Penelope the wife of Wm. Miller - that said John Clarey died intestate & without issue or any other distributee or next of kin than the said Penelope and Virginia -- That after the death of the said John Clarey the said Wm. Miller sold and conveyed all his right and interest in the said slaves in right of his wife to Wm. A. Bassett the Petitioner which may be seen by exhibit marked (A) Now your

Petitioners are desirous that partition shall be made of the said slaves, And your Worships to order and decree that partition be made accordingly and that you will from time to time make all such other and further orders and decrees in the premises as may to your Worships seem meet and proper and as in duty bound &c.
Johnston & Brooks, Solrs.

State of North Carolina } Court of Pleas and Quarter Sessions
Pasquotank County } December Term 1859

To the Worshipful the Justices of said Court, The Petition of C.B. Brothers & Wm. A. Bassett respectfully sheweth unto your Worships that they are tenants in common of the following slaves to wit: Woman Jane & her two Children, John Wesley and George Nolly**[?]**, Your petitioners further show, that they desire to hold their shares of said slaves in severalty, and to that end they pray your Worships to appoint three free holders unconnected with them by consanguinity or affinity to divide the said slaves into two equal shares and to allot and set apart to each of your petitioners one of said shares in severalty, and to report their proceedings in due form of Law to the next Term of this Court. And your Petitioners as in duty bound will ever pray.
G. W. Brooks, Attorney for Petitioners

State of North Carolina } Court of Pleas and Quarter Sessions
Pasquotank County } December Term 1859

To the Sheriff of Pasquotank, Greeting:
You are hereby commanded to summon Daniel Richardson, Seth Morgan & James Whedbee Commissioners to divide the slaves named in the petition into two equal shares and to allot to each of the petitioners one share thereof in severalty and to report proceedings thereof in due form of Law to the next Term of this Court.

Witness, James W. Hinton, Clerk of our said Court this the first Monday of December in the 84th year of our Independence A.D. 1859.
Issued the 19th day of December 1859.
J.W. Hinton, Clk
By Chas. G. Elliott, D.C.

Pasquotank County
Petitions to sell or Divide Slaves

C.B. Brothers als to the Court
Order to divide Slaves
Executed, see report within
W.E. Mann, Shff
By J. Wilcox, DShff

In the matter of C.B. Brothers	} Court of Pleas & Quarter Sessions
To the Court	} December Term 1859

This Cause being heard the Court doth declare that the Petitioner CB Brothers & W.A. Bassett are tenants in common: Each being Entitled to one Moiety in value of the slaves whose names are mentioned in this Petition of said slaves, It is therefore ordered by the Court that Partition of said slaves be made between the Petitioners in as Equal shares as may be and that the more valuable share be assessed with a sum to be paid to the share or lot of loss value sufficient to make the shares of each Equal in value -- And the Court doth appoint Daniel Richardson, Seth Morgan and JM Whedbee Commissioners to examine value and make partition accordingly - & make report to the next Term of this Court.

In obedience to the above order, We the Commissioners Seth Morgan, D. Richardson & J.M. Whedbee met at C.B. Brothers & after being duly sworn, did proceed to value & divide the negroes named in the annexed order as follows.

Woman Jane $800, John Wesley $600, Geo Nolly $525, Total $1925.

To W.A. Bassett one of the Petitioners we give Woman Jane, Geo. Nolly
To C.B. Brothers the other Petitioner John Wesly.
Bassett to pay Brothers three Hundred & Sixty Two Dollars & Fifty cents ($362.50)
Witness our Hands & Seals the 20th Decr 1859
Seth Morgan (Seal)
Danl. Richardson (Seal)
J.M. Whedbee (Seal)

****

Pasquotank County
Petitions to sell or Divide Slaves

A. L. Wadsworth & Wife and others
Petition for Division of Slaves
The Court
December Term 1859

State of North Carolina } Court of Pleas & Quarter Sessions
Pasquotank County } December Term 1859

To the Worshipful the Justices of said Court:
The Petition of A.L. Wadsworth and wife Helen, Wm. F. Martin and Wife Elizabeth Burguin Trustee, and of Marion M. Morine, respectfully showeth unto your Worships that they are tenants in common of the following slaves, which they inherited from their ancestor Martha M. Morine to Wit: John, Jacob, Hamlet, Hannah, Manuel, Cynthia, Charles, Fanny & her children Mary Ann, Alice, Cynthia, Matthew, p[?], & Charles, Sarah & her child Lucious, Mana, Penny, Louisa, Juliann, Rosanna & her child Jim Wilson, Nancy Francis, Margaret & her child Ellen, Isaac, Hamlet, Mabel, Edmund, Tim, Joanna, Tom, Minerva & her children Wilson & Joe, Cornelius, Noah, Albert, Jim, George.

Your Petitioners further show, that they desire to hold their shares of said slaves in severalty, and to that end they pray your Worships to appoint five freeholders unconnected with them by consanguinity or affinity, they or any three of them to divide the said slaves into thee equal shares, and to allot and set apart to each of your Petitioners one of said shares in severalty, and to report their proceedings in due form of law to the next Term of this Court - And your Petitioners as in duty bound will ever pray.
L. D. [?], Sol.

State of North Carolina } Court of Pleas and Quarters Sessions
Pasquotank County } December term 1859

To the Worshipful the Justices of said Court,
The Petition of A.L. Wadsworth & Wife Helen, Wm. F. Martin & Wife Elizabeth by Trustee of Burguin of Marion M Morine respectfully sheweth unto your worships that they are tenants in common of the following slaves to Wit: John, Jacob, Hamlet, Hannah, Manuel, Cynthia, Charles, Fanny & her children Mary Ann, Alice, Cynthia, Matthew, Ipsey & Charles, Sarah & her child Lucious, Maria, Penny, Louisa, Julianne, Rosanna & her child

Pasquotank County
Petitions to sell or Divide Slaves

Jim Wilson, Nancy, Francis, Margaret & her child Ellen, Isaac, Hamlet, Mabel, Edmund, Lem, Joanna, Tom, Minerva & her children Wilson & Joe, Cornelius, Noah, Albert, Jim & George.. Your Petitioners further show, that they desire to hold their shares of said slaves in severalty, and to that end they pray your Worships to appoint five free holders unconnected with them by consanguinity or affinity to divide the said Slaves into three equal shares and to allot and set apart to each of your petitioners one of said shares in severalty, and to report their proceedings in due form of Law to the next Term of this Court. And your petitioners as in duty bound will ever pray.
L.D. Starke, Attorney for Petitioners.

State of North Carolina } Court of Pleas and Quarter Sessions
Pasquotank County } December term 1859

To the Sheriff of Pasquotank, Greeting:
You are hereby commanded to Summon Geo W. Brooks, F.M. Charles, G.W. Charles, Timothy Hunter & James W. Hinton Commissioners to divide the slaves named in the petition into three equal shares and to allot to each of the petitioners one share thereof in severalty and to report proceedings thereof in due form of Law to the next Term of this Court.

Witness, James W. Hinton, Clerk of our said Court this the first Monday of December in the 84th year of our Independence, A.D., 1859.
Issued the 19th day of December 1859.
J. W. Hinton, Clk
By Chas G. Elliott, D.C.

On Motion Geo. W. Brooks, F.M. Charles, J. W. Charles, Timothy Hunter & J.W. Hinton, freeholders, are appointed Commissioners they or any three of them to divide the slaves named in the petition into three equal shares, and to allot to each of the petitioners one share thereof in severalty, and to report their proceedings in due form of Law to the next Term of this Court.
Test, J.W. Hinton, Clk
By Chas G. Elliott, D.C.

State of North Carolina }

Pasquotank County
Petitions to sell or Divide Slaves

Pasquotank County }

The undersigned, appointed Commissioners by the Court of Pleas and Quarter Sessions, December Term, 1859, of the County aforesaid, to divide the slaves named in the petition of A.S. Wadsworth & Wife Helen, Wm. F. Martin and Wife Elizabeth by trustee Burguin & Marion McMorine, (said petition having been made to said Court at the Term aforementioned) into three equal shares, and to allot to each of the petitioners one share thereof in severalty, respectfully report.

That on the 21st December, 1859, they (the said Commissioners) met and proceeded to divide and allot the slaves referred to in the said petition and in the order of the Court appointing them. They divided and appropriated said slaves as follows to Wit: Lot No. 1, Margaret & Ella, $940.00, Hamlet Jr. $50.00, Julian $1300.00, Isaac $1100.00, Fanny & Children Mary Ann, Alice, Cynthia, Matthew, Ipsey & Charles & Hamlet Jr. $4140.00 $1000.00, Deduct charges on Estate, Viz: $8930.00, Cynthia $200.00, Pay to Lot No. 2 $188.34, Total $8541.66 --- Lot No. 2, Joanna $310.00, Minerva & 2 children $1510.00, Jacob $200.00, Cornelius $1400.00, Albert $1040.00, Louisa $1100.00, Rosanne & son Jim 41550.00, Edmund $850.00, Tom $525.00, $8485.00, Manuel $200.00, Paid by Lots No. 1 & 2 $256.67, Total $8541.67, Lot No. 3, Sarah & Lucious $1300.00, Penny $1200.00, John $150.00, Jim $1400.00, George $1270.00, Maria $1100.00, Nancy Frances $800.00, Sem $800.00, Mabel $950.00, $8970.00, Hannah $360.00, Pay to Lot No. 2 $8610.00, paid by Lot No. 1 & 2 $68.33, Total $8541.67.

They (The said Commissioners) appropriated and assigned the slaves named in Lot No. 1 to Wm. F. Martin & Wife Elizabeth, (SS Burgwin trustee) those named in Lot No. 2 to A.S. Wadsworth & Wife Hellen; and those in Lot No. 3 to Marion McMorine in severalty.

The said Commissioners further report that the slaves Charles & Noah though at present a charge upon the estate, are young and likely, and may possibly recover from the diseases with which they are afflicted and again become valuable. They have not included them in the preceding schedule, and recommend that they be retained in common among the petitioners, All which is respectfully Submitted

G. W. Brooks, Geo W. Charles, T. Hunter, James W. Hinton & F.M. Charles, Commissioners.

Pasquotank County
Petitions to sell or Divide Slaves

****

Joseph B. Shaw Admr et al
Petition for Sale of Slaves
The Court
Report made to March Term 1859

North Carolina }
Pasquotank County }

To the Worshipful the Justices of the County Court of Pasquotank, March Term 1859.

Pursuant to the annexed order of Court to me directed I did proceed after due advertisement according to said order to sell the slaves mentioned as the property of the Estate of Miles Commander for distribution between his next of kin on the 31st day of Decr 1858 at Newbegan Creek on a Credit of six months with interest fro date, And the said slaves were offered at public sale to the highest bidder at the time & place & upon the terms aforesaid and they were bid off by the following named persons and at the following prices respectfully and in the following order.

Man Ned to Mordacai Morris	$77.00
Man Driver to Mordacai Elliott	$212.00
Man Bob to Wm. Banks	$1110.00
Man Ambrose to T.D. Pendleton	$910.00
Boy Isaac To Same	$1055.00
Boy Frank to W.W. Kennedy	$915.00
Girl Rose to Thos Markham	$1015.00
Woman Sarah to Mordacai Morris	$25.00
	$5319.00

There were many bidders assembled and many bids were made, there was much Competition in the bidding and the bids as herein before stated were the last & highest bids obtained, all of which is respectfully submitted.
Jos. B. Shaw

****

Jos Harris's Petition for Partition

Pasquotank County
Petitions to sell or Divide Slaves

Mary C White & Jno. L. Wood
Filed Sept Term 1859
Service Accepted
John L. [?] & Jno. L. Wood
Brooks

North Carolina	} Court of Pleas & Quarter Sessions
Pasquotank County	} September Term 1859

To the Worshipful the Justices of the Court aforesaid
The Petition of Joseph Harris humbly complaining respectfully sheweth unto your Worships that he is tenant in Common with Mary Caroline White for whome John L. Wood is Guardian and the said John L. Wood of a certain slave named Jack - that the said slave belongs to the petitioner & the said Wood & his said Ward in the following proportions One third part to the Petitioner. One Fourth to the said Mary Caroline, and the balance to the said Wood, That Your Petitioners share in said slave bequeathed to Your Petitioners Wife by her late father John Thompson, Your Petitioner is desirous that partition be made so that he may Enjoy his share in severalty and therefore prays your Worships to order and direct a sale of said slave to be made for that purpose upon such time as Your Worships may seem meet and proper - And to that end Your Petitioner prays Your Worships to order Copies of this Petition to give to the said Jno L. Wood that he may be and appear &c then & there &c.

And that you will from time to time make all such other orders and decrees in the premises as to your Worships may seem meet and proper and as in duty bound &c.
G.W. Brooks, Solr.

Jos Harris Vs. M. C. White
& Jno. L. Wood

Court of Pleas & Quarter Sessions	}
September Term 1859	}

This Cause coming on to be heard upon the Petition, evidence &c And it appearing to the Court that the allegations in the petition are true - The Court doth order and decree that the petitioner is entitled to partition of said slave Jack be sold at public sale before the Court House door in

Elizabeth City thirty days notice of sale on a credit of six months with interest from date -- and the Court doth appoint Jno. L. Wood Commissioner to make such advertisement and sale and take bond of the purchaser and report to the next Term of this Court.
Test, J.W. Hinton, Clk
By Chas G Elliott, D.C.

Jos Harris
Order on Petr. For Partition
Mary C. White & Jno L. Wood
Report Dec. Term 1859

Hinton	2.25
Brooks	4.00
	$6.25

To the Worshipful the Justices of the Court of Pleas & Quarter Sessions, Novr Term 1859

We the undersigned did pursuant to the order of Court to me directed first duly advertise the sale to be made at the Court House in Elizabeth City and pursuant [?] did offer Negro Man Jack at public sale to the highest bidder on a credit of six months with interest from date on the 6th day of Decr. 1859 when and where William Palen appeared and bid for the said slave fourteen Hundred and twenty five dollars which was the highest and last bid then and there where the said Wm. Palin became the purchaser of the said slave at the said sum, all of which is respectfully submitted.
John L. Wood, Commissioner

****

Cornelius Trueblood et als
Petition to the Court

State of North Carolina } Court of Pleas & Quarter Sessions
Pasquotank County } September term AD 1859

Pasquotank County
Petitions to sell or Divide Slaves

To the Worshipful the Justices of said Court, the Petition of Cornelius Trueblood, Thomas Reed, Benjamin [?], Newton Sawyer and Isadora Raper an infant under twenty one years of age by her Guardian Newton Sawyer, Admr. of Jos Trueblood Dec'd respectfully showeth to Your Worships that they are tenants in Common of Certain Slaves to Wit (Woman Kate and her child Frank) Your Petitioners further show that they desire to have the said Slaves divided among them according to their respective rights and interests in the same, but that a division in kind cannot be made without injury to the parties concerned, Your Petitioners therefore pray Your Worships to order a sale thereof on such terms as to Your Worships shall seem best and that the proceeds of the sale may be divided among them according to their respective rights and interests in said slaves And Your Petitioners as in duty bound will ever pray.
J.L. Ball Attorney for the Petitioners.

North Carolina }
Pasquotank County Court } Sept Term 1859

Cornelius Trueblood & als, Petition to sell Slaves

It appearing to the satisfaction of the Court that the Petitioners are tenants in common of the slaves (Woman Kate and her child Frank) named in the petition, and that the said slaves cannot be divided in kind among the parties interested, it is therefore ordered, adjudged and decreed that Thomas Reed be appointed a Commissioner to make sale of said slaves and it is further ordered that after advertisement of the sale at the Court House Door in the town of Elizabeth City and three more public places in the County of Pasquotank for at least twenty days, he proceed to sell said slaves at the Court House aforesaid to the highest bidder at public auction upon a credit of six months first takeing bond with approved security for the payments of the purchase money. It is further Ordered that the said Commissioner make his report to the next term of this Court.
Test, J.W. Hinton, Clk
By Chas G. Elliott, D.C.

Cornelius Trueblood & als
Order to Sell Slaves
Reprt & Return to Dec. Term 1859

Hinton	2.25
Ball	4.00
	$6.25

In Pursuance of the within order I did proceed to sell the Negroes therein named at the Court House door in Eliz. City on Monday the 5th day of December 1859 after first advertising said negroes for twenty days, when and where L. G. Eddings appeared and bid for the same Eight Hundred and fifty five Dolls. upon the terms herein contained and was then & there declared the purchaser of said negroes all of which is respectfully Submitted
Allowed $10

****

B.B. Reed Admr.
Petr for sale of Slaves
The Court
Filed to Sept Term 1859

North Carolina } Court of Pleas & Quarter Sessions
Pasquotank County } September Term 1859

To the Worshipful the Justices of the said Court.
The Petition of Benj B. Reed Admr. of E.B. Reed humbly complaining respectfully sheweth unto Your Worships that he find the Estate of his intestate so much indebted as to render a sale of all slaves belonging to said Estate necessary - And therefore prays Your Worships to order and direct a sale to be made of Old Woman Hannah and Fillis and her two Children Wilson and Sally for the purpose aforesaid, on such terms and conditions as to Your Worships may seem meet & proper -- And that you will from time to time make all such other and further orders and decrees in the Premises may to Your Worships seem meet & proper and as in duty bound &c.
G.W. Brooks, Solr.

B.B. Reed Admr.
Order to sell Slaves

Ret. & Report Decr. Term 1859

Hinton	$2.25
Brooks	4.00
	$6.25

North Carolina }
Pasquotank County }

County Court Sept Term 1859

This Cause coming on to be heard and it appearing that a sale of all the slaves whose names are Mentioned in the Petition (Viz: Old woman Hannah, and Fillis and her two Children Wilson & Sally) is necessary for the payment of debts. It is therefore Ordered that the Petitioner sell the said Slaves Hannah & Phillis and her two children; On a credit of six months with interest from date, That he duly advertise the sale for thirty days and make report - to the next term of this Court.
Test, J.W. Hinton, Clk
By Chas. G. Elliott, D.C.

North Carolina }
Pasquotank County }

To the Worshipfull the Justices of said County.

The Undersigned did pursuant to an order of Court to me directed to proceed to advertise a sale to be made of the slaves named therein as as directed and pursuant thereto did offer at the Court House door in Elizabeth City on the 5th day of decr. 1859 on a credit of six months with interest from date to the highest bidder - the said slaves as follows and sold same as follows

Negro Woman Hannah to J.C. Johnston	450.00
Fillis & Child to W.W. Ball	300.00
Boy Wilson to Jos B. Reed	521.00
	2271.00

All of which is respectfully Submitted
B.B. Reed, Admr. of Edwin Reed Dec'd

****

Pasquotank County
Petitions to sell or Divide Slaves

Order of Court To Chas. Harris
To Sell the Slave of Brite Cartwright, Dec'd 1859

State of North Carolina } Court of Pleas & Quarter Sessions
Pasquotank County } Decr. Term 1858

Chas. Harris Admr.
Petition to Sell **[Torn]**

This Cause coming on to be heard, upon the petition **[Torn]** ordered and decreed that the Petitioner **[Torn]** Harris's sell the slaves (girls) **[Torn]** belonging to the Estate of Br **[Torn]** at the Court House door in the County of Pasquotank on a credit of Six months with interest from date after giving due advertisement **[Torn]** the **[Torn]** **[Smudged]** take bond with approved security and report make to the next term of this Court to be held for this **[Torn]** of Pasquotank at the C.H. in E. City on the 1st Monday in March A.D. 1859.
Issued **[Torn]** 16th day of Decr. 1858.
J.W. Hinton, Clk
By Chas G. Elliott, D.C.

****

Order of Court to Chas Harris
To Sell the Slaves of
Lavinia & Victoria Cartwright, 1858

State of North Carolina } Court of Pleas & Quarter Sessions
Pasquotank County } Decr. Term 1858

This cause coming on to be heard, upon the petition it is ordered adjudged & Decreed that the Petitioner Chas Harris, sell the slaves Cynthia & Christian belonging to the Petitioner; before the Court House in E.City on the 1st day of Jany 1859, on a credit of six months with interest from date - that he take bonds from purchaser with approved security & due report make at the next term of this Court to be held for Pasquotank County Eliz. City on the 1st Monday in March AD 1859.
Issued 12th day of Decr. 1858.
James W. Hinton, Clk

Pasquotank County
Petitions to sell or Divide Slaves

By Chas G. Elliott, D.C.

****

Timothy Morgan Admr. of W. [A]. McDonnell
Pet for sale of Slaves
The Court
Filed to Sept Term 1860
Brooks

North Carolina } Court of Pleas & Quarter Sessions
September Term 1860 } September Term 1860

To the worshipful the Justices of the Court aforesaid
The Petition of Timothy Morgan Admr. of W. A. McDonnell humbly complaining respectfully sheweth unto your Worships, that Your petitioner finds the Estate of his Intestate so much indebted as to render a Sale of one of the slaves belonging to said Estate necessary, And therefore prays Your Worships to order and decree a sale to be made of Girl Mary belonging to the Estate of his Intestate to enable your Petitioner with the proceeds of such sales to pay off and discharge the debts remaining now unpaid & the proper costs attending Administration of said Estate, And that such Sale be made as your Worships may think proper and that you will from time to time make all such other and further orders and decrees in the premises and the nature of your Petitioners case may require, and as in duty bound &c.
G.W. Brooks Solr for Petitioner.

In the Motion of Timothy Morgan
Admr of Wm. A. McDonnell
To the Court
September Term 1860

Upon the hearing of the Petition in this cause and it appearing to the satisfaction of the Court that the allegations in the Petition are true, it is therefore ordered by the Court that the Petition sell said slave Mary after due advertisement for the space of 30 days at the Court House door in Elizabeth City & three other places in said County, on a credit of six months with interest from date of sale to be made at the Court House door in Elizabeth City, and that he make report.

Pasquotank County
Petitions to sell or Divide Slaves

****

R. Jackson & Wife Mary
& Thos. H.. Mayfield et al
Petition for Sale of Slave for Division
The Court
Pet. Filed to Decr. Term 1860

North Carolina } Court of Pleas & Quarter Sessions
Pasquotank County } December Term 1860

To the Worshipful the justices of the said Court, The Petition of Robinson Jackson & Wife Mary and Thomas Henry Mayfield of full age James O. Mayfield infant by his next friend Thos. H. Mayfield humbly complaining sheweth that they are tenants in Common of a Slave named Susan, that the said Slave is the same owned by Roger Mayfield at his death and your Petitioner mary being his widow at his death & Your Petitioners Thos. H. & James Obering [?] his only children living at the death of said Roger, they derived title to the said slave as tenants in Common of equal interest by the delivery over to Your Petitioners of the said Slave by the Admr of said Roger.

Your Petitioners are desirous that partition be made of said slave and inasmuch as partition can only be made by sale of said slave for that purpose Your Petitioners pray that you will hear this their petition & complaint and that you will order and direct that a sale of said slave Susan be made so that each of your petitioners may have and enjoy their proper shares & portion in value of said Slave in severalty, and that you will from time to tim make all such other and further orders and decrees in the premises as the nature of your Petitioners case may require, And as in duty bound &c
G. W. Brooks (Seal)

In the Matter of R. Jackson & Wife et als
To the Court
December Term 1860

Upon the hearing of this petition it is adjudged and considered by the Court that the petitioners are Entitled to Partition of the slave Susan whose name

is mentioned in the petition in the Cause, And it is ordered and decreed by the Court that the said slave be sold for that purpose on a credit of twelve months at the Court House door after twenty days advertisement of the time & place of sale at three or more public places in said County of which places the Court House door shall be one, that note be required with good security with interest from such sale, And the Petitioner Robinson Jackson is hereby appointed by the Court to make the sale accordingly & make report.
Issued Dec. 12th 1860
Test J.W. Hinton, Clk
By C. G. Elliott, D.C.

North Carolina }
Pasquotank County }

To the Worshipful the Justices of the Court of Pleas & Quarter Sessions March Term 1861.

The Undersigned beg leave to report that he did pursuant to the annexed order of Court to me directed advertise the slave Susan mentioned therein as therein directed and did pursuant to such advertisement offer said slave at public Sale before the Court House door in Elizabeth City on the 1st day of January last When and Where there were many persons assembled, And there was then & there bid for the said Slave the sum of Five hundred and fifty dollars, Which was the best & highest bid which could be obtained for the same and the said slave was struck off to D.D. Raper at the said sum, all of which is respectfully submitted.
Robinson Jackson.

Susan at $530 to D.D. Raper
Paid Butt 1.00 for auctioneering slave
$549.00
Costs of Pet $6.25
$542.75

****

A.C. Albertson
Order to Divide Slaves
Return Mch Term 1861

Pasquotank County
Petitions to sell or Divide Slaves

Exd, See Report within
W.E. Mann, Shff
By J. Wilcox, DShff

Hinton	2.25
Mann	3.10
Starke	4.00
	$9.35
	3.11
	6.24

1/3 pd Mch 2/
/3.11 by L. W. Stokely

A.C. Albertson & others
Petition to divide Slaves
The Court
December Term 1860
Starke

State of North Carolina } Court of Pleas & Qr. Sessions
Pasquotank County } December Term 1860

To the Worshipful the Justices of said Court.
The Petition of Alferd C. Albertson, Franklin Stokely and wife Sarah, and Elsbery Albertson, an infant under twenty one years of age, by his guardian, Elias Carver, respectfully Showeth unto your Worships that they are tenants in common of the following slaves to Wit: Mack, Charles, Tom, Martha, Winny, Mary, March, Anderson, John and Jacob.

Your petitioners further show, that they desire to hold their shares of said slaves in severalty, and to that end they pray your Worships to appoint three freeholders, unconnected with them by consanguinity or affinity, to divide said slaves into three equal shares, and to allot and set apart to each of your petitioners one of said Shares in severalty, and to report their proceedings in due form of law to the next term of this Court, And your Petitioners, as in duty bound will ever pray &c
L.D. Starke, Atty for Petitioners

State of North Carolina } Court of Pleas and Quarter Sessions

Pasquotank County
Petitions to sell or Divide Slaves

Pasquotank County }

To the Worshipful the Justices of said Court.
The Petition of Alfred C. Albertson, Franklin Stokely, & Wife Sarah & Elsbery Albertson an infant by Elias Carver Guardian respectfully sheweth unto your worships that they are tenants in common of the following slaves to wit: Mack, Charles, Tom, Martha, Winney, Mary, March, Anderson, John and Jacob.

Your petitioners further show, that they desire to hold their shares of said slaves in severalty, and to that end they pray your Worships to appoint three free holders unconnected with them by consanguinity or affinity to divide the said slaves into three equal shares and to allot and set apart to each of your petitioners one of said shares in severalty, and to report their proceedings in due form of Law to the next term of this Court. And your petitioners as in duty bound will ever pray.
L. D. Starke Attorney for Petitioners.

State of North Carolina } Court of Pleas and Quarter Sessions
Pasquotank County } December term 1860

To the Sheriff of Pasquotank, Greeting:
You are hereby commanded to summon Wilson Spence, Wm. Williams Junr., & James M. White Commissioners to divide the slaves named in the petition into three equal shares and to allot to each of the Petitioners one share thereof in severalty and to report proceedings thereof in due form of Law to the next term of this Court.

Witness, James W. Hinton, Clerk of our said Court this the first Monday of December in the 85th year of our Independence, A.D., 1860.
Issues the 11th day of December 1860.
J.W. Hinton, Clk
By C.G. Elliott, D.C.

North Carolina }
Pasquotank County }

In obedience to the annexed order we the undersigned Commissioners did on the 2nd day of Jany 1861 meet at the School House at Newland & having the slaves mentioned in said order present after being sworn proceeded to value & divide them as follows to wit.

To Alfred C. Albertson we allot & set apart	
March valued at	$500
Winny valued at	$600
Charles valued at	$100
	$1200
To Franklin Stokely & Wife Sarah	
Mary & Jacob valued at	$800
Anderson & 300 - John $200	$500
Lot No. 2 has to pay Lot No. 3 $100	$1300
	$100
Leaving Lot No. 2 worth$	$1200
To Ellsbury Albertson an Infant by Elias Carver Guardian	
Tom Valued at $800 - Mack $250	$1050
Martha valued at	$50
Lot No 3 receives from Lot No. 2	$1100
	$100
Making Lot No. 3 worth	$1200

& making all the Lots equal
All of which is respectfully submitted, Given under our hands & Seals the day & date above written. In Presence of J. Wilcox
James M. White (Seal)
Wm. Williams (Seal)

****

Eliz Crawford
Pet. To Sell Slaves
In Equity
Spring Term 1861
Fall T. 1866 Petition
An the papers in this case are
Filed within Nov 1868
V Docket F. 1. 1866, Martin

State of North Carolina } In Equity
Pasquotank County } Spring Term 1861

Pasquotank County
Petitions to sell or Divide Slaves

To the Honorable the Judge of the Court aforesaid:

Humbly complaining respectfully sheweth unto your Honor, the Petition of Eliz. Crawford of the County aforesaid - that she is a Widow, and has four Children, all of whom are dependant upon her for support. That she has a life estate in two negroes, Bill & Manuel, both negro men - the remainder interest in both of whom is owned by her said children - Your Petitioner further showeth that her annual income is insufficient to enable her to properly provide for the support and maintenance of her children - That she owns, absolutely, a tract of land in the County aforesaid, but that she is unable to sell the same for a proper price, and therefore Your Petitioner prays Your Honor to grant an order authorizing her to sell one of the said slaves, to wit Manuel aged 19 years at private sale, that with the proceeds of such sale she may properly provide for the support of her children, Your Petitioner asks for the support of her children, Your Petitioner asks for this relief and as in duty bound will ever pray.

Martin, Sol for Petr.

This Cause coming to be heard upon petition and report of Master, the Court doth adjudge and decree that the Master shall sell the negro in the pleadings named, at public auction before the Court House Door, upon a credit of six months with interest from the purchase from date money saving sufficient to pay the costs in this behalf incurred which shall be paid in cash, having first advertised said slave according to Law for the space of twenty days, take bond & approved security for the purchase money and report to the next term of this Court. It is further ordered, adjudged and decreed that the Master shall inquire and ascertain the value of the life estate of the petitioner, Elizabeth Crawford, in the fund arising from the sale of said slave, and report the same to the Court, to the end that her share in said negro may be paid to her in cash.

The Clerk & Master respectfully reports he is personaly well acquainted with the said Elizabeth Crawford, her means of supporting herself & her four children, That with the exception of a little household Kitchen furniture, she has no other property but that is mentioned in the within petition but the land mentioned therein, is already under a mortgage or

Deed of trust for the sum of $600 and which under [?] circumstances It is very [?] whether it would sell for more than [?]
Jos C. Ehringhaus, Clk & M

Chapter Two

Pasquotank County

Civil Actions

North Carolina State Archives
Pasquotank County Records
Records of Slaves and Free Persons of Color
C.R.075.928.10

Cartwright Vs Broshiers [1792]
Ansr to Peto for an Injunction
To stay with
Pasquotank County
June Term 1792

State of North Carolina }
Pasquotank County } Sessions

The [?] of Clement Cartright **[Faded]**
This Defendant **[Faded]**
For Answer to the said Petition or to so much thereunto he Answereth and saith that he admits that he [?] the Negroe Slaves mentioned in the Petition of the petitioner together with their increase otherwise set forth, He also

admits that **[Faded]** the said Slaves were sold but does not **[Faded]** they were sold by him altho he conceives he has **[Faded]** a right to dispose of the Interest which he in right of his Wife possesses therein provided he does not carry them **[Faded]** without the jurisdiction of the State, This Defendant **[Faded]** that on the coming of age of Thomas Broshier **[Faded]** Heirs of legatees of the said John - Broshier **[Faded]** his advertisement & Promotion this defendant **[Torn]** relinguish to him his right in three of the said**[Torn]** to wit, Jacob, Davis & James, that the said Thomas **[Torn]** sold the Negroe Jacob to Enoch Relph Esquire by & **[Torn]** the consent of Thomas Jonathan Banks Executor **[Torn]** said John Broshier Dec'd & former Guardian to the **[Torn]** and **[Torn]** James to **[Faded]** of the town of **[Torn]** the County of Bertie Merchant **[?]** this Defendant **[Torn]** reason to believe by and with the consent of the said Jonathan and this Defendant avers that the said **[Torn]** slaves are all that **[Faded]** out of his Possession and this Defendant saith that there are now in Possession of the said Negroe Slaves with their increase Ten Without that &c &c Prays &c &c.
Wm. Blair Pro Deft.

Clement Cartwright Maketh Oath that the **[Faded]** in the above Answers **[Faded]** are true[**Faded]** & the rest he believes are true.
Sworn to in Open Court, June 6th 1792

****

Governor Vs. William Luffman [1797]
Civil Action
Pasquotank County

The Governor of the State Vs. William Luffman
Office £ 7"6
£" 7"15
Ret to March Term 1797
Note **[?]**, J Banks

State of North Carolina
To the Sheriff of Pasquotank County Greeting:

Whereas we by our writ to you directed have Commanded you that you Should Cause to be made of the Goods & Chattels, Lands & Tenements of William Luffman the Sum of Seven pounds fifteen Shillings which lately in our County Court of Pleas & Quarter Sessions the

Governor of the State recovered against him for Damage, Whereof the said William Luffman is liable as to us appears of record, besides your fees for this Service, So that you have the said monies before the Justices of our said Court, to be held for the County of Pasquotank at the Court House in Nixonton on the first Monday in Sept next then & there to render the Said Governor his Said Debt -- And you that day returned to us that by virtue of our Writ to you directed for that purpose have taken into Your hands & Possession one Negro Man Peter and you the monies have with Seven Shillings & Ten pence Costs) before the Justices of our Said Court, at the Court House in Nixonton on the first Monday in March next, to render to the said Governor his Debt aforesaid, Herein fail not & have you then & there this Writ & Have you [?] execution the Same. Witness Enoch Relfe, Clerk of our EP at Decr. £ 3"9
Plures N Expo 3"9
Ball of Judgt £ 7"6
XXV January

****

White and Nixon Vs. Joseph Scott [1803]
Civil Action
Pasquotank County

White and Nixon
Will: T. Muse Pltff in fact
Vs. Joseph Scott
Pasquotank, June Term 1803
Rec'd my Fee, W Blair

State of North Carolina
To the Sheriff of Pasquotank County Greeting:
Whereas we, by our writ commanded you, that of the goods and chattels, Lands and Tenements of Joseph Scott Esquire in your bailiwick, you should cause to be made the sum of two hundred and twenty five pounds five shillings & 2d which lately in our County Court of Pleas and Quarter Sessions, held for the County of Pasquotank, White and Nixon recovered against him for debt and damages as also the sum of six pounds ten shillings and two pence for costs and charges by them in their suit in that behalf expended, whereof the said Joseph Scott Esquire is convicted and liable as to us appears of record, besides your own fees for that service; and

that you have the said money before the Justices of our said Court, at Elizabeth City, the first Monday of March next, after the tenth day of December in the year of our Lord one thousand eight hundred and two to render to the said White and Nixon their debt, damages, costs and charges aforesaid; and that you at that day returned on the said writ that you had levied the same on two negroes and the land of Joseph A Scott also negroe Quiller and Aaron

---

Their value received - We do Assign all our right, Title, Interest, Claim and demand of, in and to the following Judgments to William T. Muse his heirs &c

White & Nixon Vs. Jos. Scott for the sum of	£225.5.2
The Same Vs. The Same	39.7.0
Edmond White Vs The same	23.4.8
	£287.16.0

Witness our hands the 4th Sept 1802
Edm. White for White & Nixon

State of North Carolina
To the Sheriff of Pasquotank County, Greeting:
Whereas we, by our Writ commanded you, that of the goods and chattels, lands and tenements of Joseph Scott Esquire in your bailiwick, you should cause to be made the sum of Two hundred and Twenty five pounds five shillings & 2d which lately in our County Court of Pleas and Quarter Sessions, held for the County of Pasquotank, White and Nixon recovered against him for debt and damages as also the sum of Six pounds ten shillings and two pence for costs and charges by them in their suit in that behalf expended, whereof the said Joseph Scott Esquire is convicted and liable at to us appears of record, besides your own fees for that service; and that you have the said money before the Justices of our said Court, at Elizabeth City, the first Monday of March next, after the tenth day of December in the year of our Lord one thousand eight hundred and two to render to the said White and Nixon their their debt, damages costs and charges aforesaid; and you at that day returned on the said writ that you had levied the same on two negroes and the land of Joseph Scott also negroe Quiller and Aaron which remain in your hands unfold for want of Bidders. We do command you, that you expose to sale the goods and

chattels, Lands and tenements by you so as aforesaid levied upon so that you have the said Money, and six shillings and nine pence for accruing costs, before the Justices of our said Court, at Elizabeth City, on the furst Monday of June next; and we do command you further, that of the goods and chattels, lands and tenements of the said Joseph Scott Esquire (in your bailiwick) you cause to be made the residue of the said debt, damages, costs and charges, and that you have the said money before the Justices of our said Court at Elizabeth City on the day aforesaid, to render to the said White and Nixon their debt, damages, costs and charges aforesaid; and have you then and there this writ. Witness William Templeman Muse, Clerk of the said Court at, Elizabeth City, the 12th day of March in the 27th year of our Independence, and in the year of our Lord, 1803.
Issued the 15th day of March 1803
Will T. Muse, Clk

Clerk and Tax	£3.12.3
Atto WB	2
Wm Robinson writ	1.4.8
Debt	£207.9.7
Damage	£17.15
	£225.5.2

Pasquotank March 5th 1803

Whereas a Sale of my lands negroes and other Property was to have taken place on this day (Legal notice has been given by Sundry executors at the Instance of the Governor of the State returnable to the Superior Court at April Term 1803, and at the instance of Sundry other persons returnable to Pasq. March Term 1803 - And the said Parties having agreed to a [?] of the said sale, on Condition that it shall take place on Wednesday the sixth day of April Next - Now Know Ye that I the said Joseph Scott in Consideration of the indulgence given by the parties to the Suits above mentioned - Do Authorize the Shariff or his Deputy of the County aforesaid, to proceed on the sixth day of April next and to make Sale of my lands, Negroes & other property or so much thereof as will Satisfy the Executors above referred to, In Witness Whereof I have hereunto set my hand and Seal the date above Written
Test, Wm. Wilson
J Scott (Seal)

Pasquotank County
Civil Actions

Account Sales of Sundry Property sold on the 6th April 1803 belonging to Joseph Scott Esquire to Satisfy Sundry Executioners Against him

Negroes to Wit

1 Ben about 50 years of age to William T. Muse	50
2 Aaron 25 to William T. Muse	100
3 Quiller 30 years to William T. Muse	100
4 Reuben 22 years to William T. Muse	75
5 Miles 11 years, to William T. Muse	50
6 Phillis 40 years, to William T. Muse	40
7 Pleasant 16 years, To William T. Muse	40
8 Matilda 12 years, to William T. Muse	40
9 George 2 years , to William T. Muse	12.10
10 Sarah 2 & 1/2 years, to William T. Muse	12.16
11 Mourning 50 years, to William T. Muse	25

the Tract of land whereon the said Joseph Scott now lives containing 274 1/2 acres at 17/1 1/2 pr Acre sold subject to William Jordans Mortgage to Wm T. Muse

2 Horses Pitt & Shepard

25	235
	£805

Quiller & Mourning returned on Exors from the Supr Court & £12.8.1 in part of [?] Taxes - the land & other negroes returned on Exors issued from the Clks Office of Pasquotank - The Sale of the within mentioned Horses Accounted for as follows.

Bal. Of direct Taxes	12.6
Balance of costs Lockwood Vs Scott	4.15.5
Costs Dashiel Vs Scott	4.10.5
Judgt & Costs obtn by [?]	4.12.0
Part of Judgt & costs by [?]	6.19.8
Bal. Of a Judgt onto by Sol Pool	3.10
	£25

March

In obedience to the within writ, I Robert McMorine Sheriff of Pasquotank County within mentioned, did on the Sixth day of April next, after a postponement on the fifth day of March 1803 and the Teste of the within Writ as pr. Agreement hereunto annexed, enter into and upon the lands whereon the within named Joseph Scott now lives containing Two hundred and seventy four and one half Acres, And Caused the same to be sold at publick Sale or Vendue having first advertised the time and place of said Sale according to Law & when William T. Muse bid for the said lands the Sum of seventeen shillings and one penny half penny, Subject to William Jordans Mortgage Pr Acre, and being the last and highest Bidder the same was struck off to him at the price aforesaid, which satisfys two hundred and thirty five pounds of this Execution - the Balance of five pounds seven shillings and five pence including all Costs Satisfied by the Sale of Negro Aaron to the said William T. Muse for the Sum of One hundred pounds the Exors No 22.23.37 and 18 for Balance of the sale of Aaron.
£240. 7-5 Debt & all costs
April 6th 1803
W. Banks Sworn DShff for Robt. McMorine, Shff

****

Pickett Vs. Blount & al [1825]
Civil Action
Pasquotank County

Jasper Pickett Vs. John B. Blount & al
& Thos. Payner
Subpoena
L. Martin, Attorney
To be Executed on Blount & Returned

State of North Carolina } Court of Enquiry
Hertford County } Thos M. Blount Admr. of Jno B. Blount of Chowan County, Greeting: For certain causes offered before our Court of Equity for the County of Hertford, we command and enjoin you the said John B. Blount, that laying all other matters aside, and notwithstanding any excuse, you personally appear before the Honorable the Judge of Equity, at the next Court, to be held for the County of Hertford, at the Court House in Winton, on the fourth Monday in March next; to answer concerning those things which shall then and there be objected to you, in and by the Bill of

Complaint of Jasper Pickett, and further to do and receive what our said Court shall consider in this behalf. And this you shall in no wise omit under the penalty of One Hundred Pounds: and have you then and there this writ. Witness James Yancey Clerk and Master of our said Court, at Winton, the 25th day of March Anno Dom. 1825 and in the **[Blank]** year of our Independence.
Issued the 6th day of September 1825.
James Yancey CME

Jasper Pickett Vs. Jno. B. Blount & Thos Payner
Subpoena to be left with Blount

State of North Carolina } Court of Equity
Hertford County }

To Thomas M. Blount Admr. of Jno. B. Blount of Chowan County, Greeting: For certain causes offered before our Court of Equity for the County of Hertford, we command and enjoin you the said John B. Blount, that laying all other matters aside, and notwithstanding any excuse, you personally appear before the Honorable the Judge of our Court of Equity, at the next Court, to be held for the County of Hertford, at the Court House in Winton, on the fourth Monday in September next; to answer concerning those things which shall then and there be objected to you, in and by the Bill of Complaint of Jasper Pickett, and further to do and receive what our said Court shall consider in this behalf. And this you shall in no wise omit under the penalty of One Hundred Pounds: and have you then and there this writ. Witness James M. Yancey, Clerk and Master of our said Court, at Winton, the 25th day of March Anno Dom. 1825 and in the **[Blank]** year of our Independence
Issued 6th day of September 1825.
Js. M Yancey, CME

To the Honorable Judge of the Court of Equity for the County of Hertford, Your orator Jasper Pickett of Hertford County humbly complaining shews to your honor, that some time about the first of year 1820 he was the owner of and was in the possession of two slaves (among other property) named Abraham and Nimrod: and that a Judgment was obtained in Hertford County Court at the instance of William & Jos G. Reed (Benjamin Talbot in fact) Vs your orator for $329.80 to be discharged however on the payment of $164.90 with interest from the 5th June 1819 - Your orator further shews that a writ of Vendition Exponas & Fi Fa was derected to the Sheriff of Currituck County where the said slaves were to expose the said slaves among other property to sale for ready money to satisfy by said debt and that he has understood and believes a certain Thomas Sanderson then of Currituck made of said slaves, as the agent of the said Garrison M Smith, bid off the said Abraham and Nimrod in his own name Abraham at $60 and Nimrod at $65 on thr 4th day of November in the said year 1820 and did then and there on the day aforesaid take a bill of sale for said slaves in his own name; which bill of sale your orator has ready to produce when & where &c, Your prator further shews your honor that the said Thomas Sanderson not having paid any money for said slaves to the Sheriff - Your orator secured to the said Garrison M Smith his debt aforesaid by a deed in trust on property; and the said Sanderson being hereof notified sent the said slaves Abraham & Nimrod to your orator at Winton, and wrote to him that he would give him a bill of sale for them at some time after, or words to that effect and authorized your orator to keep the said negroes in his possession and apply them to his own benefit - the legal title to them being in the mean time in said Thomas Sanderson.

Your orator further shews your Honor that while the Title to the said Slaves being in Sanderson & your orator having the possession of them under the said [?] hired the said Abraham and Nimrod to Daniel Southall to fish on Chowan River in Bertie County; and that while there a certain Jonah Collins of Edenton having obtained a judgment against your orator in Chowan Superior Court of Law for about $490 execution to collect the same was put into the hands of the Sheriff of Bertie County to be levied on the said slaves; and this coming to the knowledge of the said Thomas Sanderson who claimed the legal title in the said Slaves he sent up an agent to forbid the sheriff interfering with his legal interest in the said slaves at his peril; and the Sheriff being unwilling to run any hazard went with the agent to the Josiah Collins in Edenton who directed them to Collins saying he had nothing to do with it and Blount said he had the whole control of the matter and pleed to on the subject to secure the debt agreed that if your orator would give notes that was good to secure the debt he would deliver the slaves to either Your orator or the said Thomas Sanderson whichever your orator preferred and that your orator might have any credit on the claim so that he would make the debt safe, and that he did not wish to injure your orator.

Your orator further shews that his coming to his knowledge and being very desirous of saving the said slaves if practible; but if not that the said slaves should sell for there value, he made all the efforts in his power to procure notes such as he supposed would suit the said John B. Blount: and that he obtained a note on one Daniel B. Lindsay of Currituck County which he avers was good and secure for about the amount due for Collins debt; and that on the day appointed for the sale he sent an agent with a letter to John Blount to know if he would take Lindsay's note aforesaid and release the negroes aforesaid, and the said Blount informed your orators agent that he would take the note on Lindsay; but that he would bid off the slaves and keep them for your orator to redeem at any time that he would deliver him Lindsay's note or any other good note or notes that would secure the money due: and the said John B. Blount on the day of sale publikly declared before the sale that he did not wish the negroes to be bought by any one but himself because he wanted them that your orator might redeem them: and that while the sheriff was crying the negroes & the said Blount bidding he said Blount declared that he was bidding on them for Your orators benefit that he might have an opportunity of redeeming them.

And your orator charges that there were many persons present that were capitalists and would have given the value for the said Slaves or either of them but for the declarations of the said Blount made as aforesaid.

And Your orator charges that the said slaves sold for very small sums as he has understood and believes not exceeding $100 each.

Whereas in truth and in fact either of the slaves Abraham of the value of $1200 being a valuable Mechanic were of the value of $800 in cash; and the said Blount has been offered $800 for one of the slaves frequently since the said sale.

Your orator confiding in the divers promises and declarations of the said Blount made before the sale of the said slaves; and again made and [?] at the sale of the said slaves, fell in with James Iredell Esquire at Gates Court of law next after the sale that said James Iredell having funds in hand of your oratirs to the amount of $98.50 directed said Iredell to pay the same over to said Blount on account of the redemption of the said Slaves; which your orator understands & believes he did do; and the said Blount received it as such and then by the direction of the said Blount said Iredell wrote to your orator that your orators note with good security for the balance would be recovered at any time.

Your orator confiding in these promises sent an agent to said Blount with Lindsay's note aforesaid and the record of a judgment against one Caleb Ives that was good some short time afterwards; and the agent applied to Collins, who directed the agent to apply to Blount saying he had nothing to do with it; and the agent accordingly applied to Blount who referred to take the notes but said to the agent that he would take only note of your orators made payable to Collins with good security for the balance of the debt due, and give up the slaves.

Your orator then being greatly involved in debt by losses at sea with considerable difficulty procured a note signed by your orator for the balance due Collins being four hundred and fifty five dollars and procured Garrison M Smith of Hertford County and Thomas Williams of Currituck County to become his securities: and your orator avers that the said Smith and Williams or either was and yet is ample security for the sum and a much larger sum and that he took the note to Edenton where the said Blount being the sole actor in the case he in the presence of James Iredell Esquire Tendered the said cost mentioned note to Blount and demanded the negroes; but he said Blount refused to take said note and deliver the said slaves and further declared that he would never give up the negroes until compelled by law, nor take any note whatsoever.

Your orator then unstituted suit against the said John Blount to recover the said slaves in the said in the name of Thomas Sanderson Exors who had the legal title in Currituck Superior Court of Law: and the suit depending in said Court for trial about the 10th October 1824 at the Superior Court of Law at Perquimans County the said Blount proposed to your orator to refer the right of your orator the damages &c and the right of said Blount to your orators counsel Leonard Martin and to the said Blounts counsel James Iredell & that your orator agreed thereto: and that the said arbitrators met at the Bank of Edenton about the first of April last to settle the matters refered to him; both the said Blount and your orator being notified & being present: and that the said Blount then & there fraudulently refused to lat the arbitrators proceed in the reference. Your orator then dismissed the suit in Currituck Superior Court of Law at the last term thereof.

Your orator expressly charges that the Slave Abraham hath been in the possession of said Blount ever since the Sheriff's sale in Bertie which was about the 31st May 1821 and that he is a valueable Mechanic of the value of $30 per month - and he further charges that he hath had the slave Nimrod for the same time & that he is a valuable slave of the value of $70 per annum.

Your orator further charges that he still holds the obligation signed by Smith & Williams as aforesaid in full force & ready to deliver to the said Blount or any one else should your Honor order the same to be delivered for the redemption of said slaves - or to pay any sum of money your orator may direct for the redemption of said slaves.

Your orator further charges that the said John B. Blount made all the declarations aforesaid both before & at the time of the said sale and did bid at the said sale & take a bill of sale from the Sheriff of Bertie for the slaves aforesaid in trust for your orator & to be redeemed by your orator: and that in pursuance of this trust aforesaid the said John B. Blount at the divers times aforesaid after he had bid off said slaves declared that your orator should redeem the said slaves.

And your orator expressly charges that the said slaves while in the possession of the said John B. Blount to the full knowledge of the said John B. Blount were of the value your orator hath set forth above: and that the said John B. Blount hath recovered the full value of the whole of the debt aforesaid that remained due after the payment he received of James Iredell Esquire as aforesaid from the profits work & labor of the said slaves.

Your orator further charges that the said John B. Blount hath at all times since and before he purchased the said slaves declared and given out on speeches that he should and that he had purchased the said slaves in trust for your orator and to be redeemed by him until last April when the said John B. Blount believing your orator from the death of [?] [?] would be unable to establish his right to redeem said slaves, fraudulently [?] to defraud your orator altogether of his valuable slaves aforesaid at the great sacrifice set forth in this Bill of Complaint.

In tender consideration whereof, and inasmuch as Your orator hath no relief in the premises by the strict rules of the Common and is relievable only in a Court of Equity where trusts and frauds are cognizable &c - To the end therefore that the said John B. Blount may come to a fair amount for the profits and hire of said slaves since in his possession; and that the said John B. Blount may produce said slaves; and that your orator may redeem said slaves by paying the balance of the money due if any there be due which he hereby offers to do when & where this Court may require the same; and that the said John B. Blount may deliver the said slaves to your orator & release to your orator all right and title to said slaves or by other means vest your orator with the right and title to said slaves &c Your orator prays that a copy and subpoena be served on the said John B. Blount and Thomas Payner Executor of Thomas Sanderson aforesaid returnable to the next Term of this Court, and that the said John B. Blount be compelled on his corporal oath to declare & true answer make

to all the matters charged in his Bill of Complaint in as full and ample manner as if herein again repealed by way of interogatory: and that he in special manner declare & set forth whether he did not have said execution [?] on said slaves as your orators property? And whether he did not declare before the sale of said slaves that he should bid them off as security only for said debt and that your orator should have an opportunity to redeem said slaves by securing the debt said John B. Blount while the suit aforesaid was depending in Currituck Superior Court of Law did not of his own head & motion procure your orators consent to refer the whole matters in controversy about the said slaves to James Iredell & Leonard Martin and whether last April when the said referees met at the Bank at Edenton to hear and determine the matters in controversy did not refuse to have the matters referred settled by the said arbitrators and that the said Thomas Payner **[Poyner]** show cause if any he has [?] he should not convey the legal title to said slaves to your orators - and your orator further prays that your Honor decree an account to be taken of the value of the [?] and profits of the said slaves since they have been in the said Blounts possession and that the said Blount be directed to perform his trust in the premises and deliver said slaves and that he be compelled to deliver and convey his right therein to your orator. And that your orator make such other & further decree in the premises as the value of this case requires &c
Leonard Martin Sol for Complt.

****

McMorine & Henderson Vs. Pool [1826]
Civil Action
Pasquotank County

John McMorine & Alexander Henderson Real Ptlff Vs. Richard Pool
Ven Expo
Richard Pool Esqr
Bond Debt and Interest in full, Alexander Henderson
Pasquotank, March term 1826

State of North Carolina
To the Sheriff of Pasquotank County, Greeting:
Whereas, we by our Writ, commanded you, that of the goods and chattels, lands and Tenements, of Richard Pool Esqr. (in your bailiwick) you cause to be made the sum of One hundred & Sixty Six dollars 50 cents with Int

on $141.31 from the 8th June 1825 till paid. Which lately in our County Court of Pleas and Quarter Sessions, held for the County of Pasquotank, John McMorine recovered against him for debt as also the sum of nine dollars, 77 1/2 Cents for costs and charges by him in his suit in that behalf expended, whereof the said Richard Pool is convicted and liable as to us appears of record; besides your own fees for that service; and that you have the said money before the Justices of our said Court, at Elizabeth City, the first Monday of December next, after the first Monday of September in the year of our Lord one thousand eight hundred and twenty 5 to render to the said John McMorine his debt, damages, costs; and charges aforesaid; and you at that day returned on the said Writ, that you had levied the same on the lands where Richard Pool lives joining the lands of John Bailey and others, Subject to the Execution of William Amies Executor.
Wm Gregory, Shff which remain in you hands unsold for the want of a bid.

We do therefore command you, that you expose to sale the Goods and Chattels, Lands & Tenements by you so as aforesaid levied upon, so that you have the said money, and six shillings and nine pence for accruing costs, before the Justices of our said Court, at Elizabeth City, on the first Monday of March next: and we do command you further that of the Goods and Chattels, Lands and Tenements, of the said Richard Pool his debt (in your bailiwick) you cause to be made the residue of the said debt, damages, costs and charges, and that you have the said money before the Justices of our said Court, at Elizabeth City, on the day aforesaid to render to the said John his debt, damages, costs and charges aforesaid; and have you then and there this Writ. Witness Charles Grice, Clerk of the said Court, at Elizabeth City, the first Monday of December in the 50th Year of our Independence, and in the Year of our Lord one thousand eight hundred and twenty five.
Issued the 17th day of December 1825.
Charles Grice, Clk.

Amount Sales of Negroes sold on 8th Feby. 1826 on account of Execution in my hands against Richd Pool Esqr - to be bid off by John Pool - in the following manner.

Negroe Woman Charlotte & George To Jno Pool	50.00
Negroe Child George to Jno Pool	40.00
Negroe Woman Mary & Child Elijah	
Boy Jacob to Jno Pool	20.00

Girl [?] to Jno Pool	10.00
Child Eady to Jno Pool	10.00
Old Robin to Jno Pool	10.00
	$140.00

The above negroes were delivered by me and sold by William Gregory on the day & year above.

8th July 1826
And on the same day the Land of Richd Pool was sold to satisfy an Execution in favour of Jno McMorine, Alexander Henderson in fact against said Pool.
Two hundred and seven acres of Land @ 50 Pr acre To Jno Pool Jr.
$103.50

Satisfied by the sale of Richard Pools Land and negroes on the 8th Feby 1826 - filed within which satisfies this Execution & fifty seven dollars & four cents paid on an Execution from [?] Richd Pool from Northampton County & the Clk [?]
W Gregory, Shff

Debt & Damage $166.50 with Int on $111.31 from the 1st June 1825 till paid

Clerk	$4.67 1/2
Atto	4.00
J DS	1.10
	$9.77 1/2

****

Morris & Jackson Vs. Commander [1827]
Civil Action
Pasquotank County

Account of Sale of the Negroes of Thos Commander dec'd sold by virtue of [?] Excution To June Term 1827 one in favor of Caleb Morris & one in favor of Benj. M Jackson & Wife Nancy sold on the 20th March 1827.
Sold for cash

Pasquotank County
Civil Actions

Betty & Child To John Hollowell $138.00 Sold by Consent of Parties at Six Months Credit Interest to be Deducted.
Man Andrew -- to Alderson Whidbee $250.00
Girl Catherine -- To John Pool $103.00
Esther & Boy Ben --Perthina Commander $65.00
Boy Jim -- William **[Faded]** --$187.50
Girl Maria -- Benj. Jackson -- $142.00
725.08
Ad the woman sold for cash 138.00
$863.08

Wm Gregory, Shff
By Joshua A Pool, DShff

****

Wilson Vs. Trueblood [1830]
Civil Action
Pasquotank County

Thomas Wilson, Asignee & Rich H. Ramsey in fact
Ven Expo
Exum Trueblood et al
Pasquotank, March Term 1830

State of North Carolina
To the Sheriff of Pasquotank County, Greeting:
Whereas, we by our Writ, command you, that of the Goods and Chattels, Lands and Tenements of Exum Trueblood & his Wife Nancy, John M. Jackson and Nathan Morris of Mordacai (in your bailiwick) you should cause to be made the sum of One hundred & Ninety four Dollars 20 cents with Interest from 17 June 1828 till paid, which lately in our County Court of Pleas and Quarter Sessions, held for the County of Pasquotank, Thomas Wilson assignee recovered against them for Debt, as also the sum of One dollar & 33 cents, costs and charges by Him in His suit in that behalf expended, whereof the said Exum & others are convicted and liable as to us appears of record; besides your on fees for that service; and that you have the said money before the Justices of our said Court, at Elizabeth City, the first Monday of December next, after the first Monday of September in the year of our Lord one thousand eight hundred and 29 to render to the said Thomas his Debt, damages, costs and charges aforesaid;

and that you at that day returned on the said writ, that you had levied the same on Sundry Negroes of Exum Trueblood subject to Anderson, John C. Ehringhaus Executioners.
Jas. A. Pool, Shff

Which remain in your hands unsold. For the Want of a Bid. We do therefore command you that you expose to sale the goods and Chattels, Lands & Tenements by you so as aforesaid levied upon, so that you have the said money, and six shillings and nine pence for accruing costs, before the Justices of our said Court, at Elizabeth City, on the first Monday of March next; and we do command you further, that of the goods and chattels, lands and tenements of the said Exum & others (in your bailiwick) you cause to be made the residue of the Said Debt, damages, costs and charges, and that you have the said money before the Justices of our said Court, at Elizabeth City, on the day aforesaid, to render to the said Thomas his Debt, damages, costs and charges aforesaid; and have you then and there this writ. -- Witness Charles Grice, Clerk of the said Court at Elizabeth City, the first Monday of December in the LIII year of our Independence, Anno Domini 1829
Issued the 22nd day of December 1829.
Charles Grice, Clk

After Due & Legal Notice of the Time & Place of Sale on the first Day of March 1830 at the Court House Door for Ready Money the following Negroes to Witt; Woman Murell, Gene, Child Dolly [?] Rachael and Boy Chute, Luke When Richard H. Ramsey by Joseph H. Pool Bid for the same the sum of two Hundred and sixty Six Dollars & was the best Bidder and they were struck off to him and the Money applied as follows the sum of Sixty Six Dollars & twelve cents to the Payment of No. 25 which is in full for debt Court Cost & Shff Cannady in favour of Anderson Morris to this Term the Sum of Fifty Nine Dollars & 98 to the Payment of No. 38 in favor of John C. Egringhaus to the Term which is [?] [?] Court Cost & Shff Canna and the sum of [?] Jail fees the Balance say one Hundred & Thirty Seven Dollars & 90 Cents to the payment of this Execution, Given under my hand & Seal this 1st Day of March 1830.
Joshua Pool, Shff (Seal)

Pasquotank

Pasquotank County
Civil Actions

March Term 1830

Satisfaction for the Sum of one Hundred & Thirty Seven Dollars & 90 Cents for Returns filed within, Advertised at the Court House Door Newbegan Creek & [?] Creek and Nixonton & no Sale of the Land for want of a Bid
Joshua A. Pool, Shff

January the 14th 1830 levied on a tract of Land Belonging to Exum Trueblood & his Wife Nancy [?] the Lands of Benj M Jackson & others also his [?] & Wifes in the Lands where he [?] the Lands of Josiah C. Blount & others
Joshua Pool, Shff
Debt $194-20 With Int from the 17 June 1828 till paid
Clerk $ 1--35

****

Williams Vs. Kelly [1831]
Civil Action
Pasquotank County

Account of Sale of the goods & Chattels, Lands & Tenements of John Kelly sold on the 25th May 1831.

1 Negro Girl Mary to Abner Williams	$5.00
House & Lott " "	25.00
	30.00

The above Sum applied to the Payment of the Cost of sold Execution & are in favor of the [?] of the Court To June 1831 No 67 - and the costs of this Execution and cause a Levy the Balance say $11.75 being aplied to the Debt as per the Property [?] of by Pltff.
Joshua A Pool, Shff

****

White Vs. Davis [1835]
Civil Action
Pasquotank County

Pasquotank County
Civil Actions

Account of Sale of the Negroe belonging to Jesse Davis dec'd sold on the 11th Day of February 1835 by Virtue of Sundry Execution Returnable to March Term 1835

Woman Dorcas To William Glover	$439.00
Girl Sarah To William Glover	336.00
Boy Daniel To Frederick Whitehurst	400.00
	$1175.00

Joshua A Pool, Shff

The above Sum of $1175 approved as follows To Wit.

Lemuel Jennings } Debt & Tracts	$135.75
Miles White in fact} Bill to Pltff	17.75
To the use of Max[?] Harris} Clerk & Shff	2.75
Lemuel Jenning } Debt & Int	$269.83
Frederick Whitehurst} Bill of Cost	1550
In fact Vs. same } Shff	$28533
David Nicholson} Debt & Int }	$123.50
Guardian to the use of Bill of Cost}	11.60
Joseph Richardson}	$135.10
Charles Harrill } Debt & Int	$110.35
Vs Same } 8.20	$119.05
Same } Debt & Int	$12.06
Vs Same}	6.60
}	$1866
Miles White} Debt & Int	$158.18
Vs} Bill of Cost	20.75
Same}Shff	$178.93
Amoutn Carried over	893.32

****

Sutton Vs. Gordan [1842]

Pasquotank County
Civil Actions

Civil Action
Pasquotank County

Account of Sale of the goods & Chattels of S. Gordan sold on the 9th day of August 1842 by Virtue of an Execution in favor of Benj Sutton Guardian[?] the use of James W Mullen Returnable to September Term of the County Court 1842.

1 Negro Girl Rachael to William Gordan	$10.00
1 Bay Mair to William Gordan	10.00
1 Mule to William Gordan	5.00
2 Lands & Calfs to William Gordan	1.00
24 Head Hogs to William Gordan	5.00
1 Latt Oat to William Gordan	1.00
1 GiG & honey to William Gordan	5.00
2 [?] to William Gordan	1.00
4 feather Beds to William Gordan	5.00
Soaking Glass to William Gordon	.50
Bura[?] to William Gordan	5.00
Ditto to William Gordan	.50
Candle Stand to William Gordan	.50
Latt Chares To William Gordan	1.00
Cook [?] to William Gordan	1.00
Dutch Oven to William Gordan	1.00
All the remainder of the Kitchen Furniture William Gordan	.50
1 Latt [?] To William Gordan	.50
4 Plans	.5
$55.50	

****

[Small Vs Pool [1848]
Civil Action
Concerning Soundness of Slave Tamer
Pasquotank County

Edwin Small Vs. Joseph H. Pool
Transcript
Jordan's fee for Plff

Pasquotank County
Civil Actions

Elliott's Fee for Defendant

State of North Carolina }
Pasquotank County }

Transcript of the Record of the Proceedings had in the Court of Pleas and Quarter Sessions, held for the County of Pasquotank, commencing the first Monday of June 1847 at the instance of Edwin Small.
Plaintif's, Vs Joseph H. Pool
Defendants -- as follows:

State of North Carolina.
To the Sheriff of Pasquotank County, Greeting:
You are hereby commanded to take the body of Joseph H. Pool (if to be found in your bailiwick,) and him safely keep, so that you have him before the justices of the Court of Pleas and Quarter Sessions, at the next Court, to be held for the County of Pasquotank, at the Court House in Elizabeth - City, on the first Monday in June next, then and there to answer unto Edwin Small in a plea of trespass on the Case to his damage Four hundred Dollars.

Herein fail not, and have you then and there this writ. Witness, Wm. W. Griffin, Clerk of our said Court, at Elizabeth - City, the first Monday of March in the 71st Year of our Independence, A.D. 1847.
Issued the 19th day of April 1847.
W.W. Griffin, Clk.

Which Writ was returned endorsed, Executed
Joshua A Pool, Shff
To which suit the defendant appeared by his attorney G. Elliott Esqr and pleaded the [?] issue - Payment & set off - leave to add, R & J. -- and at Sept Term 1847 this Case Coming on to be heard, Plaintiff called an new suit - appeal prayer to the Superior Court of Law which prayer was granted, and at the same time it was agreed by both parties concerned that the case go up, without further [?].

Edwin Small Vs. Joseph H. Pool
Bill of Costs

Writ, [?] & Tax	2.40
2 Subpoenas	.30
Termination	.75
Order for appeal	.20
Transcript & Seal	1.25
Fees due W W Griffin	4.90
J. A Pool, Shff	1.65
W. Hasket (Wit) J.A. P[?]	1.94
S.H. Roach	.30
John Small wit	1.62
D.D. Raper	1.50
Jesse Morgan	1.70
Attorney	4.00
	$17.61

I W. W. Griffin Clk of the Court of Pleas & Quarter Sessions held for the County ofPasquotank, do hereby certify that the foregoing is a true & perfect Copy of the record of proceedings had in the above stated Case -- In Testimony whereof I have hereto affixed the seal of said Court at 14th Septr 1847
W.W. Griffin, Clk

Edwin Small Vs. Joseph H. Pool

This was an action on the case in Court in which the Plaintiff declared;
First - For a deceitful representation of the soundness of a negro slave by the name of Tamer, which the Defendant sold to the Plaintiff and, Secondly for a false warranty of the soundness the said slave at the time the defendant sold her to the Plaintiff - The plaintiff proved that on the 1st of January 1846, the defendant sold at public auction some fifteen or twenty slaves, some four or five of which belonged to him individually, and the vendue to an estate of which he was executor - that at said sale the plaintiff purchased Tamer, which was one of the slaves which belonged to the defendant in his own right - It was further in evidence that before the sale commenced, the auctioneer recommended the slaves generaly as sound and healthy, with the exception of one or two old negroes. It was further in evidence that whilst the sale was in progress, the bidders would occasionaly inquire if the particular slave then being sold was sound and healthy, and that when such enquiry was made the answer was in the affirmative: That no such enquiry was made when Tamer was sold, The

auctioneer was introduces who stated that he had no distinct recollection of what did occur at the sale, but that whatever representation he made was by the authority of the defendant that he understood, that the negroes generally as he understood was sold as sound, with the exception of the old negroes - A Witness was then introduced, by the plaintiff who proved that he had been overseer of the defendant, that this negroe did not work out, that she had picked peas on one occasion, and complained of being unwell. It was further in evidence, that the defendant did not work out in the farm - the plaintiff then proved that in the month of March after the sale, the slave complained of pains in her arms, which she said was rheumatism and that her wrist was swollen - and that at that time in the opinion of two witnesses she had about half common sense -- It was further in evidence, that the difference in value between such a slave as Tamer was, if she had been sound and such as she was one half - The defendant's proposed to prove what the negroe sold for in first January, 1846 and what the plaintiff afterwards sold her for in Richmond, which was objected to by the Court Plaintiff and ruled out by the Court there was no objection to the charge of his Honor Judge Dick then was a verdict for the Plaintiffs - Rule discharged because of refusing proper evidence **[Faded]** no Security required

---

Small Vs. Jos. H. Pool
Subpoena
Ret. To Term 1848
Executed
Joshua A Pool, Shff

State of North Carolina,
To the Sheriff of Pasquotank County, Greeting:
You are Hereby Commanded to Summon Jesse Morgan, Willis Hasket & D.D. Raper, personally to be and appear before the Judge of the Superior Court of Law, at the next Court to be held for the County of Pasquotank, at the Court House in Elizabeth City, on the fourth Monday after the fourth Monday in Sept. next, then and there to testify and the truth to say in behalf of the Pltff in a certain matter of controversy in the said Court depending, and then and there to be tried, wherein Small is Plaintiff, and Jos. H. Pool is Defendant: and this you shall in no wise omit, under the penalty by law enjoined. Witness, John Pool, Clerk of the said Court, at

Pasquotank County
Civil Actions

Elizabeth City, the fourth Monday after the fourth Monday in March in the 72nd year of our Independence, Anno Dom. 1848.
Issued the 6th day of Sept 1848.

Edwin Small Vs. Jos. H. Pool
Subpoena for Willis Haskett
To Pasquotank Sept Ct.
Ret. Fall Term 1848
Not to be found in Chowan but lives
I understand in Perquimans County
T.S. Foskins, Shff

State of North Carolina
To the Sheriff of Chowan County, Greetings:
You are hereby Commanded to Summon Willis Hasket personally to be and appear before the Judge of the Superior Court of Law, at the next Court to be held for the County of Pasquotank, at the Court House in Elizabeth City, on the fourth Monday after the fourth Monday in Sept next, then and there to testify and the truth to say in behalf of the Plaintiff in a certain matter of controversy in the said Court depending, and then and there to be tried, wherein Edwin Small is Plaintiff, and Joseph H. Pool is Defendant: and this you shall in no wise omit, under the penalty by law enjoined. Witness, John Pool, Clerk of the said Court, at Elizabeth City, the fourth Monday after the fourth Monday in March in the 72nd year of our Independence, Anno Dom. 1848.
Issued the 3rd day of May 1848.
John Pool, Clk

Edwin Small Vs. Jos. H. Pool
Subpoena
Ret Immediately
Not to be found
Joshua A Pool, Shff

State of North Carolina
To the Sheriff of Pasquotank County, Greeting:
You are hereby commanded, to summon George D. Pool personally to be and appear before the Judge of the Superior Court of Law, at the next

Court, to be held for the County of Pasquotank, at the Court House in Elizabeth City, on the fourth Monday after the fourth Monday in September next, then and there to testify and the truth to say in behalf of Edwin Small in a certain matter of controversy in the said Court depending, and then and there to be tried, wherein Edwin Small is Plaintiff, and Joseph H. Pool is Defendant; and this you shall in no wise omit, under the penalty by law enjoined. Witness, G.W. Brooks, Clerk of our said Court, at Elizabeth City, the fourth Monday after the fourth Monday in the 72nd year of our Independence, Anno Domini, 1847.
Issued the 29th day of October 1847.
Wm. F. Martin, Clk

Edwin Small Vs. Jos. H. Pool
Subpoena
Ret Fall Term 1847
Executed
Joshua A Pool, Shff

State of North Carolina,
To the Sheriff of Pasquotank County, Greeting:
You are hereby commanded to Summon Darias Raper & Jesse Morgan & Geo D Pool personally to be and appear before the Judge of the Superior Court of Law, at the next Court, to be held for the County of Pasquotank, at the Court House in Elizabeth City, on the fourth Monday after the fourth Monday in Sept. next, then and there to testify and the truth to say in behalf of the Plaintiff in a certain matter of controversy in the said Court depending, and then and there to be tried, wherein Edwin Small is Plaintiff, and Joseph H. Pool is Defendant; and this you shall in no wise omit, under the penalty by law enjoined. Witness GW Brooks Clerk of the said Court, at Elizabeth City, the fourth Monday after the fourth Monday in March in the 72nd Year of our Independence, Anno Domini 1847.
Issued the 30th day of Sept 1847.
G. W. Brooks

Edwin Small Vs. Jos. H. Pool
Subpoena
Ret Fall Term 1848
Not to be found in my County

Pasquotank County
Civil Actions

Tho Riddick, Shff

State of North Carolina

To the Sheriff of Gates County, Greeting:

You are hereby Commanded to Summon Willis Hasket personally to be and appear before the Judge of the Superior Court of Law, at the next Court to be held for the County of Pasquotank, at the Court House in Elizabeth City, on the fourth Monday after the fourth Monday in Sept next, then and there to testify and the truth to say in behalf of Edwin Small in a certain matter of controversy in the said Court depending, and then and there to be tried wherein Edwin Small is Plaintiff, and Joseph H. Pool is Defendant: and this you shall in no wise omit, under the penalty by law enjoined. Witness, John Pool, Clerk of the said Court, at Elizabeth City, the fourth Monday after the Fourth Monday in March in the 72nd year of our Independence, Anno Dom. 1848.

Issued 2nd day of May 1848.

John Pool, Clk

Small Vs. Pool

Subpoena

Ret immediately

Executed on R V Pool

The 25th October 1848

Joshua Pool, Shff

State of North Carolina.

To the Sheriff of Pasquotank County, Greeting:

You are hereby commanded to summon Richard Pool personally to be and appear before the Judge of the Superior Court of Law, then and there to testify and the truth to say in behalf of Jos H. Pool in a certain matter of controversy in the said Court depending, and then and there to be tried, wherein Edwin Small is Plaintiff & Jos. H. Pool is Defendant; and this you shall in no wise omit, under the penalty by law enjoined. Witness, John Pool, Clerk of the said Court, at Elizabeth City, the fourth Monday after the fourth Monday in March in the 72nd year of our Independence, Anno Domini 1848.

Issued the 25th day of Oct 1848

John Pool, Clk

Edwin Small Vs. Joseph H. Pool
Subpoena
Ret Fall Term 1847
Executed
Joshua A Pool, Shff

State of North Carolina
To the Sheriff of Pasquotank County, Greeting:
You are hereby commanded, to summon John Small & Willis Hasket personally to be and appear before the Judge of the Superior Court of law, at the next Court, to be held for the County of Pasquotank, at the Court House in Elizabeth City, on the fourth Monday after the fourth Monday in Sept next, then and there to testify and the truth to say in behalf of the Plaintiff in a certain matter of controversy in the said Court depending, and then and there to be tried, wherein Edwin Small is Plaintiff, and Joseph H. Pool is Defendant; and this you shall in no wise omit, under the penalty by law enjoined. Witness G.W. Brooks, Clerk of our said Court, at Elizabeth City, the fourth Monday after the fourth Monday in March in the 72nd year of our Independence, Anno Domini, 1847.
Issued the 5th day of October 1847
G.W. Brooks

Small Vs. Jos. H. Pool
Ret to Term 1848
Executed on David Kenyan
18th October 1848'
Joshua A Pool, Shff

State of North Carolina
To the Sheriff of Pasquotank County, Greeting:
You are hereby commanded to Summon Daniel H. Kinyan personally to be and appear before the Judge of the Superior Court of Law, at the next Court to be held for the County of Pasquotank, at the Court House in Elizabeth City, on the fourth Monday after the fourth Monday in Sept next, then and there to testify and the truth to say in behalf of the Defendant in a certain matter of controversy in the said Court depending, and then and there to be tried, wherein Small is Plaintiff, and Jos. H. Pool is Defendant: and this you shall in no wise omit, under the penalty by law enjoined.

Witness, John Pool, Clerk of the said Court, at Elizabeth City, the fourth Monday after the fourth Monday in March in the 72nd year of our Independence, Anno Dom. 1848.
Issued the 13th day of Oct, 1848
John Pool, Clk

Edwin Small Vs. Jos. H. Pool
Subpoena
Ret. Spring Term 1848
Willis Hasket not to be found
Executed on all the next
Joshua A. Pool, Shff
Fashine, Peyton, Boston, Peyton

State of North Carolina
To the Sheriff of Pasquotank County, Greeting:
You are hereby commanded to summon Jesse Morgan, Darius Raper, Jno. Small & Willis Hasket personally to be and appear before the Judge of the Superior Court of Law, at the next Court, to be held for the County of Pasquotank, at the Court House in Elizabeth City, on the fourth Monday after the fourth Monday in March next, then and there to testify and the truth to say in behalf of the Plaintiff in a certain matter of controversy in the said Court depending, and then and there to be tried, wherein Small is Plaintiff, and Jos. H. Pool is Defendant; and this you shall in no wise omit, under the penalty by law enjoined. Witness, John Pool, Clerk of our said Court, at Elizabeth City, the fourth Monday after fourth Monday in Sept. in the 72nd year of our Independence, Anno Domini, 1847.
Issued the 8th day of April 1848.
John Pool, Clk

Small Vs. Pool
Notice
Copy to be returned
A Copy left with John Small
The 24th October 1848
Joshua A.Pool Shff

To John Small
Sir,
You are hereby notified to produce the bill of Sale for negro girl Thamer given to you by me that the same may be used if required, on the trial of the Suit at your instance, now pending in Pasquotank Superior Court, against me, or parol evidence will be offered in Reference thereto.
October 24th
Joseph H Pool
Per Gilbert Elliott, Atty.

Small Vs. Jos. H. Pool
Subpoena
Ret T. Term 1848
Executed
Joshua A Pool, Shff

State of North Carolina
To the Sheriff of Pasquotank County, Greeting:
You are hereby Commanded to Summon John Small personally to be and appear before the Judge of the Superior Court of Law, at the next Court to be held for the County of Pasquotank, at the Court House in Elizabeth City, on the fourth Monday after the Fourth Monday in Sept next, then and there to testify and the truth to say in behalf of the Pltff in a certain matter of controversy in the said Court depending, and then and there to be tried, wherein Small is Plaintiff, and Jos. H. Pool is Defendant: and this you shall in no wise omit, under the penalty by law enjoined. Witness, John Pool, Clerk of the said Court, at Elizabeth City, the fourth Monday after the Fourth Monday in March in the 72nd year of our Independence, Anno Dom. 1848
Issued the 6th day of Sept. 1848.
John Pool, Clk

Small Vs Pool
Notice
Copy to be returned
A Copy left With Small
The 25th October 1848
Joshua A Pool, Shff

Edwin Small
Sir
Take notice, you are notified to produce the Bill of Sale given you by me for Negro girl Thamer to be used as evidence in the Suit now pending at your instance against me, in Pasquotank Superior Court, or Parol testimony will be offered, as to the contents of said Bill of Sale.
Oct 25th 1848
Jos. H. Pool

State of North Carolina,
Supreme Court - December Term 1847
Edwin Small Vs. Joseph H. Pool } 105 Pasquotank

Nash, I --The case presents but a single point. The plaintiff claims damages of the defendant for a fraud in the sale of a slave named Tamer. In order to show the amount to which he was entitled, the plaintiff introduced witnesses who testified that "the difference in value between such a slave as Tamer was if she had been sound & such as she actually was one half." So far as is disclosed by the case, this was all the evidence upon that point given to the jury. Our consideration is confined to the case as it is. The Defendant offered to prove what the plaintiff gave for the negro in January & what he sold her for in the succeding July in Richmond. This evidence was objected to by the plaintiff & rejected by the Court. This decision is the error complaining of by the Defendant. We think his [?] erred, that the testimony ought to have been received. In actions [?] in damages, the Jury in general have a discretionary power in awarding them, subject to the control of the Court. But in a case of deceit in the sale of property the law has adapted as the rule by which the Jury are to be governed the damages estimated, the difference in the value of the article sold, as sound or unsound at the time of the sale. The price given by the purchaser & that for which he sold it, does not conclusively fix the amount of damages. But it is competent as some evidence of the value of the property at the respective times of the purchase & the sale, & as such the Jury had a right to hear it. Clare & Maynard 32 EG I R 714. It does not establish the value, but may aid & assist the jury in their enquiries upon the point. More particularly was it admissable in this case, as the plaintiff had punished the Jury with no evidence upon which they could understandingly act. He did not show what sum Tamer was worth at the time of the sale either as sound or unsound Judgment is reversed & venire de[?] awarded.

Judgment

This cause came on to be argued upon the transcript of the record from the Superior Court of Law of Pasquotank County upon consideration whereof this Court is of opinion that there is error in the proceedings of the said Superior Court, therefore, It is considered & adjudged by the Court here that the said judgment be & the same is hereby reversed - and it is ordered that this judgment with the opinion of this Court as delivered by the honorable Frederick Nash one of the Judges thereof be certified to the said Superior Court to the intent that a venire de novo be awarded & further proceedings had therein accordingly, And it is considered & Adjudged that the defendant recover against the said Edwin Small the Plaintiff the sum of $5.25 the costs in this Court incurred & Execution issue therefor.

Certified by E.B. Freeman, Clk

Small Vs. Pool } Pasquotank Superior Court of Law
} Fall Term 1847

These are to certify, that D.D. Raper hath attended this Court
5 days this Term, as a Witness for the Pltff in this Suit

Attending 5 days at 6/ shillings per day	3.00
Travelling 10 miles at 6/ shillings per day	.20
Ferriages	
Certificate and Probate	.10
	3.30

Sworn to before me
Geo W. Brooks for Jno Pool

Small Vs. Pool } Pasquotank Superior Court of Law
} Fall Term 1848

These are to certify, that Jno Small hath attended this Court
1 day this Term, as a Witness for the Ptf in this Suit

Attending 4 days at t shillings per day	2.40
Travelling 18 miles at 6 shillings per thirty miles	.36
Ferriages	
Certificate and Probate	.10

2.86

Sworn to before me, John Pool

Small Vs. Pool } Pasquotank Superior Court of Law
} Fall Term 1848

These are to certify, that Jesse Morgan hath attended this Court 4 days this Term, as a Witness for the Pltff in this Suit

Attending 4 days at 6 shillings per day	2.40
Travelling 16 miles at 6 shillings per thirty miles	.32
Ferriages	
Certificate and Probate	.10
	2.82

Sworn to before me, John Pool, Clk

Small Vs. Pool } Pasquotank Superior Court of Law
} Springl Term 1848

These are to certify, that Jno Small hath attended this Court 3 days this Term, as a Witness for the Pltff in this Suit

Attending 3 days at shillings per day	1.80
Travelling 9 miles at **[Blank]** shillings per thirty miles	.36
Certificate and Probate	.10
	2.26

Sworn to before me, John Pool, Clk

Small Vs. Pool } Pasquotank Superior Court of Law
} Fall Term 1847

These are to certify, that W.W. Hasket hath attended this Court 4 days this Term, as a Witness for the Pltff

Attending 4 days at 6 shillings per day	2.40
Travelling 32 miles at 6 shillings per thirty miles	.64
Ferriages	
Certificate and Probate	.10
	3.14

Sworn to before me Wm. F. Martin for G.W. Brooks

Small Vs. Pool } Pasquotank Superior Court of Law

} Fall Term 1848

These are to certify, that D.D. Raper hath attended this Court 4 days this Term, as a Witness for the Pltff

Attending 4 days at 6 shillings per day	2.40
Travelling 9 miles at 6 shillings per thirty miles	.18
Ferriages	
Certificate and Probate	.10
	2.68

Sworn to before me, John Pool, Clk

Small Vs. Pool } Pasquotank Superior Court of Law
} Spring Term 1848

These are to certify, that D. Raper hath attended this Court 3 days this Term, as a Witness for the Pltff in this Suit

Attending 3 days at 6/ shillings per day	1.80
Travelling 5 miles at 6 shillings per thirty miles	.20
Ferriages	
Certificate and Probate	.10
	2.10

Sworn to before me John Pool, Clk

Small Vs. Pool } Pasquotank Superior Court of Law
} Fall Term 1848

These are to certify, that D.D. Raper hath attended this Court 1 day this Term, as a Witness for the Defd in this Suit

Attending 1 day at 6 Shillings per day	.60
Travelling 9 miles at **[Blank]** shillings per thirty miles	.18
Ferriages	
Certificate and Probate	.10
	.88

Sworn to before me, John Pool, Clk

Small Vs. Pool } Pasquotank Superior Court of Law
} Fall Term 1847

These are to certify, that Jno. Small jath attended this Court 5 days this Term, as a Witness for the **[Blank]** in this suit

Attending 5 days at 6/ shillings per day	30

Travelling 18 miles at 6/ shillings per thirty miles .36
Ferriages
Certificate and Probate .10
Sworn to before me G W Brooks, Clk for Jno. Pool **[?]**

Small Vs. Pool } Pasquotank Superior Court of Law
} Fall Term 1847

These are to certify, that Jesse Morgan hath attended this Court 5 days this Term, as a Witness for the Pltff in this Suit.

Attended 5 days at 6 shillings per day	3.00
Travelling 18 miles at **[Blank]** shillings per thirty miles	.36
Ferriages	
Certificate and Probate	.10
	3.66

Sworn to before me G.W. Brooks pr W.F. Martin

****

Grandy Vs. Sanders [1849]
Civil Action
Pasquotank County

J.J. Grandy Vs Lancaster R. Sanders
Fi Fa
Ret. M. T. 50
Satisfaction in part of Debt for $328.85
And all Costs & Shff **[?]** as per Acct of Sale filed
In No. 10 to this Term
& Fees paid in office
Joshua A Pool, Shff

State of North Carolina

To the Sheriff of Pasquotank County, Greeting:

You are hereby Commanded, That of the goods and Chattels, Lands and Tenements of Lancaster R. Sanders (if to be found in your bailiwick,) you cause to be made the sum of Three Hundred Twenty Two Dollars 34/100 with Int from Oct 15th 1829 which J. J. Grandy lately in our County Court of Pleas and Quarter Sessions, held for the County of Pasquotank, at the Court House in Elizabeth City, recovered against him for debt, as also the

sum of $7.50 for his costs and charges in the said suit expended, whereof the said L. R. Lancaster is convicted and liable as to us appears of record. And have you the said monies before the Justices of our said Court on the first Monday of March next, then and there to render to the said J.J. Grandy his debt and interest, costs and charges aforesaid. Herein fail not, and have then and there this writ. Witness, William W. Griffin, Clerk of the said Court, at Elizabeth City, the first Monday in Decr. In the 74th year of our Independence, Anno Domini, 1849.
Issued the 11th day of Decr. 1849.
W.W. Griffin, Clk.

Record of JA Pool three hundred & Twenty Eight 85/100 Dollars in part for this Execution
Jhn J. Grandy

Judgt $322. 34 pence Oct 15th 1849
5.15 to Decr 21/49
7.50 Court Costs
9.12 Shff Court Levy
$344 11/100

Levied this Fi Fa on the following negroes, the goods & Chattels of Lancaster R. Sanders to Wit Woman Penny, Girl Ellen, Boy Albert & Boy Charly this 21st Decr. 1849.
Joshua A. Pool, Shff

Also on the same day all the Interest of Lancaster **[Faded]**

****

Jackson Vs. McLain [1850]
Civil Action
Pasquotank County

State of North Carolina.
To the Sheriff of Pasquotank County, Greeting:
You are hereby commanded to Summon Mary Ann Jackson (if to be found in your bailiwick before the Justices of the County Court of of Pleas and Quarter Sessions, at the next Court to be held for the County of

Pasquotank, at the Court House in Elizabeth City, on the first Monday in June next, then and there to answer unto John McLain & wife Lourany of a Plea that she render unto them one negro woman Ann, of the value of five hundred dollars, & one negro boy Bill, of the value of four hundred dollars, & one negro girl Mary Jane, of the value of four hundred dollars, & one negro child Aley of the value of four hundred dollars; which she detains to their damage two thousand dollars.

Herein fail not, and have you then and there this writ. Witness William W.Griffin, Clerk of the said Court at Elizabeth City, the first Monday of March in the 74th year of our Independence, A.D. 1850.
Issued the 8th day of April 1850.
W.W. Griffin, Clk.

State of North Carolina,

To the Sheriff of Pasquotank County, Greeting:
You are hereby commanded to summon Elizabeth Sawyer & William Sexton personally to be and appear before the Justices of the County Court of Pleas and Quarter Sessions, at the Court House in Elizabeth City, on the first Monday in Sept next, then and there to be tried, wherein John McLain & Wife are Plaintiffs and Mary Ann Jackson is Defendant. And this you shall in no wise omit, under the penalty by law enjoined. Witness, William W. Griffin, Clerk of the said Court at Elizabeth City, the first Monday of June in the 73rd year of our Independence, Anno Domini 1850.
Issued the 20th day of Augt. 1850.
W.W. Griffin, Clk
I hereby bind myself, heirs, executors, and administrators, jointly and severally for the costs of this suit
John Pool

McLain Vs. M. A. Jackson } Pasquotank County Court
} Sept. Term, 1850

These are to certify that Wm. Sexton hath attended this Court 4 days this Term, as a Witness for the Pltff in this suit.

Attending 4 days at **[Blank]** shillings per day	2.40
Travelling 32 miles at **[Blank]** shillings per thirty miles	.64
Ferriages	
Certificate and Probate	.10

3.14

Sworn to before me
W.W. Griffin, Clk

****

Pool & Gasking Vs. Jackson [1851]
Civil Action
Pasquotank County

Aplide to J.H. Pool Execution $653.56 - Tax for 1849 on C.C. Jackson $9.70 [?] of Mrs. Turner Tax $2.00 also on C.C. Jackson Tax for 1850 & 6.32
Balance &73.40 to [?] & [?] to this
Joshua A Pool, Shff

Account of sale of Negro Man Manuel the goods & Chattels of C.C. Jackson sold on the 11th July 1851 at Mr Fletcher's Store for cash
Man Manuel To George Pool & that
Trading under the firm of Pool & Gaskins.
Joshua A Pool, Shff

****

Small Vs. Raper [1852]
Civil Action
Pasquotank County

North Carolina }
Pasquotank County }

Edwin Small personally appears before me, Danl. Richardson, Clerk of the Superior Court of law for said County, who being solumnly sworn on the Holy Evangelist of almighty God, says, that he has been in the Lawful possession of the negro slave boy Ison, within the last two years next preceding this date (& within the last six months preceding the date hereof) & that he has been deprived of the possession of the said boy, Ison, without his permission or consent & as he believes, by Darius D. Raper - and that the value of the boy, Ison, to this affiant is supposed to be

about Eighty dollars & this Affiant is made to obtain a Writ of Replevin against said Raper for said taking up said boy, Ison.
Edwin Small
Sworn & Subscribed to before me Jany 31st 1852
Daniel Richardson, Clk

State of North Carolina
To the Sheriff of Pasquotank County, Greeting:
You are hereby commanded to summon DR Perry & Chas B Brothers personally to be and appear before the Judge of the Superior Court of Law, at the next Court, to be held for the County of Pasquotank, at the Court House in Elizabeth City, on the fourth Monday in Sept next, then and there to testify and the truth to say in behalf of Deft. In a certain matter of controversy in the said Court depending, and then and there to be tried, wherein E.Small is Plaintiff, and D D Raper is Defendant; and this you shall I no wise omit, under the penalty by law enjoined. Witness, Daniel Richardson, Clerk of the said Court, at Elizabeth City, the fourth Monday after the fourth Monday in March in the 76th year of our Independence, Anno Domini, 1852.
Issued the 29th day of Sept. 1852.
Daniel Richardson, Clk.

State of North Carolina.
To the Sheriff of Pasquotank County, Greeting:
You are herebt commanded to summon John Small, Robert Small, Mary Louisa Salton[?], H.R. Perry Esqr, John D. Weeks & William Shannon personally to be and appear before the Judge of the Superior Court of law, at the next Court, to be held for the County of Pasquotank, at the Court House in Elizabeth City, on the fourth Monday after the fourth Monday in Sept next, then and there to testify and the truth to say in behalf of the Plaintiff in a certain matter of controversy in the said Court depending, and then and there to be tried, wherein Edwin Small is Plaintiff, and Darius D. Raper is Defendant; and this you shall in no wise omit, under the penalty by law enjoined. Witness, Daniel Richardson, Clerk of the said Court, at Elizabeth City, the fourth Monday after the fourth Monday in March in the 75th year of our Independence, Anno Domini 1852.
Issued the 2nd day of Oct 1852.
Daniel Richardson, Clk.

North Carolina }
Pasquotank County }

To the Sheriff of Pasquotank County: Greeting:
Whereas Edwin Small has this day entered into Bond, as required by law, for the institution of a suit in replevin, against Darius D. Raper, for the recovery of a slaves boy named Ison, about seven years old, three & a half feet high, of a black complexion - stout built - valued at Eighty dollars, now being in the possession of the said D.D. Raper, Defendant, enter into bond with approved security in the sum of one hundred & sixty dollars, made payable to the Plaintiff, with a condition to perform the final Judgment which shall be rendered in this case; You are hereby commanded to take into custody the slave aforesaid, if to be found in your County, & him deliver to the said Edwin Small, Plaintiff, without delay.

And you are further commanded to take the body of Darius D. Raper, (if to be found in your County) & him safely keep, so that you have him before the Judge of the next Superior Court of Law to be held for said County, on the Fourth Monday after the fourth Monday in March next, then & there to answer unto Edwin Small of a further plea that he has detained the said slave, Ison, as aforesaid, to his damage two hundred dollars

Herein fail not; & have you then and there the Bond aforesaid to be given by the said Defendant; & also this Writ.
Witness Danl. Richardson, Clk.

North Carolina }
Pasquotank County }

Know all men by these presents, that we, Edwin Small & John Small, are held & firmly bound unto Darius D. Raper, in the sum of one hundred dollars, to be levied of our goods & chattels, Lands & tenements, to the full payment of which we hereby bind ourselves, our heirs, Executors & administrators, jointly & firmly & by these presents

The Condition of the above Bond is such, that, whereas, the above bounden Edwin Small, has this day prayed that a Writ of Replevin shall issue from the Superior Court of Law for said County, against said Raper **[Roper]**, , to obtain the possession &c of a negro slave boy, Ison which he alleges said Raper has forcibly, without his consent, taken from his possession, within the last two years - Now therefore if said Edwin Small shall perform the final Judgment on said Writ, which is about to issue agreeable to Law, then this Bond is to be void otherwise to remain in full force & virtue.

Given under our hands & Seals this 30th January 1852 In presence of John Pool.

Edwin Small (Seal)
Jno. Small (Seal)

North Carolina }
Pasquotank County }

Know all men by these Presents that we Darius D. Raper & **[Blank]** are held & firmly bound unto Edwin Small in the sum of one hundred & sixty dollars, to be levied of our goods & Chattles, Lands & Tenements to the full payment of which we hereby bind our heirs, Executors & Administrators, jointly & Firmly by these Presents.

This is the Condition of the above Bound - Whereas, a Writ in Replevin has been issued on negro boy, Ison in possession of said Raper, at the Instance of Edwin Small & the said Roper has applied, under the Statute, to take said boy out of custody upon giving bond & approved security.

Now therefore if said Raper shall abide by & perform the final judgment of the Superior Court of Law of said County, to which said Writ is returnable - this bond is to be void otherwise to remain in full force and virtue.

Given under our hands & Seals this 7th of Feby 1852.
Witnesses
Wm. Newbould, Shff
D.D. Raper (Seal)
Thos. Banks (Seal)

State of North Carolina

To A.R. Smith, Esqr.

Know Ye, That we reposing especial trust and confidence in your fidelity and prudent circumspection, do command, authorize and empower you, or any of you, that at such time and place as you shall appoint, you call and cause to come before you Emaline White and diligently examine on the Holy Evangelist of Almighty God, what she may know in and about a certain matter of dispute now at issue in the Superior Court of Law, made in a cause, wherein Edwin Small is Plaintiff, and D.D, Raper is Defendant, as well on the part of the Plaintiff as the Defendant, and such examination and deposition by you so taken, you are to send closed up under your seal, to our said Court, to be held for the County of Pasquotank, at the Court House in Elizabeth City, on the fourth Monday after the fourth Monday in September next, and this you are in no wise to omit.

Witness Danl. Richardson, Clerk of the said Court, at Elizabeth City, under his Hand and Seal of Office, the fourth Monday after the Fourth Monday in March in the 76th Year of the Independence of the said State, Anno Dom. 1852.
Daniel Richardson, Clk.

State of North Carolina
To
Know Ye, That we reposing especial trust and confidence in your fidelity and prudent circumspection, do command, authorize and empower you, or any of you, that at such time and place as you shall appoint, you call and cause to come before you Emaline White, Wife of Thos. White and diligently examine on the Holy Evangelist of Almighty God, what she knows in and about a certain matter of dispute now at issue in the Superior Court of Law, made in a cause, wherein Edwin Small is Plaintiff, and D.D. Raper is Defendant, as well on the part of the Plaintiff as the Defendant, and such examination and deposition by you so taken, you are to send closed up under your seal, to our said Court, to be held for the County of Pasquotank, at the Court House in Elizabeth City, on the fourth Monday after the fourth Monday in Sept next, and this you are in no wise to omit.

Witness D. Richardson, Clerk of the said Court, at Elizabeth City, under his Hand and Seal of Office, the fourth Monday after the Fourth Monday in March in the 76th Year of the Independence of the said State, Anno Dom. 1852
Danl. Richardson, Clk

Deposition taken pursuant to the annexed Commission at Deep Creek by me Isaiah Cheny **[Cherry]** one of the Justices of the of Norfolk in the State of Virginia on the 12th day of June 1852 to be read in evidence in a suit

now pending in the Superior Court of Law for the County of Pasquotank, State of North Carolina whereon Edwin Small id Pltff and D.D. Raper is Defendant (Notice moved by Pltff) Emaline White wife of Thomas White witness for Defendant being duly sworn upon the Holy Evangelist of Almighty God deposeth and says as follows, Viz. That some time in the month of January 1851 she was at the House of Doctr[?] R. Perry and heard a bargain or contract made between Mrs. Raper formerly Mrs. Perry, and Edwin Small in relation to negro boy Isom Viz. That Small should take the boy for the term of five years, for his victuals and clothes, and it was further agreed between the parties that in the event of the Marriage death & of Mr. Perry, Mrs. Small should surrender the boy for his support &c and further this deponant saith not
Witness &c
Emeline White
Done before me at Deep Creek on the day and date first above written.
Witness my hand and Seal Isaiah Cheny (Seal)

Edwin Small Vs. D.D. Roper

Interrogatories propounded by the Plaintiff to the witness Emeline White 20th of October 1852 (Notice waived by Defendant)

Int 1st At the conversation between the Plaintiff and the present wife of Defendant deposed to by you at your former examination in this case, who was present besides yourself and the parties named? In what part of the house did it take place, and at what time? State the month, year, day and time of day.
Answer D.R. Perry and wife, Mr. Small and wife, and Mrs. Perry, now the wife of Defendant were present. The conversation took place in the piazza on Sunday afternoon in the year 1851, and I think in the month of January.

Int. 2nd Did you know whether the parties were in earnest? Was it not a conversation carried on in jest?
Answer I think they were in earnest, and do not believe the conversation to have been in jest.

Int. 3rd Did you ever hear any conversation between the same parties on the same subject, before or after that time, and in those conversations was

any thing said in reference to what should be done in case of the marriage of the wife between the parties on that subject.
Answer But at that time Small said to Mrs. If she were to die in the time that he had the boy, what would be done with him. - She answered that the heirs could take him and pay Mr. Small for the time he kept him whatever was just or right -- Then Small asked her if she were to die married in the time - what then. She replied that she would take him and pay whatever was right - He then said well.

Int 4th Before your former examination, had you any conversation with the Defendant or his wife, in reference to the matter testified to by you, and if so, was your recollection of the substance of your deposition based upon your memory of the facts, or upon the conversation with the Defendant and his wife?
Answer I had no conversation with the Defendant or his wife in reference to the matter, and the substance of my deposition was based upon my own recollection of the facts.

Int 5th To your reccolection of the substance of the conversation deposed to by you at a former examination, clear and distinct, together with all the circumstances?
Answer Yes

Int 6th Did Defendant ever confess having taken the boy Isom from the Plaintiff, to you or in your presence?
Answer I heard Mr. Raper say that he had taken the boy Isom from Mr. Small, and offered to pay him for him some time before he took him.

Int 7th State all you know further which you think would benefit the Plaintiff in this suit?
Answer I know nothing further in regard to the matter
Emeline White

Norfolk County To Wit:
This day Emeline White personally before me, Arthur R. Smith, a Judtice of the peace for the County aforesaid, and made oath to the truth of the above depositions -- As witness my hand and Seal this 20th day of October 1852.
Arthur R. Smith, J.P. (Seal)

Small Vs. Raper } Pasquotank County Superior Court of Law
} Fall Term 1852
These are to certify that Wm. Shannon hath attended this Court 2 days this term, as a witness for the Pltff in this suit.
Attending 2 days at **[Blank]** shillings per day
1.20
Travelling **[Blank]** miles at **[Blank]** shillings per thirty miles
Ferriages
Certificate and Probate .10
1.30
Sworn to before me, D Richardson, Clk.

Small Vs. Raper } Pasquotank County Superior Court of Law
} Fall Term 1852
These are to certify that Jno Weeks hath attended this Court 3 days this term, as a witness for the Pltff
Attending 3 days at **[Blank]** shillings per day
1.80
Travelling 12 miles at **[Blank]** shillings per thirty miles .24
Ferriages
Certificate and Probate .10
2.14
Sworn to before me, D.Richardson, Clk

Small Vs. Raper } Pasquotank County Superior Court of Law
} Fall Term 1852
These are to certify that Mary Louisa **[?]** hath attended this Court 2 days this term, as a witness for the Ptlff in this suit.
Attending 2 days at **[Blank]** shillings per day
1.20
Travelling 12 miles at **[Blank]** shillings per thirty miles .24
Ferriages
Certificate and Probate .10
1.54
Sworn to before me, D. Richardson, Clk

Rec'd of D. Richardson Two Dollars & seventeen cents in full for my witness Mary in the cause, E. Small Vs. D.D. Raper. June 10th 1853, Jno Weeks.

E Small Vs. DDRaper

Writ, Tax & bond	2.40
Afsd 20 cents & [?]	1.20
45 Judjt 75	1.20
4.80 DR, Clk	4.80
W Newbould, Shff	1.00
W [?] D.S.	2.40
Brooks atty	4.00
M Louisa Sattenstall	1.54
W. Shannon	1.30
Jno Weeks	2.14
	17.18

D.D. Raper
Charge for taking deposition $150
A.R. Smith

****

Raper Vs. Williams [1852]
Civil Action
Pasquotank County

Sale 2 slaves by [?] For acct of Mrs D D Raper 1852 against agt. For Mr. W W Williams.

Oct 16th man Jesse & his Wife Sucky to Mr. Isaac Overby $600
Charges

Bond of Jesse 15th September to 16th Oct 31 days 21 [?]	7.75
Sucky	7.75
Receive & release fee upon negroes	.50
Paid for bringing above negroes from Rickets	.25
Hat $1.50, Shirt 44 & Blanket for Jesse	2.94
Shoes Handkerchief & Blanket for Sucky	2.25

Soup Furnished above negroes .30
Commission upon sale of above negroes .10
Enclosed is the WP Strothers check No 89 drawn on Norfolk in my favour & by my advertisement made payable to order of Mrs D D Raper for Sedrum Grady
Richmond 16th Oct 1852
31:74
$568.26

NB In filling up the bill of sale I Excepted (after the words sound & healthy) her left ankle. They [?] that you would have all their bidding & any thing else which they had that you may consider worth it sent to them -- Viz. Sent up to me so their present master can get it for them -- They have up the James River in this State some hundred miles - They were hard cases & well sold.

****

Pool & Gaskins Vs. Hinton [1858]
Civil Action
Pasquotank County

Jos H. Pool use of Thomas Gaskin Vs. Jno M. Hinton et al
Return March Term, 1858
Satisfaction full debt & Int paid Plaintiff by the
Sale of Sundry Negros sold at the Court House Door
In Eliz City March 1st 1858 see acct of sale
Filed within Cost paid in office
Wm Newbould, Shff

State of North Carolina
To the Sheriff of Pasquotank County:
Whereas, we by our writ commanded you, that of the Goods and Chattels, Lands and Tenements of John M. Hinton, J.W. Hinton & W.W, Griffin (if to be found in your bailiwick) you cause to be made the sum of Three thousand Dolls, a credit of four hundred and eighty seven & 50/100 dols. Sept 8th 1859 with interest from the 21st day of May 1855 which J.H. Pool & T.Gaskins in fact lately in our County Court of Pleas and Quarter Sessions, held for the County of Pasquotank, recovered against them for

Debt, as also the sum of $11.50 for costs and charges by him in his suit in that half expended, whereof the said defendant is convicted and liable, as to us appears of record, besides your own fees for that service; and that you have the said money before the Justices of our said Court, at Elizabeth City, on the first Monday in Decr., next, in the year of our Lord one thousand eight hundred and fifty seven to render to the said plaintiff his Debt, costs and charges aforesaid; and you at that day returned on the said Writ, that you had levied the same on the House & Lot where Jno. M. Hinton now lives adjoining the Lot of J.W. Hinton & W.P. Matthews, Oct 24th 1857
Wm. Newbould, Shff which remain in your hands unsold.

We do therefore Command You, that you expose to sale the Goods and Chattels, Lands and Tenements, by you so as aforesaid, levied upon, so that you have the said money, and 65 cents for accruing costs, before the Justices of our said Court, at Elizabeth City, on the 1st Monday of March next; And we do Command you further, That of the Goods and chattels, lands and tenements of the said Hinton et als, (in your bailiwick) you cause to be made the residue of the said debt, damages, costs and charges, and that you have the said money before the Justices of our said Court, at Elizabeth City, on the day aforesaid to render to the said Gaskins his Debt, costs and charges aforesaid. And have you then and there this Writ.

Witness, James W. Hinton, Clerk of our Court, at Elizabeth City, the first Monday in Decr. And in the 82nd year of our Independence, Anno Domini 1857.
Issued the 20th day of January 1858.
J. W. Hinton, Clk
By Chas. Elliott, D.C.

Act Sales of negros belonging to John M. Hinton sold under execution my hands issuing from December Term 1857 Pasquotank County Court returnable to March Term 1858.

Man Charles to John Hinton	1000
Girl Mabel To D D Raper	835
Woman & 2 Children To JC Ehringhaus	950
Louisa & Gint[?] to J.C. Ehringhaus	
Boy Isaac To A H. Lindsay	520
Man Cooper to Da Da	1085

Man Fred Jno L Hinton	300
	$4690

Wm Newbould, Shff

Rec'd of Wm. Newbould, Shff three thousand & nine Dollars & Eighty Eight Cents in full for the Balance, Debt & Int of this Execution
March 5th 1858, T. Gaskins

Judgment for $3000, acres of 487.50 Sept 8th 1857 with interest from the 21st day of May 1858

J.W. Hinton$	350
Tax	100
Wm. Newbould	300
Pool Attorney	400
	$1150

Chapter Three

Pasquotank County

Concealment of a Slave

North Carolina State Archives
Pasquotank County Records
Records of Slaves and Free Persons of Color
C.R.075.928.9

State of North Carolina
Pasquotank County

Transcript of the record of Proceedings, had in the County Court of Pleas and Quarter Sessions, held for the County of Pasquotank, begun on the first Monday of December 1852 at the instance of P.a. R.C.Cohoon Plaintiff Vs. R. K. Speed et als Defendant, as follows, to wit:

State of North Carolina
To the Sheriff of Pasquotank County, Greeting:
YOU are hereby commanded to take the bodies of Rufus K. Speed, William P. Matthews & John Hoy[?] (if to be found in your bailiwick) and them safely keep so that you have them before the Justices of the County Court of Pleas and Quarter Sessions, at the next Court to be held for the County of Pasquotank, at the Court House in Elizabeth City, on the first

Monday in December next, then and there to answer unto Philip A. R. C. Cohoon on a plea of trespass & his damage five thousand Dollars.

Herein fail not, and have you then and there this writ. Witness, W.W. Griffin, Clerk of the said Court at Elizabeth City, the first Monday of June in the 76th year of our Independence, A.D. 1852.

Issued the 29th day of October 1852, which writ was returned endorsed executed, J. Newbould, Shff, W.W. Griffin, Clk., To which the Deft appeared by his Counsel B. Ehringhaus due **[?]** & pleaded "General rule -- leave to add" - and at March Term 1853 this case coming to be heard -- Plff called a Non suit-& appeal prayer & granted by the Plff entering into bond in the sum of two hundred dollars with surety - bond execited with W.W. Griffin, G W Brooks sureties.

P.A. R. C. Cohoon Vs R.K. Speed et al
T.D. M. T. 53 No 65
Subscribed for all
Witnesses in County Court
Ehringhaus & Jordan } Pool, Martin
Vs. Plff } Smith for Defds
P.a. R. C. Cohoon Vs. R.K. Speed et als

Writ & **[Torn]**	$1.40
Tax	1.00
J.W. Hinton for Transcript	2.65
Newbould	3.15
John Bray	3.10
Attorney	4.00
	$15.30
Afd Dr J. Flemming	3.10
	$18.40

State of N. Carolina }
Pasquotank County }

I James W. Hinton Clerk of the Court of Pleas & Quarter Sessions held for the County aforesaid do hereby Certify that the foregoing is a true & perfect Transcript of the record Received of proceedings had in the above stated

In Testimony whereof set my hand & affixed the Seal of the sd Court this the 18th day of April 1853, James W. Hinton, Clerk

Pasquotank County
Concealment of a Slave

North Carolina, SS
Supreme Court - June Term 1855
P.A R. C. Cohoon Vs RK Speed et al

This Cause came on to be argued upon the Transcripts of the record from the Superior Court of Law of Pasquotank County - upon consideration whereof this Court is of opinion that there is no error in the records & proceedings of the said Superior Court - Therefore, It is considered & adjudged by the Court here that the said judgment be & the same is hereby in all things affirmed - and that the plaintiffs recover against the said R. K. Speed & W.P. Matthews the sum of six pence besides his costs in & about the said suit in the said suit in the said Superior Court incurred to be taxed in the same Court & also the sum of $14.66 the costs in this Court incurred - and let the plaintiff have execution for the costs of this Court as well as for his said damages from this Court to be issued - & let the judgment here be certified to the said Superior Court to the interest that execution for the costs in that Court incurred may issue according to the Statute in such case made & provided.
Certified by E.B. Freeman, Clerk

Mr. Charles Will see on Execution[?] that he has made a mistake in the dots of the Conmmission, It Should read September 1853 instead of 1854. Please make the correction
E B [?]

State of North Carolina
To S S Stubbs

Know Ye, That we reposing especial trust and confidence in your fidelity and prudent circumspection, do command, authorize and empower you, or any of you, that at such time and place as you shall appoint, you call and cause to come before you Wm. Hodges and diligently examine on the Holy Evangelist of Almighty God, what he may know, in and about a certain matter of dispute now at issue in the Superior Court of Law, made in a cause, wherein P.A. R. C. Cohoon Vs. R.K. Speed, Wm. P. Matthews & J. W. Hoy are defendants, as well on the part of the plaintiff as the defendant,

and such examination and deposition by you so taken, you are to send closed up under your seal, to our said Court, to be held for the County of Pasquotank, at the Court House in Elizabeth City, under his Hand and Seal of Office, the fourth Monday after the fourth Monday in March in the 78th Year of the Independence of the said State, Anno Dom. 1853.
F.W. Charles, Clk.

Cohoon Vs. Speed et als
Notice
To be Returned

A True Copy of the within left with R R Speed & JW Hoy & and a copy of same left at the residence of W P Mathews this 16th Sept 1854.
Wm. Laboy [?]

Dr R. K. Speed, Wm. P. Matthews & Jno W Hoy

You are hereby notified that the depositions of R.A. Baker, Wm. Hodges & others will be taken in the City of Norfolk at the Hotel of B B Walters on Friday the 29th of this Month between the hours of 11 AM & 4 O'clock PM of said day to be read in evidence in a suit now pending in the Superior Vourt of Law of Pasquotank County Wherein P.A. R. Cohoon is Plaintiff and R R Speed, Wm. P. Mattews and J.W. Hoy are defendants, when & where you are requested to appear and then and there produce a warrant - issued by R K Speed to Wm. P. Mattews or some other officer to enter the instance or buildings of the Plff said Warrant dated sometime in August or September 1852, otherwise real evidence will be taken of the [?] of the contents of said Warrant &c
Jordan & Brooks, Attys for the Plff.

Question
The deposition of William Hodges of lawful age taken at the Hotel of B.B. Walters in the City of Norfolk Virginia on Friday the 29th day of September 1854 between the hours of 11 AM & 4 O'clock PM of said day, pursuant to the annexed Commission & notice, before Simon S. Stubbs a Justice of the peace in and for the City of Norfolk Virginia, to be read in evidence in a suit now pending in the Superior Court of Law for Pasquotank County North Carolina, wherein P.A.R. C. Cohoon is plaintiff and R.K. Speed, William P. Matthews and John W. Hoy are defendants.

Pasquotank County
Concealment of a Slave

The deponant, a witness for the plaintiff, being first duly sworn deposeth & saith by George W. Brooks Exqr. Counsel for the plaintiff. Did you have any conversation with Dr. Speed , or did you hear D. Speed in connection with any other person, in relation to a warrant under which the premises of D. Cohoon had been entered & searched; If yes, state what that conversation was.

Answer. I heard D. Speed say in my presence that he had issued a warrant to search the premises of Dr. Cohoon for a runaway slave, believing at the time that the negro was there, and under [?] Circumstances he would do the same thing again.

By the Same. Did you in that conversation, or any other, hear Dr. Speed speak in a disrespectful manner of Dr Cohoon. (This Question was objected to by John Pool Esqr. Counsel for the Defendants.)

Answer. I have heard Dr Speed say to the best of my recollection that Dr Cohoon had no Character to lose; I do not recollect that this remark of Dr Speed was made in the Conversation above alluded to. But think it was.

By the Same. When and where did this conversation occur?

Answer. It ocurred in Elizabeth City, the time I do not remember, but it was at a time Dr Speed Called upon me to know my authority for having said that the difficulty involved in this suit was settled, I think it was in the year 1853.

Cross Examined by John Pool Esqr. Counsel for the defence

Question. By the defendant's Counsel. Is not the general reputation of D. Cohoon very bad in the County of Pasquotank? This question was objected to by the Counsel for the plaintiff.

Answer. I have heard many persons speak in his favour. I think I have heard more speak against him than in his favour.

By the same. What did they say against him? (This question was objected to by the plaintiffs Counsel, and sustained by the Justice.

By the Same. Did you not in the town of Elizabeth City, in the presence of Jno. J. Grandy, William P. Matthews, and W.W, Griffin, say that D.P.A.R. C. Cohoon was a scoundrel, and speak otherwise disrespectful of him?

Answer. I have not.

Examined again by the Plaintiff's Counsel

Were there reports against the character of D. Cohoon, to which you have alluded, most frequently heard by you from D. Speed and others whom you know to be imtimate with D. Speed?

Answer. I have heard Dr Speeds friends speak very disrespectful of D. Cohoon, and I think these reports [?] most generally from D. Speed and his friends, I have heard others

---

The Deposition of Hamlin L. Eppes, David O. Duke and Owen R. Flynn taken before me, Richard L. Brewer, a Justice of the Peace for the County of Nansemond, State of Virginia, pursuant to notice hereto annexed at the Washington Hotel in the town of Suffolk, Nansemond County, on the 27th day of September, between the hours of 11 A.M. and 4 P.M. to br read as evidence in behalf of P.A.R.C. Cohoon in a certain action at Law depending in the Superior Court of Law for the County of Pasquotank, State of North Carolina wherein P.A.R.C. Cohoon is Plaintiff and Dr R.K. Speed, John W. Hoy & Wm. P. Matthews are Defendants

Present: John R. Rilby and G W Brooks, Counsel foor plaintiffs, James E. Jenkins and John Poole, Counsel for Defendants

Hamlin L. Epps being duly sworn on the Holy Evangelist of Almighty God, deposeth and saith as follows;
1st. Question by John R. Rilby, attorney for Plaintiff. How old are you, and where do you reside;
Answer: I am sixty years old, and reside in the County of Nansemond.
2nd Do you know Dr P.A. R.C. Cohoon, and if so, how long have you known him?
Answer. I know Dr. Cohoon, and have known him for the last sixteen or eighteen years.
3d. What is and has been his general character for veracity, honesty and deportment in the estimation of the public?
Answer. As far as my knowledge extends he was viewed by the public as a gentleman.
This Question and answer are excepted to on general grounds by Defendant's Counsel
4th What is your own opinion as to Dr Cohoon's character as a gentleman?
Excepted to by Defendant's Counsel because an individual the question is an illegal one.
Answr My own opinion is, that Dr Cohoon was a gentleman, and I have always looked upon him as such and never had any good reason to change that opinion.

5th Was Dr Cohoon a practising physician when you first knew him and did he continue such until he left Nansemond County?
Answr. He was a practising physician when I first knew him, and continued such until he left Nansemond County.
6th About what time did Dr Cohoon leave the County?
Answr. He left fourteen or fifteen years ago.
7th Was it not generally reported, that Dr Cohoon shot a Mr. Daughtrey in this County, and that he left the place in consequence of it, there being a warrant out for his arrest at the time of his departure.
Excepted to as irrevelant and illegal by Plaintiff's Counsel.
Answr it was so reported.
8th (Recorded by request of Plaintiff's Counsel) Was it not reported that Dr Cohoon defrauded some of his creditors on leaving the County?
Answr Not to my knowledge.
9th Have you known the reputation of Dr Cohoon since he left the county, and how often have you seen him since?
Answr I have not, - and have met with him but once, and was with him a few minutes And Farther the deponent saith not.
D, S, Eppes

David O. Duke being duly sworn on the Holy Evangelists of almighty God, deposeth and saith as follows;
1st Question by John R. Rilby attorney for Plaintiff. How old are you and where do you reside?
Answr I am forty nine years old and reside in the town of Suffolk, Nansemond County.
2nd Do you know Dr P.A.R.C. Cohoon, and if so, how long have you known him?
Answr I do know him and have known him some twenty years or more.
3rd What is an and has been his character for honesty, veracity and general deportment?
Answr I have never known or heard any thing derogatory to his character while in Nansemond County.
4th Was Dr Cohoon a practising physician while he resided in Nansemond County?
Answr He Was
5th Did Dr. Cohoon have an extensive practice as a physician? Whilst in Nansemond County?
Answr Excepted to by Defendant's Counsel as illegal and irrevelant.

Answr My opinion is he had an extensive practice.
6th Were you acquainted with the first wife of Dr Cohoon? If so, how long have you known her.
Excepted to by Defendant's Counsel as irrevelant.
Answr I was well acquainted with her, and was for eight or ten years previous to her removal from Suffolk.
7th Did you ever reside in the family of Dr Cohoon?
Answr I did some two months whilst he lived in Suffolk.
8th Were the relations which existed between Dr Cohoon and his wife affectionable and respectful whilst they resided in this county?Excepted to by Defendant's Counsel as irrevelant.
Answr Whilst I lived I never saw two persons appear to live more affectionately together, and never heard any thing to the contrary during my acquaintance with them.
Questioned by the Plaintiff's Counsel
Were the children of Dr Cohoon small when he left the county of Nansemond and was it owas it not reported that Miss Ann Skinner went to live with Dr. Cohoon to take care of his children.
Answr The Children were very small, and after the death of his wife it was reported that she did go to take care of those children.
And further the deponent saith not
D O Duke

Captain Owen R. Flynn being duly sworn on the Holy Evangelists of Almighty God, deposeth and saith as follows:
1st Question by John R. Kilby, attorney for Plaintiff
How old are you and where do you reside?
Answr I am fifty years old and am a resident of Suffolk.
2nd Do you know Dr. P.R. C. Cohoon and if so how long have you known him?
Answr I have known him from a small boy.
3rd What is and has been his general character for veracity, honesty and general deportment?
Answr In this community his character was fair and while a citizen of Suffolk he conducted himself with propriety -- I knew nothing against his character except that he was irritable. He resided in Suffolk some two years or more and was received as a gentleman in the best society.
4th was he a practising physician whilst a resident of this County and had an extended practise

Excepted to by the defendant's Counsel as illegal and irrevelant
Answr He was a practising physician whilst residing in this County and had some practise in Town and County, and it was increasing when he left.
5th Whilst Dr. Cohoon lived in Suffolk was he a married man?
Answr He was.
6th Did you know or hear of any difficulties between himself and wife?
Answr I never did.
Questioned by the defendant's Counsel.
1st How far does Andrew McHister live from this place, and is Mrs. Daniel Brinkley in the Town of Suffolk?
Ans. His place of business is adjoining this Hotel and Mrs Danl. Brinkley is in the Town of Suffolk. This last question excepted to on accounts of irrelevancy by Plaintiff's Counsel
2nd Did he reside in Suffolk whenn he left this State in 1838
Answr He Did
3rd Have you heard it as a rumor in Nansemond County that he has been living in adultry with Miss Ann Skinner since he left the County.
Answr I have heard such a rumor but not from any authentic source.
4th Have you heard it reported in Nansemond County that after he left Suffolk he caused the death of his first wife by poison
Excepted to by the Plaintiff's counsel as irrevelant & illegal.
7th Was Dr Cohoon a successful physician, and had he an extended practise in the county of Nansemond?
Excepted to by Defendant's Counsel as irrevelant.
Answr. I do not know that he was a successful physician of my own knowledge nor do I know of my own knowledge that he had an extended practise.
8th Was Dr Cohoon generally considered a successful and as having an extended practise whilst living in Nansemond County?
Excepted to as illegal and irrevelant by defendant's Counsel.
Answr. Such was the impression made upon my mind that he had and was.
9th Do you know Miss Ann Skinner and how long have you known her?
Excepted to as irrevelent by defendant's Counsel.
Answer I knew her and have known her from childhood.
10th Do you know, and if so, how long have you known her general reputation for chastity, and virtuous deportment?
Excepted to as irrevelant by defendants Counsel.
Answr Up to the time she left Nansemond County, I did know her general reputation which was in eighteen thirty eight or nine.

11th What was that general reputation for chastity and virtuous deportment?
Answr It was very good as far as I know or believe.
12th Did Miss Ann Skinner reside in the family of Dr Cohoon a married man from this County, and was Dr Cohoon a married man at that time or not?
Answr She did, and Dr Cohoon was married to his first wife.
13th Was the first wife of Dr Cohoon living at the time he removed from Nansemond County, and was she the mother of Dr Cohoon's children?
Answr She was.
14th Was Miss Ann Skinner, whilst she resided in Nansemond County, received into respectible society?
Answr She was most assuredly.

Questioned by Defendant's Counsel

1st Question Were you personally intimate with Dr Cohoon, and had you an opportunity thus of knowing the man and his reputation?
Answr I was very well acquainted with him while living in Suffolk, and I think I had something of an opportunity of learning something about the Gentleman and his reputation
2nd Did you ever employ him in your family as a physician?
Answr I did not
3rd Did Dr Cohoon practise extensively in your neighbourhood?
Answr I have know knowledge of the fact but am of opinion he did not.
4th Do you know that he had any practise in that neighbourhood?
Answr I do not know of my own knowledge but the presumption is he had.
5th Are you connected by marriage or otherwise with Miss Ann Skinner, and how?
Answr I married her Aunt.
6th Have you not heard rumors derogatory to the virtuous character of Miss Ann Skinner, particularly in connection with the Plaintiff, Cohoon, since her leaving this County?
Excepted to by the Plaintiff's Counsel because it does not seek to prove her general character
Answr I have heard rumors supposing they were intimate in a criminal way - but cannot tell from whom or from how many I heard it, but they were from men who are in the habit of talking freely; and do not know that

it has prevented her from being received into society when she has come here since she left

---

The Defendant's Attorney (James E. Jenkins) moved the Justice to allow him to take testimony under the same notice and commission, attached hereto, which was objected to by John R. Rilby, Plaintiff's Attorney, because no notice had been given to the Plaintiff by the defendant of such intentions, whereupon the Justice refused to allow such testimony to be taken.
Richard L. Brewer, JP

State of Virginia
Nansemond County, To Wit
I Richard L. Brewer, a Justice of the peace for the county aforesaid, in the said State, do hereby certify that the foregoing depositions were duly taken, sworn to and subscribed before me at the time and place mentioned therein. Given under my hand this 27th day of September 1854
Richard L. Brewer, JP

Speak disrespecfully of D. Cohoon
By the Deft.'s Counsel, Do you know who the intimate friends of D. Speed are?
Answer I think I do
By the same, who are they?
Answer: I decline naming them.
And further the deponent saith not.
Virginia, City of Norfolk, to wit
Subscribed and sworn to before me Simon S. Stubbs, Mayor of the City of Norfolk Virginia and EX offices, a Justice of said City, at the time and place and for the purpose in the Caption of this deposition written. In testimony whereof I hereunto subscribe my name and affix my seal of Office this 29th day of September 1854.
Simon S. Stubbs, Mayor & Ex Officio a Justice of the peace for the City of Norfolk
Fee for taking deposition $5, Postage - Charles, 15 cts.

State of North Carolina

Pasquotank County
Concealment of a Slave

Pasquotank County

Know all men by these presents, that we P. A. R. C. Cohoon & W.W. Griffin & Geo W. Brooks are held and firmly bound tunto R.R. Speed & W. P. Matthews in the sum of Two hundred dollars current money, to be paid to the said R R Speed & W.P. Mathews, his Heirs, executors, administrators, or Assigns -- To the which payment well and truly to be made we bind ourselves, our Heirs, Executors, Administrators, jointly and severally, firmly by these Presents. Sealed with our Seals, and dated this the Eleventh day of March Anno Domini one thousand eight hundred and fifty three.

The Condition of the above obligation is such, that whereas in a suit brought by P A R C Cohoon against R R Speed & W. P. Mathews in the County Court of Pleas and Quarter Sessions, held for the County aforesaid on the first Monday in March was ordered by this Court to be called & upon default non suit was entered & Judgment against the Plff for the costs of suit. And whereas the said P. A. R. C. Cohoon hath prayed for and obtained an appeal from the said judgment to the next Superior Court of Law, to be held for the County of Pasquotank on the 4th Monday after the 4th Monday in March 1853. Now in case the said P. A. R. C. Cohoon doth well and truly prosecute his said appeal with effect, or in case he fail and be cast therein, shall well and truly pay all such damages, costs and charges, as shall be awarded against him by the Superior Court, and also fulfil and perform the sentence, judgment and decree of the said Court; then the above Obligation shall be null and Void, otherwise to remain in full force and virtue.
Sealed and Delivered in the Presence of J. W. Hinton
Philip A R C Cohoon (Seal)
W.W. Griffin (Seal)
G W. Brooks (Seal)

Cohoon Vs Speed & als
T. Q. C. [?]

We Claim damages against the defendants on some of them on the following State facts.
1st Court

Pasquotank County
Concealment of a Slave

The entering upon the premises of Dr Cohoon by defendants and breaking his out house open under the pretence of search of a Runaway Slave. He charges this was done maliciously to injure Pltff in his feelings and good name. He charges this was done without authority well knowing Cohoon had no store or stolen property Concealed on his premises. He Charges the premises were entered and house broken opened by two of defendants with the authority and assent and concurrence of all [?] [?] to injure the feelings and reputation of Plaintiff. He charges this was done wantonly and with [?] to cause Plaintiff to be Suspected of harbouring and concealing Runaway Slaves and stolen property and thereby to injure Plaintiffs practise of Medicine. He charges they was well [?] Plantiff was from his house with the notorious [?] to frighten the female portion of his family.

Cohoon Vs. Speed & others, Trepass

The plaintiff P A R C Cohoon being duly sworn doth depose and say that he cannot safely go to trial in this Cause without the testimony of Dr Hodges who formerly resided in the County of Pasquotank and since the last term of this Court has removed to the State of Virginia and is now there as this Affiant is informed and believes and is not in attendance of this Court. Said Witness has been Subpoened & was in attendance at the last Term of this Court and is not kept away by any [?] or concurrence of this Plaintiff. This Plaintiff expects to prove by said Witness that the trespass committed by the Defendant Should and [?] if by this Plaintiff and that said Speed did the acts [?] of maliciously and without lawful excuse, this affiant further States this affidavit is not made for delay but to obtain Justice & therefor prays a certiori to the next term of this Court at which time he [?] procure the testimony of said Witness. Plaintiff further saith That [?] Flemming is also a material witness for him - has been duly subpoened and is not in attendence at this Court and kept away by this [?] this affiant expects to prove by said witness their trepass [?] of Pltff and that it was done without lawful & [?] and also [?] this affiant expects to procure his testimony by next Term if this Court afsd is not made for delay.
Subscribed & sworn before me, F.M. Charles, Clk
Cohoon Vs Speed & others affsd
Philip A R C Cohoon

Pasquotank County
Concealment of a Slave

State of North Carolina

Be it remembered that at a Superior Court of Law, began and held for Hertford County, at the Court house in Winton, on the fourth Monday of September Anno Dom 1839, Came Washington J. Moore, by his Atto Aug. Moore Esqr and brought into the said Court his writ against Philip A.R. C. Cohoon, which writ in the following words & figures, to Wit --

State of North Carolina,

To the sheriff of Hertford County, Greeting: You are hereby Commanded to take the body of Philip ARC Cohoon, (if to be found in your Bailiwick and him safely keep so that you have him before the Judge of the Superior Court of Law, at the next Court to be held for the County of Hertford, at the Court House in Winton, on the fourth Monday of September next, Then & There to answer unto Washington J. Moore in a plea of trespass on the Case for defamation to his damage &c Five thousand Dollars. Hereunto fail not, And have you then and there this Writ -- Witness, John A. Anderson, Clerk of our said Court at Winton, the fourth Monday of March in the year of our Lord 1839 And in the 63rd year of the Independence of the said State issued the first day of April 1839.
John A. Anderson, Clk

We bind ourselves to be the Plaintiff's security, for all such Costs & damages as may be awarded against him in this suit in case he shall fail to prosecute the same with effect according to act of Assembly, Witness our hands & Seals
(Signed) Saml B. Pope (Seal)
Sheriff's endorsement & return thereon, Came to hand April 1st 1839 Ed. R. Jeggets, Shff, executed April 5th 1839 Ed R. Jeggets, Shff, By F.R. Jeggets, DShff
And at the Court aforesaid, to wit Fall Term 1839, the Plaintiff filed his declaration, the following is the same.

State of North Carolina } Superior Court of Law
Hertford County } Fall Term 1839

Washington J. Moore complains of Philip ARC Cohoon being in custody &c for that whereas the said Washington J Moore now is a good, true, [?] and faithful citizen of the State aforesaid, and, as such has always behaved and conducted himself, and until the committing of the several grievances by him the said Philip ARC Cohoon as hereinafter mentioned, was always reported, esteemed and accepted and amongst all his neighbours and other good and worthy citizans, to whom he [?] any [?] known to be a person of good name, farmer, and credit, to wit at the County aforesaid.

And whom also, the said Washington J. Moore hath not ever been guilty, or until the time of the committing of the said several grievances, by the said Philip A.R. C. Cohoon as herein after mentioned, been suspected to have been guilty of injury, or any other such crime. By means of which said [?], he the said Washington J. Moore upon the committimg of the said grievances by the said Philip ARC Cohoon as hereinafter mentioned, had deservidly obtained the good opinion and credit of his neighbours, and other good and worthy citizens, to whom he was in any while known, to wit, at the County aforesaid.

And whereas also before the committing of the several grievances by the said Philip ARC Cohoon as hereinafter mentioned a certain bill of indictment has been depending in the said Superior Court of Law held for the County aforesaid, wherein the State of North Carolina was Plaintiff, and the said Philip ARC Cohoon Perigrine P. Clements & Jas M Boon were defendants, and while said indictment had been then lately tried at the Spring Term 1839 of said Court in amd for the County aforesaid, and as such trial the said Washington J. Moore had been and was examined on oath, and hath given his evidence as a witness for and on behalf of the said State, to wit at Hertford County aforesaid yet the said Philip ARC Cohoon [?] knowing the premises, but greatly enjoying the happy state and condition of the said Washington J Moore, and contriving, and wickedly and maliciously intending to injure the said Washington J Moore in his said good name and credit, and to bring him into public scandel, infamy and disgrace with and amongst all his neighbours, and other good and worthy citizens, and to cause it to be suspected and believed by those neighbours and citizens that he tho said Washington J Moore had been and was guilty of perjury, and to subject him to the pains and humilities by the laws of the said state made and provided against and [?] upon persons guilty thereof, and to hex, harrass [?] and wholly ruin him the said Washington J Moore, his [?] to wit, on the 31st day of March in the year aforesaid, at the County [?] in a certain [?] which the said Philip ARC Cohoon, then and there had in the presence and hearing of one Jesse Harriss well of divers other good and worthy citizens of the said State, he the said Philip ARC Cohoon further contriving and intending as aforesaid, then and there in the presence and hearing of the said last mentioned citizens falsely and maliciously spoke and published of and concerning the said Washington J Moore and of and concerning the said indictment, which have been so depending as aforesaid, and of and concerning the evidence by him, the said Washington J Moore given on the said trial as such witness as aforesaid, [?], Scandulous, Malicious and defamatory words following, that is to say, Washington J Moore(meaning him the said Washington J Moore) swears to a damn lie, and thereby then and there meaning, that he the said Washington J Moore in giving in his evidence as such witness on the trial aforesaid, had committed wilful and corrupt perjury. By means of the committing of which said several grievances by the said Washington J Moore hath been and is greatly injured in his said good manner, and credit, and brought into public scandal, infamy and disgrace, with and amongst all his neighbours and other good citizens of the said state, inso much that divers of good and worthy neighbors and citizens to whom the integrity of the said Washington J Moore in the premises were unknown, have on occasion of the committing of the said grievances by the said Philip ARC Cohoon as aforesaid, from [?] hitherto suspected and believed and still do suspect and believe the said Washington J Moore to have been, and to be a person guilty of perjury, and have by reason of the committing of the said grievances by the said ARC Cohoon as aforesaid, from thence hitherto wholly [?] and still do refuse to have any transaction acqaintance or discourse with him the said Washington J. Moore, as they were [?] and accustomed before to have, and otherwise would have, and the said Washington J Moore hath been, and is by means of the premises, otherwise greatly injured, to wit, at the County aforesaid. To the great damage of the said Washington J Moore of five thousand dollars, and therefore he brings his suit.

2nd And afterwards to wit on the 31st day of March aforesaid in a certain other discourse which the said Philip ARC Cohoon then and there had in the presence and hearing of the said Jesse Harriss and of divers other good and worthy citizens of the said State, he the said Philip ARC Cohoon further contriving and intruding, as aforesaid, then and there in the presence and hearing of the said last mentioned citizens falsely and maliciously spoke and Published of and concerning the said Washington J Moore, and of and concerning the said indictment which had been depending as aforesaid, and of and concerning the evidence by him the said Washington J Moore given on the said trial as such witness as aforesaid then and there [?] false, scandulous, malicious and defamatory words following, that is to say he (Meaning the said Washington J Moore) swore to a damn lie, and thirdly then and there meaning, that he the said Washington J Moore in giving in his evidence as such witness on the trial aforesaid, had committed wilful and corrupt perjury, by means of the committing of which said several grievances by him the said Philip ARC Cohoon as aforesaid, in the said Washington J Moore hath been and is greatly injured in his said good name **[?]** and credit, and brought into public scandal, infamy and disgrace, with and amongst all his neighbours and citizens of this State, inasmuch that divers of these good and worthy neighbours and citizens to whom the **[?]** and integrity of the said Washington J Moore in the premises were **[?]** , have an occasion of the committing of the said grievances by the said Philip ARC Cohoon as aforesaid, from thence hitherto to suspected and believed and still do suspect and believe the said Washington J Moore to have been and to be a person guilty of perjury, and have by reason of the committinof the said grievances by the said Philip ARC Cohoon as aforesaid, from thence hitherto wholly refused and still do refuse to have any transaction, acquaintence or discourse with him the said Washington J Moore, as they before were used and accustomed to have, and otherwise would have, and the said Washington J Moore hath been and is by means of the premises, otherwise greatly injured, to wit, at the County aforesaid, To the great damage of the said Washington J Moore of five thousand dollars.

[Faded] Atty for Plff
3rd And afterwards to wit on the 31st day of March aforesaid at the County aforesaid in a certain other discourse which the said Philip ARC Cohoon then and there had in the presence and hearing of the the said Jesse Harrile and of divers good and worthy citizens of the said State, he the said Philip ARC Cohoon further contriving and intending as aforesaid, then and there in the presence and hearing of the last-mentioned citizens falsely and maliciously spoke and published of and concerning the said indictment which had been depending as aforesaid, and of and concerning the witness by him the said Washington J Moore given on the suit trial as such witness as aforesaid, **[?]** other false, scandulous, malicious and defamatory words, that is to say **[?]** (meaning the said Washington J Moore) sworn to a damn lie, and thereby then and there meaning that the said Washington J Moore in giving in his evidence un such witness on the trial aforesaid, had committed wilful and corrupt perjury

4th And afterwards, to wit on the 31st day of March aforesaid at the County aforesaid in a certain other discourse which the said Philip ARC Cohoon

then and there in the presence and hearing of the said Jesse Harrill and of divers other good and worthy citizens of the said State, he the said Philip ARC Cohoon further contriving and intending as aforesaid, then and there in the presence and hearing of the said last mentioned citizens falsely and maliciously spoke and published of and concerning the said Washington J Moore, and of and concerning the said indictment which had been depending as aforesaid and of and concerning the evidence by him the said Washington J Moore given on the said trial as such witness as aforesaid **[?]** other false, scandulous, malicious and defamatory words, that is to say **[Smudged]** (meaning the said Washington J Moore) sworn to a damn lie, and thereby then and there meaning that the said Washington J Moore in giving in his evidence as such witness on the trial aforesaid, he the said Washington J Moore hath been and is greatly injured in his said good name, **[?]** and credit, and brought into public scandal, infamy and disgrace, with and amongst all his neighbors and and other good and worthy citizens of the said State, inasmuch as divers of the good and worthy neighbours and citizens to Whom the **[?]** and integrity of the said Washington J Moore in the premises were unknown, have an occasion of the committing of the said grievances by the said Philip ARC Cohoon as aforesaid from thence wholly refused and still do refuses to have any transaction, acquaintance or discourse with him the said Washington J Moore, as they were used and accustomed before to have, and otherwise would have, and the said Washington J Moore hath been and is by means of the premises, otherwise greatly injured, to wit at Hertford County aforesaid To the great damage of the said Washington J Moore of five thousand dollars. And therefore he brings his Suit.
Cluny**[?]** & Morriss, Atto for Pltf

Washington J Moore Vs. P. A. R. C. Cohoon

By means of the committing of which said several grievances by the said Philip ARC Cohoon as aforesaid, he the said Washington J Moore hath been and is greatly injured in his said good name **[?]** and credit, and brought into public scandal, infamy and disgrace, with and amongst all his neighbours and other good and worthy citizens of the said State, inasmuch that divers of these good and worthy neighbours and citizens to whom the innocense and integrity of the said Washington J Moore in the premises were unknown, have on occasion of the committing of the said grievances by the said Philip ARC Cohoon as aforesaid, from thence hitherto suspected and believed and still do suspect and believe the said Washington J Moore to have been, and to be a person guilty of perjury, and have, by reason of the committing of the said grievances by the said Philip ARC Cohoon as aforesaid, from thence wholly refused and still do refuse to have any transaction, acquiantence or discourse with him the said Washington J Moore, as they were used and accustomed before to have, and otherwise greatly injured, to wit, at the County aforesaid To the great damage of the said Washington J Moore of five thousand dollars.

Copy of Bail Bond

State of North Carolina }
Hertford County }

Know all men by these presents that we Philip A.R.C. Cohoon, Andrew J. Askew & William T. Bynum, all of the County aforesaid are held & firmly bound unto Edward R. Leggett **[Jeggett]** Sheriff of the County aforesaid, to be paid unto the said Edward R. Jegetts Sheriff, his heirs, administrators, executors or assigns, for the true performance whereof we bind ourselves, our heirs, Administrators, executors, or assigns jointly & severally, firmly and by these presents, Sealed with our seals, & dated this 5th day of April 1839.

The Condition of the above obligation is such, that if the above bounded Philip A.R.C. Cohoon, do well and truly make his personal appearance at our next Superior Court to be holden for the County of Hertford on the fourth Monday in September next, at the Court House in Winton, then & there to answer unto Washington J Moore in a plea of trespass on the case for Defamation to his damage &c Five Thousand Dollars -- and then and there stand to & abide by the judgment of the said Court, and not depart the said Court without leave, then the above obligation to be void, otherwise to remain in full force and virtue
Signed, Sealed & delivered in the presence of Frances W. Leggets
Philip A.R. C. Cohoon (Seal)
Andrew J. Askew (Seal)
Wm. T. Bynum (Seal)

Pasquotank County
Concealment of a Slave

I Ed. R. Jeggets[?] Sheriff of Hertford County, do hereby assign over the within obligation and Condition to Washington W. Moore - The Plaintiff therein named, his executors and Administrators, to sue for recovery agreeably to an Act of Assembly in such Case made & provided.

Given under my hand & Seal this 5th day of April 1839

Ed. R. Jegett, Shf.

And at the Court aforesaid to wit: Fall Term 1839 the said Philip A.R.C.Cohoon by his Atto. David Outlaw Esqr comes & defends the wrong & injury where &c and pleads.

General issue, justification Stat. Limitations; R. & J.

Therefore let a jury thereupon Come before the Judge &c. at Winton on the fourth Monday of March aforesaid to wit Spring Term 1840, the said Philip A.R.C. Cohoon filed the following affidavit for the removals of the Cause, to wit:

Moore Vs. Cohoon

The defendant in this Case maketh oath, that from what he has understood from many sources, and fully believes he cannot come Safely to the trial of his cause in this County, affiant has every reason to believe, that, that this Case has been the subject of much remark in the County of Hertford and that efforts have been made to his prejudice and which are calculated seriously to effect a decision of the Case before the Jury. And in particular that affiant believes that one John A. Anderson a man of wealth and influence in the County, in whose employment the plaintiff was at the time of bringing of the action, and now is has used such efforts against this affiant as to have much prejudiced the minds of a large portion of the Community against him. For these reasons affiant believes he cannot come safely to trial in this County, affiant further states that these facts has come to his knowledge since the last term of this Court.

Sworn & subscribed in open Court --Philip A.R.C. Cohoon

John A. Anderson, Clk, by L.M. Cowper

Spring Term 1840

Upon the hearing of the defendants affidavit, the Court orders this Cause to be removed to Gates County

State of North Carolina,

Pasquotank County
Concealment of a Slave

I John A. Anderson clerk of the Superior Court of Law for Hertford County, do hereby certify the foregoing to be a true and correct Transcript of the proceedings had in the Case of Washington J. Moore Vs. Philip A.R.C. Cohoon, which Case is by order of the Court removed to the County of Gates. In Testimony whereof I have hereunto set my hand & affixed the seal of my office at Winton, this 4th Monday of March A.D. 1840. John A. Anderson, Clk, (Seal)

State of North Carolina } Superior Court of Law
Gates County } Spring Term 1840

Transcript from Hertford County into office 2nd Apl 1840 - H. Gilliam, Clk
Washington J. Moore Vs. Philip A.R.C. Cohoon, Continued.

And at the next Term of this Court, to wit: Fall Term 1840 this Cause was Continued by defendants paying Costs of said Term and it was ordered that Ca. [?] issue to the County of Edgcomb for same.

And at the next Term of this Court, to wit: Spring Term 1841 this Cause was continued.

And at the next Term, of this Court, to wit: Fall Term 1841, The following letter (of which this is a Copy) was received, to wit:

Washington J Moore Vs. Philip A.R.C. Cohoon, Suit in Gates Superior Court for Slander or Defamation.

Whereas Philip A.R. C. Cohoon, having entered into bond, payable to me this day, with William T. Bynum & Andrew J. Askew securoties for the payment of all costs of every discription incurred or taxable to the same, as well as for the payment of my Lawyer's fee's in consideration of which I have Consented to dismiss the same, the said P.A.R.C. Cohoon first signing a Certificate of the falsity of his slanderous expressions, The Clerk of the Superior Court will therefore please dismiss the same by there paying the costs as above stated
Winton May 22nd 1841.
Witness, John A. Anderson & Pleasant Jordan -- W.J. Moore

And at the present Term to wit: Fall Term 1841, this Cause was dismissed at the Defendants Costs

Pasquotank County
Concealment of a Slave

State of North Carolina

I William L. Boothe Clerk of the Superior Court of Law in & for Gates County, do hereby Certify, that the foregoing is a true & correct Transcript and exemplification of the proceedings had in the Case of Washington J Moore Vs. Philip A.R.C. Cohoon, as appears of record. In Witness whereof I have hereunto set my hand & affixed the seal of my office, at Gatesville, this 22nd day of April A.D. 1854.
Wm. L Boothe, Clerk

E. City N. Carolina, March 20th 1854

Sir

You are hereby notified that on Wednesday the 5th day of April 1854 and from [?] Thereafter until [?] between the hours of 10 A.M. and 5 P. M. at the Central Hotell in Suffolk Va. [?] to be taken by defendants to be read as evidence in a suit now pending in the Superior Court of Law of pasquotank County which you are pltf and Rufus k Speed, W.R. [?] an aforesaid you can be present and Cross Examine the witness if you desire.
Dr CARC Cohoon, Pool & Martin Elizabeth City attorneys for the Defendant.

State of North Carolina

To W.B. **[Smudged]** Justices of the Peace for the Court of Nansemond and State of Virginia.

Know Ye, That we reposing especial trust and confidence in your fidelity and prudent circumspection, do command, authorize and empower you, that at such time and place as you shall appoint, you call and cause to come before you R.H. Webb & R H Parker, Edward C. Riddick, Jethro Riddick, Daniel Brinkley Thos Hall, W.S. Riddick, J H Doughty [?], & M.H. Watkins and diligently examine on the Holy Evangelist of Almighty God, what they know in and about a certain matter of dispute now at issue in the Superior Court of Law, made in a cause, wherein P.A.R.C. Cohoon is plaintiff, and R.K. Speed et al are defendants as well on the part of the plaintiff as the defendant, and such examination and deposition by you so taken, you are to send closed up under your seal, to our said Court, to be held for the County of Pasquotank, at the Court House in Elizabeth City, on the fourth Monday after the fourth Monday in March next, and this you are in no wise to omit -- Witness F.M. Charles, Clerk of the said Court, at

Pasquotank County
Concealment of a Slave

Elizabeth City, under his Hand and Seal of Office, the fourth Monday after the Fourth Monday in September in the 78th Year of the Independence of the said State, Anno Dom. 1854
F.M. Charles, Clerk.

The depositions of Robert H. Webb and others to wit: Richd. H. Parker, Edward C. Riddick, Jethro Riddick, Daniel Brinkley, Thos. Hall, Willis S. Riddick, J.K. Daughtrey, Wm. T. Braton[?] and Col. Meshak H. Watkins.

Taken before me W.B. Wellons a justice of the peace for the County of Nansemond Pursuant to a Commission and notice hereto annexed at the Central Hotel in the town of Suffolk in Virginia on the 5th day of April 1854 between the hours of 12 and 6 P.M. to be read as evidence on behalf of Rufus K Speed and others in a Certain action at Law depending in the Superior Court of Law for the County of Pasquotank in North Carolina wherein PA. R.C. Cohoon is Plaintiff and Rufus K Speed and others are defendants

Present James E. Jenkins attorney for defendant, John R Kelly attorney for Plaintiffs

Dr Robert H Webb being duly Sworn on the holy Evangelists of almighty God deposeth and Saith as follows

1st Question by Defendant's Counsel, What is your age and Profession? I was 58 years old last birth day and by profession a Physician.

2nd Question by same, Did you Know Dr. PARC Cohoon during his residence in Nansemond County, and what was his general reputation and character?
This question excepted to by John R. Kilby atto for P.A.R.C. Cohoon because it does not specify what kind of general character and because the question of character is not proper to investigate in the case between the parties.
Answer I knew Dr Cohoon when he was a resident of Nansemond County, But after commencing the practice of Medicine he went away, and when he went to directly [?] afterwards he lived in the upper part of Nansemond and there practiced Medicine from thence he went to Suffolk and resided there two or three years I think, this was 17 or 18 years ago. He left Suffolk

about 16 years ago, where he went to don't know. I had little connection with Dr Cohoon personally, but believe he was a man generally disposed to [?] and dispute, and according to my recollection I think he was so regarded by the community

3rd by same - What was his general character for veracity?
This question excepted to for reasons assigned to second question (by same)
Answer Really I cannot tell you what his character for veracity was in the Community

4th Question Did you regard him as a man of veracity?
Excepted by plts atto for reasons assigned in the other exceptions & because specific enquiries or individual opinions are illegal.
Answer Cohoon at one time had some transactions with me and did not comply with his promises and I thought treated me badly. At the time of [?] I did not regard him as a man of veracity, but afterwards I did.

5th Question by same. Did or did not Dr Cohoon during his residence in Nansemond County establish a general reputation?
Excepted by Ptls atto because of the indefiniteness of the question & for reasons assigned in first exception.
Answer I don't know Sir

6th Question You spoke of his leaving Suffolk some 16 or 17 years ago - was it generally said he left the County to prevent prosecution for a violation of the Criminal law of the State?
Excepted to by plts atto, because the question seeks to prove some particular act or fact not proper to be done in the case.
Answer I believe, myself, that he left to prevent a criminal prosecution, I think that was the belief of the Community but not certain of that fact.

7th Question Did or did not Dr Cohoon establish a reputation amongst his professional brethren - and if so what was that reputation?
Excepted to by Plts atto: For reason assigned in first exception
Answer I believe that Dr. Cohoons reputation amongst his professional brethren was not good.

8th Question Was there any reports in circulation in Suffolk affecting the reputation of Dr. Cohoon for chastity.

Excepted because wholly irrevelant to the issue (by Ptls atto.)
Answer I do not know that there was any such report circulated generally in Suffolk, but I heard such a report [?] whether it was true or not.

9th Question Did you know one Miss Ann Skinner
Answer I did not.

10th Question have you ever heard a report relative to the intimacy of Dr. Cohoon with a young lady living in his house.
Excepted to by Plts atto: because it seeks a specific answer to a particular fact
Answer No Sir

11th Question Was he, Dr. Cohoon not regarded as a suspicious man?
Excepted to by Plts atto: because indefinite, and not revelant to the issue.
Answer I could answer that question for myself but cannot answer it for others. I did not regard him as such, Do not know how other people regarded him.

1st Question by the Plts atto: you have said in answer to the 6th Quest by Defts: That you believed Dr. Cohoon left Nansemond County because of some criminal prosecution against him - Please state if you know, whether such prosecution, if any was for any infamous offence, or for some personal encounter with some one?
Answer It was for a personal encounter

Question by Defendants Counsel: Please state the nature or that Encounter and whether or not it would have subjected him to confinement in the public Jail and penetentiary?
Excepted to by Plts atto: because the Deft has no right to investigate any such specific fact
Answer It was said that Dr. Cohoon and a man named Daughtery had a fight and he (Cohoon) shot at Daughtery. My impression is if convicted it would have sent him to the penetentiary, but I do not know that fact.
Further this deponent Saith not
Signed Ro: H. Webb

The taking of these depositions is adjourned till Thursday 6th April 1854
W.B. Wellon JP
The taking of these depositions is adjourned till Friday the 7th April 1854

Pasquotank County
Concealment of a Slave

W.B. Wellon, JP.

Dr. Richard H. Parker another witness being duly sworn on the Holy Evangelists of Almighty God deposeth and saith as follows.

1st Question by Defendants Counsel, What is your age and occupation?
Answer I am 52 years old a Practicing Physician in the town of Portsmouth

2nd Question By same: Did you know Dr. P.A.R. C. Cohoon during his residence in Nansemond County or elsewhere; and what was his general reputation?
Excepted to by Ptls atto because it does not state what kind of reputation; and because the enquiry as to reputation is not such as can be made in a suit such as is depending between the parties.
Answer I knew Dr. Cohoon personally when a young man, perhaps 25 years since perhaps I have seen him once in one occasion only 15 years ago & to general reports or rumors for the last 15 years his reputation has not been very Commendable, for my estimation, from the rumors not that I know any thing about Cohoon personally.

Question by same -- Have there not been reports currently circulated and generally believed, affecting his character as a gentleman and impugning his character for veracity and honesty of purpose.
Excepted to by Plts atto because of the objection contained in last paragraph of first exception.
Answer I could state that there has been reports circulated and generally believed affecting his character as for morals are concerned as to his character for veracity -- I know nothing. As to his honesty of purpose [?] is impossible for me to state.

Question by Same: Have there not been reports in circulation and those reports believed, charging him with dishonesty in his dealings with his fellow men.
Excepted to for reasons assigned above by Plts atto and because of its leading character
Answer I don't know particulars in this case except that of his exorbitant charges in his profession of them I know nothing personally. I heard that he charged $750 for one amputation: I consider that making those exorbitant charges was very unprofessional

Question by same -- What was his reputation for chastity?
Excepted to by Plaintiffs Atto.
Answer So far as one particular case is concerned he cannot be very Chaste

Question What case was that?
Excepted to by the Ptls atto because of the fact that the question seeks to prove a particular fact.
Answer It was rumoured generally and believed that he lived with an unchaste woman

Question by same: Give her name?
Excepted to by Ptls atto because it seeks to prove a particular fact, & by mere rumor.
Answer A Miss Skinner, Miss Ann Skinner I think.

Question by same: What was her general reputation?
Excepted to by Pltfs atto, for reasons assigned in first exception
Answer Her general reputation was that she was unchaste. When I knew her she was then living in the house of Willis F. Riddick about 15 years ago. I had not then learned that she was unchaste but since that time my mind has become perfectly satisfied of the fact.

Question by same: What do you mean by Saying She was unchaste?
Excepted to by Plaintiffs Atto
Answer I was satisfied in my mind that certain young men did have connections with her

Question by same: What was Dr. Cohoons reputation amongst Gentlemen of his Profession
Excepted to by Plaintiffs Counsel
Answer Dr. Cohoons reputation generally amongst his Profession has not been very good. He has been accused of putting up quack medicines and sending them out which has been considered generally un professional.

Question Has he not been charged with mal Practice in his Profession?
Excepted to by Plaintiffs Atto
Answer Not that I know particularly

Question by same: Was it not Currentlyl reported and generally believed that Dr. Cohoon and Miss Ann Skinner were criminally intimate.
Excepted to by Plaintiffs Atto
Answer All that knew Cohoon and his Lady knew the circumstances generally believed the fact.

Question by Plaintiff's Atto: Please explain what you meant by quack medicine?
Answer We consider any one medicine which any Physician sends out as a cure for all diseases or a cure for the for all Disease in all persons in all persons is a quack medicine.
Further this deponent saith not
Signed Richd Parker

The Taking of these depositions is adjourned to Saturday the 8th day of April 1854
Capt. Edward C. Riddick being duly sworn deposeth and saith.

1st Question by Defendants Attorney - What is your age and occupation?
Answer I am in my 47th year by occupation a farmer.

2nd Question by same: Were you acquainted with Dr. P.ARC Cohoon during his residence in this part of the Country and what was his general reputation in the Community in which he lived?
Excepted to by Plts Atto, because it does not specify what kind of a reputation or what for.
Answer I was acquainted with him when he lived in the town of Suffolk, and while he lived in the upper part of the County. I have known him ever since he commenced practicing medicine. So for my own knowledge extends I regarded him as a gentleman. I have heard people speak slightly of him, do not know whether they had cause for doing so or not.

2nd Question by the same: Was, or was he not regarded as a suspicious man by many of his neighbors?
Excepted to by Plaintiffs Atto for reasons told above.
Answer I have heard people say about the time he had an affray with Mr. Doughtery that he would not speak the truth at all times. I do not know whether they were his enemies or not.

3rd Question Was, or was he not regarded as a troublesome and dangerous man by many of his acquaintences?
Excepted to by Plaintiffs Atto for reasons told above and because of its leading character
Answer That is a hard question to answer, he never was troublesome, I do not know whether he or they were at fault.

4th Question by same: Were there not general rumors affecting his character for chastity?
Excepted to by Plaintiffs Atto.
Answer I am bound to say yes; there were general rumors to affect his character for chastity, but as for my own self I do not know whether they were true or not. I do not know whether there was any fornications for such rumors or not.

5th Question by same: Did those rumors allude to his illicit intercourse with any particular female, or for general unchaste conduct.
Excepted to by Ptls Atto because the question seeks to establish a general reputation by proving particular fact
Answer Rumor said he was not chaste with one, that was public opinion; of my own knowledge I do not know any thing about it.

6th Question by now, Who was that one?
Excepted to by same, because of the reason assigned in last exception.
Answer Miss Ann Skinner was the person that it was about.

7th Question by same: What were the rumors affecting her reputation for Chastity?
Excepted by Plts atto.
Answer All that I can say that public opinion was against her.

Question by same, Did public opinion allude to unchaste Conduct with others than Cohoon?
Excepted to by Plts atto.
Answer No Sir, I knew of no other besides Cohoon, that is I never heard of others.

Question -- With reports like these in circulation would you not have felt a delacacy in introducing Such a physician into the private chaimber of any one of your female relations.

Excepted to by Plts Atto: because of its seeking to find the witness's individual opinion, and because it seeks to prove a particular fact in order to establish general character - and for other reasons.
Answer I never employed him in my family because I had another family physcian, I had never give the matter any thought, If I could have known he was man that some people **[Torn]**

Question **[Creased]** reports in circulation about **[?]** can you then say he bore the reputation of not being a suspicious and dangerous now?
Excepted to by Plts Atto because of its leading character
Answer If reports about him be true I should regard him as suspicious and dangerous, but I know nothing about the reports myself.

Question When did he leave Nansemond County?
Answer I do not know exactley, I suppose some 15 or 16 years ago.

Question What were the circumstances under which he left?
Excepted by the Ptls Atto, because it seeks to prove particular facts.
Answer I Know nothing about it of my own knowledge.

Question State what public opinion said was the cause of his leaving?
Excepted to by Plts Atto
Answer Public opinion said he left to escape the penalty of the law.

Question by Plts atto: You have said in answer to a Question by Defts Atto that with certain rumors about Dr. Cohoon, if known to you to be true, you would not have him to attend your family -- with such rumors, and also with the knowledge of his superior ability to other physcian near you would you not send for him?
This question is excepted by the Defendants Counsel because the **[Creased]** this question avers a fact which no where appears in the evidence, is intended as a leader to elicit an answer which the witness otherwise under a general question would not be given
Answer If he had been a superior Physcian to others **[?]** him I should have sent for him to attend my family in a difficult case.
Firther this deponent saith not, Signed.
Edward C. Riddick & W.B. Wellons JP

The taking of these depositions is adjourned until Monday the 10th day of April 1854.

Pasquotank County
Concealment of a Slave

The taking of these depositions is adjourned until Tuesday the 11th day of April 1854, W.B. Wellons JP.

Capt Jethro Riddick, another witness being duly sworn on the Holy Evangelists of Almighty God deposeth and saith as follows.

Question by Defendant's Counsel - what is your age - occupation, and in what part of Nansemond County do you live?
Answer I am 50 years old by occupation a Farmer and reside in the Cypress District 10 miles from Suffolk.

Question by the same. Did you know one Philip ARC Cohoon during his residence in Nansemond County, And what his general reputation?
Excepted to by Plaintiff's Counsel.
Answer I knew him personally when I saw him. He always treated me as a Gentleman, I Know nothing of his reputation only from reports

3rd Question were there not current rumors generally believed affecting his general reputation?
Excepted to by Plaintiff's Counsel because it does not specify what kind of a reputation.
Answer There was a great many rumors going about, I cannot say whether they were generally believed or not or whether they effected his general reputation much. It has been so long I have forgotten the particulars.

4th Question by same: Was his general reputation for veracity and general fair dealing in his business transactions good?
Answer I do not know.

5th Question Did you know one Miss Ann Skinner?
Excepted to by Plaintiff's Atto
Answer I did.

6th Question What was her general reputation in the Community in which she lived when you knew her.
Excepted to by Plaintiff's Atto
Answer It was said she was a pretty girl.

7th Question What was her general reputation for chastity?

Excepted to by Plaintiffs Atto.
Answer There were unfavourable rumors about her but I do not know now exactly what they were excepted in one particular case

8th Question Did those rumors affect her reputation for chastity.
Excepted to Plaintiffs Atto.
Answer They might or Might not, I do not now recollect.

9th Question Was she not charged in the community with having criminal connection with some one?
Excepted to by Plaintiffs Atto because it seeks to prove a particular fact and for other reasons.
Answer It was so rumored.

10th Question Were there rumors general?
Answer I do not know whether they were general or not, they were talked about by some individuals.

11th Question Did rumor point to any particular person as the one with whom she had illicit intercourse or was it believed to be general.?
Excepted to by the Plaintiffs atto, because it seeks to prove a particular fact.
Answer It was thought she had intercourse with one man.

12th Question Who was that man?
Excepted to by Plaintiffs Atto for same reason or the [?].
Answer Dr P. A R C Cohoon.

13th Question She being charged with illicit intercourse with a married man, can you say that her reputation for chastity was good?
Excepted to by Plaintiffs Atto because the facts assumed was not proved, and because they are irrelavant
Answer Not as far as report went.

14th Question With those reports in circulation about Cohoon can you say Cohoons general reputation was good?
Excepted to by Plaintiffs Atto because of its leading Character.
Answer I cannot, so far as Miss Skinner's case is concerned.

15th Question Were there not other charges brought against him?

Excepted to by Plaintiffs Atto because it seeks to prove a particular fact.
Answer Yes. There were other charges brought against him.

16th Question What were they?
Excepted to by the Plaintiffs atto for the **[?]**
Answer It was said he had an affray with Matthew Daughtery.

17th Question Was he not charged with a general disposition to enough and **[?]**?
It was said he was.

18th Question Was he not charged with not telling that **[?]**
Excepted by Plaintiffs Atto because it is a Question and because it seeks to prove a general reputation by a particular fact.
Answer He might or might not, I do not now recollect.

19th Question When does Capt Edward C Riddick live?
Answer In my own immediate neighbourhood.

20th Question From the reputation of Miss Ann Skinner would you have suffered her to be friend and associate for your daughter?
Answer I should not if I could have helped it
Question by the Plaintiff Atto. How long since Dr Cohoon left this County?
Answer I do not know exactly
Question by same How long has it been since these rumors were in existence about Dr Cohoon?
Answer It was before he left Nansemond and since and since he left.

21st Question by Defendants Atto. State under what circumstances he left.
Answer It was said he shot Mathew Daughtery and a warrant was issued for his arrest.

22nd Question Was it not generally believed that if he had remained he would have gone to the penetentiary?
Answer If the report was true I reckon he would

23rd Question by Plaintiffs Atto: Can you state of your own knowledge whether he was guilty of any penitentiary or other serious offences in his affray with Mr Daughtry?

Answer I Cannot
And futher this deponent sait not.
Signed Jethro Riddick

Daniel Brinkley another witness being duly sworn upon the Holy Evangelists of Almighty God deposeth and saith as follows.

Question by Defendants Attorney. What is your age, occupation and place of residence?
AnswerI am 47 years old by occupation a Farmer and reside in the Cypress District 9 miles from Suffolk.

2nd Question Did you know one PARC Cohoon during his residence in Nansemond County and what was his general reputation for veracity and general conduct and citizenship?
Answer I did know him. I know nothing about his reputation for veracity. I have heard rumors going about as to the way in which he and others lived, In other respects he was always spoken very highly of until he had the affray with Mr. Daughtery.

3rd Question After the affray with Daughtery did you not hear many reports and were they not believed, affecting his reputation for veracity and general fair dealings?
Answer I do not recollect that I ever did, I did not hear much about him after the left here.

4th Question Did you know one Miss Ann Skinner?
Answer I did

5th Question What was her general reputation for chastity?
Excepted to by Plaintiffs Atto as irrevelant.
Answer Rumor said it was not first rate as to my own part I know nothing about it.

6th Question Was she charged with criminal connection with any person?
Excepted to because it seeks to prove a particular fact.
Answer It was supposed to be the case with a particular man

Question Who was that man?

Excepted to by Plts Atto - for the same so the [?]
Answer Dr. Cohoon

Question Was she not charged with general unchaste conduct?
Excepted to by Plts Atto
Answer Not general only with the one mentioned.

Question With such reports in circulation and generally believed would you have suffered her to become an associate for your female relatives?
Answer I could not.

Question Were these reports generally believed?
Answer They were generally believed.

Question With such reports in circulation and generally believed about Cohoon would you not have hesitated in introducing him unto the private chamber of any of your female relatives as a Physician?
Excepted to by Plts Atto because of its leading character and for other reasons.
Answer I should not if they were sick!

Question When did Cohoon leave Suffolk?
Answer I do not recollect exactly some 15 or 16 Years ago.

Question Have you heard the cause of his leaving and how he left?
Answer I understood that he and Matthew Daughtery had a fight at the Court House and he shot Daughtery and a warrant of arrest was gotten and he left the State to prevent arrest, I do not know how he left.

Question Was it not generally believed that if he had remained he would have been sent to the Penitentiary?
Excepted to by Plts Atto
Answer I think it was generally believed.

Question Have you heard of any other charges against him ?
Excepted to by Ptls Atto because it seeks to prove particular facts.
Answer Not that I can recollect.
And farther this deponent saith not
Signed, Daniel Brinkley Sr.

Pasquotank County
Concealment of a Slave

The Taking of these depositions is adjourned till Wednesday 12th April 1854, W.B. Wellons

Thomas Hall, another witness being duly sworn on the Holy Evangelists of Almighty God deposeth and saith as follows.

1st Question by Defendant's Atto. What is your age, occupation and place of residence?
Answer I am 46 years old, and by occupation a Farmer and Sheriff of Isle of Wight County in which County I reside.

2nd Question by same: Did you know one P.A.R.C. Cohoon during his residence in Isle of Wight County, and how did his neighbors regard him?
Excepted to Ptls Atto because it is indefinite and assumes a particular fact which is not proven
Answer I knew Dr Cohoon and have heard that he lived in Isle of Wight County, but cannot sat on my oath that I knew him when he lived there. This was some 17 or 18 years ago and before I was an Officer. I cannot answer as to how his neighbors regarded him.

3rd Question Have you met with and known him since?
Answer I have.

4th Question State what reputation he bore at this time then mentioned.
Excepted to by Ptls Atto
Answer With a portion of the people he bore not a very good reputation with others a tolerable good reputation, I knew very little about him myself.

5th Question Was he regarded by the Community as a peaceable and quiet citizens, or as and dispised to [?] and quarell?
Excepted to by Plts Atto.
Answer I know that he was engaged in two law suits in Isle of Wight County, which produced considerable excitement
This answer is Excepted to by the Plts Atto because ot is wholly iresponsive to the question proposed.

6th Question Did these suits produce and wrangling and quarreling in which he was a participant?

Excepted to by Plts atto because it seeks to prove a general reputation by particuler facts and because irrevalant to the issue.
Answer I think they did as I have understood from others.

7th Question From the reports or rumors generally in circulation was Cohoon not considered in fault?
Excepted to by Plts Atto because it is a leading question and seeks to prove a particular fact.
Answer In the suits - I think he was considered at fault having been tried by a jury twice and in both cases decided against him.
This answer is Excepted to because the witness speaks of a fact which can be proved by record testimony.

8th Question Were not the verdicts of those juries generally approved as being correct.?
Excepted to by Plts Atto because the fact proved is foreign from the issue and for other reasons.
Answer They were.

9th Question In the wrangling and quarreling [?] on those suits was not Cohoon generally considered at fault?
Excepted by Tlts Atto because it seeks to prove a general reputation by particular facts and because of its leading character.
Answer I think so for as I heard it was considered he was in the wrong or mistaken.

10th Question Was he not then regarded as a troublesome man?
Excepted to by Plts Atto for the same reasons as the last.
Answer I think he was in so far as those two suits were concerned.

11th Question After he left Isle of Wight County state how long you knew him.
Answer A very short time.

12th Question During that short time did his reputation improve, or was he engaged in further difficulties?
Excepted to by Plts Atto because it seeks to prove a general reputation by particular facts
Answer I do not think his reputation in Isle of Wight improved any, as to further difficulties I know nothing about.

13th Question Do you know, or have you heard from reliable information that he left Suffolk, and if so for what cause.
Excepted to by Plts Atto because it seeks to prove particular facts.
Answer I heard from reliable information that he left Suffolk for shooting Matthew Daughtery.

14th Question From what you have learned of this shooting and the opinion of the Community generally do you not suppose the offence would have sent him to the penitentiary?
Excepted to by the Plts Atto because of its leading character and because it seeks to prove a particular fact by hear say to establish a general reputation.
Answer I have heard some people who spoke of it say that they supposed it would.

15th Question Were there charges brought against him for not telling the truth?
Excepted to by Plts Atto because it seeks to prove specific fact
Answer I never heard of any except in the case of Daughtery.
And further this deponent saith not.
Signed, T Hall

The taking of these depositions is adjourned to Thursday the 13th April 1854, W.B. Wellons

Capt Willis S. Riddick another witness being duly sworn on the Holy Evangelists of Almighty God deposeth and saith as follows.

1st Question by Defendant's Attorney. What is your age, occupation and place of residence?
Answer I am 84 years old by occupation a farmer and reside 7 miles from Suffolk in Nansemond County.

2nd Question Did you know one P.A.R.C. Cohoon during his residence in this County, and what reputation did he bear in the Community in which he lived?
Excepted to by Plaintiffs Atto for its uncertainty.

Answer Yes I knew him when he lived in this County, I knew nothing of his reputation except hear say.

3rd Question What reputation did rumor or hearsay assign him in the Community in which he lived?
Excepted to by Plts Atto for its uncertainty.
Answer His general reputation was tolerably bad, some spoke of his having treated them very well and others badly.

4th Question What was his general reputation for veracity and general fair dealings
Answer I have never heard any thing about his veracity, some accused him with making too large accounts for his Medical services, others said his charges were no larger that other Doctors.

5th Question What was his general reputation for chastity?
Excepted to by Plts Atto as irrevalant
Answer I cannot say that I ever heard any thing about his Chastity when he lived in Suffolk, but I heard a great deal after he left . I have heard a great deal about his Chastity since he left and may have heard about it before but cannot be certain.

6th Question State what you heard?
Excepted to by Plts Atto because it seeks to prove a general reputation by particular facts.
Answer I have heard that a young lady lived in his house by the name of Miss Ann Skinner and it was thought that he was to fond of her, that he had intercourse with her and kept her.

7th Question In what manner did rumor say he kept her?
Excepted to by Plts Atto for the same reason as above.
Answer It was said he slept with her.

8th Question Were those rumors general?
Answer I think they were.

9th Question What reputation did Miss Ann Skinner bear for chastity?
Excepted to by Plts Atto.
Answer Tolerable, bad.

10th Question Was it such as to forbid your visiting her as a Lady.
Answer It was

11th Question Did the community general regard her in this light?
Answer I think they did.

12th Question what was Dr. Cohoon's reputation for general good conduct?
Answer I never heard of his being generally a bad man.

13th Question Was he not regarded as a troublesome and disputatious man?
Excepted to by Plts Atto because of its leading.
Answer Not that I know of.

14th Question Had he any difficulties during his residence in Nansemond?
Excepted to by Plts Atto because it seeks to prove a general reputation by a particular fact.
Answer I have heard of one difficulty - he had but do not know whether it was when he resided here or not.

15th Question What was that difficulty?
Excepted to by Plts Atto for same reason as the last.
Answer I have heard that him and a man named Doughtery had a difficulty and he shot Doughtery and afterwards Doughtery knocked him down with a stick, and that Doughtery was [?] so bad but that he would have paid him well if he had been let alone.

16th Question Did the public generally regard Cohoon as having been in fault in this difficulty?
Excepted to by Plts Atto because its not a proper question to prove a general reputation
Answer I do not know which the public said was in fault.

17th Question Was it not generally believed that if he had been tried for the offence that he would have sent to the Penitentiary?
Excepted to by Plts Atto for same reasons as in the last.
Answer Not that I know of.

18th Question by Plaintiff's Attorney -- When did Cohoon move from the County of Nansemond?

Answer I do not know

19th Question How long since you knew Dr. Cohoon?
Answer It was when he lived in Suffolk some years ago, but do not know how many years, When I knew Cohoon I think I went to [?] in Suffolk and was noy 21 years old. And farther this deponent saith not.
Signed, Willis S. Riddick

Revr'd Jacob K. Daughtrey being duly sworn on the Evangelists of Almighty God, deposeth and saith as follows.

1st Question by Defendant's Attorney. What is your age & occupation and place of residence.?
Answer I an 54 years old by occupation a farmer and Minister of the Gospel and reside ten miles from Suffolk in the County of Nansemond.

2nd Question Did you know Dr. P.A.R.C. Cohoon during his residence in this part of the County and what was general reputation?
Excepted to by Plts Atto because it does not specify what kind of a reputation.
Answer I knew him while he lived in Nansemond County and also while he lived in Isle of Wight County - he seemed to have been remarkable for Controversy as he was frequently in difficulties with persons with different persons. Whether he was Plaintiff or Defendant in those Controversies I know not

2nd Question What was his general reputation for veracity?
I think his veracity in many cases was questioned by many.

3rd Question Was he regarded as a good or bad citizen?
Excepted to by Plts Atto.
Answer He was regarded rather as a troublesome man.

4th Question Was he engaged whilst living there in many difficulties?
Excepted to by Plts Atto because it seeks to prove a general reputation by proving particular facts.
Answer He was - he interupted some peaceable men that would not otherwise have been in controversies I am sure.

5th Question Was, or was he not considered a dangerous man?
Answer I think he was more mischievous than dangerous, I do not think he was a man of much moral courage.

6th Question Was, or was he not considered a man disposed to deceive generally there who had dealings with him?
Excepted to by Plts Atto
Answer The public seemed to consider him a man disposed to deceive.

7th Question Was or was he not regarded as a suspicious character?
Excepted to by Plts Atto.
Answer I am unprepared to answer the question.

8th Question Did his neighbors regard him as one who would act honestly?
Answer I do not think that they regarded him as being correct in all his dealings in transactions.

9th Question What was his reputation for chastity?
Answer I think I have heard his chastity questioned in the community; though I know nothing of it myself.

10th Question How did his professional brethren regard him ?
Answer I cannot say.

11th Question About what time did he leave this part of the Country, and why.
Excepted to by Plts Atto because it seeks to prove a general character by particular facts.
Answer I suppose he left about 12 or 15 years ago. I cannot be definite. I do not know why he left directly.

12th Question Did the community at large assign any reasons for his leaving?
Excepted to by Plts Atto for same reasons as the last.
Answer I do not remember to have heard the reasons why he left.

13th Question When did he leave Suffolk? And why?
Answer My answer to the last question will bear answer to this.

14th Question With a knowledge of the reports in circulation about him, and the general reputation he bore, would you have permitted him to become one [?] acquaintence of your family?
Answer He did visit my family, I regarded his wife as a lady and my family visited her. I also had his professional services in my family once, and then it was to a negro [?] in [?] bed.

1st Question by Plaintiff's Atto. Did you ever have a difficulty with Cohoon.
Answer No I had no difficulty with him. He did make an attack on me but I would not accept it.

2nd Question Was Cohoon in the habit of [?] with the gentlemen of the neighborhood when he resided?
Answer He was

3rd Question Whilst you knew him had he a good practice as a Physician?
Answer He had.

15th Question by Defendant's Counsel. Before he left the neighborhood did not many of the gentlemen refuse to associate with him?
Answer I believe the people associated with him excepting those who had controversies with him.

16th Question By same: Were there charges of mal-practice brought against him?
Excepted to by Plts Atto because it seeks to prove a reputation by particular facts
Answer I believe there was.

17th Question Were they believed generally?
I should think they were.

4th Question by Plaintiff's Attorney: You speak of charges against Dr Cohoon for mal practice, have you ever heard charges of a similar character brought against other Physician?
I Except to this question because the Examination of the witness has been made in cheef, he has been Cross - examined and re-examined by first question & the question is irregular and ought not to be allowed, Counsel for Defendant

Answer I Have.

5th Question by same: Although you have heard these charges against practicing Physician, Cohoon among them, did they not still continue to get as much practice as before?
Excepted to for reasons assigned before by Defendant's Atto.
Answer I believe they did.
And farther this deponent saith not
Signed, Jacob K. Daughtrey

William T Beaton **[Blaton]** another witness being dul sworn on the Holy Evangelists of Almighty God deposeth and saith as follows.

1st Question by Defendant's Attorney: What is your age, occupation and place of residence?
Answer I am 51 years old by occupation a Farmer and Constable in Isle of Wight County in which County I reside.

2nd Question Did you know one P.A.R.C. Cohoon, when did he reside when you knew him, and how was he regarded by the community in which he lived?
Excepted to by Plts Atto because indefinite.
Answer I did know him when he resided in Isle of Wight County and when he resided in Winton N.C. As a Physician I believed he stood very high while he lived in Isle of Wight. I used to hear people grumble considerably at his charges.

3rd Question Was he regarded as a peaceable and qiuet citizen or as one disposed to wrangle a Quarrell.
Answer At some times I think he was apt to wrangle and quarrell

4th Question Was he on good terms with his neighbors general?
Answer When he lived in Isle of Wight so far as I know he was on good terms with most of his neighbors. He then lived a mile and a half from me. After that he lived in 5 or 6 miles of me, I do know that I heard of only particular difficulty there except one with Matthew Daughtrey.

5th Question Think and answer if he was not in some other quarrell, dispute or vexatious suits?

Excepted to by Plts Atto because it seeks to prove a reputation by particular facts and because of its leading character.
Answer I have heard that he had a suit with Col Watkins, and his Mother. I had forgotten that at first.

6th Question Did these quarrells or suits produce much excitement?
Excepted to by Plaintiff's Atto for reasons assigned last.
Answer I should judge they did.

7th Question Did they lead to any wrangling or quarrelling and tend to disturb the peace of the neighborhood?
Excepted to by Plts Atto for same reasons as above.
Answer I cannot say of my own knowledge.

8th Question What did the community say of these quarrells and suits?
Excepted to by Plts Atto because it seeks to prove a general reputation by particular facts.
Answer So far as the the suit against Col Watkins and his Mother is concerned I believe the general opinion was that they were brought wrongfully. I think that it was generally said that Cohoon was [?] to blame in those suits.

9th Question What was the reputation of Cohoon for veracity?
Excepted to by Plts Atto as irrelavant.
Answer I do not know.

10th Question What did the community say of his reputation for veracity?
Excepted by Plts Atto for the same as the last.
Answer Some did not have the [?] of confidence in him.

11th Question Was he regarded by the community as one who would take unfair advantages of others?
Excepted to by Plts Atto.
Answer Some was of the opinion that he would.

12th Question Can you then say that he bore a fair reputation?
Excepted to by Plts Atto because it is a leading character.
Answer I should not judge he did.

13th Question was he not regarded as a suspicious character?

Excepted to by Plts Atto for same as last.
Answer I cannot answer that question.

14th Question Was his honesty not suspected by some persons?
Excepted by Plts Atto for the same as the last and for other reasons.
Answer I have heard some few doubt it.

15th Question by same: Were there not many who doubted it?
Excepted to by Plts Atto for same reason.
Answer I did not know.

16th Question Do you think probably that there were many who doubted his honesty?
Excepted to by Plts Atto.
Answer I should think ot probable there were many who doubted his honesty.

17th Question What was his general reputation for chastity?
Answer I do not know.

18th Question Were there any reports in circulation affecting his reputation for chastity?
Excepted to by Plts Atto
Answer None that I ever heard of.

1st Question by the Plaintiff's Attorney: Was Dr. Cohoon ever employed by you as a Physician?
Answer He was

2nd Question by same: Did not Cohoon have a good practice whilst in your neighborhood?
Answer He did.

3rd Question by same: Was he not thought and spoken highly of by many?
Excepted by Def. Atto for divers reasons.
Answer As a Physcian he was. When he first come then he was spoken highly of as a gentleman, After those suits he was not spoken so highly of.

19th Question by Defendant Atto: You state that he had a good practice in your neighborhood, did that practice continue to be good or did it dwindle?

Answer I think it continued to be good until he left for Suffolk.

20th Question by same: Were there not charges of mal practice brought against him?
Excepted to by Plaintiff's Atto because it [?] to prove a general reputation by proving particular facts.
I do not know
And farther this deponent saith not.
Signed, Wm. T. Beaton

Col. Merideth H. Watkins being duly sworn on the Holy Evangelists of Almighty God deposeth and saith as follows.

1st Question by Defendant's Attorney: What is your age, occupation and place of residence?
Answer I am 49 years old by occupation a Farmer and reside in Isle of Wight County.

2nd Question Did you know one P.A.R.C. Cohoon and what was his reputation during his residence in this part of the Country?
Excepted to by Plts Atto because it is indefinite.
Answer I knew him well. His reputation was bad with many.

3rd Question How was he generally regarded by the community in which he lived?
Excepted to by Plts Atto as irrevelant.
Answer He was regarded by many as a troublesome man.

4th Question Was he considered a dangerous man by the community?
Excepted to by Plts Atto
Answer I do not know that he was considered a grave man if you consider a man that will take the advantage, if another dangerous, he was dangerous I believed he was so regarded in the community.

5th Question What was his reputation for honesty and fair dealings.
Excepted to by Plts Atto as irrevelant to the issue.
Answer I cannot answer this question for the Public.

6th Question Was he regarded by many persons in Isle Wight County as an honest man?
Answer I cannot say.

7th Question Were there many who regarded him as a dishonest man?
Excepted to by Plts Atto because it seeks to prove a general reputation by the opinion of a part of the community.
Answer There were some that regarded him in that light.

8th Question From his general conduct was he considered a suspicious person?
Answer I should say he was. I thought him a very suspicious man.

9th Question What was his reputation for veracity?
Excepted to by Plts Atto as irrevelant to the issue.
Answer As for as him and myself were concerned I should say it was bad.

10th Question Was he considered a man who would do dirty tricks to accomplish and **[?]**
Excepted to by Plts Atto
Answer My own opinion is that he would. I **[smudged]** then were other persons who regarded him so too. I have heard a great many speak contemptily of him whether there was a just cause for it or not I do not know.

11th Question You of his being a troublesome man, was he often in difficulties?
Answer He was.

12th Question Who did **[?]** generally **[?]** as being the author of these difficulties?
Excepted to by Plaintiff's Atto
Answer Cohoon

13th Question Was he generally disposed to wrangle and quarrell?
Excepted to by Plts Atto
Answer I do not know.

14th Question How did he stand with his professional brethren?
Answer I do not know.

15th Question What was his reputation for chastity?
Excepted by Plts Atto as irrelevant.
Answer I have not heard any thing regarding his chastity- worthy of note.

16th Question When did he leave this part of the Country?
Answer Some 15 or 16 years ago. I cannot answer the question definitely.

17th Question Why did he leave?
Excepted to by Plts Atto because it seeks to establish a reputation by proving particular facts.
Answer Public opinion says to escape arrest.

18th Question With what offence was he charged that he should have left to prevent an arrest?
Excepted to by Plts Atto for the same reasons as the last.
Answer He was charged with shooting Matthew Daughtery.

19th Question Had he been caught what did public opinion say would have been done with him?
Excepted to by Plts Atto
Answer Sent to the penetentiary.

20th QuestionWas this opinion general?
Answer I believe it was.

1st Question by Plaintiff's Attorney: You have spoken of Cohoon's having difficulties and suit with persons, were you one of the parties?
Answer I was.

2nd Question by same: When did these difficulties occur?
Answer some 16 or 18 years ago. Cannot be definite about the date.

3rd Question When the suit occurred between you and Cohoon did it not cause great enmity between you and him and has not the same ill feelings continued until now?
Excepted to by Defendants's Atto because of its leading nature.
Answer I did, and it has but that some ill feeling has not caused me to exagerate in the statements I have made.

4th Question by same: Did not Dr. Cohoon have a good practice as a Physician whilst you knew him?
Excepted to by Defendant's Atto.
Answer I knew of but very little of his practice report, said his practice was pretty good.

21st Question by Defendant's Counsel: You say Cohoon and your self had a suit, who brought that suit?
Excepted to by Plts Atto because it seeks to establish a general reputation by proving particular facts.
Answer Dr. Cohoon.

22nd Question by same: Did you do any thing that you know of to provoke that suit?
Excepted to by Plts Atto for same reasons as before.
Answer I did not.

23rd Question What was the result of that suit?
Excepted to by Plts Atto for same.
Answer A jury decided for the Defendant on the second trial.

24th Question What was the general opinion of the community?
Answer This is a delicate question for me and I prefer that others should answer it.

25th Question Do you think that your feelings towards him would prejudice you in giving his general reputation?
Answer No

26th Question You have been asked about his practice and said you knew but little, please state a portion or the whole of that little?
Excepted to by the Plts Atto because it seeks to investigate specific facts.
Answer He intruded his practice on my wife and bled her against her will and afterward presented an account against me, through Capt Beaton for amount some where between 20 and 40 dollars which I refused to pay. This bleeding took place in my absence at the time of a collision on the Portsmouth and Roanoke Rail Road near Suffolk when the Physicians generally volunteered their services to aid the wounded. No other Physcians charge against the wounded. That being understood that the rail road company paid the expense. He treated others in the same way.

The Plaintiff's Attorney now enters an exception to the taking of all the preceding depositions, because the subject of character, is one which the Defendants should not investigate in any such action as is pending between the parties.
Further this deponent Saith not.
Signed, Meredith H. Watkins.

Amount of Charges for taking these depositions
Witness Allowance

Ro H Webb, 1 day, no mileage	.50
H. L. Eppes, 1 day	.50
R.H. Parker, 1 day, .50, 14 miles @ 4 cents each	1.06
Ed C. Riddick, 1 day 50, 2 miles @ 4c	.58
Jethro Riddick, 1 day (no mileage	.50
Danl. Brinkley, 1 day, no Mileage	.50
	$3.64
Carried Forwd	
Amt of Charges Brought forward	
	3.64
Thos Hall, 1 day & 10 miles @ 4c	.90
Willis S. Riddick, 1 day, no mileage	.50
Jacob K Daughtrey, 1 day, (do)	.50
Wm. T. Beaton, 1 day, 20 miles @4cts	1.30
Col M. H.W. Watkins, 1 day, 10 miles 4cts	.90
Wm B. Wellons Justice of the peace for 19 hours Service (in obedience to Code of VA) at 75 Cts Pr hour.	14.25
	$21.99

State of Virginia
County of Nansemond to Wit.

I William B. Wellors a justice of the Peace for the County aforesaid in the State aforesaid do hereby Certify that the foregoing depositions were duly taken and sworn to and Subscribed before me at the times and places, therein mentioned in obedience to the annexed Commission from the Superior Court of Pasquotank County and the Notice thereto appended.

Given under my hand this 14th day of April 1854.
W. B. Wellons, JP

Cohoon Vs. Speed et al
X-8249

This was an action of trespass, Tried at Spring Term, 1855, of Pasquotank Superior Court, before Person, Judge

It was in evidence that the Defendant, Matthews, the acting Constable for the town of E. City applied to the Defendant, Speed, one of the acting Justices of said County, for a warrant to search for & arrest a runaway slave, supposed to be Concealed upon the premises of the Plaintiff, &, there was evidence going to show that Speed & that Matthews acted [?] & issued the Warrant. The Defendant Matthews went to the door of a stable situated upon the premises of the Plaintiff, which opened into one of the public streets of the Town of Elizabeth City, & standing in the street, requested one hoy[?] to assist him in the taking the negro if he should find him concealed in said stable, But Matthews did not produce or mention the warrant, to the recollection of the witness, nor did the witness recollect to have heard Matthews direct anyone to go upon the premises of the Plaintiff - The Witness further stated that he believed, but was not altogether positive, that Matthews drew out, with his fingers, a staph that fastened said door, & thereupon the witness & others pushed open the door & stood in the Stable & premises but that Matthews did not enter that the stable was loose & come out of the door easily -- that servant of Cohoon was present at the time, it being the servant which had charge of the stable, & that he struck, with an axe, but did not injure, the lock of another door, but that he did not hear Mayhews direct him so to do. That the side of the stable, where the door opened, forward the [?] between the strut & the premises of the Plaintiff -- That Speed was not present during the time.

The Court instructed the Jury, that if they believed Speed issued the Warrant, as aforesaid, & that Matthews acting under the Warrant either drew the stable, as stated by the witness, or directed those who entered, to enter -- although Matthews himself did not go upon the premises -- still he would be a trespasser & liable in this action; & that Speed, who issued to him the Warrant, was also a trespasser & also liable in this action, whether present at the time the trespasser was committed, or not if Matthew was acting under that [?] that it made no difference, in this action, whether Speed was or was not a Justice of the peace.

Then was a verdict for the Plaintiff against both Defendants -- Rule upon the Plaintiff for new Trial -- Rule discharged -- Appeal prayed & granted
Saml. J. Person, Judge &c.

Cohoon Vs. Speed et als
To be Returned
A True Copy of the Notice left with Dr. R K Speed & JW Hoy
& a copy left at the residence of WP Matthews
This 16th Sept 1854, Mr [?]

To Dr. R.K. Speed, W.P. Matthews & John W. Hoy

You are hereby notified that Depositions of Hamilton L. Eppes, Mr. Daniel Brinkley, Major Andrew McAlester, Owen R Flynn, David Duke and others will be taken in the Town of Suffolk VA. On Wednesday the 27th, 28th & 29th of this month, at the Washington Hotel in town, between the hours of 10 oclock AM & four oclock PM on said days the same to be continued from day to day thereafter until completed, said depositions to be read in evidence in a suit now pending in the Superior Court of Law of Pasquotank County wherein PAR Cohoon is Plaintiff and your self, Wm. Matthews & Jno. W. Hoy are Defendants, when and where you can appear & cross examine if you see proper.
Jordan & Brooks, Attys for Plff
Sept 15th 1854.

Cohoon Vs. Speed et als
Subpoena
Return Spring Term 1854

To hand the 19th day of April 1854, Executed on Jno. A. Anderson the 20th April, Wm. Worthington not to be found. Executed on K Rayner the 21st April 1854. Jno. P. Bridges, Shff.

I deputise A.G. Britt to Execute this Subpoena on Kenneth Rayner April 20th 1854
Jno. P. Bridges, Shff

Pasquotank County
Concealment of a Slave

State of North Carolina
To the Sheriff of Hertford County, Greeting:

You are hereby commanded to summon Dr. William Worthington, John A. Anderson & Kenneth Rayner personally to be and appear before the Judge of the Superior Court of Law, at the next Court to be held for the County of Pasquotank, at the Court House in Elizabeth City, on the fourth Monday after the fourth Monday in March next, then and there to testify and the truth to say in behalf of the Defendant in a certain matter of controversy in the said Court depending, and then and there to be tried, wherein P.A.R.C. Cohoon is Plaintiff; and R.K. Speed & als are Defendants; and this you shall in no wise omit, under the penalty by law enjoined.

Witness, Francis M. Charles, Clerk of the said Court, at Elizabeth City, the fourth Monday after the fourth Monday in Sept. in the 78th year of our Independence, Anno Domini, 1853.
Issued the 4th day of April 1854.
F.M. Charles, Clerk.

Cohoon Vs. Speed & others
Spring Term 1854

Came to hand the 22nd April 1854, I have summoned Jno. A. Anderson in and others Subp. In the same case & in behalf of the Defendant Mr. Anderson not being at home to day I have Excecuted this.
J.P. Bridges, Shff.

State of North Carolina.
To the Sheriff of Hertford County, Greeting:
You are hereby commanded to summon John A. Anderson personally to be and appear before the Judge of the Superior Court of Law, at the next Court, to be held for the County of Pasquotank, at the Court House in Elizabeth City, on the fourth Monday after the fourth Monday in March next, then and there to testify and the truth to say in behalf of the Defendants in a certain matter of controversy in the said Court depending, and then and there to be tried, wherein P.A.R. C. Cohoon is Plaintiff; and R K Speed & others are Defendants; and this you shall in no wise omit, under the penalty by law enjoined.

Witness, Francis M. Charles, Clerk of the said Court, at Elizabeth City, the fourth Monday after the fourth Monday in Sept. in the 78th year of our Independence, Anno Domini, 1853.
Issued the 29th day of April 1854
F.M. Charles, Clerk

Cohoon Vs Speed
Service Accepted
Jos. B. Shaw

State of North Carolina,
To the Sheriff of Pasquotank County, Greeting:

You are hereby commanded to summon Joseph Shaw personally to be and appear before the Judge of the Superior Court of Law; immediately, to be held for the County of Pasquotank, at the Court House in Elizabeth City, on the fourth Monday after the fourth Monday in September next, then and there to testify and the truth to say in behalf of Defendant in a certain matter of controversy, in the said Court depending; and then and there to be tried; wherein PARC Cohoon is Plaintiff; and R K Speed et als are Defendants; and this you shall in no wise omit, under the penalty by law enjoined.

Witness, Francis M. Charles, Clerk of the said Court, at Elizabeth City, the fourth Monda after the fourth Monday in the year of our Independence, Anno Domini, 1853
Issued the 26th day of October 1853.
Francis M. Charles, Clk.

Cohoon Vs Speed & als
Subpoena - Defdts
Ret Fall Term 1854
Executed, C.B. Brothers

State of North Carolina,
To the Sheriff of Pasquotank County, Greeting:

You are hereby commanded to summon Mordacai Morris personally to be and appear before the Judge of the Superior Court of Law, at the next Court, to be held for the County of Pasquotank, at the Court House in Elizabeth City, on the fourth Monday after the fourth Monday in

March next, then and there to testify and the truth to say in behalf of The Defendant in a certain of controversy in the said Court depending, and then and there to be tried, wherein PAR C Cohoon is Plaintiff and R.K. Speed et als are Defendants; and this you shall in no wise omit, under the penalty by law enjoined.

Witness, F.M. Charles, Clerk of the said Court, at Elizabeth City, the fourth Monday after the fourth Monday in September in the 78th year of our Independence, Anno Domini, 1854.
Issued the 28th day of April 1854.
F.M. Charles, Clerk.

State of North Carolina,
To the Sheriff of Pasquotank County, Greeting:

You are hereby commanded to summon T. Hunter, J.J. Grandy, W.W. Griffin, Reuben Overman & John Bailey personally to be and appear before the Judge of the Superior Court of Law, at the next Court, to be held for the County of Pasquotank, at the Court House in Elizabeth City, on the fourth Monday after the fourth Monday in Sept. next, then and there to testify and the truth to say in behalf of the Defendants in a certain matter of controversy in the said Court depending, and then and there to be tried, wherein P.A.R.C. Cohoon is Plaintiff; and R.K. Speed & als are Defendants; and this you shall in no wise omit, under the penalty by law enjoined.

Witness, F.M. Charles, Clerk of the said Court, at Elizabeth City, the fourth Monday after the fourth Monday in March in the 78th year of our Independence, Anno Domini, 1854.
Issued the 23rd day of Oct. 1854.
F.M. Charles, Clk.

Cohoon Vs Speed et als
Subpoena
Ret Immediately
Executed by C. B. Brother, DShff

State of North Carolina,
To the Sheriff of Pasquotank County, Greeting:

You are hereby commanded to summon John J. Grandy and Harriet Ann Turner, personally to be and appear before the Judge of the

Pasquotank County
Concealment of a Slave

Superior Court of law, at the next Court, to be held for the County of Pasquotank, at the Court House in Elizabeth City, Immediately, then and there to testify and the truth to say in behalf of the Plaintiff in a certain matter of controversy in the said Court depending, and then and there to be tried; wherein Philip A. R. Cohoon is Plaintiff; and R K Speed et als are Defendants; and this you shall in no wise omit, under the penalty by law enjoined.

Witness, Francis M. Charles, Clerk of the said Court, at Elizabeth City; the fourth Monday after the fourth Monday in Sept. in the 78th year of our Independence, Anno Domini, 1853.
Issued the 26th day of Oct 1853.
F.M. Charles, Clk.

Cohoon Vs Speed et als
Subpoena
Return Immediately
Executed, Wm. Newbould, Shff

State of North Carolina,
To the Sheriff of Pasquotank County, Greeting:

You are hereby commanded to summon Jas. S. Long personally to be and appear before the Judge of the Superior Court of Law, at the Court House in Elizabeth City, immediately then and there to testify and the truth to say in behalf of the Plaintiff in a certain matter of controversy in the said Court depending, and then and there to be tried, wherein Dr PARC Cohoon is Plaintiff and Dr. R K Speed et als are Defendant; and this you shall in no wise omit, under the penalty by law enjoined.

Witness, F.M. Charles, Clerk of the said Court, at Elizabeth City, the fourth Monday after the fourth Monday in March in the year of our Independence, Anno Domini, 1854.
Issued the 26th day of April 1854.
F.M. Charles, Clk.

Cohoon Vs Speed et als
Subp for Defendant
Ret, S, T [?], Executed
Wm. Newbould, Shff

Pasquotank County
Concealment of a Slave

State of North Carolina
To the Sheriff of Pasquotank County, greeting:

You are hereby commanded to summon Jos. B. Shaw, William Glover, Thomas Harvy, T.H Hunter, W.W. Griffin personally to be and appear before the Judge of the Superior Court of Law, at the next Court, to be held for the County of Pasquotank, at the Court House in Elizabeth City, of the fourth Monday after the fourth Monday in March next, then and there to testify and the truth to say in behalf of the Defendants in a certain matter of controversy in the said Court depending, and then and there to be tried; wherein Cohoon is Plaintiff; and Speed et als are Defendants; and this you shall in no wise omit, under the penalty by law enjoined.

Witness, Francis M. Charles, Clerk of the said Court, at Elizabeth City, the fourth Monday after the fourth Monday in Sept in the 78th year of our Independence, Anno Domini, 1853.
Issued the 11th day of April 1854.
F.M. Charles, Clerk.

Dr. P.A.R. C. Cohoon Vs Dr. R K Speed et als

State of North Carolina
To William A. Clark & Wilson W. Williams.
Know Ye, that we reposing especial trust and confidence in your fidelity and prudent circumspection, do command, authorize and empower you, or any of you, that at such time and place as you shall appoint, you call and cause to come before you Wm. Hodges and diligently examine on the Holy Evangelists of Almighty God, what he knows in and about a certain matter of dispute now at issue in the Superior Court of Law, made in a cause, wherein Philip ARC Cohoon is Plaintiff, and R K Speed, W.P. Matthews & J.W. Hoy are Defendants, as well on the part of the Plaintiff as the Defendant, and such examination and deposition by you so taken, you are to send closed up under your seal, to our said Court, to be held for the County of Pasquotank, at the Court House in Elizabeth City, on the fourth Monday after the fourth Monday in March next, and this you are in no wise to omit - Witness F.M. Charles, Clerk of the said Court, at Elizabeth City, under his Hand and Seal of Office, the fourth Monday after the fourth Monday in Sept. in the 78th Year of the Independence of the said State, Anno Dom. 1853.

Pasquotank County
Concealment of a Slave

Notices Ret Tuesday 4th April between 10 AM & [?] at this store of W.W. Williams
F.M. Charles, Clerk.

State of North Carolina

To Richard L. Brewer, a Justice of the peace for Nansemond County, State of Virginia.

Know ye, That we reposing especial trust and confidence in your fidelity and prudent circumspection, authorize and empower you, or any of you, that at such place and time as you shall appoint, you call and cause to come before you Hamlin F. Eppes, David Duke and Owen R. Flynn and diligently examine on the Holy Evangelists of Almighty God, what they know in and about a certain matter of dispute now at issue in the Superior Court of Law, made in a cause, wherein Philip A.R.C. Cohoon is Plaintiff, and R K Speed and others are Defendant, as well on the part of the Plaintiff as the Defendant, answer such examination and deposition by you so taken, you are to send closed up under your seal, to our said Court, to be held for the County of Pasquotank, at the Court House in Elizabeth City, on the fourth Monday after the fourth Monday in September next, and this you are in no wise to omit. Witness F.M. Charles, Clerk of the said Court, at Elizabeth City, under his Hand and Seal of Office, the fourth Monday after the Fourth Monday in March in the 78th Year of the Independence of the said State, Anno Dom. 1853.
F.M. Charles, Clk.

State of North Carolina,

To the Sheriff of Pasquotank County, Greeting:

You are hereby commanded to summon Marmaduke Baker personally to be and appear before the Judge of the Superior Court of Law immediately this Court, held for the County of Pasquotank, at the Court House in Elizabeth City, on the fourth Monday after the fourth Monday in March next, then and there to testify and the truth to say in behalf of the Plaintiff in a certain matter of controversy in the said Court depending, and then and there to be tried, wherein Dr. P.A. R. C. Cohoon is Plaintiff; and Dr. R.K. Speed is Defendant; and this you shall in no wise omit, under the penalty by law enjoined.

Witness, F.M. Charles, Clerk of the said Court, at Elizabeth City, the fourth Monday after the fourth Monday in Sept. in the 78th year of our Independence, Anno Domini 1853.
Issued the 25th day of April 1854.
F.M. Charles, Clerk.

State of North Carolina

To the Sheriff of Pasquotank County, Greeting:
You are hereby commanded to summon Roberson White, Timothy Pendleton, Jno. Bray & James Flemming personally to be and appear before his Honor the Judge of the Superior Court of Law of Pasquotank County, at the next Court, to be held for the County of Pasquotank, at the Court House in Elizabeth City, on the fourth Monday after the Fourth Monday in March, then and there to testify and the truth to say in behalf of Cohoon in a certain matter of controversy in the said Court depending, and then and there to be tried, wherein Cohoon is Plaintiff and Speed & Matthews are Defendants. And this you shall in no wise omit, under the penalty by law enjoined. Witness James W. Hinton, Clerk of the County Court of Pleas and Quarter Sessions of said County at Elizabeth City, the first Monday of March in the 77th year of our Independence, Anno Domini 1853
Issued the **[Blank]** day of April 1853
James W. Hinton, Clerk

Cohoon Vs Speed et als
Subpoena
Executed by Wm Newbould, Shff

North Carolina
To the Sheriff of Pasquotank County, Greeting:
You are hereby commanded to summon Dr. Robt. Prinout**[?]** personally to be and appear before the Judge of the Superior Court of Law, at the next Court, to be held for the County of Pasquotank, at the Court House in Elizabeth City, on the fourth Monday after the fourth Monday in March next, then and there to testify and the truth to say in behalf of the Plaintiff in a certain matter of controversy in the said Court depending and then and there to be tried, wherein P.A.R.C. Cohoon is Plaintiff; and Dr. R.K. Speed

is Defendant; and this you shall in no wise omit, under the penalty by law enjoined. Witness, Francis M. Charles, Clerk of the said Court, at Elizabeth City, the fourth Monday after the fourth Monday in Sept. in the 77th year of our Indepednence, A.D. 1854.
Issued 25th day of April 1854.
F.M. Charles, Clk.

P.A.R.C. Cohoon Vs Speed & Matthews
Subpoena
Ret. Spring Term 1853
Executed by Wm. Newbould, Shff
P. A. R. C. Cohoon Vs R.K. Speed, W. P. Matthews & John W. Hoy

W. P. Matthews, Sir

You are hereby Notified that the deposition of Dr. Hodges, will be taken on Tuesday the 4th April 1854, between the hours of 11 o'clock AM & 4 o'clock PM, in the Town of Elizabeth City, at the Store off W.W. Williams, Esqr. to be read in evidence in the suit now pending in the Superior Court of Law of Pasquotank wherein I am Plaintiff and you, R.K. Speed & John W Hoy Defendants, when and where you can appear and cross examine, if you see proper, This 31st March 1854.

Dr. Cohoon Vs Speed et als
Ret. Immediately
Wm. Newbould, Shff

State of North Carolina

To the Sheriff of Pasquotank County, Greeting:
You are hereby commanded to summon Dr. Hodges personally to be and appear before the Judge of the Superior Court of Law, at the next Court, to be held for the County of Pasquotank, at the Court House in Elizabeth City, on the fourth after the fourth Monday in March next, then and there to testify and the truth to say in behalf of the Defendants in a certain matter of controversy in the said Court depending, and then and there to be tried; wherein P.A.R.C. Cohoon is Plaintiff; and R.K. Speed et als are Defendants; and this you shall in no wise omit, under the penalty by law enjoined.

Witness, Francis M. Charles, Clerk of the said Court, at Elizabeth City, the fourth Monday after the fourth Monday in Sept. in the 78th year of our Independence, Anno Domini 1853.
Issued the 1st day of April 1854.
F.M. Charles, Clerk.

Cohoon Vs Speed & als
Subpoena for Defendant
Ret. Spring term 1854
To hand Apr. 3rd 1854
Executed, J.F. Jinkins, Shff
By W.A. Jones DShff

State of North Carolina
To the Sheriff of Edgecombe County, Greeting:
You are hereby commanded to summon Joseph John Porter, Robert Norfleet & C.L. Dicken, personally to be and appear before the Judge of the Superior Court of law, at the next Court to be held for the County of Pasquotank, at the Court House in Elizabeth City, on the fourth Monday after the fourth Monday in March next, then and there to testify and the truth to say in behalf of the Defendant in a certain matter of controversy in the said Court depending, and then and there to be tried; wherein P.A.R.C Cohoon is Plaintiff; and R.K. Speed & als are Defendants; and this you shall I no wise omit, under the penalty by law enjoined.

Witness, Francis M. Charles, Clerk of the said Court, at Elizabeth City, the fourth Monday after the fourth Monday in Sept. in the 78th year of our Independence, Anno Domini, 1853.
Issued the 24th day of March 1854.
F.M. Charles, Clerk.

Chohoon Vs. Speed et als trespass
Notice To Matthews, to be Returned
A True Copy of the within delivered to
WP Matthews, March 31st 1854
C B Brothers
P.A.R.C. Cohoon Vs R.K. Speed, Wm P Matthews & others

Pasquotank County
Concealment of a Slave

Take notice that on the trial of this cause now pending in the Supr Court of Pasquotank County you will be required to produce & deliver a Certain Warrant Commonly Called a Search Warrant issued to R.K. Speed one of the Defendants and placed in the hands of WP Matthews the other Defendant to search the Premises of the said Plaintiff for a runaway Slave and in default thereof I shall offer secondary Evidence of its contents.
April 25th 1854
Brooks & Jordan, Atty for Plts.

Cohoon Vs Speed & als
Subp for Defendant
Ret. Spring Term 1854
To Hand April 8th
Executed, Robt. R. Tayloe, DShff

State of North Carolina
To the Sheriff of Bertie County, Greeting:
You are hereby commanded to summon Dr. A.J. Askew personally to be and appear before the Judge of the Superior Court of law, at the next Court, to be held for the County of Pasquotank, at the Court House in Elizabeth City, on the fourth Monday after the fourth Monday in March next, then and there to testify and the truth to say in behalf of the Defendant in a certain matter of controversy in the said Court depending, and then and there to be tried, wherein P.A.R.C. Cohoon is Plaintiff; and R.K. Speed & als are Defendants; and this you shall in no wise omit, under the penalty by law enjoined.
Witness, Francis M. Charles, Clerk of the said Court, at Elizabeth City, the fourth Monday after the Fourth Monday in Sept. In the 78th year of our Independence, Anno Domini, 1853.
Issued the 4th day of April 1854.
F.M. Charles, Clerk.

Cohoon Vs Speed & als
Supb for Defendant
Ret. Spring Term 1854
Executed 22nd April 1854
Asa Hill, Shff
Came to hand 21st April 1854

Pasquotank County
Concealment of a Slave

State of North Carolina,

To the Sheriff of Gates County, Greeting:

You are hereby commanded to summon Benj. Saunders, Barnes Goodman & Marmaduke Baker personally to be and appear before the Judge of the Superior Court of Law, at the next Court, to be held for the County of Pasquotank, at the Court House in Elizabeth City, on the fourth Monday after the fourth Monday in March next, then and there to testify and the truth to say in behalf of the Defendants in a certain matter of controversy in the said Court depending, and then and there to be tried; wherein P.A.R. C. Cohoon is Plaintiff; and R.K. Speed & als are Defendants; an this you shall in no wise omit, under the penalty by law enjoined.

Witness, Francis M. Charles, Clerk of the said Court, at elizabeth City, the fourth after the fourth Monday in Sept. in the 78th year of our Independence, Anno Domini, 1853.

Issued 11th day of March 1854.

F.M. Charles, Clerk.

Cohoon Vs. R.K. Speed & als
Subpoena
Ret. Spring
Executed, Newbould, Shff

State of North Carolina

To the Sheriff of Pasquotank County, Greeting:

You are hereby commanded to summon Dr. W Hodges personally to be and appear before the Judge of the Superior Court of Law, at the next Court to be held for the County of Pasquotank, at the Court House in Elizabeth City, on the fourth after the fourth Monday in March next, then and there to testify and the truth to say in behalf of Plaintiff in a certain matter of controversy in the said Court depending, and then and there to be tried, wherein PARC Cohoon is Plaintiff and R.K. Speed et als are Defendants: and this you shall in no wise omit, under the penalty by law enjoined. Witness, Daniel Richardson, Clerk of the said Court, at Elizabeth City, the fourth Monday after the Fourth Monday in Sept. in the 77th year of our Independence, Anno Domini, 1852.

Issued the 25th day of March 1853.

Danl. Richardson, Clerk.

Pasquotank County
Concealment of a Slave

Cohoon Vs. R.K. Speed et als
Subpoena
Ret. Pasquotank Sup. Court Spring Term 1855
To Hand April 19th 1853
Executed, J. F. Jenkins, Shff
By WA Jones Dep. Shff

State of North Carolina

To the Sheriff of Edgecombe County, Greeting:

You are hereby commanded to summon Joseph R. Porter, Robert Norfleet and C.L. Dixon personally to be and appear before the Judge of the Superior Court of Law, at the next Court, to be held for the County of Pasquotank, at the Court House in Elizabeth City, on the fourth Monday after the fourth Monday in March next, then and there to testify and the truth to say in behalf of Defendants in a certain matter of controversy in the said Court depending, and then and there to be tried, wherein P.A.R.C. Cohoon is Plaintiff and Dr. R.K. Speed et als are Defendants; and this you shall in no wise omit, under the penalty by law enjoined.

Witness, F. M. Charles, Clerk of the said Court, at Elizabeth City, the fourth Monday after the fourth Monday in September in the 79th year of our Independence, Anno Domini 1854.

Issued the 13th day of April 1855.

F.M. Charles, Clk.

Cohoon Vs Speed et als
Notice
To Speed to be returned
Executed by delivering a true copy of the within
To Dr. Speed on the 31st March 1854
C B Brothers, DShff
PARC Cohoon Vs R K Speed, W. P. Matthews & Jno. W. Hoy

R K Speed Sir,

You are hereby notified that the deposition of Dr. Wm. Hodges will be taken on Tuesday the 4th April 1854 between the hours of 11 o'clock AM & 4 o'clock PM in the town of Elizabeth City at the store of W W Williams Esqr. - to be read in Evidence in the suit now pending in the

Pasquotank County
Concealment of a Slave

Superior Court of Law of Pasquotank wherein I am Plaintiff & you WP Matthews & John W Hoy are Defendants, When and where you can appear and Cross Examine if you see proper, This 31st March 1854.

State of North Carolina, Pasquotank County.
Superior Court of Law, Spring Term 1853
Dr. Cohoon Vs. Dr. Speed et als

These certify that T.D. Pendleton hath attended this Court
[?] days this Term, as a Witness for the Plff in this suit

Attending 3 days at six shillings per day	1.80
Travelling 48 miles at six shillings per thirty miles	.66
Ferriages	
Certificate and probate	.10
	$2.46

Certified to before me, F.M. Charles, Clk.

State of North Carolina, Pasquotank County
Superior Court of Law, Spring Term 1853
Dr Cohoon Vs Dr. Speed et als

These certify that T.D. Pendleton hath attended this Court 3 days this Term, as a Witness for the **[Blank]** in this Suit.

Attending 3 days at six shillings per day	1.80
Travelling 24 miles at six shillings per thirty miles	.48
Ferriages	
Certificate and Probate	.10
	2.38

Sworn to before me, F.M. Charles, Clk & JW Hinton

State of North Carolina
Pasquotank County Superior Court of Law, Spring Term 1853
Cohoon Vs Speed et als

These are to certify that T.D. Pendleton hath attended this Court 2 days this Term as a Witness for the Pltf

Attending 2 days at 6 shillings per day	1.20

Travelling **[Blank]** miles at six shillings per thirty miles
Ferriages .52
Certificate and Probate .10
1.82

Sworn to before me, J. W. Hinton Dep Clk

State of North Carolina
Pasquotank County Superior Court of Law, Spring Term, 1853
Cohoon Vs Speed et als

These are to certify that Dr Printout hath attended this Court one day this Term, as a Witness for the Pltff in this suit.

Attending 1 day at six shillings per day .60
Travelling **[Blank]** miles at six shillings per thirty miles
Ferriages
Certificate and Probate .10
.70

Certified to before me F.M. Charles, Clk

Pasquotank County Superior Court of Law, Spring Term, 1853
Cohoon Vs. Speed et als

These are to certify that J. Flemming hath attended this Court 5 days this term, as a Witness for the Pltff in this suit.

Attending 5 days at **[Blank]** shillings per day 3.00
Travelling **[Blank]** miles at **[Blank]** shillings per thirty miles
Ferriages
Certificate and Probate .10
3.10

Sworn to before me D. Richardson, Clk

State of North Carolina
Pasquotank, Superior Court of Law **[Blank]** Term 1854
Cohoon Vs. Speed et als

These certify that Jas. S. Long hath attended this Court three days this Term, as a Witness for the Pltff in this suit.

Attending 3 days at six shillings per day	1.80
Travelling **[Blank]** miles at six shillings per thirty miles	
Ferriages	
Certificate and Probate	.10
	1.90

Certified t before me, F.M. Charles, Clerk.

State of North Carolina
Pasquotank County Superior Court of Law, Fall Term 1854.
Cohoon Vs Speed et als

These certify that John W. Hoy hath attended this Court one day this Term, as a Witness for the Pltff in this suit.

Attending 1 day at six shillings per day	.60
Travelling **[Blank]** miles at six shillings per thirty miles	
Ferriages	
Certificate and Probate	.10
	.70

Certified to before me, F.M. Charles, Clerk

State of North Carolina
Pasquotank County Superior Court of Law, Spring Term 1855
P. A.R. Cohoon Vs. Speed et als

These are to certify that R. Norfleet hath attended this Court three days this Term, as a Witness for the Defendt in this suit

Attending 3 days at six shillings per day	3.00
Travelling 360 miles at six shillings per thirty miles	10.80
Ferriages	
Certificate and Probate	.10
	13.90

Certified to before me, F.M. Charles, Clerk

State of North Carolina
Pasquotank Superior Court of Law, Spring Term, 1854
Cohoon Vs. R.K. Speed et als

Pasquotank County
Concealment of a Slave

These certify, that R. Norfleet (of Edgecombe Co.) hath attended this Court on day this Term, as a Witness for the Defts in this suit.

Attending **[Blank]** day one dollar	1.00
Travelling 360 miles one dollar per thirty miles	12.00
Ferriages	
Certificate and Probate	.10
	13.10

Sworn to before me, F.M. Charles, Clerk

State of North Carolina
Pasquotank County Superior Court of Law, Spring Term, 1853
P.A. R. C. Cohoon Vs. R. K. Speed et als

These certify that Jas. S. Long hath attended this Court this day, this Term, as a Witness for the Pltff in this suit

Attending 3 days at six shillings per day	1.80
Travelling **[Blank]** miles at six shillings per thirty miles	
Ferriages	
Certificate and Probate	.10
	1.90

Certified to before me, F.M. Charles, Clerk

State of North Carolina
Pasquotank County Superior Court of Law, Spring Term, 1853
Cohoon Vs. Speed et als

These certify that J.J. Grandy hath attended this Court this day this Term, as a Witness for the Plff in this suit.

Attending 3 days at six shillings per day	1.80
Travelling **[Blank]** miles at six shillings per thirty miles	
Ferriages	
Certificate and Probate	.10
	1.90

Certified to before me, F.M. Charles, Clerk

State of North Carolina
Pasquotank County Superior Court of Law, Spring Term, 1853

Pasquotank County Concealment of a Slave

Dr. Cohoon Vs. Dr. R.K. Speed

These certify that D. W. Hodges hath attended this Court This day, this Term, as a Witness for the Pltff in this suit.

Attending 3 days at 10 shillings per day	3.00
Travelling 80 miles at 10 shillings per thirty miles	2.40
Ferriages	
Certificate and Probate	.10
	5.50

Certified to before me, F.M. Charles, Clerk, Witness lives out of the County.

State of North Carolina
Pasquotank County Superior Court of Law, Fall Term 1854
Cohoon Vs. Speed et als

These certify that J.J. Grandy hath attended this Court this day, this Term, as a Witness for the Pltff in this suit.

Attending 3 days at six shillings per day	1.80
Travelling **[Blank]** miles at six shillings per thirty miles.	
Ferriages	
Certificate and Probate	.10
	1.90

Certified to before me, F.M. Charles, Clerk

State of North Carolina
Pasquotank County Superior Court of Law, Spring Term, 1853
Cohoon Vs. Speed et als

These certify that John J. Grandy hath attended this Court This day, this Term, as a Witness for the Defdt in this suit.

Attending 3 days at six shillings per day	1.80
Travelling **[Blank]** miles at six shillings per thirty miles	
Ferriages	
Certificate and Probate	.10
	1.90

Certified to before me, F.M. Charles, Clerk

Pasquotank County
Concealment of a Slave

State of North Carolina
Pasquotank County Superior Court of Law, Fall Term, 1854
Cohoon Vs. Speed et als

These certify that John J. Grandy hath attended this Court This day, this Term, as a Witness for the Defdt in this suit

Attending 3 days at six Shillings per day	1.80
Travelling **[Blank]** miles at six shillings per day.	
Ferriages	
Certificate and Probate,	.10
	1.90

Certified to before me, F.M. Charles, Clerk

State of North Carolina
Pasquotank County Superior Court of Law, Spring Term, 1854.
Cohoon Vs. Speed et als

These certify that J.J. Porter hath attended this Court 3 days, this Term, as as a Witness for the Defdt Speed in this suit

Attending 3 days at 10 Shillings per day	3.00
Travelling 360 miles at six shillings per thirty miles.	10.80
Ferriages	
Certificate and Probate	.10
	13.90

Sworn to before me, F.M. Charles, Clerk

State of North Carolina
Pasquotank County Superior Court of Law **[Blank]** Term 1854.
Cohoon Vs. Speed et als

These certify These certify, that Jos Shaw hath attended this Court two days this term, as a Witness for the **[Blank]** in this suit.

Attending 2 days at six shillings per day,	1.20
Travelling 36 miles at six shillings per thirty miles	.72
Ferriages	
Certificate and Probate	.10
	2.02

Sworn to before me, F.M. Charles, Clerk

State of North Carolina
Pasquotank County Superior Court of Law, Fall Term, 1853
Cohoon Vs. R.K. Speed

These certify, that Dr. Wm. Hodges hath attended this Court 5 days this Term, as a Witness for the **[Blank]** in this suit.

Attending 5 days at six shillings per day	3.00
Travelling miles at six shillings per thirty miles	
Ferriages	
Certificate and Probate	.10
	3.10

Sworn to before me, F.M. Charles, Clk

State of North Carolina
Pasquotank County Superior Court of Law, Spring Term, 1854
Cohoon Vs. Speed et als

These certify, that Thos Harvey hath attended this Court Two days this Term, as a Witness for the Defdt in this suit.

Attending 2 days at six shillings per day	1.26
Travelling 32 miles at six shillings per thirty miles	.64
Ferriages	
Certificate and Probate	.10
	1.94

Sworn to before me, F.M. Charles, Clk

State of North Carolina
Pasquotank County Superior Court of Law, **[Blank]** Term 185**[?]**
Cohoon Vs. R.K. Speed et als

These certify, that J.J. Porter (of Edgecombe County) hath attended this Court one day this Term, as a Witness for thr Defdt in this suit.

Attending 1 day one dollar per day	1.00
Travelling 360 miles one dollar per thirty miles	12.00
Ferriages	

Certificate and Probate	.10
	13.10

Sworn to before me, F. M. Charles, Clerk

State of North Carolina
Pasquotank County Superior Court of Law, Spring Term, 1854
Cohoon Vs. Speed et als

These certify, that Marmaduke Baker (out of the Co.) hath attended this Court Two days this Term, as a Witness for the Defdt in this suit.

Attending 2 days one dollar per day	2.00
Travelling 120 miles one dollar per thirty miles.	4.00
Ferriages	
Certificates and Probate,	.10
	6.10

Sworn to before me, F.M. Charles, Clerk

State of North Carolina
Pasquotank County Superior Court of Law, Spring Term, 1855
Cohoon Vs. R.K. Speed et als

These certify, that Jos. H. Shaw hath attended this Court, This day, this Term, as a Witness for the Defdt in this suit

Attending 3 days at six shillings per day	1.80
Travelling 38 miles at six shillings per thirty miles	.76
Ferriages	
Certificate and Probate	.10
	2.66

Certified to before me, F.M. Charles, Clerk.

State of North Carolina
Pasquotank County Superior Court of Law, Spring Term, 1854
Cohoon Vs. R.K. Speed et als

These certify, that C. L. Dickson **[Dicken]** (of Edgecombe County) hath attended this Court one day this Term, as a Witness for the Defdt in this suit

Pasquotank County
Concealment of a Slave

Attending 1 day one dollar per day	1.00
Travelling 360 miles one dollar per thirty miles	12.00
Ferriages	
Certificate and Probate	.10
	13.16

Sworn to before me, F.M. Charles, Clerk

State of North Carolina
Pasquotank County Superior Court of Law, Spring Term, 1854
Cohoon Vs. Speed Vs. et als

These certify, that C. L. Hunter hath attended this Court three days this Term, as a Witness for the Defdt in this suit.

Attending 3 days at six shillings per day	1.80
Travelling **[Blank]** miles at six shillings per thirty miles	
Ferriages	
Certificate and Probate	.10
	1.90

Sworn to before me, F.M. Charles, Clk.

State of North Carolina
Pasquotank County Superior Court of Law, Spring Term, 1854
Cohoon Vs. Speed et als

These certify, that Mr. Baker (out of the County) hath attended this Court two days this Term, as a Witness for the Pltff in this suit.

Attending 2 days one dollar per day	2.00
Travelling **[Blank]** miles at six shillings per thirty miles	4.00
Ferriages	
Certificate and Probate	.10
	6.10

Sworn to before me, F.M. Charles, Clk

State of North Carolina
Pasquotank County Superior Court of Law, Fall Term, 1854
PARC Cohoon Vs. R.K. Speed et als

Pasquotank County
Concealment of a Slave

These certify that J.J. Porter hath attended this Court 3 days this Term, as a Witness for the Defdt in this suit.

Attending 3 days at six shillings per day,	3.00
Travelling 360 Miles at six shillings per thirty miles	10.80
Ferriages	
Certificate and Probate	.10
	13.90

Sworn to before me F.M. Charles, Clerk

State of North Carolina
Pasquotank County Superior Court of Law, Fall Term, 1854
Cohoon Vs. Speed et als

These certify that John Br[?] hath attended this Court four days this Term, as a Witness for the Pltff in this suit

Attending 4 days at six shillings per day	2.40
Travelling **[Blank]** miles at six shillings per thirty miles	
Ferriages	
Certificate and Probate	.10
	2.50

Sworn to before me, Clerk

State of North Carolina
Pasquotank County Superior Court of Law, Spring Term, 18[?]
Cohoon Vs. Speed et als

These are to certify, that Dr. Hodges hath attended this Court 4 days this Term, as a Witness for the Pltff in this suit.

Attending 4 days at six shillings per day	3.40
Travelling **[Blank]** Miles at six shillings per thirty miles	
Ferriages	
Certificate and Probate	.10
	3.50

Sworn to before me, D. Richardson, Clk

State of North Carolina
Pasquotank County Superior Court of Law, Fall Term, 1854.

Pasquotank County
Concealment of a Slave

Cohoon Vs Speed et als

These certify that Marmaduke Baker hath attended this Court This day, this Term, as a Witness for the Pltff in this suit.

Attending 3 days at six shillings per day.	3.00
Travelling 120 miles at six shillings per thirty miles	3.60
Ferriages	
Certificate and Probate	.10
	6.70

Sworn to before me, **[Blank]**

State of North Carolina
Pasquotank County Superior Court of Law, Fall Term, 1854
Cohoon Vs. Speed et als

These certify, that Jas W. Hinton hath attended this Court three days this Term, as a Witness for the Defdt in this suit

Attending 2 days at **[Blank]** shillings per day	1.20
[Blank] miles at six shillings per thirty miles	
Ferriages	
2 **[?]** at 10 cts Each	.20
Certificate and Probate	.10
	1.50

Sworn to before me, F.M. Charles, Clk

State of North Carolina
Pasquotank County Superior Court of Law, Fall term, 1854
Dr Cohoon Vs et als

These certify that Capt. T. Hunter hath attended this Court three days this Term, as a Witness for the **[Blank]** in this suit

Attending 3 days at six shillings per day,	1.80
Travelling **[Blank]** miles at six shillings per day	
Ferriages	
Certificate and Probate	.10
	1.90

Sworn to before me, F.M. Charles, Clk

Pasquotank County
Concealment of a Slave

State of North Carolina
Pasquotank County Superior Court of Law, Fall Term, 1854
Cohoon Vs. Speed et als

These certify that John Baily hath attended this Court one day this Term, as a Witness for the Defdt in this suit.

Attending 1 day at six shillings per day	.60
Travelling 16 miles at six shillings per thirty miles	.32
Ferriages	
Certificate and Probate	.10
	1.02

Sworn to before me, F.M. Charles, Clk

State of North Carolina
Pasquotank County Superior Court of Law, Fall term, 1854
Cohoon Vs. Speed et als

These certify that Jos. B. Shaw hath attended this Court three days this Term, as a Witness for the Defdt in this suit.

Attending 3 days at six shillings per day,	1.80
Travelling 36 miles at six shillings per thirty miles	.72
Ferriages	
Certificate and Probate	.10
	2.62

Sworn to before me, F.M. Charles, Clk.

State of North Carolina
Pasquotank County Superior Court of law, Fall Term, 1854
PARC Cohoon Vs. R K Speed et als

These certify that C. L. Dickens hath attended this Court 3 days this Term, as a Witness for the Defendant in this suit.

Attending 3 days at **[Blank]** Shillings per day.	3.00
Travelling 324 miles at six shillings per thirty miles.	9.80
Ferriages	
Certificate and Probate	.10
	12.94

Sworn to before me, F.M. Charles

State of North Carolina
Pasquotank County Superior Court of Law, Fall Term, 1854
Cohoon Vs. Speed et als

These certify that T.D. Pendleton hath attended this Court four days this Term, as a Witness for the Pltff in this suit.

Attending 4 days at six shillings per day.	2.40
Travelling 28 miles at six shillings per thirty miles.	.56
Ferriages	
Certificate and Probate	.10
	31.06

Sworn to before me, F.M. Charles, Clerk.

State of North Carolina
Pasquotank County Superior Court of Law, Fall Term, 1853
Cohoon Vs. Dr. R. K. Speed

These certify, that Timothy Pendleton hath attended this Court Five days this Term, as a Witness for the **[Blank]** in this suit.

Attending 5 days at six shillings per day	3.00
Travelling 14 miles at six shillings per thirty miles	.28
Ferriages	
Certificate and Probate	.10
	3.38

Sworn to before me, F.M. Charles, Clk

State of North Carolina
Pasquotank County Superior Court of Law, Spring Term 1855.
Cohoon Vs. Speed et als

These certify that John W. Hoy hath attended this Court This day, this Term, as a Witness for the Pltff in this suit.

Attending 3 days at six shillings per thirty miles.	1.80
Travelling **[Blank]** Miles at six shillings per thirty miles	
Ferriages	

Certificate and Probate,	.10
	1.90

Sworn to before me, F.M. Charles, Clk

Chapter Four

Pasquotank County

Patrol Records

North Carolina State Archives
Pasquotank County Records
Records of Slaves and Free Persons of Color
C.R.076.928.10 -C.R.075.928.10

Rec'vd Payment From B. Sutton, Jeremiah King.
This may Certify that Jeremiah King Capt of Patrol, NC -- Were ordered to patrol the streets of Elizabeth City one Night in this year & by an order of the [?] he is intitled to one Dollar & fifty cents the treasurer will pay the same, December 24th 1834
Abner Williams, Clk.

Rec'vd payment from B. Sutton Treasurer, George Kellenger[?].
This Certifys that George Kellenger Capt. Of Patrol No - 2 have been ordered out three Nights to patrol the Streets of Elizabeth City in this year & agreeable to an order of the Commissioner of the Sd. Town he is allowed one Dollar & fifty cents for Each Night, the treasurer will pay the same, December 22nd 1834

Abner Williams, (C M)

Rec'd payment from Benj. Sutton, Treasurer, Alfred A Turner
This may certify that Alfred Turner, Capt. December 12th 1834 of the Patrol No 7 were ordered out Tues. Nights in this present year to Guard the Town & agreeable to an order of the Commissioners he is Intitled to one Dollar & fifty cents Each Night & the Treasurer will pay the same out of the funds
Abner Williams (C M)

Received pay for the within Decr. 22nd 1834, Jno Burcher.
This Certifys that John Burcher Capt of Patrol No 14 have been ordered out three Nights in this year to Patrole the Streets of Elizabeth City & agreeable to an order of the Commissioners of the Town he is allowed one Dollar & fifty cents for each Night, the Treasurer will pay the same, December 22nd 1834.
Abner Williams

Rec'd payment from Benjamin Sutton, Treasurer.
This may Certify that John McMorine Capt. Of Patrol No **[Blank]** were ordered out two Nights to Patrol the Streets of Elizabeth City by an order of the Commissioners of the Sd. Town, he is Intitled to one Dollar & fifty Cents Each Night, the treasurer will pay the same, December 26th 1834.
Abner Williams.

Recv'd Payment from Benjamin Sutton, Treasurer.
Elizabeth City Dec. 22nd 1834. Whereas it appears that William Glover, Captain of Patrol did with his Company Patrol the Town of Elizabeth City on the night of June 27th 1834, ordered at a Meeting of the Comms. of the Town held this day that the Treasurer pay the said William Glover the sum of one dollar & fifty cents.
Test., A.C. **[?]**, Clk.

Dismissed appearing at Decr. Term '49

Pasquotank County
Patrol Records

Ordered by the Court that D.D. Raper, Ed. Chauncy, J B. Skinner, J. Sharp and Morris White and Benoni Morris be appointed patrolers for District No 3 -- The Court

---

Ja. S. Relf Patroller, allowed by the Court, 1816.
Personally came before me James S. Relf & qualified as Patroller in District No. 4 for the Year 1815. Wm T Relf Pd., Order.

State of North Carolina }
Pasquotank County } March Term 1815
I Certify that James S. Relfe was appointed a Patroller for District No 4 at this Term and as far as I know did his duty as such.
Test, Richard Muse, DC.

Charles Bailey -- $4.00, Allowed to John Pool $4

State of North Carolina }
Pasquotank County } SS
I Certify that Charles Bailey was appointed a Patroller in District No. 7 at December Term 1816 and as far as I know did his duty as such.
Will: J. Muse, Clk.

State of North Carolina }
Pasquotank County } September Term 1816.
Ordered that John Davis be appointed Patroller in the room of Hardy White for District No. 2.
Teste, Richard [Muse] DC
John Davis, Patroller No. 2, Executed, John Pool.

State of North Carolina }
Pasquotank County } SS
I Certify that Rowan Barclift was appointed a Patroller in District No. 7 at September Term 1816 - and as far as I know did his duty as such.
Rowan Barclift Allowed at $4 to John Pool.
Teste, Will T. Muse, Clk., Sep. 19th 1818.

Pasquotank County Patrol Records

State of North Carolina }
Pasquotank County } September 1816

Ordered that Rowan Barclift, George Bailey, Thomas Newbould be appointed Patrollers in District No. 7.
R. Barclift, No 7., Executed, John Pool, Shff.
Teste Richard Muse, DC.

State of North Carolina }
Pasquotank County } September Term 1819

Orderd that Benjamin B. Lowry, James Gregory, Francis Fletcher, John Cartwright and Harvey Luton be appointed patrollers in District No. 1
Will: T. Muse, Clk.

State of North Carolina }
Pasquotank County } June Term 1825

Ordered that Robert Bailey, Addison Whedbee, Noah Hollowell, Henry Moore, and Henry Raper be appointed Patrollers in District No. 3.
Teste, Charles Grice, Clk
Patrollers No. 3, June Term 1825. Executed By William Gregory, Shff by Joshua Pool, DShff
Benjamin B. Lowery, Excuted, Richd. Pool, DS

State of North Carolina } Court of Pleas & Quarter Sessions
Pasquotank County } Decemr. Term 1828

Ordered that Mordecai Gregory, William Sanderlin, Henry Pendleton, Wilson Aydlet, Thomas Jordan Junr. And Robert Bailey be appointed Patrolls for District No. 4.
Teste, Charles Grice
The Within [?] was [?] Before me 20th of January 1829.
Thomas Jordan
Patroll No . 4, Ordered that the within named persons be allowed the Payt. For their services as the Law directs

---

Decr. Term 1849, Ordered that Martin Hariss be allowed Ten dollars as parol for 1849.

Teste W.W. Griffin, Clk
No 426, Ma. Harris, $10

North Carolina } March Term 1861
Pasquotank County }

To the Worshipful, the Justices of the Court of Pleas and Quarter Sessiond for said County.

In pursuance of an order of Your Worshipful Court, passed at December Term last, appointing the undersigned a patrol Committee for District No. 4 in said County we have appointed the following Gentleman as a Patrol for said district, and have duly notified them of their said appointment, Viz., Henry Raper, Geo. W. Pendleton Junr. & Fred Leaff, William **[Torn]** All of which is respectfully submitted.
Feb. 14th 1861
Committee, Geo D. Pool, C.W. Hollowell & R.B. Creecy.

No. 206, C.B. Brothers
Decr. Term 1846, Ordered that Charles Brothers be allowed twelve Dollars as Patrol in District No. **[?]**
Teste, W.W. Griffin, Clk
Canceled

No. 207, J. E. Weeks, $12
James E Weeks
Decr. Term 1846, Ordered that James E. Weeks be allowed Twelve Dollars as Patrol in District No. 7
Teste, W.W. Griffin, Clk
Canceled

No. 344, Isaac Nash, $10, M T. 49
Elizabeth Nash for Isaac Nash
March Term 1849 - Ordered that Isaac Nash be allowed Ten Dollars as patrol for the **[?]**
Teste, W.W. Griffin, Clk.

Pasquotank County
Patrol Records

No. 352, A. Jackson, $10, M. T. 49, Wm. A. Jackson
March Term 1849, Ordered that Anderson Jackson be allowed Ten Dollars as patrol for 1848.
Teste, W.W. Griffin, Clk
Canceled

Moses H. Overman
No. 319, Moses Overman, $20
Sept. Term 1848 - Ordered that Moses Overman be allowed Twenty Dollars as patrol in District No. 4.
Teste, W.W. Griffin, Clk
Canceled.

No. 383, D.D. Raper, $10, DD Raper
Sept Term 1849, Ordered that D.D. Raper be allowed Ten Dollars as patrol for 1848.
Teste, W.W. Griffin, Clk
Canceled.

No. 318, Tim Gregory, Timothy P. Gregory
Sept. Term 1848 Ordered that Timothy Gregory be allowed Twenty Dollars as patrol in District No. 4.
Teste, W.W. Griffin, Clk
Canceled.

No. 388, Jno L. Wood, J. L. Wood.
Sept. Term 1849, Ordered that Jno. L. Wood be allowed Ten Dollars as patrol for 1848.
Teste, W.W. Griffin, Clk
Canceled

No. 427, D. Whitehurst, $10, Davis Whitehurst
Decr. Term Ordered that Davis Whitehurst be allowed ten Dollars as patrol for 1849
Teste, W.W. Griffin, Clk

No. 349, S. Pendleton, $10, Stephen Pendleton
March Term 1849 - Ordered that Stephen Pendleton be allowed Ten Dollars as patrol for 1848
Teste, W.W. Griffin, Clk
Cancel

No. 203, D.D. Raper, $10, D D Raper, D. T. 46.
Decr. Term 1846 Ordered that D.D. Raper be allowed Twelve Dollars as Patrol in District No. 7
Teste, W.W. Griffin, Clk
Canceled

$1.70
Sept. Term 1848 - Ordered that J. Pool, Shff be allowed one Dollar as over charges in the place of Ed. Pendleton for 1846 - also the amt. of the Poll tax of John James on the list of 1847.
Teste, W.W. Griffin, Clk
Canceled.

No. 204, A. Alexander, $12, D. T. 4, Anthony Alexander.
Decr. Term 1846, Ordered that Anthony Alexander be allowed Twelve dollars as a patrol in District No. 7.
Teste, W.W. Griffin, Clk.
Canceled

No. 202, R. Maxfield[?], $12, Roger Maxfield, Decr T. 46
Decr. Term 1846, Ordered that Roger Maxfield be allowed Twelve Dollars as Patrol for District No. 7.
Teste, W.W. Griffin, Clk
Canceled

No. 205, Jno Small, $12, D. T. 46, Jno Small

Pasquotank County
Patrol Records

Decr. Term 1846, Ordered that John Small be allowed Twelve Dollars as patrol in District No. 7
Teste, W.W. Griffin, Clk
Canceled

No. 345, Reuben Pendleton, $10, M. T. 49, Reuben Pendleton.
March Term 1849 ordered that Reuben Pendleton be allowed Ten Dollars as patrol for 1848.
Teste, W.W. Griffin, Clk
Canceled

For Charles Davis
Delivered a copy to Chas. Davis, W.[?], Shff by J. Wilcox, DShff
State of No. Carolina }
Pasquotank County }

P. You Charles Davis Capt, Wm Thomas, Willis Casey, Samuel Gregory and James Snell are hereby notified you are appointed a patrol to patrol from Knobs Creek, Pasquotank River, the North and part of the West boundaries of Elizabeth City (say to the middle of Geo. W. Charles land lying between Georgetown & the Babtist Church) extending west to the Swamp above where Charles Davis formerly lived - you will therefore qualify and proceed to the discharge of your duties - By order of the patrol Committee, Feby 1861.
John Black, Chairman

No. 347, Jos. Pendleton, $10, M. T., 49
March Term 1849 - Ordered that Joseph Pendleton be allowed Ten Dollars as patrol for 1848.
Teste, W.W. Griffin
Canceled

No. 394, A. Banks, $10, Ambrose W. Banks.
Sept. Term 1849 - Ordered that Ambrose Banks be allowed Ten Dollars as patrol for 1848.
Teste, W.W. Griffin, Clk
Canceled

No. 384, Ed. Chancy, $10
Sept. Term 1849 - Ordered that Ed. Chancy be allowed Ten Dollars as patrol for 1848.
Teste, W. W. Griffin
Canceled

No. 389, Ed White, $10, Edmund White.
Sept Term 1849, Orderd that Edmnd White be allowed Ten Dollars as patrol for 1848.
Teste, W.W. Griffin
Canceled

No. 478, Peter Pugh, $12, Novr 14th 1850 pay the within amt to Peter Pugh
Sept Term 1850 - Ordered that Peter Pugh be allowed Twelve Dollars as Patrol in District No. one.
Teste, W.W. Griffin, Clk
Canceled

No. 387, J. Wilcox, $10, J. Wilcox
Sept. Term 1849 - Ordered that J. Wilcox be allowed Ten Dollars as patrol for 1848
Teste, W.W. Griffin, Clk
Canceled

No 425, M. Pritchard, $10.00, Martin Pritchard
Decr. Term 1849 - Ordered that Martin Pritchard be allowed Ten Dollars as patrol for 1849.
Teste, W.W. Griffin
Canceled

No. 481, R. Pendleton, $12, Reuben Pendleton.
Sept. Term 1850 Ordered that Reuben Pendleton be allowed Twelve Dollars as patrol in District No. one.

Teste, W.W. Griffin, Clk
Canceled

No. 317, Jos. Bradshaw, $20, Joseph R. Bradshaw.
Sept. Term 1848 - Ordered that Joseph Bradshaw be allowed Twenty Dollars as patrol in District No. 4.
Teste, W.W, Griffin, Clk
Canceled

No. 346, H. Delou**[?]**, $10, M. T. 49, Harvy X Delon.
March Term 1849 - Ordered that Harvey Delon be allowed Ten Dollars as patrol for 1848
Teste, W.W. Griffin, Clk
Canceled

No. 385, B.N. Overman, $10, B N Overman
Sept. Term 1849 - Ordered that Benja. N. Overman be allowed Ten Dollars as patrol for 1848.
Teste, W W. Griffin, Clk
Canceled.

Patrol for District No. 2 **[Faded]** Send a Copy of this order on Wm H. Davis, Wm **[Faded]**, Shff
North Carolina } Court of Pleas and Quarter Sessions
Pasquotank County } March Term 1859

Ordered that Wm H. Davis, Jos B. Shaw, Thomas Harvey & Jesse Rogerson be, and they are hereby appointed Patrol for District No. 2 the ensuing year Issued Mch 18th 1859.
Teste J.W. Hinton, Clk, By Chas G. Elliott, DC

Order for Patrol To Marmaduke Cartright & others
A Copy left With M Duke Cartright the 13th June 1835
Joshua A Pool, Shff
State of North Carolina } Court of Pleas & Quarter Sessions
Pasquotank County } June Term 1835

Pasquotank County
Patrol Records

Ordered By the Court that Marmaduke Cartright, James Cartright, Charles Bright, Mager **[Faded]**, Robert Simpson be appointed Patrol for District No. 5
Teste, Stephen Charles, Clk

Patrole District No C., Decr Term 1831, all the orders Delivered to Lodwick Williams, Teste, **[?]**
Job Car**[?]**, Thos Tempe**[?]**, Joseph Pritchard appeared before me and were qualified as patrolls agreeable to Law May 11th 1832, Wm**[?]**

Personally come before me William A Pritchard, Frances White & Frances Ackiss and qualified as patrollers
Thos Bell, Personally cam before me William Mundin and qualified as a Patrol

---

Nathan Small, JP
Personally come before me Charles Ber**[?]** & qualified as a patroller, Oct 1st day 1830

Personally come before me Thomas Bell JP Simon Overman and qualified as a patroller 1st day 1830
Thos Bell, JP

State of North Carolina } Court of Pleas and Quarter Sessions
Pasquotank County } September Term 1830

Ordered that Francis White, Francis Ackiss, Simon Overman, William Pritchard, Charles Brite, William Mundin be appointed Patrol for District No. 7
F. Charles Grice, Clk

State of North Carolina } Court of Pleas and Quarter Sessions
Pasquotank County } December Term 1831

Pasquotank County
Patrol Records

Ordered that John Richardson, Lodawick Williams, Jeremiah Stokely, Joseph Prtichard, Thos. Temple and Job Carver be appointed Patrol in District No. 6
Test, Charles Grice, Clk

State of North Carolina } Court of Pleas & Quarter Sessions
Pasquotank County } June Term 1835

It is ordered by the Court that Francis Fletcher, Addison Whidbee, William C. Banks, John S. Bailey, Benjamin White & Thomas Banks be appointed Patrollers for the District No. 3.
Teste, Stephen Charles, Clk
Order apointing Francis Fletcher, Addison Whedbee, Will C. Banks, John Bailey, Benjamin White, Thos Banks patrol for District No. 3.
A Copy left with Adderson Whidbee the first Day of July 1833, Joshua A Pool, Shff

---

Order for Patrol in District No 6, Jeremiah Stokely & others, June Term 1835. Executed by delivering a coppy of this, June 13th 1835
M. W. Jones
State of North Carolina } Court of Pleas & Quarter Sessions
Pasquotank County } June Term 1835

Ordered By the Court that Jeremiah Stokely, Saml Jordan, Thomas Temple, Joseph Pritchard, Daniel Spence, Joseph Davis, Daniel Williams and Lodawick Williams, be appointed Patroll in District No. 6.
Teste, Stephen Charles, Clk

E W Albertson, Executed by carrying a Copy of this notice with E.W. Albertson, 1860
North Carolina
Pasquotank County Court, December Term 1860.

Ordered that E.W. Albertson, Abel Spence, & Wm. Williams Junr. Be appointed a Committee to order out such persons as may be subject to patrol duty in District No. 6, at such times as they may deem necessary to patrol said District. Issued Dec. 15th 1860
Teste, J.W. Hinton, Clk by CG Elliott, DC

Pasquotank County
Patrol Records

No 424, Eph Harris, Ephraim Harris,
Decr. Term 1849 - Ordered that Ephraim Harris be allowed Ten Dollars as patrol for 1849.
Teste, W.W. Griffin, Clk

Patrol order for District No 5. A Copy of the within left at the House of Grandy Harris the 29th June 1836, Joshua A Pool, Shff
State of North Carolina } Court of Pleas & Quarter Sessions
Pasquotank County } June Term 1836

Ordered by the Court that Davis Whitehurst, Grandy Harris, Philip Pritchard, John Harris Junr., Ephraim Brite of Jesse be appointed Patrols in the District No. 5.
Teste, Stephen Charles, Clk

M S Dance
Delivered a Copy to M. S. Dance, W E Mann, Shff by JW[?], DShff
North Carolina
Pasquotank County Court, December Term 1860

Ordered that M.S. Dance, D. D. Raper and Edmund Chancey be appointed a Committee to order out such persons as may be subject to patrol duty in District No. 3, at such times as they may deem necessary to patrol said District. Issued Dec. 15th 1860.
Test: J.W, Hinton, Clk by C G Elliott, DC

For Grandy Harris
Delivered a Copy Feby 16th 1861, W E[?], Shff by J Wilcox, DShff.
State of North Carolina } Grandy Harris Capt
Pasquotank County } Evan Pritchard, John Jackson, Simeon Harris and Thomas Bland are hereby notified you are appointed a patrol to patrol from Grandy Harris's mill to Elizabeth City and on either side of said road viz. (West of where he formerly lived) and the Center of Geo. W. Charles fields to the town line and on the West to the [?] and midway between said road & run quarter road to the town line, you will therefore quantify and proceed to the discharge of your duties, By order of the Patrol Committee, Feby 1861.
John Black Chairman

Pasquotank County Patrol Records

Copy Returned
Wm E Mann, Shff
North Carolina
Pasquotank County Court, June Term 1860

Ordered that George Sawyer, Dr. Chas. A. Riddick, James Price, Thomas Harrell, Wm Davis be and they are hereby appointed Patrol for District No. 3, Issued June 1860
J. W. Hinton, Clk by CG Elliott, DC

Mager Bell
Delivered a Copy to Jno Black
W.E. Mann, Shff by J Wilcox, DShff
North Carolina
Pasquotank County Court, December Term 1860.

Ordered that Mager Bell, Jno S. Burges & John Black be appointed a Committee to order out such persons as may be subject to patrol duty in District No. 5 at such times as they may deem necessary to patrol said district. Issued Dec 15th 1860
Test: J W Hinton, Clk by Chas G Elliott, DC

A Copy of this notice has been Served
Wm E. Mann, Shff
North Carolina
Pasquotank County Court, December Term 1860.

Ordered that Jno. Cartwright, Benoni Cartwright & Barney Berry be appointed a committee to order out such persons as may be subject to patrol duty in District number One, at such time as they may deem necessary to patrol said District, Issued Dec. 14th 1860.
Test: J.W. Hinton, Clk by C G Elliot, DC

Copy Served, Wm E Mann, Shff
North Carolina
Pasquotank County Court, June Term 1860

Ordered that Henry Perry, Wm. Miller, James Eason, D.D. Raper, Robinson Jackson, & Wm B. Overman be and they are hereby appointed Patrol for District No. 7, Issued June 1860
Test: J W Hinton, Clk by C G Elliot, DC

Wm. Banks & als, District No. 5, served a duplicate Copy of this notice on Wm. Banks as Capt of Patrol. Wm E Mann, Shff
No. Carolina
Pasquotank County Court June Term 1859, Ordered that Wm Banks, D.D. Raper, Southey Jackson, Wm Jackson, W.W. Perry & Wm. Blount be and they are hereby appointed a patrol for District No. 5 the lower part. Issued June 1859
Test: J W Hinton, Clk by Chas G Elliott, DC

Patrol in District No. 7
Sent to [?] White by Joshua Low, June 11th 1859
W.E. Mann, Shff by J Wilcox, DShff
North Carolina } County Court
Pasquotank County } June Term 1859

Ordered that Willis Brite, Malachi Jackson, Daniel Brite, John Wood, Ambrose White & Stephen Harris be appointed patrol for District No. 7, Issued June 11th 1859
Test: J W Hinton, Clk by Chas G. Elliott, DC

Patrol for Dist No. 4, John Shirley
A Copy left with Leml Jackson
W.E. Mann, Shff by Wilcox, DShff
North Carolina } Court of Pleas & Quarter Sessions
Pasquotank County } March Term 1859

Ordered that John Shirley, Lemuel Jackson, William Stephenson & Stephen Scott be, and they are hereby appointed Patrol for District No. 4 for the ensuing year. Issued March 18th 1859
Test: J W Hinton, Clk by Chas Elliott, DC

Chapter Five

Pasquotank County

Insurrection Papers

North Carolina State Archives
Pasquotank County Records
Records of Slaves and Free Persons of Color
C.R.075.928.10

State Vs Sundry Negroes
Subpoena
Ret. Immediately
Executed
State of North Carolina

To the Sheriff of Pasquotank County, greeting;

You are hereby commanded to summon Mark Delon personally to be and appear before the Justices of our Inferior Court of Pleas and Quarter Sessions, at the Court House in Elizabeth City, immediately, then and there to testify and the truth to say, in behalf of **[Blank]** in a certain matter of controversy in the said Court depending, and then and there to be tried, wherein the State is Plaintiff, and Sundry Negroes are Defendants; and this you shall in no wise omit, under the penalty by law enjoined. Witness

William T. Muse, Clerk of the said Court, at Nixonton the ninth day of June in the XXVI Year of our Independence, Anno Dom. 1802.
Will: T. Muse, Clk

The State Vs. Negro Moses
10th June 1802 a Copy Delivered to William Albertson
Wm Banks, DS

Pasquotank, June 10th 1802

To Mrs Wm. Albertson, Guardian to Elizabeth Sutton, You are hereby noticed that the Trial of Negroe Moses will be on the 22nd day of this month in the Courthouse in Elizabeth City for a charge of conspiracy, you will therefore attend the Trial of the said negro & make defence if you think proper.
Robt McMorine, Shff

State Vs. Sundry Negroes
Ret. Immediately

State of North Carolina
To the Sheriff of Pasquotank County, greeting:

You are hereby commanded to summon Jesse Symons personally to be and appear before the Justices of our Inferior Court of Pleas and Quarter Sessions, at the court house in Elizabeth City, immediately, then and there to testify and the truth to say, in behalf of the State in a certain matter of controversy in the said Court depending, and then and there to be tried, wherein the State is Plaintiff, and Sundry Negroes are Defendants; and this you shall in no wise omit, under the penalty by law enjoined. Witness William T. Muse, Clerk of the said Court, at Elizabeth City, the 9th day of June in the 26th Year of our Independence, anno Domini 1802.
Will: T. Muse

State Vs Sundry Negroes
Sup.
Joshua Trueblood
Executed, Robert McMorine

Pasquotank County Insurrection Papers

State of North Carolina

To the Sheriff of Pasquotank County, Greeting:

You are hereby commanded to summon Joshua Trueblood personally to be and appear before the Justices of our Inferior Court of Pleas and Quarter Sessions, at the Court House in Elizabeth City, immediately, then and there to testify and the truth to say, in behalf of **[Blank]** in a certain matter of controversy in the said Court depending, and then and there to be tried, wherein the State is Plaintiff, and Sundry Negroes are Defendants; and this you shall in no wise omit, under the penalty by law enjoined. Witness William T. Muse, Clerk of the said Court, at Elizabeth City, the Ninth day of June in the XXVI Year of our Independence, Anno Dom 1802.
Will T. Muse Clk

State Vs. Sundry Negroes
Subpoena
Ret. Immediately
Executed on Charles Adams **[Addison]** & John Baily
T. Banks, Shff

State of North Carolina

To the Sheriff of Pasquotank County, greeting:

You are hereby commanded to summon Zachariah Nixon, John Commander, John Baily personally to be and appear before the Justices of our Inferior Court of Pleas and Quarter Sessions, at the court house in Elizabeth City, immediately, then and there to testify and the truth to say, in behalf of the State in a certain matter of controversy in the said Court depending, and then and there to be tried, wherein the State is Plaintiff, and, and Sundry Negroes are Defendants; and this you shall in no wise omit, under the penalty by law enjoined. Witness William T. Muse, Clerk of the said Court, at Elizabeth City immediately day of 8th June in the 26th Year of our Independence, Anno Dom. 1802.
Will: T. Muse

The State Vs. Supr Vs Sundry Negros
Ret Immediately
Executed on Charles Overman & John McDaniel
W. Banks, Shff

Pasquotank County Insurrection Papers

To John [?] to Execute, Robt. McMorine

State of North Carolina

To the Sheriff of Pasquotank County, Greeting:

You are hereby commanded to summon John McDanil, Charles Overman Senr., John Poole son of James & Mary Stone personally to be and appear before the Justices of our Inferior Court of Pleas and Quarter Sessions, at the Court House in Elizabeth City immediately, then and there to testify and the truth to say, in behalf of the State in a certain matter of controversy in the said Court depending, and then and there to be tried, wherein the State is Plaintiff, and Sundry Negros are Defendants; and this you shall in no wise omit, under the penalty by law enjoined. Witness William T. Muse, Clerk of the said Court, at Elizabeth City immediately, 8th day of June in the 26th year of our Independence, Anno Dom. 1802.

Will T. Muse

The County of Pasquotank with William: T. Muse
The County of Pasquotank
To William: T. Muse

1802

May 22nd

To my attendance at a special Court held in May } £5

Had for the Trial of Slaves charged with Conspiracy

Decr. 10th

My fees for the Trial of Negro Sarah at this Time 1.10

Cash Pd Edward Myrick of Norfolk for Sundry blank Books for the use of the Clks Office $34

P Bill & Rec't, 17

Cash per part of M Spences Expt to Norfolk after Books, 3

Cash Pd for [?] Entries & Heywoods manual by Mr. Cotter at Raleigh 12 1/2 Dolls 6.5

£ 32.15

Amt allowed, Baily Jackson, Keaton & [?] Scott

Wm T. Muse exhibited his Account for books furnished for the use of the Clks Office, and for Sundry Services performed by him Amounting to the sum of Thirty two pounds fifteen shillings. Ordered that the same be allowed, and that the County Treasurer pay the same and be allowed therefore in the **[?]** of his amounts.

Deposition of Silla
Discharged by the Court on Examination

Silla, property of Benjamin Powers on oath declared, that Davis, belonging to Cannons Estate, told her, that he heard that the **[?]**, and that the Negroes were a going to Rise, & Tann Property of Anthony Markham, said that if the Negroes did Rise he would have that Neck to himself. Davis said have he Reconed they would Kill all the Black folks that would not join them, this **[?]** took place at B. Powers since the 27th April.
Before me, Charles Grice
16 May 1802.

The County of Pasquotank with Robert McMorine
Allowed June Term 1802
Will: T. Muse, Clk
County of Pasquotank
To Robert McMorine **[Faded]**

May
4 day, Tony belonging to Thos Harvey
3 Joe, the Estate of D. George
2 Tom Do of John **[Faded]**
8 Sol & Mose of Joseph Trueblood
4 Adam of Thos Waymouth
32 Mose The Estate of Ashley Sutton
15 Mingo of W. Leigh
15 Seaser of Wm. Knowles
15 Cooper of John Grantham
2 Ned of John graves
24 Bob of Sullivans Estate
4 Luke of John Boyd
4 Will of Keaton
7 Isaac of Damrons Estate
4 Andrew of Wm Slate
16 of 2 Negroes of Jesse Redding
16 of 2 do Mrs. Redding

48 of 6 do Saml. Johnston
25 Sampson a Free Negro
10 of 2 negroes of Saml. Cobbs
2 Will of Bailey Jackson
2 Tom of Mr Mosely
2 Aaron of Jas [?]
305 Days of the above prisoners @ 2/£30 .10
Comitment & release of 24 Negroes @ 5/4 6.8
Whiping 4 negroes & Cutting the ear of one 5/ 1
37.18

John M. Donald his Peto for Compensation in the late insurrection of the negroes.

Petition of John McDonald & others

To the Worshipful, the County Court of Pasqt.

The Memorial of the Subscribers Humbly sheweth to youe worshipful Body, that in the late insurrection of the negroes, they were engaged in Suppressing the same; and being Called out upon duty at a busy Season of the Year; Suffered much from the neglect of their domestic concerns, but Viewing with Horrow the then impeading danger, they were prompted on in the exercise of that duty, to Save their County from the rapear & plunder, of those infatuated Creatures, to which it was exposed. Your Memorialist & a few others of patriotick Principal, turned out to circumvent the approaching mischief but at that time there was no law for rewarding publick Virtue of this kind, the Legislature at their las Session passed a Law authorizing your Worshipful body to raise a fund by way of tax to compensate your Memorialists for their Services - but your Memorialists have to lament, that that provision has been in sum measure neglected, to the great Discouragement of others who may engage in the like Service in future time. Your Memorialists farther to represent to your worshipful Body that Some persons have come forward and Drawn their pay, but by what authority they no not, or whether they were more intitled than others, now your Memorialists wish to petition your worshipful Vody for an equal Share of right and Law to which they are intitled with the rest of their fellow Citizens and as in duty bound they will ever Pray &c.

Pasquotank County Insurrection Papers

John McDonald, Thomas Jordan, Laml. War[?], Jos L. Brothers, Ben Ackiss[?], Josiah Relf, John Sawyer, Wm. Stott, Joab Jackson, E. Bailey, Daniel Shirley, Jas.L. Shannonhouse, Benj S. Overman, Jas Sawyer, [?].

Chapter Six

Pasquotank County

Negroes Taken Up

North Carolina State Archives
Pasquotank County Records
Records of Slaves and Free Persons of Color
C.R.075.928.10

This may Certify to some, it May Consarn that thair is a Negro Wench and Child the wench by the Name of Hanner and the Child by the Name of Ester is apperhined and Committee to the County Jail of Pasquotank County and is said To be the Property of Aron Dades[?] and therfour this Cirtify to Give you Notis to Com to Next suceding Cort Which is the first Monday in December Next then and ther to com and Claim if you have Any, November 10th 1794
John Baily for Ro. McMorine, Shff

Pasquotank County Feby 24th 1796

To Aaron Morris

Pasquotank County
Negroes Taken Up

Sir, there is a Negro Woman by the name of Dinah & Four Children Viz Plizent, Franke, William & Milli, in custody & said to be liberated, You are hereby noticed to attend at the next Court to be held for the said County at the Court House in Nixonton on the first Monday in March next & make Claim (if any you have) or they will be sold during the setting of the said Court at the Court House Door

I am &c.

Robt. McMorine, Shff

Pasquotank County Novr. 25th 1793

Friend Charles Overman

There is a negro Man by the Name of Job formerly your property apprehended as a manumitted Slave, & in Custody

You are hereby Noticed to attend & make Claim to the same (if any you have) at the Next Court, which will be held for the County of Pasquotank on the first Monday in Decr. Next or he will be sold during the term, at the Court House Door.

I am &c

Robt. McMorine, Shff

State of North Carolina

To William Simpson Dr

To finding Negro Isaac in confined in the Jail at Elizabeth City from the tenth of May unto the twenty fifth of June forty Seven Days at 2/8 per Day, 5.7.6, To Turning Key on said Negro 2/8 - 0.2.8.

The above are of five pounds ten Shillings and two pence is allowed the [?], £5 1 0.2

August 29th 1796

Taken up and put in Goal a Negro Woman by the Name of Frank 15 Days Board att 1/6 per Day

Turning the Key 5/4 £1.7.10

Pasquotank County
Negroes Taken Up

August 29th then taken up and put in Goal a Negro Woman by the Name of Ruth

Five Days Board att 1/6 per Day -	£0.7.6
Turning the Key	0.5.4
	0.12.10

August 29th Taken up and put in Goal a Negro Girl By the name of Jinny

15 Days Board att 1/6 per Day	£1.2.6
Turning the key	0.5.4
	£3.8.6

The Negro woman that has been put to Bed att my house I Leave it to the Gentleman of the **[Faded]** to Give me What they think is Right as I have had a great Deal talk **[Torn]**

State of North Carolina
Pasquotank County SS
September Term 1793

The State Vs.

The Defendant having been manumitted previous to the passing of the Act of the General Assembly prohibiting the manumission of Persons held as Slaves acquired the rights and priveleges of a Freeman of and no subsequent Act of the Legislature could deprive him of those privilidges, but the Court having decided that the said Act of the General assembly should operate respectively so as to bring the Case of the Defendant within the same I do Certify that the decision of the Court is unconstutional and illegal which I conceive to be a Sufficient reason for an Appeal to the Superior Court.
W Blair, Atto

Friend John lane I set out from house yesterday, to Come down to Court Concerning that Negro woman that the informed me was in Jail at Nixonton, but being in a poor state of health and she being so difficult I did not think it safe at any rate for me to attend Court, But may inform the that the same Negro hath been several times taken in our County and Tried at Court, but the circumstance of the Case was such that she was aquited and I should willingly hope the Court would not order her Sold without it

was Clearly proved that she was free which I believe Cannot be done Pleas to inform the Court this much and oblige thy friend.
Caleb White the 5th 3d 1793.

Mr. Aaron Morris

I hereby give you Notice that a Negro Woman called Doll (&(held)) was Apprehended as a Liberated Slave said to be Your Former Property and proceedings to be had thereon at our Next Court held at Nixonton on the Third Monday in the present Month according to Law.
Jno Lane Shff, 9 March 1790.

Mr. Aaron Morris Junr.

Sir

Notice is hereby given that there is a negro woman by the name of Easter said to be liberated by you taken up & will be Proceeded agt. Agreeable to Law at our Next Court to be held for the County of Pasquotank on the 1st Monday in Sept. Next.
Augt. 23rd 1793, Robt. McMorine, Sheriff.

Pasquotank County Novr. 25th 1793

Friend Josiah Trueblood

There is a negro man by the Name of Samson formerly your Property apprehended as a manumitted Slave in Custody.

You are hereby noticed to attend & make Claim to the same (if any you have) at our Next Court which will be held for the County of Pasquotank on the first Monday in Decr. Next, or he will be sold during the term at the Court House Door.
I am &c, Robt. McMorine, Sheriff.

Pasquotank County May 20th 1790

To Mr. Thomas Nicholson

Sir

There is a negroe man by the name of **[Torn]** in the Custody and said to be liberated, you are hereby noticed to attend at the next Court to be held for

the said County at the Court House in Nixonton on the first Monday in June next & make Claim (if any you have) or he will be sold during the sitting of said Court at the Court house Door.
I am &c, J Banks, D Sheriff.

Pasquotank County Novr. 25th 1793

Friend Aaron Morris

There is a Negro Woman & two Children by the names of Beck, Jacob, & Penny in Custody Supposed to be liberated by you if you have any Claim to the above Negroes you are hereby noticed to attend at our next Court & make claim or they will be Sold during The Courts Sitting which will Commence on the first Monday in December Next.
Robt. McMorine, Sheriff.

Pasquotank County Mar. 1st 1790

To Mr Aaron Morris

Sir

There is a negro woman by the name of Peg & her child Henry in Custody & said to be liberated, You are hereby Noticed to attend at the next Court to be held for the said County at the Court House in Nixonton on the first Monday in this present month & make Claim (if any you have) or they will be sold during the sitting of this said Court at the Court House Door.
I am &c, Rob McMorine, Sheriff

Pasquotank County Feb 1790

Sir

There is a negro man by the name of Isaac in Custody & said to be liberated, You are hereby noticed to attend at the next Court to be held for the said County at the Court House in Nixonton on the first Monday in March Next & make Clame (if any you have) or he will be Sold During the sitting of the said Court at the Court House Door.
I am &
Ro. McMorine, Sheriff
To Nathn Person }

Pasquotank County
Negroes Taken Up

Randolph County}

Mr. William Overman

I hereby Give You Notice that a Negro Woman Called Rose was Apprehended as a liberated Slave said to be your former Property; and Proceedings to be had thereon at our next Court held at Nixonton on the third Monday in the present month According to Law.

J Lane, Shff 8th March 1790.

Pasq - Nixonton May 12th 1802

Mr. James White Senr.

Sir, you are hereby notified that the trial of Negro Hannah said to be manumitted by you will be at our next Court to be held for the County, in Elizabeth City on the first Monday in June next, You will therefore attend if you think proper.

Robt McMorine, Sheriff

A Copy of the above delivered to Jas White May 12th 1802

Robt. McMorine, Shff

Nixonton June 4th 1802

Mr. Ph**[Faded]** Albertson & Aaron Albertson

You are hereby noticed that the trial of Negro Woman Named Mariah & five Children said to be manumitted by John Trueblood Dec'd will be had at our next Court to be held for the County of Pasquotank in the Court House in Elizabeth City during the sitting of said Court, You will therefore attend the trial of said Negroes & make Claim if you think proper.

Robt. McMorine, Shff

Negroes Apprehended as Liberated Slaves

By Sale of Rose	£33
Patience & Children	20.6
Jonas	56.4

Pasquotank County
Negroes Taken Up

Doll & Child	37.0
Job	44
Edeus[?]	40.12.6
Rose	42.3
	273.5.6
Ball & Contra	220.3.2
Ball Contra Due the State	£162.9.3

Errors Excepted p Jno Lane, Shff
March Term 1790

Rec'd of John Lane twenty nine pounds Thirteen Shillings & 1" in Cash & Ninety one Pounds 12/1 in obligations, Amounting to One hundred & twenty One Pounds five shillings & ten Pence being in part of the Within balance due the Public as within Stated.
Rec'd by me This 22nd July 1793
Enoch Relfe, CCC

An Accot: of Expences of the Guard & Negroes. Considered by This Court under an act of the Late General Assembly
1777 - Sep 10th

To Cyder for the Guard & Negroes	£1.3.0
To Toddy at the Sale10.0	
To Mr. Thomas Relfe's Bill	4.2.6
To Summoning 12 Men	1.12.0
To Commitment releasing 12 Negroes	3.4.0
To Wages of the Guard for tending two nights	5.4.0
To John Richardson for keeping the Amt of Sale other services	15.5.6

Pasquotank, Sept 12th 1777, Thos Riding, Shff

1790
Dr. The State of North Carolina for Expences on Negroes

To Jaylors Bill on the whole Bill	£13.1
Sheriff for Warrants [?] Notices & Services whole	9.6.8
Clerks fees on the whole	9.
Witness Certificate on Tryal of Job	18

Pasquotank County
Negroes Taken Up

Atto Fees	14
Commiss on the sale Amt to 273.5.6 [?]	6.16.8
Ball due	220.3.2
	273.5.6

To Paid the Takers up Pr Receipts	
One fifth Part of the Balance	44.0.8
To Commis on doing the busines of taking Calculations Giving receipts & & & on the Whole	13.13.3
Balance due the State in Obligations Payable at 9 Months	
	162.9.3
	220.3.2

Produced & allowed in open Court, Enoch Relfe CCC
June Term 1790, Errors Excepted.

State Vs. Negroe Hannah
Subpoena & Notice
Pasquotank, June Term 1802

Notice	£.5.4
Subp	1.6.8
Comitment & Release	5.4
4 Days in Goal	10.0
Calling Jury	1.4
Execution for Sale	5.4
Bail Bond	2.0
Coms. On Sale	2.10
	£5.6
Clk fees	1.10
My Do	2.0
	£8.16
4/5 Int proceeds to the State	72.19.3
1/5 of Do to the taker up in the hands of Jos Banks	18.4.9
	£100

By Sale of Negroe Hannah £100
State of North Carolina Dr.
To Robt. McMorine, Sheriff

Pasquotank County
Negroes Taken Up

June Term 1802
Sheriffs fees on the trial of 15 Slaves taken up as manumitted Slaves & discharged by Court & to be paid out of the above Balls. Due the State agreeable to an order of the County Court of Pasquotank at this Term 40/8
30.10

Gaolars fees 36 Days of Albertson's Tom	4.10
Chs Overman witness ticket	11.5
Saml. Newbould's do	10
State Atty fees @ 40/1	30
Clk of Court do 30/	22.10
Supra Cm.	£88.11.5
By the pounds of Hannah as above	£72.19.3
Balance due the Officers	15.12.2
	£88.11.5
W Blevins	29.10
W Muse	19.5
Shff	29.4.3
	72.19.3

Robt. McMorine, Sheriff

State of North Carolina }
Pasq County }

Know all men by these presents, That I Josiah Perry are held and firmly bound unto Robert McMorine, Sheriff of the County aforesaid, in the Sum of Two Hundred pounds to which payment well and truly to be made, I bind my self, my Heirs, Administrators and Assigns, severally by these Presents. Sealed with My Seal and Dated this 1st Day of October One Thousand, seven Hundred & Ninety Three.

The Condition of this Obligation is such, That ir Negro Job formerly belonging to Charles Overman being apprehended as a Manumitted Slave do make his personal appearance before the Justices of the County Court of Pleas and Quarter Sessions, to be held at the Court House in Nixonton on the 5th Monday in Decr. There stand and abide by the Judgment of the said Court, and not depart without licence be obtained then this **[Torn]** in full Force and Virtue. Signed, Sealed, and Delivered in the presence of J. Lane & Josiah Perry.

State of North Carolina }

Know all Men by These Presents, That I William Jordon are held and firmly bound unto Robt McMorine, Sheriff of the County aforesaid, in the Sum of Two hundred pounds to which payment well and truly to be made, I bind My self, My Heirs, Administrators and Assigns, Severally by these Presents, Sealed with my Seal **[Missing]** this 18th Day of Novr. One Thousand, Seven Hundred and ninety three.

The Condition of this Obligation is such, That if Negro Woman Tamer formerly the property of Henry Parker**[?]** being apprehended as a manumitted Slave do make her personal appearance before the Justices of the County Court of Pleas and Quarter Sessions, to be held at the Court House in Nixonton on the 1st Monday in Decr. Next, and there stand and abide by the Judgment of the said Court, and not depart without Liberty, first had and obtained, then the above obligation to be void, otherwise to remain in full Force and Virtue.
Signed, Sealed, and Delivered in the Presents of Andrew Knox.
Wm Jordan.

State of North Carolina }
Pasquotank County }

Know all men by these presents that we Josiah Relfe and Benjamin Davis takers up of Milly and her six Children and Joseph Relfe and Fredk Davis are held and firmly bound unto Abraham Symons in the sum of One hundred & fifty Pounds current money, to be paid to the said Abraham Symons his heirs, Executors, Administrators, jointly and severally, firmly by these Presents. -- Sealed with our Seals, and dated this 6th day of Decr. Anno Dom. 1809.

The condition of the above obligation is such, that whereas in a suit brought by the State Pr Josiah Relfe & Benja. Davis against Milly & six Children belonging to A. Symons in the County Court of Pleas and Quarter Sessions, held for the County aforesaid, on the first Monday in December instant, judgment was recovered by the Defendant by having the above Negroes discharged by the Court and costs of suit. -- And Whereas the said Josiah Relfe & Benja. Davis hath prayed for and obtained an

appeal from the said judgment to the next Superior Court of Law, to be held for the district of Edenton, on the sixth day of April next: Now in case the said Josiah Relfe & Benjamin Davis doth well and truly prosecute his said appeal with effect, or in case he fail and be cast therein, shall well and truly pay all such damages, costs, and charges, as shall be awarded against him by the said Superior Court, and also fulfil and perform the sentence, judgment, and decree of the said Court: then the above obligation shall be null and void, otherwise to remain in full force and virtue.
Sealed and delivered in the presence of Will T. Muse
Josiah Relfe (Seal)
Benja Davis (Seal)
Joseph Relfe (Seal)
His
Fred X Davis (Seal)
Mark

Transcript of the record and proceedings had in the County Court of Pasquotank, begun and held at the Court House in Elizabeth City on the first Monday in September in the year of our Lord One Thousand Eight hundred and four at the Instance of the State against **[Blank]** and her Children as follows.

State of North Carolina }
Pasquotank County SS } September four 1804

On motion by John Hamilton in regard of Milly and her six Children Vizt Ferebee, Suckey, Demcey Tamer, Aaron and Mary, (Demcey and Ferebee being in the possession of Josiah Relfe) Easter and her six Children Patty, Betty, Frank**[?]**, Nancey, and Delilah (Patty being in possession of Benjamin Davis supposing them illegally liberated and the matter standing for some time without notice on the Owner or refuted owner, it is ordered that the Sheriff do take these negroes in his possession and Custody and deliver them unto Pl**[Faded]** Albertson taking Security for the appearance of the negroes at the next Term and that the cause between the State and these negroes do stand for Trial at the next Term, as usual in the like Case.
Acap**[?]** Wm. Spence DC

Pasquotank County
Negroes Taken Up

Not Executed by reason Benjamin Davis and Josiah Relfe refuseth to give up the negroes mentioned in this writ and I did not know the said negroes nor did the Pltff attend to shew them to me
J Banks, DShff

And at a Succeeding Term of the said Court to wit December Term 1804, On argument the above negroes Discharged, from which Judgment Benjamin Davis and Josiah Relfe the takers up pray'd an appeal to the next Superior Court of law to be held at Edenton for the District of Edenton on the 6th day of April must which was granted them on reasons being filed and entering into bond in the sum of One hundred and fifty pounds with Joseph Relfe and Frederick Davis as Securities for prosecuting their said appeal with effect.

In Testimony whereof I have hereunto set my hand and the publick Seal of my office the 7th day of December anno Dom. 1804 and in the 29th year of American Independence.
Will: T. Muse, Clk

State vs Milly & her Children } Costs	
1804, Decr. Clks fees	[?]
Order for appeal	12
Official Bond	6
Stay on the appeal	8
Transcript of Proceedings	8
County Seal	2.6
	£2.16.6
Atto	8.6
Shff	3.5
Shff	

Rec'd from messrs Davis & Relfe, £3.5 for Clerks & Shff fees
Will: T. Muse, Clk

Chapter Seven

Pasquotank County

Criminal Actions

North Carolina State Archives
Pasquotank County Records
Records of Slaves and Free Persons of Color
C.R.075.928.9 & C.R.075.928.10

King Vs. Negro Dick [1734
Criminal Action
Felony
Pasquotank County

Perquimans
The Examination of Zebulon Clayton & ye Negro Dick before me Moses Speight Esqr : one of his Majesty's Justices of ye Peace for ye Sd. Precinct the 7th day of Feb: 1734

The Sd. Negro Dick being Charged before me, by Ellinor Hall of Pasquotank Precinct Widow, That the said negro Dick together with one Wm. Taylor a white Servt. Of his Masters did on the 24th of Jany. Last past in ye night of the same day feloniously break open & Enter her ware house

& Cellar thereunto belonging, and thence did take, Steal and Carry away, Rum, Sugar, Callico, Garlick, and other Goods, to the value of Twenty Pounds in fresh Pork &c Saith That Ye Sd. Wm: Taylor had been a long times Importuning him to go a privateering with him, did one Friday night, being ye day afsd.: go with ye Sd, Taylor to Wm: Barclifts and taking his canoe, Came up to Nathl. Hall Esqrs landing where was lying a Boat out of which ye Sd. Taylor took two Glass Bottles and being about half full of Rum, one Rug and one Pr. Of Trowzers, and & out them in the Canoo they came in, afterwards he goes to ye Dwelling house almost **[?]** then returning he goes to ye Ware house Door and Shuged agt. It; which not opening he goes to ye Cellar Door wch being lock't, he took a piece of a broken paddle & Broke it open and entering he drew a dram out of a Cask of Rum thence standing in a bason that stood under ye Cask & brought to him this Examint wch he drank, then taking a handle of **[?]** yt. Stood in ye Sd. Cellar, he filled it about three parts full with rum, then standing upon ye top of the Cellar Door with a piece of a **[?]** he broke & Wrenched open a window that open'd into the ware-house above. And thence throw out some sugar wrapt up in a Deer Skin, also some Garlicks, some Callico, some **[?]** Knives, 4 penknives in sheaths, some Gartering, some Benches of Pins & some in a brown Paper, and somethings in his bosom & so going away they landed where they took up ye Canoo from, and then taking ye Goods they Carried them away into the woods, and ye dry Goods in a hollow Tree, and ye Rundlet ye Sd. Taylor sunk in ye water in a blown up root
Taken before me the day and year above Sd., Moses Speight

His
Negro X Dick
Mark

****

King Vs. Negro Ben [1746
Criminal Action
Felony
Pasquotank County

Warrt. For Negro Ben

North Carolina }
Pasquotank County }

Pasquotank County
Criminal Actions

Whereas Complaint being maid to me one of his Majesty's Justices by Thos Pendleton That a Negro man Slave named Ben belonging to Mrs. Sarah Palen, has lately marked a hogg belonging to the Complainent it beig Contrary to an Act Concerning **[Smudged]** Killing, marking or mismarking a hoggs and Cattel &c

These are therefore in His Majesties Name to will and Command you On Site hearof to apprehended the said negro man slave Ben and him safely hold well you have him before me or sum one of his Majesties Justices of the County order that he may delt with According to the Act of Assembly in that Case made and provided herein fail not as you will Answer the Contrary -- Given under my hand and Seal This 8th Day July 1746
Cornelius Relfe (Seal)

To the High Sheriff & his Deputy. You must Summon Ken **[Smudged]** **[Smudged]** for the Complainent

This may Satisfy that I having Summoned Thos Relfe, John Scarborough, Isaac Stokely & John Hodges[?] to atend at the Court House on Thurrsday the 10th this Instant In Order to try a Negro man slave for marking a Hog after the above warrant.

You must Summon Lamuel Bunday to appear at the Court House as an Evidence Concerning a matter now Depending between Thos Pindleton and a Negro on [?] for marking a hogg about a matter that you may know.

You are hereby Ordered to in his Majesty's Name to Summon Sarah Palin personally To appear Thursday Eight of the Clock This Instance to Appear in behalf of her negro slave Ben On An Information and Complaint against him by Thos. Pindleton for marking One hog of the said Thos Pindleton, if she has or can Lawfully say any thing in behalf of her Afsd Negro
C.K.
Executed by Saml Height

****

King Vs. Negro Essex [1769
Criminal Action
Crime not Given
Pasquotank County

Pasquotank County
Criminal Actions

North Carolina }
Pasquotank County } SS.

At a Court brgun opened and held at the Court House at Windfield according to Act of Assembly in such Case made and Provided for the Tryal of Essex Negroe, a Slave of the Property of Richard Brownrigg squire of Chowan County the tenth Day of November in the year of our Lord One Thousand Seven hundred and Sixty Nine

Present The Worshipful William Boyd.

Justices, Thomas Macknight, Matthias Ellgood, Isaac Gilford, Abram Sumors[?], John Sawyer.

Free Holders, Owners of Slaves, William Reid, Joseph Redding, Trimagain Redding, Benjamin Shadrick[?]

The above Negroe Essex aforsaid being Tried and found Guilty was valued to the sum of Eighty Pounds Current Money, It was then and there Ordered that he be Carried to the Place of Execution and on 13th]?] Instant being Monday Between the hours of Twelve and One O'Clock be hanged by the nexk till he be Dead Given under our Hands and Seals the day & year above Written

John Sawyer (Seal), William Reid (Seal), Joseph Reding (Seal), Benj Sedrick (Seal) [?], Trimagain Reding (Seal), Wm Boyd (Seal), Thos Macknight (Seal), Mathias Ellgood (Seal), Isaac (Seal), Abram Sumors (Seal)

****

King Vs. Negro Jack [1774
Criminal Action
Crime not Given
Pasquotank County

North Carolina }
Pasquotank County }

Pasquotank County
Criminal Actions

At a Court begun opened and held at the Court House at Windfield according to Act of Assembly in such Case made and Provided for the Tryal of Jack a Negro Slave of the property of John Hosea of the County and Province aforesaid the 5th day of July in the Year of our Lord One Thousand Seven Hundred & Seventy Four.

Present the Worshipful Justices & Esqrs.

Justices: Lamuel Sawyer, Thomas Reding, Robert Jordan, John Gray, Abner Harrison.

Free Holders of Slaves: Edmund Chancey, Joseph Reding, John Watkins, Thomas Relfe.

The above Negro Jack aforesaid being tried and found Guilty &c. It was then and there Ordered that he be Carried to the goal from Whence he came and from there to the publick Whipping post and there to have Fifty two Lashes on his Bare Back well Laid on. [?] to pay all Lawful Costs. Given under our hands and Seals this 5th Day of July Anno Domini 1774.

Leml. Sawyer (Seal), Thos Reding (Seal), John Gray (Seal), Abner Harrison (Seal), Edmd Chancey (Seal), Jos Reding (Seal), Thos Relfe (Seal)

****

King Vs. Negro Martin [1774]
Criminal Action
Felony
Pasquotank County

North Carolina }
Pasquotank County }

At a Court begun Opened and held at the Court House at Windfield according to Act of Assembly in such Case made and Provided for the Tryall of Martin a Negro Slave of the Property of Miriam Jones Orphans of Griffeth Jones Dec'd of the County and Province aforesaid in theYear of our Lord One Thousand Seven Hundred and Seventy Four for feloniously Stealing Linen Cloth valued at Fifteen shillings Proclamation Money, August

Present the Worshipful Justices: Robert Munden, John Crawford, Enoch Relfe, Tremagain Reding

The Above Negro Martin aforesaid being Tried and found Guilty was Valued to Eighty Pounds Proclamation Money, It was then and there Ordered that he be Carried to the Goal or place of confinement from whence he came and from thence to the Common Place of Execution and on Thursday the 18th of this Instant Between the Hours of Twelve and Two O'Clock be hanged by the Neck till he be dead. Given under my hand and Seals the day and year above written.

Thomas Reding (Seal), Abner Harrison (Seal), John Gray (Seal), Thomas King (Seal), Robert Munden (Seal), John Crawford (Seal), Enoch Relfe (Seal), Trimagin Reding (Seal).

****

King Vs. Negro Doll [1774]
Criminal Action
Crime not Given
Pasquotank County

North Carolina }
Pasquotank County } SS

At a Court begun Opened and held at the Court House at Windfield according to Act of Assembly in such case made and Provided for the Tryal of Doll Negro Slave of the property of Robert Hosea of the County and Province aforesaid in the Year of our Lord One Thousand seven Hundred and Seventy four.

Present the Worshipful Justices & Esquires

Justices: Lemuel Sawyer, Thomas Reding, Robert Jordan, John Gray, Abner Harrisson,

Gentlemen and Freeholders, Owners of Slaves: Edmund Chancey, Joseph Reding, John Watkins, Thomas Relfe.

The above Negro Doll aforesaid being Tried and found Guilty - It was then and there Ordered that She be Carried to the Goal from whence She Came from Thence to the Public Whiping post and there Receive Thirty Nine Lashes on her bare Back well laid on, Given under our Hands and Seals the 5th Day of July Anno Domini 1774. Master to Pay all Lawful Costs.

Edmd Chancey (Seal), Jos. Reding (Seal), John Watkins (Seal), Thos Relfe (Seal), Leml Sawyer (Seal), Thos Reding (Seal), Robt. Jordan (Seal), John Gray (Seal), Abner Harrison (Seal).

****

King Vs. Negro Richard [1775]
Criminal Action
Felony
Pasquotank County

Pasquotank SS

Whereas Richard - a negro Man belonging to Joseph Jones Esqr. of the County afsd. Has this day been brought before us at the Complaint of James Ferebe for Stealing from himself & [?] some Rum out of their Cellar.

These are therefore to command you to Take into your Custody the Said Negro man Richard & him & in Safety Carry to the County Goal & there him Keep untill the Time appointed for his Tryall. Given under our Hands & Seals this 6th January 1775
Demsey Burgess JP (Seal)
Dempsey Sawyer JP (Seal)
To the Sheriff of Pasquotank County

North Carolina }
Pasquotank County } SS

At a Court begun opened and held at the Court House at Windfield According to Act of Assembly in such Case made and Provided for the Tryal of Richard a Negro Slave of the Property of Joseph Jones of the County and Province aforesaid in the Year of our Lord One thousand Seven Hundred and Twenty five January 7th

Present the Worshipful Justices & Esquires

Justices: Lemuel Sawyer, Jonathan Banks, Edward Everigain, Isaac Sawyer.

Freeholders & owners of Slaves: Robert Palmer, Isaac Jones, John Palin, Isaac Murden

The above Negro Richard aforesaid being Tried and found Guilty & was then and there Ordered that he be Carried to the Publick Whiping Post and Receive Forty Lashes on his Bare Back and have his Right Ear Nailed to the Post and Cut off, Given under our hands and Seals the day and year above written.

Leml Sawyer (Seal), Jon Banks (Seal), Edw. Everigan (Seal), Robert Palmer (Seal), John Palin (Seal), Isaac Murden (Seal).

****

King Vs. Negro Jacob [1775]
Criminal Action
Killing a Horse
Pasquotank County

North Carolina }
Pasquotank County } SS

At a Court begun Opened and held at the Court House at Windfield According to Act of Assembly in such Case made & Provided for the Tryal of Jacob a Negro Slave of the Property of Joseph Salsbury of the County and Province aforesaid in the year of our Lord one Thousand Seven Hundred and Seventy Five, for a Confession of Killing a Horse the Property of Alexander McClain Equal in Value to [?]

Present the Worshipful Justices & Esquires

Justices: Jonathan Harring, Robert Murden, William Scarborough.

Free Holders, Owners of Slaves: Thomas Relfe, Enoch Relfe, Spencer Ripley, Demsey Gregory.

The above Negro Jacob being Tried and found Suspected Guilty - It was then & there Ordered the said Negro Jacob be carried to the Publick Whipping Post & there Receive Eighteen lashes on his bare back well laid on by the Constable & his Master pay all Lawful Costs.

Jon Harring (Seal), Rob Murden (Seal), Wm Scarborough (Seal), Enoch Relfe (Seal), Demcey Gregory (Seal), Spencer Ripley (Seal), Thos Relfe (Seal).

****

King Vs. Negroes London & Dave [1776]
Criminal Action
Felony, Stealing
Pasquotank County

North Carolina }
Pasquotank County } SS

To Thomas Relfe Special Constable to Execute & make return -- Whereas Complaint hath been made to me one of his Majesties Justices of the peace for the County that a Certain Negroe fellow the Property of Mrs. Mary Blount named London And another Negroe fellow the Property of William **[Torn]** named Dave have on the nights of the 23rd & 24th of February last feloniously broke into a Warehouse at Windfield & Stole from there Sundry Articles such as Pork, Rum & Sugar the Property of William McCormich - These are therefore to Warrant you to take said Negroes into your Custody & Safely keep untill released, Given under my hand & Seal This 2nd March 1776.

To Isaac Gregory Esqr. Sheriff &c

You are hereby required to Summon three Justices of the Peace & four Freeholders & Owners of Slaves in Order to hold a Court for the Tryal of

Pasquotank County
Criminal Actions

Negroes London & Dave Committed to Goal for Feloniously Stealing & Breaking Houses, Given under our Hand & Seals this [?] day of March.
Robert Murden

In obedience to the within precept, I have Sum'd John Gray, Robert Murden & Edward Evergain Esqr. & Joseph Reding, David George, Spencer Ripley & Thomas Humphries Free holders.
Isaac Gregory, Shff. Executed & Returned to Robert Murden this 4th March 1776.

To Thomas Relfe Special Constable & Goal Keeper, You are hereby required to receive into your Custody the Bodies of Negroes London & Davy and them Commit to the County Goal there safely keep them untill Reman'd from further Tryall -- Given under my hand & Seal this 4th day of March 1776
Robert Murden.

0: 18.8 for the Court.	
Commt	2.8
Releasment	2.8
Goalers fees	3.0
Two Witnesses	5.4
	1.12.4
Warrant	2.8
	£1.15.0

****

State Vs. Negro Dave [1776]
Criminal Action
Felony
Pasquotank County

North Carolina }
Pasquotank County }

At a Court Begun Opened & held at Windfield Monday 4th March 1776 having been Summoned by the Sheriff by order of Robert Murden Esqr. for the Tryall of Negro Dave the Property of Mr William Reed Charged with Felony.

Present the Worshipful Esquires and Justices.

Justices: John Gray, Robert Murden, Edward Evergain.

Freeholders, Owners of Slaves:Joseph Reding, Mr David George, Mr. Spenser Ripley, Mr. Thomas Humphries.

The Sheriff agreeable to Law Brought into Court Negro Dave charg'd with felony Committed on the Property of William McCormick Esqr by Breaking open a ware house & Taking from Sundry articles as Pork, Rum, Sugar &C &C &C the **[Faded]** of the 23rd of February 24th February.

The Above Negro Dave being Tried was found Guilty -- It was then and there ordered that the said Negro Dave be **[Faded]** by the to a distance not **[Faded]** than Fifty **[Torn]** from the County & give Bond with Mr Joseph Redding & Mr Spencer Ripley Securitys in the Sum of Five Hundred Pounds **[Faded]** Money payable to the Vestry of the Parish of St. Johns & then **[Faded]** in office for the time being to be **[Faded]** by them or any Parte Injured, & that the said Negro Dave be not released from his Bonds untill he be so transported -- This Transportation to be made within thirty days -- Given under our hands & Seals this 4th Day of March at Windfield Anno Dom

Jos Reding (Seal), Spencer Ripley (Seal), Tho Humphries (Seal), Edwd. Evergain (Seal), John Gray (Seal), Robert Murden (Seal), David George (Seal).

****

State Vs. Negro Jack [1776]
Criminal Action
Felony
Pasquotank County

North Carolina }
Pasquotank County }

At a Court begun opened & held at Windfield in the Court House this 8th June 1776 agreeable to act of Assembly in such case made &

Provided for the Tryall of Negro Jack the Property of Mr. John Watkins of the County & Province aforesaid, for Breaking open A House & Stealing out a quantity of Bacon Value Twenty Shillings, the Property of Mr John Crawford.

Present The Worshipful Esquires & Justices

Justices: Abram Symons, Thomas Redding, Edward Evergain

Freeholders, Owners of Slaves: Joseph Redding, Thomas Relfe, Henry Pendleton, Spencer Ripley

The above negro man Jack offering to disclose all the [?] of his Comrades & become Evidence against them. The Court Conceiving him Guilty discharged him without Punishment.

Abram Symons (Seal), Thomas Redding (Seal), Edward Evergain (Seal), Thos Relfe (Seal), Henry Pendleton (Seal), Spencer Ripley (Seal).

****

State Vs. Negro Cheschire [1777]
Criminal Action
Felony, Stealing
Pasquotank county

The State of North Carolina }
Pasquotank County }

At a Court begun Open & held for to Try Negro Cheschire belonging to the Orphans of Josiah Richardson Dec'd at the Court House at Windfield this 27th day of June 1777 who Being committed to Goal by Thomas Relfe for taking uot of a certain Schooner called the John sundry goods the property of Messrs Crawford & Speers.

Present

Justices, Esquires: Thomas Relfe, Joseph Redding, John Palin.

Freeholders & Owners of Slaves: John Smithson Junr., Alexander McClane, Peter Adams, Spencer Ripley.

Then the Court proceeded to Value the Sd. Negroe Cheschire and valued hm accordingly to Eighty Pounds Proclamation Money. Then the Court proceeded upon the Tryal of the Negroe Cheschire and ordere'd that the Sheriff of the County take him to the Common whiping Post and give him Eighty lashes on his bare back according to the Judgment of the County.

Thomas Relfe (Seal), Jos Reding (Seal), John Palin (Seal), John Smithson Junr. (Seal), Alexr McClane (Seal), Spencer Ripley (Seal), Peter Adams (Seal).

****

State Vs. Negro Jack [1783]
Criminal Action
Assault
Pasquotank County

State of North Carolina }
Pasquotank County }

At a Special Court Begun & held at the Court House in Windfield on Friday the fourteenth day of November in the Year of our God one Thousand seven hundred Eighty three in the eighth Year of the Independence of the said State for the Tryall of negro man Jack the property of Andrew Brothers for maliciously Stabing with a Jack knife Beating a negro man Jacob the property of Richard Brothers so that his Life was despared of **[?]**.

Present The Worshipfull Justices

Justices: Thomas Reding, Joseph Reding, Thomas Relfe, William Jordan,

Free Holders, Owners of Slaves: Saml Swann, Thomas Palin, Robert Hall.

Who being Qualified & took their places according to an Act of Assembly of the said State, Negro John Being Brought to the Bar and **[Smudged]** evidence be produced who proved the above accusation against John to Be

Tried **[Faded]** then they proceeded to the value of the said John who was appraised agreable to Law to Eighty Pounds Then the Court Unanimously agreed again Judgement in the following Manner Viz, That Negro John aforesaid Be taken to the Publick Whipping post where the Sheriff then give him one Hundred Lashes on his Bare Back well layed on with whips. Then the aforesaid orders were Read & Signed by the following Gentlemen.
Test, Thomas Relfe CC

Will: Jordan (Seal), Sam Swann (Seal), Thomas Palin (Seal), Robert Hall (Seal), Thos Reding (Seal), Jos Reding (Seal), Thos Relfe (Seal).

****

State Vs. Negro Quake [1783]
Criminal Action
Threatening to Poison
Pasquotank County

State of North Carolins }
Pasquotank County }

At a Special Court held at the Court House at Windfield on Friday 21st November in the Year of our Lord One Thousand Seven hundred and Eighty Three and in the Eighth year of the Independence of the said State for the Tryall of Negro Quake for threatening to poison and punish the Wife of John Symons and her Mother Mrs Elender White.

Present The Worshipful Justices & Esquires

Justices: Abram Symons, Thomas Relfe, John Smithson

Free Holders & Owners of Slaves: William Jordan, Robert Haul, Thomas Palin, Emperior Mosley.

Who being Qualified, took their Seats accordingly Negro Quake being brought to the Bar summoned and Plead not Guilty, that the Court then proceeded to examine Sundry evidence Relative to the matter and found the said Negro not Guilty and so he is Discharged, Plantiff to pay the Costs

Thomas Palin (Seal), Robert Hall (Seal), William Jordan (Seal), A. Symons (Seal), John Smithson (Seal), Thomas Relfe (Seal), Emperor Mosely (Seal).

****

State Vs. Negro John [1783]
Criminal Action
Assault
Pasquotank County

State of North Carolina }
Pasquotank County }

To the Sheriff of the County Afsd his Debety, You are here By Commanded to Take the Body of a Negro Man Named John the Property of Andrew Brothers and him have Before me or Some other Justice of the Peace for this County to answer the Complaint of Richard Brothers who Saith the sd. Negroe John Did Some time Last September Fall on his Neagro Jacob and Beat wound and Injure the Sd Neagro so that his Life was Despared of. Given under my hand and Seal this 8th of October 1783.
Tho. Reding (Seal)

Summons for **[Faded]** Hezekiah Cartwright and Jacob Belonging to Andrew Brothers.

Nov 13th 1783 You are here by Commanded to Summon three Justices and Four Freeholders and Master and owners of Slaves to meet at the Court House in Windfield on Friday the 14th of Instant to sett and trie the within Neagro, Thos Reding
To John Palin, Sheriff

Warrant for Negro Jack, A. Brothers
Executed and Returned, By John Palin Sheriff.

****

State Vs. Negro Tony [1784]
Criminal Action
Crime Not Given

Pasquotank County Criminal Actions

Pasquotank County

State of No. Carolina }
Pasquotank County }

To any lawful Officer to Execute
Whereas Complaint hath been made this Day to me one of the States Justices for the County Afsd. By John Davis, that a Certain Negro man Toney now under the Command of Thomas Ackis, Did this morning Bind in with him the Sd. John Davis, & him Did **[Faded]** Strike Sundry Times with his fist & Allso with a Large Club & then Preceded to Choke him; until he had Assistance Coming up, These are therefore to Command you to Bring the Body of the said Negro Toney before me or sum other Justice of the Peace for said County as he may be delt with as the Law Directs. Herein fale not to **[?]** Return, Givin under my hand & Seal this 11th Day of October 1784.
Abram Symonds
Summond for the Plaintiff Benjamin Newby, **[?]** Overman, Hosea Gregory.

October 16th 1784, from the evidence of Sundry Witnesses, the within negro Toney appears to be gilty of the Charge against him, He Therefore stands Committed To the Sheriff of the County of Pasqt. County you are hereby Commanded to Take the said Negro into your Custidy & him Safely Keep until he can have a fair Tryal as the Law Directs, You are further Commanded to Summon three Justices & four freeholders, owners of Slaves to meet, at the Court House on Monday Next in order Tony the said Slave, Herein fail not & this shall be your sufficient Warrant, given under our hands & Seals the Day & Date above Written} The above executed By **[?]** (Seal)
Othniel Lassell (Seal)
Joseph Riding, Sheriff.
Executed and Returned by David Bailey.

State of North Carolina }
Pasquotank County }

At a Special Court held at Windfield in the Court House of the Sd. County the 19th day of Octo. In the Year of our Lord one Thousand Seven hundred & Eighty four in the ninth year of our Independence of the Sd.

Pasquotank County
Criminal Actions

State to Try Negro Toney the property of the Late Samuel Warner Dec'd; for viciously Striking & Beating and Wounding of John Davis yeoman of the said County

Present the Worshipful Justices & Esquires

Justices: Edward Evergain, Abraham Symons, Othniel Lassell.

Gentlemen Freeholders, Owner's of Slaves: Samuel Swann, Alex McLean, John Swann, Aaron Harkins.

Being qualified took their places accordingly, Negro Toney being Brought to the Bar and Valued to Eighty pounds currency. It is Ordered that Negro Tonny be carried to the publick Whipping Post and Then Receive on his bare Back Fifty Lashes and have part of his Left Ear Cut off. Ordered that Thomas Ackis pay all Costs and that the Negro Be Kept in Custody until paid and that the Clerk Certify the Amount to the Admrs. and that he Allowed the same out of his Heir. Then the Afsd orders were read & Signed by the following Gentlemen
E[?], Abram Symonds, Othniel Lassell, Saml Swann, Alexr McLean, Aaron Harkins & John Swann Senr.
Teste Enoch Relfe, Clk

Constable	9.4
Sheriff	2.4.4
	3.13.8

****

State Vs. Negro Everet or Enoch [1787]
Criminal Action
Felony, Stealing
Pasquotank County

State of North Carolina }
Pasquotank County }

At a Special Court held in the Court House of the Sd. County on the Nineteenth day of June in the Year of 1787 for the Tryall of Negro Everet the property of Alex.d Stafford of Perquimans County for feloniously Stealing and breaking open of a Certain House & the property of Colo. Benjamin Harvey did take of his [?] six & half Bushels out and carried away of Indian Corn.

Present The Worshipfull Justices

Justices: Abraham Symons, Joseph Reding, Thomas Relfe, John Blackstone, Devotion Davis.

Freeholders and Owners of Slaves: John Stevenson, John Poynter, Rowan Howell.

The above Gentl. Being Qualified Took their seats and proceeded to the Tryall of the said Everet, when it is ordered & that the Sheriff or his Deputy take him to the Publick Whiping post and there Give him One hundred Lashes on his Bare Back then Cut off half his Right Ear and Brand him in the forehead with the Letter T and that his Master pay all Costs and this Be Executed in One Hour and that he Stand Committed and fed only Bread and for Ten days and then all Cost be paid..

Jos Reding, Abram Symons, J Blackstone, Devotion Davis, John Stevenson, Rowan Hawett [Howell].

****

State Vs. Negro Enoch [1787]
Criminal Action
Felony, Stealing
Pasquotank County

State of North Carolina }
Pasquotank County }

At a Special Court held at the Court House in Nixonton the 21st of June in the year of our Lord One thousand Seven hundred and Eighty seven for the Tryal of Negro Enoch the property of a Certain Nancy Stafford of Perquimans County who is charged for the [?] and going in to the Smoke House of Major John Blackstone and there Stealing taking out and carried away to the amount of three Hundred Weight of Pork & Bacon.

Present

Justices: Edward Evergan, Othniel Lassell, John Lane

Gentl. Freeholders & owners of Slaves: Demsey Connor, William Jordan, Thomas Davis, Benjmn. Leonard

Who was Summoned by the Sheriff for the Tryall of the said negro and after Being Aworn Took their Seats and proceeded on his Tryall uppon the Examination of Sundry Witnesses We find that he is not Guilty of the Charge above ledged against him But Stands Committed to all Cost be paid.

Edw Evergan, Othniel Lassell, Demsey Conner, Thos Davis, William Jordan & B Leonard.

****

State Vs. Negro Ben [1789]
Criminal Action
Felony, Stealing
Pasquotank County

Pasquotank County }

At A Special Court held for the Tryall of Negro Ben at the Court House in Nixonton on the Twenty seventh day of July in the Year 1789 agreeable to an act of the General Assembly in that Case made & provided the Property of William Overman in the said County.

Present the Worshipful Justices

Justices: Joseph Keaton, Anthony Markham, Thad Freshwater

Gentl., Freeholders, Owners of Slaves: Demsey Conner, Abraham Kn[?], William Lane, Joseph Commander.

That negro Ben Being brought to the Barr and after Being Examined and Sundry Evidences was found Guilty of going into the House of Isaac Jordan and the Taking out ten yards of Linen and one Jack Knife. Ordered that Negro Ben on his Bare Back Thirty nine Lashes and then to have his Right Ear Cut off ordered that William Overman his Master pay all Costs which it is Tax'd

T Freshwater (Seal), Joseph Keaton (Seal), Anthony Markham (Seal), Demsey Conner (Seal), Abraham Kno[?], (Seal), W. Lane (Seal), Jos. Commander (Seal).

****

State Vs. Negro Dick [1790]
Criminal Action
Felony, Stealing
Pasquotank County

State of North Carolina }
Pasquotank County }

At a Special Court held at the Court House in Nixonton the sixteenth Day of November in the year of our Lord one Thousand Seven hundred & Ninety for the Tryall of a Negro man Slave the property of [?] named Dick where being Charged with Feloniously by Stealing & Taking of the House of Kiziah Carver Sundry Goods the Property of the said Kiziah Carver

Present the Worshipfull Justices

Justices: Robert McMorine, William Jordan, William Lane.

Gentl., Freeholders, Owners of Slaves: Ambros Knox, Thomas Ackis, Devotion Davis Junr., Enoch Overman.

The above Gentlemen Justices of the Peace and Gentl being Qualified agreeable to Law Took their Seats -- & Ordered that the prisoner Dick be Brought to the Barr -- Dick Being Brought to the Barr his Sundry Charges being read to him he pleaded Guilty & the Court then ordered that the Witneses Both against and for the prisoner be Sworn, whereas appeared and after being Qualified agreeable gave in their Several Witnesses To Say Hezekiah Carver & Thomas Brothers. Ordered that the Shariff take Negro Man Dick and him Carry to the publick Whiping Post and there give him twenty Seven Lashes on his bare Back well laid on and then put him in the [?] there to stand for half hour and him to keep into Custody Till all the Cost is paid.

Robt. McMorine, Wm Jordan, William Lane, Ambrose Knox, Enoch Overman, Thomas Ackis, Devotion Davis

****

State Vs. Negro Nero [1790]
Criminal Action
Felony, Stealing
Pasquotank County

Pasquotank County }

At a Special Court begun and held in the Court House at Nixonton The Second day of February in the year of our Lord one Thousand Seven Hundred & Ninety for the Tryall of Negro Man Nero the property of Joshua Markham of the said County who stands charg'd for feloniously Stealing Takeing & Carrying away one hog the property of James Leonard of the County

Present the Worshipfull Justices

Justices: Joseph Keaton, William Jordan, William Lane.

Gentlemen, Owners of Slaves: Demsey Connor, Devotion Davis, James Barns, Thos Davis.

The above Gentlemen after being Qualifyed Proceeded to the Tryall of the said Negro Man Nero and he was ordered Brought to the Barr and after being Brought & was Examined and he plead Guilty & Ordered that the said Negro Nero be carried to the Publick Whipping Post and there to receive Thirty Nine Lashes on his Bare Back and have his right Ear Cut off - Given under our hands & Seals the Day & Year above Written.

Demsey Connor (Seal), Devotion Davis (Seal), Jas. Barns (Seal), Thos Davis (Seal), J Keaton (Seal), Wm. Jordan (Seal), Wm Lane (Seal).

****

State Vs. Negro Doll & Pleasant [1792]
Criminal Action
Felony, Stealing
Pasquotank County

State of North Carolina }
Pasquotank County }

At a Court opened & held at the Court House in Nixonton on the 6th day of Decemr. 1792 agreeable to Act of Assembly in Such Cases made & Provided for the Tryall of Negro Woman Pleasant & Doll the property of James Leonard & Joseph Wilson of the State and County aforesaid for Running away & Telling Lyes -- & Stealing some **[?]** from James **[Smudged]**

Present the Worshipfull Justices

Justices: William Lane, Joseph Richardson, David Pritchard.

Gentlemen, Owners of Slaves: William Lufmen, John Sawyer, Frederick Pendleton, Benja Leonard.

The above Negro Woman Pleasant & Doll brought to the Barr and was arained and on their own Confession and the Testimony Given against them before the Said Court, It was Ordered that they receive Twelve Lashes each on their bear Back & then to be set at Liberty on Payment of Cost.

John Sawyer (Seal), Fred Pendleton (Seal), William Lufmen (Seal), David Pritchard (Seal), Joseph Richardson (Seal), Wm. Lane (Seal), Benja. Leonard (Seal).

****

State Vs. Negro Joe [1792]
Criminal Action
Inciting Slaves to Escape
Pasquotank County

Pasquotank County
Criminal Actions

State of North Carolina }
Pasquotank County }

At a Court begun opened and held at the Court House In Nixonton the 6th day of December 1792 agreeable to Act of Assembly in such Cases made & Provided for the Tryall of Negro Man Joe the Property of Britton Brown in Sounth Hampton County, State of Virginia for Indeavouring to Seduce Sundry negros Belonging to the Inhabitants of Pasquotank County to make them Escape to the North.

Present The Worshipful Justices

Justices: William Lane, Joseph Richardson, David Pritchard.

Gentlemen, Owners of Slaves: William Lufman, John Sawyer, Benj. Leonard, Frederick Pendleton.

The above Negro Man Joe being Brought to the Barr and was arained and on his own Confession and the Testimony Given against him before the said Court, It was Ordered that he receive Twenty five Lashes on his Bear Back and then to be carried Back to the Goal and there to continue under the Direction of the Sheriff & Jailor agreeable to Law

John Sawyer (Seal), Wm. Lufman (Seal), Fred Pendleton (Seal), B. Leonard (Seal), David Pritchard (Seal), Jos. Richardson (Seal), Wm Lane (Seal).

****

State Vs. Negro George [1792]
Criminal Action
Felony, Stealing
Pasquotank County

North Carolina }
Pasquotank County }

At a Court begun opened & held at The Court House in Nixonton the 6th day of Decemr. 1792 agreeable to act of Assembly in such Case made and provided for a Negro man George the Property of Tabitha Marsh[?] of Caswell County in the aforesaid State for Stealing of a Hogg & a Shirt from Joshua White.

Present the Worshipful Justices

Justices: William Lane, Joseph Richardson, David Pritchard.

Gentlemen, Owners of Slaves: William Lufman, John Sawyer, Benj. Leonard, Frederick Pendleton.

The above Negro Man George being brought to the Barr and was arained and on his own Confession & the Testimony gave against him he was by the said Court Ordered to be carried to the Publick Whipping Post and there receive on his Bare Back Twenty Lashes and then carried back to the Goal & to be under the Directions of the Sheriff & Goalar agreeable to Law.

Wm Lufman (Seal), Jn. Sawyer (Seal), Fred Pendleton (Seal), B. Leonard (Seal), David Pritchard (Seal), Wm. Lane (Seal), Jos. Richardson (Seal).

****

State Vs. Negro Billy [1792]
Criminal Action
Felony, Stealing
Pasquotank County

North Carolina }
Pasquotank County }

At a Court begun opened and held In Pasquotank County in the Court House in Nixonton the 6th day of Decemr. 1792 agreeable to Act of Assembly in such Cases made & Provided for the Tryal of a Negro Man Billy the property of Samuel Brown **[Lamuel?]** of the County of Hertford in State aforesaif for Stealing of Leather from Robert Rainer & a great Coat from James Overman.

Present the Worshipfull Justices

Justices: William Lane, Joseph Richardson, David Pritchard.

Gentlemen, Owners of Slaves: William Lufman Senr., John Sawyer, Benjamin Leonard, Frederick Pendleton.

The above Negro Man Billy being Brought to the Barr and on his own Confession and the Testimony given against him before the said Court He was oedered that he receive Thirty Nine Lashes on his Bare Back and then to be carried Back to the Goal and there Continue under the Directions of the Sheriff & Goaler agreeable to Law.

Wm. Lufman (Seal), Jno. Sawyer (Seal), Fred Pendleton (Seal), B Leonard (Seal), David Pritchard (Seal), Jos Richardson (Seal), Wm Lane (Seal).

****

State Vs. Negro Aaron [1793]
Criminal Action
Felony, Stealing
Pasquotank County

State of North Carolina }
Pasquotank County }

The Worshipfull William Jordan, John Lane & Joseph Scott at a Special Court held this day in the Court House of the said County Agreeable to an Act of Assembly pass'd the Second day of December in the year of our Lord God One Thousand Seven hundred and Ninety Three for the Trial of Negroes Aaron a Negro Man the Property of Will Farange Merchant of the said County who being accused and Committed to the Goal of the County by William Lane Esquire the eighth day of June for Feloniously Stealing and takeing away Sundry Goods The Property of John Shaw & Co. of [?] Value.

The Following Persons being Summoned by the Sheriff of the County for the trial of Said said Slave, Fredk. Sawyer, Holland Lockwood, John McDonald, Samuel Palen, John A Jordan, John Stevenson, James Perry, Benj Davis, Benj. Lowry, Robert Pendleton, John Bailey and Devotion Davis Junr. Who being impannelled and Sworn Say that the Said Negro Man Aaron is not Guilty Do Says Fed Sawyer Forman. Ordered that the

Cost of the Prosecution be paid by the County and that the Clerk of the County make a County Charge of the same and Number the same in his Books. The aforesaid orders were Read & **[Smudged]**
Test, Enoch Relfe, Clk.

****

State Vs. Negro Will [1793]
Criminal Action
Felony, Stealing
Pasquotank County

Pasquotank County }
} Decr. 7th 1793

At a Special Court held this day for the Tryall of Negro Man by the name of Will for feloniously Stealing and Takeing one hog the property of Solomon Pool.

Present

Justices: Bartley Jackson, Thaddeus Freshwater, Josiah Perry.

Gentlemen, Owners of Slaves: Reuben Davis, Saml. Stewart, Devotion Davis, Simon Leary

Who being sworn to Tryd the sd. Negro man Will and Will being set to the Barr and Plead not Guilty. The Court after the Examination of Sundry Witenesses do say that the said negro man Will is Guilty of the Charge against him. And do order and adjudge that the said negro man Will Receive Thirty Nine Lashes on his Bare Back at the Whipping Post Immediately and that his Master pay all lawful Costs, Given under our hands & Seals the day and year above Written.

Bartley Jackson (Seal), Joshua Perry (Seal), Thadeus Freshwater (Seal), Devotion Davis (Seal), Saml. Stewart (Seal), Simon Leary (Seal).

****

State Vs. Sundry Negros [1795]

Criminal Action
Arson
Pasquotank County

State of North Carolina }
Pasqtk County }

Whereas Complaint hath been made by John Archdale Jordan to me Joseph Scott one of the Justices of the Peace for the said County that Dick, a Slave belonging to the Estate of Joseph Scott Dec'd & Pomp a Slave belonging to William Jordan & Ben a Slave belonging to Lemuel Palin, that has Great Cause to Suspect the said Negroes of having Willfully & feloniously set fire to a Barn Containing a Quantity of Oats & Flax which was burnt on Wednesday night the Twenty nineth of July Last -- These are in the name of the State to Command you to bring the Said negroes to wit; Dick, Pomp, Ben & Bryan, before me or some other Justice of the said County, to be dealt with as the Law directs, Given under my hand & Seal the 11th August 1795.
J. Scott, JP

Pasquotank County }

At a Special Court begun opened & held at the Court House in Nixonton This 25th day of August in the Year 1795 agreeable to the Act of the Genl. Assembly in such cases made and Provided For the Tryall of Sundry Slaves for Feloniously Setting Fire and Burning Down the Out House of John A Jordan.

Present The Worshipfull Justices

Justices: Rowan Howett, William Lane, Josiah Perry

The said Proclamation be made there **[Faded]** Return the Following **[Faded]** to Serve as Jurors to Witt

1. John Mullen, 2. John Commander, 3. Joseph Relfe, 4. Holland Lockwood, 5. William **[?]**, 6. William Banks, 7. Benjamin Lowry, 8.William Farange, 9. Joseph Commander Senr., 10. Joseph Commander Junr., 11. Devotion Davis, 12. Hugh Knox, 13. William Stott , 14. John Brouher**[?]**, 15. Thomas Davis, 16. Patrick Pool, 17. Joab Jackson, 18.

Benj. Davis, 19. Samuel Whedbee, 20. William Lufman, 21. Fredk Pendleton, 22. Fredk B Sawyer, 23. John Smithson, 24. Caleb Pendleton.

Negro Man Dick being Brought to the Barr who being Charged with the felony of Burning the house of John A Jordan Being Arrained Pleads not Guilty and for his Tryall he doth Put him self upon God and his Country and the following Persons whereas the Jurors for his Tryall and were duly Qualified to Wit: Joab Jackson, Fredk B Sawyer, John L. Bosher, William Stott, Frederick Pendleton, Patrick Pool, Caleb Pendleton, William Banks, John Mullen, Joseph Commander Junr., Benjamin Davis, Joseph Relfe Say upon their oaths that he is not Guilty of the Felony he is charged with in the Warrant

Negro Pompy and Benjamin Being Brought to the Bar who being Charged With Concerned in the Fellony of Burning the house and no person appeared to Prosecute. It is Ordered by the Court rendered that they be Discharged, and that the County pay the Charges and all Expences of this Court. The aforesaid orders were read and [?] the Following Genl. Justices. Rowan Howett, Wm. Lane, & J Perry.

****

State Vs. Negro Frank [1798]
Criminal Action
Attempted Rape
Pasquotank County

To the Sheriff of the County of Pasquotank

I herewith Send you the Body of Negro Frank (Said to be the Property of the Orphans of William Robinson Dec'd being Charged with Attempting a Rape on Peninah Wood Daughter of Thomas Wood, And I do hereby Command you to receive him into the Jail of your County & him Safely Keep without Bail or Mainprize untill he be from thence Discharged by due Course of Law -- Given under my hand & Seal this 30th July 1798.
Jos. Lane
Thos. Wood Prosecutor

Mr. Aaron Morris

Sir you are hearby Noticed that there is a Negro Man by the name of Frank Said to be the Property of the Orphans of William Robertson

which you are Guardian or Executor to the Estate which Negro is now in Custidy and Charged with attempting a Rape on the Body of Peneah Wood Daughter of Thomas Wood Which is to be Tried agreeable to act of Assembly on Satturday the 11th August Next at the Court in Nixonton you may attend if you think **[?]**
Pasquotank County
30 July 1798
J Banks, DS

****

State Vs. Negro David [No Date]
Criminal Action
Felony, Stealing
Pasquotank County

North Carolina }
Pasquotank County }

At a Special Court Begun opened & held at the Court House in Windfield according to Act of Assembly in such case made & Provided in for the Tryall of Negro Man David the Property of John Watkins of the County & Province aforesaid, for feloniously Breaking open a house & taking therefrom, Bacon to the value of Twenty Shillings or upwards the Property of Mr. John Crawford of said County.

Present the Worshipfull Justices

Justices: Abraham Symons, Thomas Redding, Edward Evergan.

Gentlemen, Owners of Slaves: Joseph Redding, Henry Pendleton, Thomas Relfe, Spencer Ripley.

The Above Negro man David being tried was found Guilty & was valued to the sum of Seventy Pounds **[Faded]** Money. Ordered that the said negro David be taken to the publick Whipping post there to have his right ear nailed to the pillow & Cut off before which he shall have Laid on' on his Bare Back fifty Lashes.

Given under our hands & Seals this Day above Written.

A. Symons (Seal), Tho Reding (Seal), Edwd. Everigan (Seal), Thomas Relfe (Seal), Henry Pendleton (Seal), Spencer Ripley (Seal), Jos. Reding (Seal).

****

State Vs. Negro Aaron [1809]
Criminal Action
Hiring his own Time
Pasquotank County

State of North Carolina } Court of Pleas & Quarter Sessions
Pasquotank County } September Term 1809

The Jurors for the State upon their oaths of their knowledge present That negro slave Aaron the property of Joseph Keaton now is & for a long time past, to wit, from the first day of January in the year of our Lord one thousand eight hundred and nine up to the day of taking this inquisition on the sixth day of September in the same year at Pasquotank County aforesaid hath been permitted by his said Master to go at large having hired his time contrary to the Act of the General Assembly in such cases made & provided, to the evil example of all others in the like cases offending and against the peace & dignity of the State.
Will Blair, Attorney for the State.

State of North Carolina
To the Sheriff of Pasquotank County, Greeting:
You are hereby commanded to take the body of Negro Aaron a Slave belonging to Joseph Keaton Esquire, if to be found in your bailiwick, and him safely keep, so that you have him before the Justices of the County Court of Pleas and Quarter Sessions, at the next Court, to be held for the County of Pasquotank, at the Court House in Elizabeth City, on the first Monday in December next, who from the information of the Grand Jury is Running at large and is Supposed to have hired his own time Contrary to an Act of Assembly in Such Cases provided. Herein fail not; and have you then and there this writ. Witness William Templeman Muse, Clerk of the said Court, at Elizabeth City, the 9th day of September in the XXX4 year of our Independence, Anno Dom. 1809.
Issued 26th day of September 1809.
Will T. Muse, Clk.

State of North Carolina,
To the Sheriff of Pasquotank County, Greeting:
You are hereby commanded to summon Benoni Cartwright personally to be and appear before the Justices of the County Court of Pleas and Quarter Sessions, at the next Court, to be held for the County of Pasquotank, at the Court House in Elizabeth City, on the first Monday in December next; then and there to testify and the truth to say in behalf of the State in a certain matter of controversy in the said Court depending, and then and there to be tried, wherein The State is Plaintiff, and Negro Aaron the Property of Joseph Keaton is Defendant. And this you shall in no wise omit, under the penalty by law enjoined, Witness William Templemam Muse, Clerk of the said Court, at Elizabeth City, the 9th day of September in the XXX4 year of our Independence, Anno Dom. 1809.
Issued the 20th day of September 1809.
Will T. Muse, Clk.

To the Worshipful Court of Pasquotank County this may Certify that I Axcept of the notice of the Tryal of my Negro Man Aaron that was prested by the Grand Jury at the Last Term & will be tried at Decr. Term next.
10th of Novr. 1809
J. Keaton.

We the Grand Jurors present negroe Aaron the property of Joseph Keaton for Running at large and supposed to hire his time id trading for him self by Information of Benoni Cartwright.

The State Vs. Negro Aaron } Pasquotank County Court
} December Term, 1809

These are to Certify, that Benoni Cartwright hath attended this Court one day this Term as a Witness for the State in this Suit.

Attending one day at four shillings per day	4
Travelling 30 miles at eight shillings per thirty miles	8
Ferriages	
Certificate and Probate	8
	£.12.8

****

Pasquotank County Criminal Actions

State Vs. Negro Prince [1814]
Criminal Action
Hiring his own Time
Pasquotank County

State of North Carolina }
Pasquotank County } June term 1814

The Jurors for the State upon their oaths present that Negro Prince the property of Deborah Jennings late of the County of Pasquotank with force and arms since 1st Oct. 1813 and from that time up to the finding of this inquisition, has been going at large in the County aforesd. Hiring his own time, Contrary to Act of Assembly in such Cases made & provided, and Agt. The peace & Dignity of the State.
Jas. Norfleet, Solr. County

****

State Vs. Negro Moses [1814]
Criminal Action
Arson
Pasquotank County

State of North Carolina }
Pasquotank County }

To any lawful Officer to Execute.
Whereas Ambrose Knowle and William Crutch hath Complained to us John Mullen Esquire and Thomas Jordan Esquire two of the Justices of the Peace for this County that Moses the Property of Col. Thomas Banks, did on the 25th Inst. Wilfully and feloniously set fire to a quantity of Flax Oats Fodder & of them the said Ambrose Knowle and William Crutch, with intent to burn and destroy the same -- These are in the name of the State to Command you to bring the said Moses before us, or some other Justice of this County to be dealt with as the law directs.

Given under our hands and Seals the 27th day of October 1814.
Benjamin B Loury and William C. George Witness
Aaron, Witness
Thomas Jordan (Seal), John Mullen (Seal)

Pasquotank County
Criminal Actions

October 28th 1814. The Defendant Moses having been brought before us, and it Appearing to be a Capital Offence, Ordered that he be Committed to Jail for further trial with lawful Costs.
John Mullen & Thomas Jordan
Executed by Wm. Freshwater.

State of North Carolina
To the Sheriff of Pasquotank County, Greeting:
You are hereby commanded to summon Nehimiah Pendleton, Thomas S. Jordan & William Gaskins personally to appear before the Justices of our County Court of Pleas and Quarter Sessions, at the Court house in Elizabeth City, immediately, then and there to testify and the truth to say, in behalf us our Solicitor Tho. **[Faded]** in a certain matter of controversy in the said Court depending, and then and there to be tried, wherein We are Plaintiffs & Negroe Moses the property of Tho. Banks Esq. Is Defendant; and this you shall in no wise omit, under the penalty by law enjoined -- Witness William Templeman Muse, Clerk of the said Court, at Elizabeth City, the 6th day of december in the 39th year of our Independence, Anno Dom. 1814.
Will T. Muse, Clk.

****

State Vs. Negro Sanders [1820]
Criminal Action
Destroying Property
Pasquotank County

James S. Relfe & Timothy Pendleton
Warrant for Negro Slave Sanders
Executed by J.K. Jordan

State of North Carolina }
Pasquotank County } To any lawful Officer to Execute & return.

Whereas James S. Relfe & Timothy Pendleton have complaint on oath before me John C. Ehringhaus, one of the Justices of the Peace for said County, that Negro Slave Sanders the property of Lydia Sawyer **[?]** them some private injury such as to destroy their property. These are

therefore to command You to apprehend the said Negro Slave Sanders and him have before some Justice of the Peace for said County to be dealt with agreeable to law. Given under my hand & Seal at my Office in Elizabeth City September the 7th 1820.
Summons for Mordacai Gregory
John C. Ehringhaus, (Seal)

State of North Carolina }
Pasquotank County } To the Jailor of said County, Greeting:

The within named defendant, not being able to give Security for his good behaviour, You are therefore commanded to receive the said Negro Slave Sanders & him safely keep untill he find two goos securities in the sum of two hundred and fifty pounds for good behaviour **[Torn].** To the next County Court to be held for this County on the first Monday of December next. Given under our hand & Seal this 8th September 1820.
John C. Ehringhaus, JP & Leml. Moore, JP.

State of North Carolina }
Pasquotank County }

Agreeable to the annexed order on the 23rd day of Apl. In the year of our Lord 1821, personally came before me W. T. Relfe one of the Justices of the said County Liddia Sawyer of the County aforesaid & acknowledged that she is indebted to the State in the sum of Two hundred dollars to be levied of her goods & Chattels lands & Tenements, to the use of the State if default is made in the performance of the condition herein under written.

The Condition of the above recognizance is such that if the above bounden Liddia Sawyer shall Cause negro Sandy her property to appear before the Justices of the County Court of Pleas & Quarter Sessions to be held for the County aforesaid at the Court House in Elizabeth City on the first Monday in June next to do & receive what shall be then & there enjoined agst said negro Sandy by the said Court & that she suffer him not to depart the same with out leave in the mean time she Cause him the said negro Sandy to keep the peace towards the good people of this State but especially toward Timothy Pendleton & Jas. S. Relfe then the above recognizance to be void otherwise to remain in full force & virtue.
Teste, Wm. T Relfe
Her

Liddia X Sawyer (Seal)
Mark

State of North Carolina,
To the Sheriff of Pasquotank County, greeting:
You are hereby commanded to summon Joseph Sawyer personally to appear before the Justices of our County Court of Pleas and Quarter Sessions, at the Court House in Elizabeth City, immediately, then and there to testify and the truth to say, in behalf of the State in a certain matter of controversy in the said Court depending, and then and there to be tried, wherein the State is Plaintiff, and Negro Sanders the property of Lydia Sawyer is Defendant; and this you shall in no wise omit, under the penalty by law enjoined. Witness William Templeman Muse, Clerk of the said Court **[Torn]** year of our Indepencence, Anno Dom. 1820.
Will T. Muse, Clk.

State Vs. Negro Sanders, March Term 1821

Ordered that negro Sanders be discharged upon Lydia Sawyer giving bond in the sum of $200 to be taken before any Majistrate of the County for the good behaviour of said Negro until said appearance at next Court and Costs
Test, Richard Muse, DC

****

State Vs. Negro Bob [1831]
Criminal Action
Hiring his own Time
Pasquotank County

State of North Carolina }
Pasquotank County } To any Lawfull Officer to Execute.

We are given to understand that Negro Man Bob the property of Saml. Halstead Esqr. is now hiring his time and is not under the protection of any person and that his conduct has been of such a nature as to excite some suspicion as to his evil **[?]** These are there fore to command you forthwith to arrest said Slave and him have before me or some other Justice

of the Peace for said County to be further dealt with. Given under my hand & Seal at Eliza City 28th August 1831.
Leml Moore (Seal) & Jas Relfe (Seal).

State of North Carolina }
Pasqr County } to the Jailor of said County

You are hereby Commanded to receive the within named Bob in your Jail and him safely Keep untill he shall be discharged agreable to Law, Given under my hand & Seal this 28th August 1831.
Leml Moore (Seal) & Jas S. Relfe (Seal).

****

State Vs. Nancy Jefferson [1833]
Criminal Action
Illegal Migration
Pasquotank County

State of North Carolina }
Pasquotank County } To any lawful Officer to execute and Return.

Whereas information has been lodged with me that one Nancy Jefferson a free negro has migrated into this State from the State of Virginia contrary to the Act of Assembly passed in the Year 1826, which Act is entitled "An Act to prevent free persons of colour from Migrating into this State, for the good government of such persons resident in the State and for other purposes " these are therefore to command you to inform the said Nancy Jefferson that she must remove out of this State within Twenty days after the date of this warrant otherwise she will be subject to incur the penalty of $500 inacted by said act -- herein fail not to make due return agreeable to Law -- Given under my hand and Seal at Elizabeth City this 15th day of August A.D. 1833.
Jas S. Relfe, JP (Seal).

****

State Vs. Betsey Wilson [1833]
Criminal Action
Ilegal Migration

Pasquotank County

State of North Carolina } To any lawful Officer to Execute & Return.
Pasquotank county }

Whereas information has been lodged with me that one Betsey Wilson a free negro has migrated into this State from the State of Virginia contrary to the Act of Assembly passed in the year 1826 which Act is Intitled "An Act to prevent free persons of Colour from Migrating into this State, for the good Government of such persons residents in the State and for other persons" These are therefore to command you to inform the said Betsy Wilson that she must remove out of this State within Twenty days after the date of this Warrant otherwise she will be subject to & incur the penalty of $500 inflicted by said Act -- Given under my hand and Seal at Elizabeth City this 15th day of August A.D. 1833.
Jas. S. Relfe, JP (Seal).

****

State Vs. Benjamin Allin [1844]
Criminal Action
Felony, Stealing
Pasquotank County

State of North Carolina
Pasquotank County

To Joseph Shaw for want of a a Legal officer.

Whereas James White of the State and in the County aforesaid free Man of Colour hath this day made information and complaint upon oath before me James W. Mullen Esquire one of the Justices pf the Peace for the said County that on the 7th day of the present month divers goods of him the said James White to wit mony have feloniously been stolen , taken and carried away from the house of him the said James White in the County aforesaid and that he hath just cause to suspect and doth suspect that Benjamin Allin of the County aforesaid free man of colour feloniously did steal take and carry away the same, These are therefore to command you to apprehend him the said Benjamin Allin and to bring him before me or some other Justice of the Peace of the County aforesaid to answer unto

the said information and Complaint, and to be further dealt with according to Law. Here in fail not, given under my hand and Seal this Jny 22nd 1844.
James W. Mullen (Seal)

State of North Carolina
To the Sheriff of Pasquotank County, Greeting:
You are hereby commanded to summon John Bailey Jr. personally to be and appear before the Justices of the County Court of Pleas and Quarter Sessions, at the Court House in Elizabeth City, immediately, then and there to testify and the truth to say in behalf of Ben Allin in a certain matter of controversy in said Court therein depending, and then and there to be tried, wherein, the State is Plaintiff, and Ben Allin is Defendant. And this you shall in no wise omit, under the penalty by law enjoined.

Witness W.W. Griffin, Clerk of our said Court, at Elizabeth City, the 2nd day of Sept. in the LXVII II year of our Independence, Anno Domini 1844.
Issued the 2nd day of Sept. 1844
W.W. Griffin, Clk.

State, Warrant for Benjamin Allen

You are hereby ordered to summons as witnesses to give testimony in this process to be present at the time of trial, Joseph Commander, Robert Raper, John Baily, and George the property of Wilson Williams.
The above witnesses have been sworn by Jos B. Shaw.

The within **[?]** has been duly examined by Joseph Shaw and the within Charged Benjamin Allen **[Faded]** for his appearance at the next Court to answer to the within charge where in he has been delivered out of custody by giving sufficient secirity August 26th 1844
James W. Mullen, JP

State of North Carolina }
Pasquotank County }

Be it remembered that on the 26th day of August in the year of our Lord one thousand eight hundred and forty four Benjamin Allen of Colour of the County aforesaid and Robert Raper and Phillip Cohoon both of the aforesaid County came before me James W. Mullen one of the Justices of the peace for the said County and severally acknowledged themselves to owe to the State of North Carolina that is to say the said Benjamin Allin fifty dollars **[Faded]** Robert Raper and Phillip Cohoon twenty five dollars **[?]** to be respectively levied of their lands and Tenements goods and chattels if the said Benj Allin shall make defalt in the performance of the **[?]**. The conditions of this recognizance is such that if the within bound Benjamin Allen shall personally appear before the Justices of the court of please and quarter sessions in and for the said County at the next court of Pleas and Quarter Sessions to be held for the County at Elizabeth City the first Monday in September next or the Judges of the Superior Court of Law to be held for district at the court house in Elizabeth City on the 4th Monday after the 4th Monday in September next for ans concerning the feloniously taking and Stealing of money the property of James White of colour of the county aforesaid with the suspicion whereof the said Benj Allin stands charged before me the said justice & to do and **[Faded]** what shall be by the said Court then and there enjoined him and shall not depart the Court without leave then the above written recognizance to be void. In the presence of

Benjamin X Allen (Seal)
Robert Raper (Seal)
Phillip A.R.C.Cohoon (Seal)

****

State Vs. Elizabeth Hall [1855]
Criminal Action
Ilegal Cohabitation
Pasquotank County

North Carolina }
Pasquotank County }

Know all men by these Presents. That we Elizabeth Hall & E.W. Sanders acknowledge ourselves indebted to the State aforesaid, in the full and just sum of Fifty dollars each, to be levied on our Goods and Chattels, Lands and Tenements; but nevertheless to be void if the above bound Elizabeth Hall make their personal appearance before the Judge of the Superior Court, in and for the County of Pasquotank to be held on the Fourth Monday after the Fourth Monday in Sept. next, and stand and abide by the Judgment of the said Court and not depart without leave first had and obtained from the said Court, otherwise to remain in full force and virtue.

Acknowledged before me, this 6th day of Oct. 1855

T.W. Banks
Elizabeth X Hall (Seal)
E. W. Sanders (Seal)

Witnesses, Augustus a Slave of Mrs. Martin, Robert A. Sar[?], W.P. Matthews, Elizabeth [**Faded**], Sworn & Sent.
F.M. Charles, Clk.
Susan Hall of Color, A H Burches, A True Bill, Joseph Jennings, Foreman.

Pasquotank County } Superior Court of Law
SS } Spring Term 1855

The Jurors for the State upon their oath present that Elizabeth Hall, being a free woman of color, late of said County, at and in Pasquotank County aforesaid, on the 1st day of April, in the year 1855 did cohabit and live, and thence continually hitherto hath cohabited and lived and still do cohabit and live together as man and wife, with a certain negro slave, a man, named Augustus and that said cohabiting and living together took place since the 1st day of March AD 1845 contrary to the form of the Statute in such case made and provided and against the peace and dignity of the State.

And the Jurors aforesaid upon their oath aforesaid do further present that the said Elizabeth Hall, a free woman of Color as aforesaid, afterwards to wit on the 1st day of January, in the year 1855 at and in Pasquotank County aforesaid, did cohabit and live, and thence hitherto up to the taking this inquisition hath cohabited and lived, and still does cohabit and live together as man and wife, with one Augustus, a man and a slave, at said County, and that said cohabiting and living together took place since the 1st day of March A. D. 1845, Contrary to the form of the Statute in such case made and provided and against the peace and dignity of the State.
W. N. H. Smith, Solr.

State of North Carolina

To the Sheriff of Pasquotank County, Greeting:
You are hereby commanded to summon Mrs. Sophia Martin, to produce her slave Augustus personally to be and appear before the Judge of the Superior Court of Law, at the next Court, to be held for the County of Pasquotank, at the Court House in Elizabeth City, on the fourth Monday after the fourth Monday in March next, then and there to testify and the truth to say in behalf of the State in a certain matter of controversy in the said Court depending, and then and there to be tried, wherein the State is Plaintiff and Eliz. Hall is Defendant; and this you shall in no wise omit, under the penalty by law enjoined.

Witness, F. M. Charles, Clerk of the said Court, at Elizabeth City, the fourth Monday after the fourth Monday in September in the 80 year of our Independence, Anno Domini 1855.
Issued the 1st day of Novr. 1855.
F.M. Charles, Clerk.

State of North Carolina

To the Sheriff of Pasquotank County, Greeting:
You are hereby commanded to summon Mrs S. Martin to produce her slave Augustus, Robert A. Sawyer, W.P. Matthews, Susan Hall (of Col.), A.H. Burches personally to be and appear before the Judge of the Superior Court of Law, at the next Court, to be held for the County of Pasquotank, at the Court House in Elizabeth City, on the fourth Monday after the fourth Monday in September next, then and there to testify and the truth to say in behalf of the State in a certain matter of controversy in the said Court depending, and then and there to be tried, wherein the State is Plaintiff and Elizabeth Hall is Defendant; and this you shall in no wise omit, under the penalty by law enjoined.

Witness F.M. Charles, Clerk of the said Court, at Elizabeth City, the fourth Monday after the fourth Monday in March in the 79th year of our Independence, Anno Domini, 1855.
Issued the 13th day of June 1855.
F.M. Charles, Clerk.

State of North Carolina

To the Sheriff of Pasquotank County, Greeting:
You are hereby commanded to summon W.P. Matthews personally to be and appear before Grand Jury at the next Court to be held for the County of

Pasquotank, at the Court House in Elizabeth City, on the fourth Monday after the fourth Monday in March, then and there to testify and the truth to say in behalf of the State in a certain matter of controversy in the said Court depending, and then and there to be tried, wherein **[Blank]** Plaintiff and **[Blank]** is Defendant; and this you shall in no wise omit, under the penalty by law enjoined.

Witness F.M. Charles, Clerk of the said Court, at Elizabeth City, the fourth Monday after the fourth Monday in Sept. in the 79th year of our Independence, Anno Domini 1854.
Issued the 28th day of April 1855.
F.M. Charles, Clerk

North Carolina

To the Sheriff of Pasquotank County, Greeting:
You are hereby commanded to take the body of Elizabeth Hall [if to be found in your bailiwick] and her safely keep, so that you have her before the Judge of the Superior Court of Law, to be held for the County of Pasquotank, at the Court House in Elizabeth City, on the fourth Monday after the fourth Monday in Sept. next; then and there to answer unto the State of North Carolina to a charge of misdemeanor brought against her.

Herein fail not, and have you then and there this writ. Witness, F.M. Charles, Clerk of the said Court at Elizabeth City, the fourth Monday after the Fourth Monday of March in the 79th year of our Independence, Anno Domini, 1855.
Issued the 13th day of June 1855.
F.M. Charles, Clerk.

The Grand Jurors on their oaths present Augustus, Slave of Mrs. Sophia S. Martin for Marrying or living together as man & Wife a free woman of Color by the name of Elizabeth Hall at the present time.
Witneses, Robert A. Sawyer, J Fearing Jr. & Wm. P Matthews..

State of North Carolina, Pasquotank County
State Vs. Eliz. (of Col.)
} Superior Court of Law
} Fall Term 1855
These certify, that R.A. Sawyer hath attended this Court

2 days this Term, as a witness for the State in this suit.

Attending 2 days at **[Blank]** shillings per thirty miles	1.20
Travelling **[Blank]** miles at six shillings per thirty miles	**[Blank]**
Ferriages	
Certificate and Probate	.10
	$1.30

Sworn to before me, F.M. Charles, Clk

State of North Carolina, Pasquotank County
State Vs. Elizabeth Hall
} Superior Court of Law
} Fall Term 1855
These certify that W.P. Matthews hath attended this Court
2 days this Term, as a Witness for the State in this suit.

Attending 2 days at six shillings per day	1.20
Travelling **[Blank]** miles at six shillings per thirty miles	
Ferriages	
Certificate and Probate	.10
	1.30

Certified to before me F.M. Charles, Clerk

State of North Carolina -- Pasquotank County
State Vs. Elizabeth Hall
} Superior Court of Law
} Spring Term 1856
These certify, that Robt Sawyer hath attended this Court
1 day this Term, as a witness for the State in this suit

Attending 1 day at six shillings per day	.60
Travelling **[Blank]** miles at six shillings per 30 miles	
Ferriages	
Certificate	.10
	.70

Sworn to before me F. M. Charles , Clerk

State of North Carolina - Pasquotank County
State Vs. Eliz. Hall
} Superior Court of Law.

} **[Blank]** Term 1855

These certify that W.P. Matthews hath attended this Court
Two days this Term as a witness for the State in this suit.

Attending 2 days at six shillings per 30 miles	1.20
Travelling **[Blank]** miles at six shillings per 30 miles	
Ferriages	
Certificate	.10
	1.30

Sworn to before me **[Blank]**

****

State Vs. Susan Hall [1855]
Criminal Action
Ilegal Cohabitation
Pasquotank County

Pasquotank County } Superior Court of Law
SS } Spring Term 1855

The Jurors for the State upon their oath present that Susan Hall, a free woman of Color, late of said County, on the 1st day of January in the year 1855 did cohabit and live, and thence continually hitherto hath cohabited and lived, and still does cohabit and live together as man and wife with one Richard, Alias, Dick, a man and a slave, at and in Pasquotank County aforesaid, and that said cohabiting and living commence since the 1st day of March 1845, contrary to the form of the statute in such case made and provided and against the peace and dignity of the State.

And the jurors aforesaid upon their oath aforesaid do further present that the said Susan Hall a free woman of color, afterwards to wit on the said 1st day of January, in the year 1855, did, and thence up to the taking this inquisition hath lived and cohabited, and still does live and cohabit, at the county aforesaid, together as man and wife with one Dick alias Richard a man and a slave and that said cohabiting and living together commenced since the 1st day of March A.D., contrary to the form of the Statute provided in such cases made.

Pasquotank County
Criminal Actions

The Grand Jurors on their oaths, present Richard, Slave of Mrs Sophia S. Martin for Marrying or living together as man & wife a free woman of color by the name of Susan Hall at the present time
Witneses Robert A. Sawyer, J Fearing Jr., & Wm. Mathews

North Carolina

To the Sheriff of Pasquotank County, Greeting:

You are hereby commanded to take the body of Susan Hall [if to be found in your bailiwick] and her safely keep, so that you have her before the Judge of the Superior Court of Law, to be held for the County of Pasquotank, at the Court House in Elizabeth City, on the fourth Monday after the fourth Monday in Sept. next; then and there to answer unto the State of North Carolina to a charge of Misdemeanor brought against her.

Herein fail not, and have you then and there this writ.

Witness F.M. Charles, Clerk of the said Court at Elizabeth City, the fourth Monday after the fourth Monday of March in the 79th year of our Independence, Anno Domini, 1855.
Issued the 13th day of June 1855
F.M. Charles, Clerk.

State of North Carolina

To the Sheriff of Pasquotank County, Greeting:

You are hereby commanded to summon R.A. Sawyer, J. Fearing, Elizabeth Hall (of col.) W.W. Griffin, & Dick alias a slave of Mrs. S. Martin personally to be and appear before the Judge of the Superior Court of Law, at the next Court, to be held for the County of Pasquotank, at the Court House in Elizabeth City, on the fourth Monday after the fourth Monday in September next, then and there to testify and the truth to say in behalf of the State in a certain matter of controversy in the said Court depending, and then and there to be tried, wherein the State is Plaintiff and Susan Hall is Defendant; and this you shall in no wise omit, under the penalty by law enjoined.

Witness F.M. Charles, Clerk of the said Court, at Elizabeth City, the fourth Monday after the fourth Monday in March in the 79th year of our Independence, Anno Domini, 1855.
Issued the 13th day of June 1855.
F.M. Charles, Clerk.

Pasquotank County
Criminal Actions

North Carolina - Pasquotank County

Know all men by these presents, That we Susan Hall & Wm. F. Martin acknowledge ourselves indebted to the State aforesaid, in the full and just sum of Fifty Dollars each, to be levied on our Goods and Chattels, Lands and Tenements; but nevertheless to be void if the above bound Susan Hall make her personal appearance before the Judge of the Superior Court in and for the County of Pasquotank to be held on the Fourth Monday after the Fourth Monday in Sept. next, and stand and abide by the Judgement of the said Court and not depart without leave first had and obtained from the said Court, otherwise to remain in full force and virtue.
Acknowledged before me, this 6th day of Oct. 1855
T. Banks

Her
Susan X Hall (Seal)
Mark
Wm F Martin (Seal)

State of North Carolina

To the Sheriff of Pasquotank County, Greeting:

You are hereby commanded to summon Mrs Sophia Martin, to produce her slave Richard personally to be and appear before the Judge of the Superior Court of Law, at the next Court, to be held for the County of Pasquotank, at the Court House in Elizabeth City, on the fourth Monday after the Fourth Monday in March next, then and there to testify and the truth to say in behalf of the State in a certain matter of controversy in the said Court depending, and then and there to be tried, wherein the State is Plaintiff and Susan Hall (of Color) is Defendant; and this you shall in no wise omit, under the penalty by law enjoined.

Witness F. M. Charles, Clerk of the said Court, at Elizabeth City, the fourth Monday after the Fourth Monday in September in the 80th year of our Independence, Anno Domini 1855
Issued 1st day of Nov. 1855
F.M. Charles, Clerk.

State of North Carolina -- Pasquotank County
State Vs. Susan Hall
}Superior Court of Law

Pasquotank County
Criminal Actions

} Spring Term 1856.
These certify, that Robt Sawyer hath attended this Court
1 day this Term, as a Witness for the State in this suit.

Attending 1 day at six shillings per day.	60
Travelling **[Blank]** miles at six shillings per 30 miles	
Certificate	.10
	.70

Sworn to before me, F.M. Charles, Clk

State of North Carolina -- Pasquotank County
State Vs. Susan Hall (of col.)
} Superior Court of Law
} Fall Term 1853
These certify that R.A. Sawyer hath attended this Court
2 days this Term, as a Witness for the State in this suit

Attending 2 days at six shillings per thirty miles	1.20
Travelling **[Blank]** miles at six shillings per thirty miles	
Ferriages	
Certificate and Probate	.10
	1.30

Certified to before me, F.M. Charles, Clerk

****

State Vs. Negro Jim [1860]
Criminal Action
Felony, Stealing
Pasquotank County

State of North Carolina
To the Sheriff of Pasquotank County, Greeting:
You are hereby commanded to take the body of Jim, a Slave the property of Wm Newbould (if to be found in your bailiwick) and him safely keep so that you have him before the Justices of the County Court of Pleas and Quarter Sessions, at the next Court to be held for the County of Pasquotank, at the Court House in Elizabeth City, on the first Monday of December next, then and there to answer unto the State of North Carolina, in a charge of Larceny. Herein fail not, and have you then and there this writ. Witness James W. Hinton, Clerk of the said Court at Elizabeth City

on the first Monday of Sept. in the 85th year of our Independence, Anno Domini 1860
Issued the 21st day of September 1860
JW Hinton, Clerk
By CG Elliott, D.C.

State of North Carolina
To the Sheriff of Pasquotank County, Greeting:
You are hereby commanded to summon Danl. Brite, & Jno. D. Hogarth personally to be and appear before the Justice of the County Court of Pleas and Quarter Sessions, at the next Court, to be held for the County of Pasquotank, at the Court House in Elizabeth City, on the first Monday in December next, then and there to testify and the truth to say in behalf of the State in a certain matter of controversy in the said Court Depending, and then and there to be tried, wherein the State is Plaintiff and Jim (a Slave) is Defendant. And this you shall in no wise omit, under the penalty by law enjoined. Witness, James W. Hinton, Clerk of the said Court at Elizabeth City, the first Monday of Sept. in the 85th year of our Independence, Anno Domini 1860.
Issued the 21st day of Sept. 1860.
J. W. Hinton, Clerk
By C.G. Elliott, DC

North Carolina } Ct. of Pleas & Qr. Sessions
Pasquotank County } Sept. Term, AD 1860

The Jurors for the State upon their oaths present that Jim, a Slave, the property of William Newbold, both late of Pasquotank County, with force and arms, in said County, on the first day of January A.D. 1860 some check muslin, handkerchief, shoes, coat and and so forth one shilling the value of one dollar of the goods and Chattels of [?] Overton, free man of color, feloniously did steal, take and carry away, against the peace and dignity of the State, and the Statute in such case made and provided.
Charles, Solr.

State of North Carolina
Pasquotank County

To any lawful Officer to execute, and return, (Within thirty days.) You are hereby commanded to arrest the body of James Mitchel and Rachael Mitchel and cause them to appear before me, or some other Justice of the Peace for said County, to answer the complaint of Jos. M. **[Faded]** in a plea of debt due by **[Faded]** the sum of thirty three dollars, & **[Blank]** cents, with interest from the 8th day of Sept. 1859. Herein fail not. Given under my hand and seal, this 21st day of November 1859.
W.W. Williams, JP (Seal)

Hertford May 12th 1860
Dr. Sir
At our Superior Court hear - the wife of Jim Mitchell of Col. against whom (Jim Mitchell & Wife) **[?]** return an appeal in my favor **[?]** last County Court, Saw Mr Brooks their Attorny when the following settlement was agreed upon.

Jim Mitchell & Wife Rachael are to pay all Cost **[Smudged]** as well as these there ascertain Amt. of Note at one year after its date -- then Credit it with $10 - and then ascertain Amount now due upon it - And take One day note payable to me for same less $4 -- which I am to be allowed them to **[?]** on paying my Costs -- Mr. Brooks requested me to write **[?]** the times so that when Mitchell & Wife go to town to Settle if - they might do so even in his Absence -- of Course I presume Mr. Brooks will.

****

Gholson Vs. Raper [1860]
Criminal Action
Crime not Given
Pasquotank County

Gholson Vs. Darius Raper

The deposition of Thos Gaskins taken by consent, on the 22nd day of August 1859, present, The plaintiff by his counsel, Geo. Brooks, The deposition being taken **[Smudged]** to be read as evidence in the above named cause, now pending in the Superior Court of Pasquotank, the said Gaskin being first duly sworn, deposes & says as follows -- to wit, says in the Month of February 1857, I sold a woman by the name of Ann, & her two youngest Children to D.D. Raper, one of whom is named Gilbert, & is the subject Matter in this suit, & says there was something the matter with Gilbert at the time I sold him to Mr. Raper that I knew of, that I had [?] however seen him for sometime, & had heard anything of his being sick. Early in March between the first & third, I rec'd a letter from Mr. Gholson, the Plaintiff in this cause, stating that he had purchased Ann, the Mother of Gilbert, & wishes to know at what price he could purchase Gilbert & also her other son George, still owned by me - who has, but one arm - I replied to the Plaintiff s letter, stating that Mr Raper the Defendant said that for the sale of uniting Gilbert with his Mother he could have him for three hundred dollars, tho he thought he was worth three hundred & twenty five or three hundred & fifty dolls; I also informed the Plaintiff that Mr. Raper said that the boy Gilbert was then a little sick, & he thought also that he was a little frost bitten, but thought he would be better in a few days, & able to travel, & I also stated in the same letter that my boy George also was sick, but was improving & would in a few days be able to travel, & that I would take for him one hundred & ten dollars, & that I would communicate to him when they both be able to travel. In a few days after writing the Plaintiff as above, I rec'd a letter from him, saying that he would take them at the price, if we, Raper & I would send them to Petersburg. I replied that he could take them if he would send for them, & we would pay half of the expence,if he would first send the money for them. I further stated in that letter that the boy George was well, & that Mr. Raper said that his boy would in his opinion, be well by the time he could send here for them. I think the letter last spoken of was dated about the 9th of March. Soon thereafter a Servant delivered to me a letter from Gholson dated March 17th 1857, in which Gholson stated that he had sent the bearer a Slave belonging to his Father from Petersburg to Elizabeth City for the two boys - George & Gilbert, & at the same time two bank checks, payable to me - one for three hundred dollars & one for one hundred & ten dollars. I was directed in the said letter to get Berry the Servant, back as soon as I could possibly. Four dollars & seventy five cents was the proportion of expences that was to be paid for Gilbert, which was handed by me to Berry under the direction of Gholson. The sane evening I Rec'd this letter by the hands of Berry, I sent my boy with a letter to Raper, informing him that Gholson had sent for the two boys, and the Servant was to return the next morning to Norfolk. The stage from Elizabeth City to Norfolk at the that season of the year left about sun rise. Raper lives about four miles from E. City, he brought the boy Gilbert the next Morning in time for the Stage; When the boy Gilbert came, he was seen to be wrapped up very well. He passed within twenty feet of me when on his way to the Stage & he seemed to be as the appearance of being a little feeble. The morning was clear, but very cold, but not near as cold as I have seen it before, and my impression is that the ground was froze. I do not remember any change of the weather that day, but at that season of the year, the weather is liable to sudden changes. I had not seen this boy Gilbert for from three weeks to a month, prior to his leaving in the Stage for Norfolk, & then only saw him as he was passing me, as described above. Raper took him in his possession a day or two after buying him from me. I have read the deposition of Martha E. Martin & Robert A. Gholson taken in this Cause in Petersburg & am satisfied that the boy Gilbert spoke of in thos depositions is the same boy sold by me to Mr. Raper, & by him to the Plaintiff. I am not however led to that conclusion by any thing stated in the deposition in regard to the disease of the boy

---

Raper on the Morning the boy left - say March 19th 1857, Executed the Bill of Sale herewith filed, Marked A, which was drawn by me in the same form as the one given by me for the Boy George
T. Gaskins
Sworn to & subscribed before me on the 22nd day of August 1859.
J.W Pool

****

State Vs. Malachi Johnson
Criminal Action
Felony, Stealing
Pasquotank County

North Carolina }
Pasquotank County }

Whereas upon complaint made before as upon the oath of Isaac Williams, that Malachi Johnson, a free Man of Color, had in his possession a Stier the property of Walter H. Riggs, alleging that the said Stier was his, and sold herein as such. This is therefore to command you to arrest the body of said Makachi Johnson of Col. and him have before us or some other Justice of the Peace to answer the said Charge.

Herein fail not, and have you then and there this precept. Given under our hands and Seals, the 28th day of August &c at 1866.

Geo. D. Pool Shff (Seal)
F. M. [?] (Seal)

Upon a hearing of the above case, and in default of bail, it is hereby ordered, that the Defendant, Mack Johnson of Col. be committed to jail until he give bail, or until the next Court of the Court of Pleas & Quarters Sessions held for this County to answer said Complaint & abide the Judgment of said Court.
Geo D. Pool Shff (Seal)

The Defendant Malachi Johnson of Col. was recognized to Office at the next Court of Pleas & Quarter Sessions for this County by giving as security in the sum of one hundred dollars, with Allen Dozier and Ben Johnson.
Test, Geo D. Pool & F.M. [?] JP
His
Ben X Johnson
Mark

His
Allen X Dozier
Mark

The Defendant in the within warrant having been recognized to appear at the next Term of the Court of Pleas & Quarter Sessions, until the jailor of the County will Release him.
Geo D. Pool, JP
Aug 25th 1866 from the want of confidence by his securities, the Defendant was recommitted to Jail.
L.C. Dashiel, Shff.

****

State Vs. John Mitchell [1835]
Criminal Action
Petty Larceny
Pasquotank County

Pasquotank County
Criminal Actions

The State Vs. John Mitchell
Hazzard Sims
Return Immediately to June Term 1835
Executed , Joshua A. Pool, Shff
By J. Keeling

State of North Carolina }
Pasquotank County }

To any lawful to Execute, Where as Henry White has made oath before me Abner Williams one of the Justices of Sd. County that John Mitchell, son of Thomas (of Colour) ware concerned in Stealing & taking away one [?] the property of Mary Morris (Widdow of Nathan) since the 24th of May 1835 this is to Command you to take the body of John Mitchell as aboved names & him and bring before me or some other Justice of the said County to answ the above charge.

Given under my hand & Seal this 28th of May 1835. Summons for Plaintiff. Henry White, Thomas Morris, Jno. Williams, Wm. Glover & Jerry Tubbs
Abner Williams (Seal)

State of North Carolina }
Pasquotank County }

Whereas Henry White of Sd. County & State of aforesaid have made oath before me Abner Williams one of the Justices of Sd County that Hazard Sims & Jeremiah Overman both men of Colour some times cald Jere Tubbs has feloniously Stolen or taken from Mary Morris Widdow of Nathan since the 24th of May 1835 one Stear or ox about four years old & Butchered Saide ox & sold the hide of Sd. ox to John McMorine Exqr this is to Command you or any lawfull officer to take the bodys of Said Hazard Sims & Jeremiah Overman some times Called Jere Tubbs & them bring before me or some other Justice of the Sd County also the Hide of Ad ox now in possession of John McMorine to answr the above Charge, Given under my hand & Seal this 27th of May 1835.
Abner Williams (Seal)

Summons for the Plaintiff, Henry White, John McMorine & Thomas Morris. Summoned William G Sawyer to aid & assert to take the Prisoners

Cost of Warrant	80
Witneses	60
William G Sawyer to Assert	20
	$1.40

State Vs. Hazard & Sims & Jeremiah Overman
Exd by Jno Shepherd

Joshua A Pool, you are hereby Commanded & to take the Body of Hazard Sims & him safely keep untill further notice May 27th 1835.
Abner Williams, JP

State of North Carolina }
Pasquotank County }

Hazard Sims brot before me & Jerry Overman alias Tubbs on examination if the Case agreeable to the within warrant & have released Jerry Tubbs - and that Hazard Sims not being able to give security - whom I think appears guilty of the charge & therefore the said Hazard I commit to Goal to stand his trial agreeable to Law -- The goaler of the County aforesaid is hereby required to receice the said Hazard into his Goal & him safely keep for his appearance to the next Supr Court to be held for the said County afsd on the fourth Monday after the 4th Monday in Sept next then and there to remain until discharged by said Court, 28th May 1835.

Thos Morris & Henry White acknowledged their **[?]** to the State aforesaid in the amount of twenty five dollars cash **[Smudged]** if they make their personal appearance & give evidence in the above case.
Abner Williams (Seal)

State Vs. John Mitchell, Son of John (of Colour)
Executed By Jno Shepherd

Henry White & Thomas Morris & (Jeremiah Overman alias Tubbs) acknowledge them selves in the sum of twenty five Dollars that they will appear at the next Superior Court & give Evidence against the said John Mitchell & there this will be void otherwise to be in full virtue.
May 30th 1835

Acknowleged before Abner Williams, JP

Joshua A Pool, Jailor

You will Receive John Mitchell & him safely keep until he is cald for to Ansr the charge, May 28th 1835
Abner Williams, JP
On examination of this Case where the State is against John Mitchell he is committed to Goal for want of bail untill the Superior Court of this County which will commence the fourth Monday after the Fourth Monday in Sept. 1835 & the Jailor are commanded to receive the Sd. John Mitchell untill he is **[?]** by bail other ways as the Law Directs.
May 30th 1835
Abner Williams, JP

Account of **[?]** of Hazard Sims & John Mitchell Two men of Color **[?]** by order of the Court of Please & Quarter sessions at June Term 1835 to pay the Cost & fine of a State Prosecution against them for Pet Larceny & **[?]** the 3rd day of June 1835.

Hazard Sims Sold to Thos W. Thompson $33.41 for ten years.
John Mitchell Sould for on year & five months. Benja. H. Charles $33.41.
Joshua A Pool, Shff

State of North Carolina } Pasquotank County Court
Hazard Sims } June Term 1835

These are to certify, that Thomas Morris hath attended this Court 1 day this Term as a Witness for the Plaintiff in this suit.

Attending 1 day at 6 shillings per day	.60
Travelling 20 miles at 6 shillings per thirty miles **[Faded]**	
Ferriages	
Certificate and Probate	.10
	$1.10

Sworn to before me, Stephen Charles, Clk.

State of North Carolina } Pasquotank County Court
Hazard Syms } June Term 1835

These are to certify that James Taylor hath attended this court 2 days this term as a Witness for the Plaintiff in this suit

Attending 2 days at 6 shillings per day	1.20
Travelling 12 miles at 6 shillings per thirty miles	.24
Ferriages	
Certificate and Probate	.10
	$1.54

Sworn to before me, Stephen Charles, Clk.

State of North Carolina } Pasquotank County Court
Hazard Syms } June Term 1835

These are to certify that Henry White hath attended this Court 9 days this term as a witness for the Plaintiff in this suit.

Attending 2 days at 6 shillings per day	1.20
Travelling 24 miles at 6 shillings per thirty miles	.48
Ferriages	
Certificate and Probate	.10
	$1.78

Sworn to before me, Stephen Charles, Clk.

State of North Carolina

To the Sheriff of Pasquotank County, Greeting:

You Are Hereby Commanded to summon James Taylor & Thomas Morris personally to be and appear before the Justices of the County Court of Pleas and Quarter Sessions, at the Court House in Elizabeth City, immediately, then and there to Testify and the truth to say in behalf of the State in a certain matter of controversy in the said Court depending, and then and there to be tried, wherein the State is Plaintiff and John Mitchell & Hazard Sims are Defendants, and this you shall in no wise omit, under the penalty by law enjoined. - Witness Charles Grice, Clerk of the said Court at Elizabeth City, the 2nd day of June in the L year of our Independence, anno Domini, 1835.
Issued the 2nd day of June 1835
Stephen Charles, Clk.

Pasquotank County Criminal Actions

State Vs. John Mitchell
Subpoena
Executed, Joshua A Pool, Shff
By [?] DShfff

State of North Carolina
To the Sheriff of Pasquotank County, Greeting:
You Are hereby Commanded to summon Henry White personally to be and appear before the Justices of the Court Court of Pleas and Quarter Sessions, at the Court House in Elizabeth City, immediately, then and there to testify and the truth to say in behalf of the State in a certain matter of controversy in the said Court depending, and then and there to be tried, wherein the State is Plaintiff and John Mitchell is Defendant, And this you shall in no wise omit, under the penalty by law enjoined -- Witness Stephen Charles, Clerk of the said Court at Elizabeth City, the 1st day of June in the L year of our Independence, Anno Domini 1835.
Issued the 1st day of June 1835.
Stephen Charles Jr., Clk.

State Vs. John Mitchell
Executed, Joshua A. Pool, Shff
By Samuel Small, DShff

State of North Carolina,
To the Sheriff of Pasquotank County, Greeting:
You Are Hereby Commanded to summon Jerry Tabbs personally to be and appear before the Justices of the County Court of Pleas and Quarter Sessions, at the Court House in Elizabeth City, immediately, then and there to testify and the truth to say in behalf of the State in a certain matter of controversy in the said Court depending, and then and there to be tried, wherein the State is Plaintiff and John Mitchell is Defendant, And this you shall in no wise omit, under the penalty by law enjoined -- Witness Stephen Charles, Clerk of the said Court at Elizabeth City, the 1st day of June. Issued the 1st day of June 1835.
Stephen Charles, Clk.

Chapter Eight

Pasquotank County

Bills of Sale

North Carolina State Archives
Pasquotank County Records
Records of Slaves and Free Persons of Color
C.R.075.928.9

No Date
Bill of Sale for Toby to Thos. Taylor

North Carolina }
Pasquotank County }

Know all men by these presents that I Henry Pendleton of the County & Province, Planter, for and in Consideration of the Sum of Twenty Pounds Lawfull money of Virginia to me in hand paid before the Ensealing hereof By Thomas Taylor Have Bargained, sold and delivered in plain open markett According to Law, a Negro boy Called Toby to the said Thomas Taylor his heirs and assigns **[Torn]** forever defend the said Negro boy to the said Taylor's heirs &c **[Torn]** in Witness whereof I the said

Henry Pendleton have hereunto sett my hand **[Torn]** the 22nd day of October, Pendleton
Witness Wm. Woodley.

****

William Brothers Bill of Sale for Cancer

North Carolina }
Pasquotank County }

Know all men by These Presents thay I William Brothers Junr. Of the County & Province afsaid Planter for & in Consideration of the valuable Sum of Thirty Pounds Current Money of the Colony of Virginia to me in hand paid by Thomas Taylor of the County & province afsaid have Sold & Delivered And by These Presents in plain and open Market According to Law have made Over my Negro Boy Called Cancer unto the said Thomas Taylor his heirs Exrs & Assigns forever Furthermore I the said William Brothers my heirs &c Doth Covenant to & with the said Thomas Taylor his heirs &c the Said Negro Boy Cancer to Warrant Secure & forever Defend, In Witness Whereof with the Delivery of the Said Negro Boy Cancer I the afsaid William Brothers have hereunto Sett my hand & Seal the 14th day of December Anno Dom 1743.
William Brothers (Seal)
Witness Present, John Morris
His
Jeremiah X Wilcocks
Mark

****

John Jones Bill of Sale to Thomas Taylor for Abraham

North Carolina }
Pasquotank County }

Know all men by These Presents that John Jones of Pasquotank County Planter for & in Consideration of the Sum of one Hundred and Eighty Pounds Current Bills of this Province afsaid in hand paid By Thomas Taylor have Bargained Sold and Delivered And by these Presents

in plain & open Markett According to Law have Sold and Delivered unto the afsaid Thomas Taylor his heirs Exrs Admrs and assigns My Negro Boy Called Abraham to Have and to hold the said Negro Boy &c And I the afsaid John Jones for myself my heirs Exrs Admrs and Every of us Doth Covenant to and with the afsaid Thomas Taylor his heirs &c the afsaid Negro Boy to Warrant Secure & for Ever Defend, In Witness whereof with the Deliverey of the said Negro Boy Abraham, I the afsaid John Jones have hereunto Sett my hand & Seal the 15th day of August Anno Dom. 1744.
Interlined between the second & third lines
John Jones (Seal)
Sign'd Sold & Delivered in the Presents of Saml. Height[?]

****

John Brown's Lease for five Negroes, Not Pd.

Know all men by these presents that I John Brown of Pasquotank county in North Carolina for and in Consideration of the Sum of one Hundred pounds Current Money of Great Britain to me in hand paid by my father Peter Brown the receipt whereof I do hereby Acknowledge and myself therewith fully and Entirely Satisfyed and paid, have Leased Setover and Delivered unto the Sd. Peter Brown for and During his Natural Life one negro Man named Frans, one negro woman named [?], one negro boy named Hill, one negro boy named Frais, and one negro boy named Dunk, and also the use and benefit of the above sd. negro man named Fraw for the use of my Motherin Law Sarah Brown During her natural Life in Witness whereof I have hereunto Set my hand & Seal this 27th Day of March 1750. Sealed Signed & Delivered in presence of us
Witness, Thomas Taylor, Henry Delon & John Brown.

****

North Carolina SS

Know all men by these Presents that I Alexander Lane of Pasquotank County in the province aforesaid Planter for & in Consideration of the Sum of ten pounds Sterling to me in hand well & truly paid at & before the ensealing & Delivery of these Presents by Robert Kingham of Edenton & Province aforesd the Receipt Whereof I do hereby acknowledge have Bargained Sold and Delivered and by these Presents do in due form of law

Bargain Sell and Deliver unto the said Robert Kingham one Negro Boy Called & Known by the Name of Jobe & every thing Else that shall be found on a Certain Plantation that I have Sold the said Robert Kingham after My Debts are paid off to the orphans of Robert Lowry Deceased to have & to hold the said negro boy Named Jobe & every thing else that is found on said Plantation unto the said Robert Kingham his heirs & assigns forever To the only Proper use & behoof of him the said Robert Kingham his heirs & assigns forever and I the said Alexander Lane the said Negro Boy named Jobe & every thing else as afsd unto the said Robert Kingham his heirs & Assigns against my self my heirs and assigns will Warrant and forever Defend by these Presents, In Witness Whereof I have hereunto Sett my hand & Seal the 25th Day of March Anno Dom 1752.
Signed, Sealed & Delivered In the Presence of George Hass & John Arnall
Alexander Lane (Seal)

****

A Bill of Sale for Pompy, Registered

North Carolina }
Pasquotank County }

Know all men by these presents that I William Woodsley of the County of Pasquotank in the Province of North Carolina, Planter, for and in Consideration of the sum of Fifteen Pounds Current money of the Colony of Virginia to me in hand well and truly paid, by Thomas Taylor, Clerk of the said County the receipt whereof I the aforesaid William Woodby Do by these presents Acknowledge my self therewith fully Satisfyed Contented and paid Have given granted Bargained and in plain and open Markett According to Law, to Bargain Sell and make over unto the said Thomas Taylor his heirs Exrs Admrs and Assigns, my half of a Negro man Called Pompey, with all the right Title Claim demand that I have to the said Negro Man Pompey by Virtue of the last will and Testament of Jonathan West, deceased, In Witness whereof I the said William Woodbey have hereunto Sett my hand, Seal the 23rd day of October Anno Dom. 1752.
Signed Sealed and Delivered in the Presents of Joseph **[?]**
William Woodly (Seal)
These may certify that the afsd bill of sale was Registered the 20th day of Octo. 1752 In Book D Fol 57

Tho Taylor, Regrs.
Test, Tho Taylor, CC

****

Account Sales of a Negro Named Jupiter by Alexander Watson

Pasquotank County SS
Novr 19th 1754

Sold one negro Man Named Jupiter formerly belonging to the Estate of Saml Williams Dec'd and now in the Possession of Alexander Watson at £51 -- Jesse[?] Delon [?]

****

Canady's Bill of Sale to Tulle Sawyer

North Carolina }
Pasquotank County }

Know all me By these Presents that I Robart Canady of the County afsd Cooper have bargend and Sold to Tulle Sawyer of the same place one Negro boy named Sam for the just Sume of Ten Pounds Cash the Title of which Negro I & my heirs Exrs Admrs shall and with for Ever Warrant & Defend to him the Sd. Tulle Sawyer his heirs & assigns for Ever as Witness my hand & Seal this 20th Day of April 1755

His
Robart R Canady
Mark
Test Benja Phillips

****

Bill of Sale of Jas Nicholson
Interest on Do May 15th 1765 to Sept 16th 1765

Know all men by these presents that I James Nicholson of Nixonton, for and in consideration of the sum of Eighteen Pounds one Shilling to me in hand paid the Receipt whereof I do hereby acknowledge

have Bargaind and Sold and Delivered, and by these presents doth Bargain Sell and deliver unto Andrew Miller of the place aforesaid a Negro Wench named Betty -- to him the said Andrew Miller his heirs and Assigns for ever -- Provided Nevertheless that if I the said James my Executors Administrators and Assigns or any of us do and shall and truly pay or cause to be paid unto the said Andrew Miller his heirs or Assigns the Sum of Eighteen pounds one Shilling on the first day of August next with Interest -then this Present Bill of Sale to be void or else to remain in full force, And it is further the Intention of these presents that in case the said James Nicholson should die before the expiration of that time that then the said Andrew Miller shall sell the said **[Torn]** at Publick Vandue and after paying himself the said sum and any other Debts or Accounts which I may hereafter once him **[Torn]** that he pay the remainder to such persons as I **[Torn]** this Province and if any over paying said Debts -- that he pay the same to my Daughter Elizabeth Nicholson In Witness whereof I have hereunto set my hand and Seal this 15th day of May 1765.
Signed Seald and Delivered in presence of James Monro.
James Nicholson (Seal)

****

Know all men by these Presents that I Matheas Ellgood Merchant of the Province of Nort Carolina and County of Pasquotank for and in Consideration of the Sum of Two hundred & ten pounds Lawful money of Virginia to me in hand paid by Neil Jamison and Company of the Colony of Virginia & Borough of Norfolk Merchants, the Receipt whereof is hereby acknowledged, Do hereby bargain, set over & deliver unto the said Neil Jamison & Company the six following negroes Vixt. Two Negro Fellows, The one Named James, the other Bacchus, Two Negro Wenches, the one named Isabella, the other Hagar, Two Negro Girls, the One named Rose and the other Kate, to have and to hold the said Negroes and their Offspring unto the said Neil Jamison & Company, their heirs, Executors, Administrators & Assigns forever and I the said Matheas Ellgood My heirs, Executors, Administrators & Assigns, by these presents, against all & all manner of Persons shall and well warrant & for ever defend the said Bargained Premises, In Witness whereof I have hereunto set my hand & Seal this Twenty first day of January, One thousand Seven hundred & sixty Seven. Seal'd & delivered in the Presence of us, Jephthah Barnard & Jno Taylor
Matt. Ellgood (Seal)

Pasquotank County
Bills of Sale

****

Bill of Sale Mathias Ellgood
For 6 negroes
North Carolina
Winton

On the 25th May 1767 Matthias Ellgood the Within Subscriber acknowledged the Within **[?]** to be his **[?]** Deed.

Pasquotank } **[?]**, Chf Just
County }

These may Certify that the within bill of sale was Registered the 2nd of June 1767.
Tho Taylor Pub Regr..
Test Thos Taylor, CC

****

Certificate to Eancell**[?]** reed **[Smudged]** Bond & Transportation

Received March 30th 1776 of William Reed a Negro man Named Davie, for which he & Joseph Riding has this day & date Given me a Bond of one Hundred pounds Proclamation Money that he is the said Reeds Property & to Defend the wright from the lawfull Claim of all Persons to Joab Cotter.

****

Account of Sales of a Negroe Wench Sold By Thos Relfe
Proved, Test, Enoch Relfe CC

Amount of Sale of a Neagro woman Named Rose the Property of Jos. & Miriam Palin Sold this 3rd day of July 1779, Sold Pr. Order of Cort, 1 Neagro Named Rose to Saml. Hollowell £2000
Thomas Relfe **[?]**

****

Pasquotank County
Bills of Sale

Bill of Sale J. Pritchard To Thos Pritchard

State of North Carolina }
Pasquotank County }

Know all men by these Presents that I John Pritchard of the County and State aforesd Planter have for an in consideration of the valluable Sum of Ten pounds to me in hand paid by Thomas Prtichard of the same State, Planter, The Receipt whereof is hereby acknowledged have sold & Deliver'd unto the Sd. Thos Pritchard a Negro man Toney formerly belonging to the Estate of Col. Erergin[?] Dec'd to the Sd. Thomas Pritchard his heirs & assigns for Ever & I the Sd. Jo Pritchard his heirs & Assigns forever & I the Sd. Jo Pritchard for my Self, my Heirs Exrts Admrs. & assigns have in plain & open manner bargained and Sold & Deliver'd unto the Sd. Thos. Pritchard, the above Tony to him and for my Self my Heirs & Warrant & ever defend the above man Tony to him & his heirs for ever & further I the Sd. J. Pritchard for my self my Heirs & ever defend the above man Tony from all & Every Person and Persons claiming by, from and under me, In Witness whereof I have hereunto put my hand and Seal this 14th Day of March 1797 [?] and Delivered in the Presents of.
John Pritchard.

****

Received from Wm. Farange Thirty Barrls Indian Corn being in full for a negro Wench call'd Little Ruth formorly the property of David George dec'd Receiv'd in full this 22nd day January 1800.
Jno McDonald

I agree to have no claim to the above Negro Wench, her Husband Stamps Jonas having paid mr the above Corn in full which I delivered to Jno. McDonald as a Purchase for said Jonas not for my Selfe & this I give as a discharge infull to him.
Wm. Farange

****

North Carolina }
Pasqk County }

Pasquotank County
Bills of Sale

This Indenture Made this twenty Second Day of January in the Year of our Lord one thousand Eight hundred between John McDonald of the one part and Job Morris of the other part witneseth that I, the Sd. John McDonald for and in Consideration of the sum of Eighty two Pounds to Me in hand paid by the said Job Morris the Receipt of which I hereby Acknowledge hath Bargained & Sell unto the said Job Morris a Negro Woman by the Name of Betty Warranting & Defending the said Negro Betty unto the said Job Morris from the Claim of Myself heirs, executors Adms or Assigns in witness whereof I have hereunto Set my hand & Seal the Day & Year above Written.
[?] Robinson
Jno. McDonald (Seal)

****

Demsey Sawyers Bill of Sale to Robt Murden

State North Carolina }
Pasquotank County }

Know all men by these presents that I Demsey Sawyer for the Consideration of one hundred and sixty five Silver dollars paid to me, by Robert Murden in the following manner viz. To pay and take in my Notes and Judgments against me to the above amount, have given & granted Bargand and Sold Set over and Deliverd in plain and open market, one halfe Negro man Named Dick aged about Eighteen Years which said Negro Dick I now Warrant Insure and for ever defend unto him the said Robert Murden his heirs Exers admrs or Assigns free and Clear from me my heirs Exrs admrs and assigns for Eaver I have put the said Robert Murden in ample and full possestion of the Said Negro by Delivery of one hat which I now deliver In the name & behalf of the said Negro, In Witness whearof I have hereunto set my hand and Seal the 15th day of April Anno Domini Eighteen hundred and one, Seald & Delivered in presence of.
Griffeth Sawyer & Susan Murden.
Demsey Sawyer (Seal)

****

Know all Men by these Presents that I Thomas Gordon of Pasquotank in the State of North Carolina Merchant, for and in Consideration of the Sum

of Four hundred Dollars, to me in hand paid the Receipt whereof I do hereby acknowledge; have bargaind sold and deliver'd and by these presents doe bargain Sell and deliver, on Negro Boy by the Name of Jerry unto Mrs. Mary Miller of Norfolk County in the State of Virginia -- and I Thomas Gordon for my self my Heirs Executors administrators and assigns, doe for ever Warrant and defend the above nam'd Negro Boy Jerry from the lawful Claim of every Person Whatsoever unto Mrs. Mary Miller, her Heirs and Assigns for ever -- In Witness whereof I have hereunto set my hand and Seal this 27th Day of March 1801
Witnesses Present, John Burnham & Barthalomew Kennedy
Thomas Gordan (Seal)

Mrs Mary Miller & her Agent Bartholomew Kennedy., 1801 March 27th to
Thomas Gordan DR To 1 Negro Boy Jerry $400
By Cash 348. 65
Ball $51. 35/100

I do hereby acknowledge the above balance to be justly due of Fifty one Dollars 35/100 unto Thomas Gordon and promise to pay the same on demand -- for Mary Miller, witness present - John Burnham Bartholomew Kennedy.

****

Bill of Sale from A. Davis to Ruth Davis

State of North Carolina }
Pasquotank County }September Term 1821

This Indenture of Sale made this second day of September Eighteen Hundred and two Between Abraham Davis of the County aforesaid of the one part and Ruth Davis of the same place of the other part Witnesseth that for and in consideration of the sum of Ten Pounds of the State aforesaid to me in hand paid by the Ruth Davis before the ensealing and delivering of these presence the Receipt of which said sum the said Abraham Davis doth hereby acknowledge himself therewith fully satisfyed and Contented hath given granted bargained & sold and by these presence doth give grant and sell unto the said Ruth Davis Her Heirs **[Torn]** and sell unto the said Ruth Davis Her Heirs **[Torn]** forever one third part of said negroe Child named Isaac To have and to hold the

aforesaid Negroes Clear and free from all Incumbrances unto the said Ruth Davis Her Heirs and assigns for ever In Witness whereof I do Hereunto set my hand and affixed my Seal the day and date above written.
Signed Seald and delivered in the Presence of us.
J Stokely
Her
Lydia X Stokely
Mark
Abraham Davis (Seal)
This Bill of Sale from Abraham Davis to Ruth Davis, was exhibited & proved in open Court by the Oath of Lydia Stokely, ordered to be registered
Teste, Will: T. Muse, Clk
Registered in the Registers office of Pasquotank County, November the 20th 1821 in Book W. Page 108.
By John C. Ehringhaus, P Regrs

****

Wm Farange's Bill, Sale of Boy Jerry

Pasquotank County }
State of North Carolina }

Know all men by these presents that I William Farrange, for and in Consideration of the Sum of Three hundred and fifty Dollars to me in hand paid and secured, the Receipt whereof I doe hereby acknowledge, have granted bargaind & Sold and by these presents doe grant bargain & Sell unto Thomas Gordon one Negro Boy by Name Jerry, and I William Farrange doe for my self my heirs Exrs Admrs. & Assigns doe Warrant & defend said Negro Boy Jerry against the lawful Claims of every Person whatsoever unto Thomas Gordon, his Heirs and Assigns for ever -- In Witness whereof I have hereunto set my hand & Seal this 31st Day of March 1806.
Wm Farrange (Seal)

****

James L. Shannonhouse's Bill of Sale To Jenny Pearson

Pasquotank County
Bills of Sale

Registered September 27th 1809 In Book S., Page 39
By Thomas Jordan, Regrs.

State of North Carolina }
Pasquotank County }

Know all men by these presents that I James L. Shannonhouse attorney for Robt. McMorine Esqr. for and in consideration of the sum of One Hundred Pounds to me in hand paid by Jenny Pearson at or before the Sealing and delivery of these presents the Receipt whereof I the said James L. Shannonhouse attorney as above mentioned do hereby acknowledge have Granted Bargained Sold and by these presents do grant bargain and Sell unto the said Jenny Pearson her Exrs Admrs and Assigns a Certain Negro Man named Dick to have and to hold the said Negro above bargained and sold and I the said James L. Shannonhouse Attorney as above do warrant and for ever defend the Title of said Negro as Attorney to Robert McMorine to the said Jenny Pearson her heirs & Assigns for ever. Witness my hand & Seal this first day of September 1809.
James L. Shannonhouse, Atty (Seal)

State of North Carolina }
Pasquotank County }

September Term 1809, This Bill of Sale from James L. Shannonhouse Attorney of Robert McMorine to Jenny Pearson was Acknowledged in Open Court. Ordered to be Registered.
Teste, Will T. Muse, Clk.

****

Samuel Warner's Bill of Sale to Margaret Warner

Know all Men by these presents That I Samuel Warner of the County of Pasquotank and State of No. Carolina of the one part and Margaret Warner of the same County & State aforesd of the other part witnesseth, I the Sd. Samuel Warner Doth Bargain & Sell unto the Sd. Margaret Warner a certain negro girl by the name of Clarasy for & in Consideration of the sum of three Hundred and twenty five dollars to me in hand paid by the Sd. Margaret Warner and secured to be paid, the Receipt whereof I do hereby acknowledge my self fully sattisfied contented and paid & I the Sd. Samuel

Warner doth for ever Warent and defend the write & Title of Sd. Negro girl unto the Sd. Margaret on her heirs forever against Claim or Claims that may hereafter arise. Signed Sealed and delivered in presents of us.
Teste, Decr. 11th 1819, J H Robertson & Richd. Chalk[?].
Samuel Warner (Seal)

****

State of North Carolina }
Pasquotank County } Sept Term 1823

This Bill of Sale from Samuel Warner to Margaret Warner was exhibited & Acknowledged in open Court & ordered to be Registered.
Test, Charles Grice, Clk
Registered in the Register's Office of Pasquotank County Book X Page 247, September 21st 1825 By John C. Ehringhaus, P Regrs.

****

Caleb Perkins's Bill of Sale to John Harris
Registered May the 30th 1820 in Book [?] 356
By John C. Ehreinghaus, P Regrs.

State of North Carolina, Pasquotank County

Know all men by these Presents that I Caleb Perkins of the County of Camden Hath Sold unto John Harriss one Negro Man By the Name of Toney for the Sum of Six hundred & Twenty five Dollars & I the said Caleb Perkins do covenant and agree to Warent the aforesaid Negroe to the said John Harriss to him & his hears and Assigns for ever [?] of the same, I have [?] unto Set my hand & Seal this 1st Day of January 1819.
Enoch Pritchard
Caleb Perkins (Seal)

State of North Carolina }
Pasquotank County } December Term 1819

The above Bill of Sale from Caleb Perkin's to John Harris was exhibited & Proved in Open Court by the Oath of Enoch Pritchard, Ordered to be Registered.
Teste, Will: T. Muse, Clk.

****

James Barnes Bill of Sale to Thomas Adams, Registered

State of North Carolina }
Pasquotank County }

Know all men by these presents that I James Barns of the County and State aforesaid have Bargained sold and by these presents do Bargin Sell & Deliver unto Thomas Adams for the Sum of three Hundred and twenty five dollars one negro girl namd Basheba which negro girl warrant and defend the Title of to the said Thomas Adams & his heirs Executors administrators or his Asigns against the Lawful Claim of all persons whatsoever which purpose I bind my self my heirs Executors & Administrators firmly by these presents in witness where unto I set my hand and Seal this the 18th day March 1818.
Teste, Willoughby Adams & Demsey Jennings
James Barnes (Seal)

State of North Carolina }
Pasquotank County }March Term 1820

This bill of Sale from James Barns to Thomas Adams was exhibited and proved in open Court by The oath of Willoughby Adams, ordered to be registered.
Teste, Will: T. Muse, Clk
Registered June the 13th 1820 in Book V. page 372 by
John C. Ehringhaus, P Regrs.

****

Thos Barnard's Bill of Sale
Boy Jess, Registered

Received 11th January 1819 of John McDonald the Sum of Six Hundred Dollars it being In full for Negroe man Jess which I sold Him this Day The Right of whom I bind myself my Heirs & Assigns to Warrant & for ever Defend witness my hand & Seal This day first above written.
In Presence of Francis Mitchell

Thos Barnard (Seal)

State of North Carolina }
Pasquotank County } March Term 1820

The Bill of Sale from Tho Barnard to John McDonald was exhibited and proved in Open Court by the Oath of Francis Mitchell, ordered to be Registered
Teste Will: T. Muse, Clk
Registered June 1820 in Book V page 368 by John C. Ehringhaus, P Register

****

Francies Wilson's Bill of Sale
[Editor's Note: This document is faded, and cannot be properly transcribed.]

The name of the Negro is Dolly --Warrant and Defend the right of to Wilson Crutch his Heirs, Exrs. --the valuation of said Negroes agreeable to an Order of Court for that purpose, Witness -- hereof I have hereunto set my hand & Seal this day and Year above mentioned.
Francis Wilson (Seal)

State of North Carolina }
Pasquotank County } March Term 1822

This Bill of Sale from Francis Wilson to **[?]** Crutch was exhibited on open Court by the Oath of Wm Wilson, Ordered to be Registered.
William T. Muse, Clk
Registered in the Register's office of Pasquotank County in Book W, page 171, March 25th 1822 by John C Ehringhaus P Regrs.

****

Jno Case to Benja. Phillips
Bill of Sale

April the 17th 1822 from Benjamin Philips Three Hundred Dollars in full payment for Negro Girl Lydia fifteen years old the wright & Title of said

Girl I do Warrant & defend unto the Said Philips to him & his heirs forever in Witness I hereunto set my hand & Seal this day & date before written.
Witness, Asa Rogerson
John Case (Seal)

State of North Carolina }
Pasquotank County } September Term 1822

This Bill of Sale from John Case to Benj. Philips was exhibited & proved in Open Court by oath of Asa Rogerson, Ordered to be Registered.
Test Will: T. Muse, Clk
Registered in the Register's office of Pasquotank County December the 27th 1822 in Book W page 234 by John Ehringhaus, P Regrs.

****

Robert Chanceys Bill of Sale for Dick

State of North Carolina }
Pasquotank County }

Know all men by these presents that I Robert Chancy do Bargan & Sell a Negro man Dick unto **[Faded]** Commander for the Sum of two Hundred & fourteen Dollars to me in hand paid By the said Commander both of said County and State aforesade and I the Sade Robbert Chancy do Warrant and Defend the said Negro Dick free and clear from the Claim or Claims of any person whereof I do hereunto Set my Hand and Seal this May 11th 1822.
Test, Carter Barnard
Robert Chancy (Seal)

State of North Carolina }
Pasquotank County } May Term 1823

This Bill of Sale from Robert Chancy to Joseph Commander was exhibited and proved in Open Court, Ordered to be Registered.
Registered May the 7th 1823 in the Register's Office of Pasquotank County May the 7th 1823
Test, Will: T. Muse, Clk
By John C. Ehringhaus, P Regrs.

****

Max Leeks Bill of Sale to D. Richardson

State of North Carolina }
Pasquotank County }

Know all men by these presents that I Maxamillian Leek **[Leek]** of the County & State afsd. For & in consideration of the Sum of four Hundred Dollars to me in hand paid by Daniel Richardson of the same place, the Receipt whereof I do hereby acknowledge my self fully satisfyed & paid, have granted bargained sold set over & delivered & by these presents absolutely grant bargain, Sell set over & delivered one Negro man named Allen aged about twenty two years unto him the Sd Daniel Richardson his heirs and Assigns forever to have & to hold the Sd. Negro Allen, unto him the Sd. Daniel Richardson his heirs & Assigns to their only proper use & benefit. And I the said Maxmillian Leek do for my self my heirs executors administrators & assigns Covenant and agree to and with the Sd. Daniel Richardson his heirs executors administrators & Assigns to Warrant and for ever defend the Aforsaid bargained and Sold Negro man Allen unto him the sd. Daniel Richardson his heirs assigns against of all & every person the claim or claims demanded In Testimony whereof I have hereunto set my hand & seal this twelfth day of November in the year of our Lord Eighteen Hundred & Twenty two. Signed Sealed & delivered in presence of us Wm. Hinton & Harvey Williams

His
Maxamillian X Leek
Mark

State of North Carolina }
Pasquotank County } June Term 1823

This Bill of Sale from Maxy Leek to Daniel Richardson, was exhibited & proved in Open Court by the Oath of William S. Hinton, ordered to be Registered.
Test Will: T. Moose, Clk
Registered in the Register's Office of Pasquotank County June the 20th 1823 in Book W pages 353.
John Ehringhaus P Regrs.

Pasquotank County
Bills of Sale

****

Spencer Sawyer's Bill of Sale of Negro Oliver

Know all Men by These presents that I Spencer Sawyer for and in consideration of two hundred and fifty received of Frederic Davis have bargained and sold unto the said Davis one negro man a slave named Oliver the right and Title whereof I do hereby bind myself to warrant and defend. In testimony whereof I have hereunto set my hand and Seal this 18th day of November A.D. 1822 in the Presence of C.R. Kinney.
Spencer Sawyer (Seal)

State of North Carolina }
Pasquotank County } January Term 1823

This Bill of Sale from Spencer Sawyer to Frederic Davis was exhibited & proved in open Court by the oath of C.R. Kinney, Ordered to be registered.
Test, Will: T. Muse, Clk
Registered in the Register's Office of Pasquotank County February the 14th 1823 in Book W page 291 by John C. Ehringhaus, P Regrs.

****

Jesse old's Bill of Sale to John Richardson Junr. For Negro boy George

State of North Carolina }
Pasqt County }

Know all men by these presents that I Jesse Old of the County of Camden and State aforesaid for and in consideration of the sum of Seventy five dollars to me in hand paid by John Richardson Junr. Of the County of Pasquotank & State aforesaid, the receipt whereof I do hereby acknowledge and my self therewith contented and Sattisfied, Have bargained & sold & by these presents do absolutely grant bargain sell & deliver unto the said John Richardson Junr. His heirs & assigns for ever a certain negro boy child named George aged about three years, the child of negro woman Jean, To have & to hold the said negro boy George unto him the said John Richardson Junr. His heirs & Assigns for ever And I do

hereby Agree & engage to Warrant & defend the Title of said Negro boy George to him the said John Richardson Junr. His heirs Assigns against the claim or demand of all & every other person or persons what ever, In Testimony whereof I have hereunto set my hand & Seal this seventh day of January in the Year of our Lord 1823.
Signed & delivered in presence of us, Lemuel Richardson jurat & James Old
Jesse Old (Seal)

State of North Carolina }
Pasquotank County } March term 1824

This Bill of Sale from Jesse Old to John Richardson Junr. Was exhibited & proved in open Court by the Oath of Lemuel Richardson, ordered to be registered.
Teste Charles Grice, Clk
Registered in the Register's office of Pasquotank County April the 5th 1824 in book W page 35
John C. Ehringhaus, P Regrs.

****

Bill of Sale from Maximillian Leek for Naney & Penny

State of North Carolina }
Pasquotank County }

Know all men by these presents That I Maximillian Leek of the County and State aforesaid for and in Consideration of the sum of one hundred Dollars to me in hand paid by David White of the State aforesaid and County of Perquimans, the receipt hereof I do hereby acknowledge and my self there with fully Satisfied Contented and paid have bargained Sold and Delivered in open Market two Negro Girls named Nanny and Penny one about two years old and the other about two months old unto the said David White his heirs and assigns for ever the above mentioned negroes Nanny and Penny and I the said Maximillian Leek for my self my heirs and assigns Doth hereby Covenant and agree to Warrant and Defend the above mentioned negroes unto the said David White his heirs and assigns from the Claim or Claims of all persons whatever, In Witness hereof I the said

Maxamillian Leek hath hereunto set my hand and Seal this the 11th day of November Anno Domini 1824.
Signed, Sealed & Delivered in the presence of us, D. Dosier.

His
Maxamillian X Leek
Mark

State of North Carolina } Court of Pleas & Quarter Sessions
Pasquotank County } September Term 1828

The Within Bill of Sale from Maxamillian Leek to David White was exhibited in open Court and proved by the oath of Dennis Dosier a subscribing Witness thereto and ordered to be Registered.
Test, Charles Grice, Clk
Registered in the Register's Office of Pasquotank County the 18th September 1828 in Book Y page 438 by John C. Ehringhaus, P Regrs.

****

Ephraim Bright to Robert Jones
Ephraim Brite's Bill to Sell

Know all men by these presents, that I Ephraim Bright of the County of Pasquotank & State of North Carolina, in consideration of the sum of three hundred & Seventy five dollars, paid me by Robert Jones of the same County & State, the Receipt whereof I do hereby acknowledge, do hereby give, bargain & sell unto the said Robert Jones, a certain negro man named Ammon, of the age of Twenty Nine years of age.

To have & to hold the said negro to him, the said Robert Jones, his heirs, executors, administrators & assigns forever, And I the said Ephraim Bright, for my self, my heirs, executors, & administrators, will warrant & defend against all persons whatsoever, unto the said Robert Jones his heirs, executors & administrators, the said bargain & sale.

In Testimony whereof, I the said Ephraim Bright have hereunto set my hand & Seal this fourteenth day of February, in the year of our Lord, one thousand eight hundred & twenty six: And I Milla, wife of the said Ephraim in Testimony of my assent to the same bargain & have hereunto set my Hand & Seal in the presence of John Richardson.

His
Ephraim X Bright (Seal)

Mark

Her
Milla X Bright (Seal)
Mark

Witness, Charles Brite

State of North Carolina }
Pasquotank county } March Term 1826

This Bill of Sale from Ephraim Brite to Robert Jones was exhibited & proved in open Court by the oath of John Richardson one of the subscribing witnesses thereto & ordered to be Registered.
Teste, Charles Grice, Clk
Registered in the Register's office of Pasquotank County March the 22nd 1826 in Book X page 340 by John C. Ehringhaus, P Regrs.

****

Lease
Thomas Banks to Solomon (Keaton)

Know all men by these presence that I Thos. Banks of the County of Pasqt. & State of North Carolina doth Bargain Sell & Convey unto (Solomon Keaton) a man of Colour a certain Negro woman By the name of Rose for & in Consideration of the Sum of fifty Dollars to me in hand paid Or Secured to be paid to have & to hold for ever the above named Woman Rose for ever in witness I hereby Set my hand & Seal this 1st Jany. 1827.
Thomas Banks (Seal)
Teste, [?] Keaton
D B Pendleton, Jurat

State of North Carolina }
Pasquotank County } March Term 1827

This Bill of Sale from Thomas Banks to Solomon Keaton (of Colour) was exhibited & proved in open Court by the oath of D. B. Pendlston one of the Subscribing witnesses thereto. Ordered to be Registered.

Test, Charles Grice, Clk

Registered in the Register's Office of Pasquotank County March 1st 1827 in Book Y page 123 by John C Ehringhaus, P Regrs.

****

Bill of Sale from Willis Casy **[Cary]** to Joseph Davis

State of North Carolina }
Pasquotank County }

Received the sixteenth day of July in the year of our Lord one thousand Eight hundred and twenty nine from Joseph Davis the sum of two hundred anf Fifty dollars in full payment for a Negro woman and child Named Phebe and Charlott the wright and title whereof I do hereby warrant secure and for ever defend unto the sd. Joseph Davis and his heirs against all Lawful claim or claims of all and Every person or persons in witness whereof I have hereunto set my hand and seal the day and date above mentioned.
Witness, James Casey
(Willis Casy) (Seal)
State of North Carolina } Court of Pleas & Quarter Sessions
Pasquotank County } September Term 1829

The foregoing Bill of sale from Willis Casey to Joseph Davis was exhibited in open Court and acknowledged and Ordered to be Registered.
Test, Charles Grice, Clk

Registered in the Register's Office of Pasquotank County Sept 30th 1829 in Book Z page 148 by John C Ehringhaus, P Regrs.

****

Exum Trueblood's Bill of Sale to Benjamin Davis

This Indenture made the 18th Oct 1829 between Exum Trueblood of the County of Pasquotank and State of North Carolina of the one part and Benjamin Davis of the same place of the other part Witnesseth that for and in consideration of the sum of two hundred and seventy five dollars to me

in hand paid by said Benjamin Davis the Receipt whereof I do hereby acknowledge my self to be contented satisfied and paid and by these presents do bargain sell convey confirm and deliver unto said Benjamin Davis his heirs executors administrators and assigns a certain negro woman Thamer and one child Charles to have and to hold the said negroes Thamer and Charles unto said Benjamin Davis his heirs and assigns forever and I the said Exum Trueblood do for my self my heirs executors Admrs. and assigns do Warrant secure and forever defend the right of said negroes of Thamer and Charles unto the said Benjamin Davis against the lawful claim or claims of all person or persons whatsoever forever in witness whereof I have hereunto set my hand ans Seal the day and year above written.
Signed Sealed and delivered in presence of Anderson Morris & RM[?]
Exum Trueblood (Seal)

State of North Carolina } Court of Pleas & Quarter Sessions
Pasquotank County } Sessions Sept Term 1830.

The foregoing Bill of Sale from Exum Trueblood to Benjamin Davis was exhibited in open Court and Ack'd and ordered to be Registered.
Test, Charles Grice, Clk
Registered in the Register's Office of Pasquotank County October 28th 1830 in Book Z page 363 by John C. Ehringhaus, P Regrs.

****

Aaron White & 6 others
Transfer for Negroes, 1830
Wilson paid

State of North Carolina }
Pasquotank County }

Know all men by these presents that we Aaron White, Edmund White, Joseph M White, Alfred White, Caleb White & Daniel Tisdale & Joseph Elliott, for & in Consideration of the love & affection which we have & do bear towards the Society of Friends or People denominated Quakers in the State aforesaid & for divers other good causes & considerations we hereunto moving, hath given granted assigned, transferred & set over Unto Joseph Parker, William Wilson, & Anderson Morris & other Trustees for said Society, all our right, title interest &

property of & in Certain Negroes. Viz. Pleasant aged about fifty years, Dolly aged about fourteen years, aaron aged about eleven years, Josiah aged about eight years, Ann aged about Sixteen years, Julia aged about four Years & Mary aged about eight months.

To have & to hold the said negroes to them & their successors in Office for the use & protection of said friends Called Quakers forever, And we the said Aaron White, Edmund White, Joseph M White, Alfred White, Caleb White, Daniel Tisdale & Joseph Elliott, for our selves, our heirs, executors or administrators doth by these presents Warrant & forever defend unto the Trustees aforesaid & their Successors in Office All our right, title & interest in & to the aforesaid negroes against the claim or claims of every Person or Persons Claiming through by from or under us or either of us Whatsoever forever -- In Witness whereof we have hereunto set our hands & Seals this 1st day of 5 mo AD 1830.

Signed, Sealed & Delivered in the presence of John Ehringhaus, jurat
Aaron White (Seal)
Edmund White (Seal)
Joseph M White (Seal)
Alfred White (Seal)
Caleb White (Seal)
Daniel Tisdale (Seal)
Joseph Elliott (Seal)

State of North Carolina } Court of Pleas & Quarter Sessions
Pasquotank County } Sessions June Term 1831

The foregoing Transfer from Aron White & others to Joseph Parker & others Trustees was Exhibited in open Court and proved by the oath of J. C. Ehringhaus a Subscribing Witness thereto and ordered to be Registered

Test, Charles Grice, Clk

Registered in the Register's Office of Pasquotank County June 18th 1831 in Book [?] page 57 by John C Ehringhaus, P Regrs.

****

C.R. Kinsey's Bill of Sale to Wm. Rogerson

State of North Carolina }
Pasquotank County }

Augt 11th 1830 }

Know all men by these presents that I Charles R. Kinsey[?] by virtue of deed in Trust to me executed by Isaiah Rogerson did according to the Terms thereof expose to sale certain negroes to wit Pomp, George, Charles & Penny and William Rogerson did there become the highest bidder for the sum of Thirty Dollars, Now Know ye that I Charles R. Kensey for & in consideration of the sum of thirty dollars to me in hand paid by William Rogerson have given granted, bargained and sold to the said William the aforesaid negroes the title to which I do hereby convey in as full amd ample a manner as they were conveyed to me by said [?] & not otherwise -- In Testimony whereof I have hereunto set my hand & Seal the day and date above written (Ack'd), C.R. Kensey (Seal)
In Presence of Miles White.

State of North Carolina } Court of Pleas and Quarter Sessions
Pasquotank County } September Term 1830

The foregoing bill of sale from Charles R. Kensey to William Rogerson was exhibited in open Court and Ack'd and ordered to be registered
Test, Charles Grice, Clk.
Registered in the Register's Office of Pasquotank County October 23rd 1830 in Book Z page 353 by John C. Ehringhaus, P Regrs.

****

I John M Skinner of Pasquotank County do hereby covenant to pay to Edmund B Harvey one thousand seven hundred and fifty dollars, in full for the price of certain negroes which he claims as distributed of his late wife Eliza and which I have this day bought from him, the said sum to be paid in the following manner, to wit, first to pay myself and give a discharge to the said Edmund for the amount he owes me, being for money paid by me in discharge of certain judgments in Pasquotank County against the said Edmund and Thomas Davis[?] as his security; and [?] pay other debts of the said Edmund to the amount of the balance of the said sum of one thiusand seven hundred and fifty dollars, the said payments to be made and proprt vouchers not exhibited to the said Edmund within two months from the time at which I shall recover or obtain possession of the said slaves and if such payments are not made and such vouchers not exhibited within the

said two months then whatever remains so unpaid I am to pay to the said Edmund his executors administrators or assigns.
Hertford, April 11th 1831.
Signed John M Skinner (Seal)
Test, Miles Elliott Junr.

****

Addison Whidbee's Bill of Sale to Venford Overton

State of North Carolina }
Pasquotank County }

Rec'd this day from Veneford Overton [?] Dollars which is in full payment for a negro man Isaac formerly the property of Lemuel Whidbe Senr. Of Perquimans County & Known by the name of Isaac Hosea about sixty years of age which I have sold the Rec't whereof I do hereby acknowledge & do hereby bind myself my heirs Executors admrs. & to warrant & defend my right & Title to her the said Vineford Overton to the above mentioned negro forever in witness whereof I have hereunto sett my hand & Seal the 24th March 1831.
Test, Abraham White, Jurat
Addison Whidbe (Seal)

State of North Carolina } Court of Pleas and Quarter
Pasquotank County } Sessions September Term 1831

The foregoing Bill of Sale from Addison Whidbee to Venford Overton was exhibited in open Court and proved by the oath of Abram White a Subscribing Witness thereto and ordered to be Registered.
Teste, Charles Grice, Clk.
Registered in the Register's Office of Pasquotank County September 25th 1831 in Book Aa page 101 by John C Ehringhaus.

****

Edmund Sanderson's Bill of Sale to Caleb Sanderson

State of North Carolina -- Pasquotank County, Know all men by these presents that I Edmond Sanderson of the County of Pasquotank and State

aforesaid has this day bargained and sold to Caleb Sanderson his Father one negro man John for three hundred and fifty Dollars one named James for three hundred and fifty one named Simon for three hundred and fifty, one named Reddick for three hundred, one named Obed for two hundred dollars, one by the name of March for one hundred and fifty Dollars, Ditto one negro woman Lowis three hundred and ten Dollars ditto one woman Grace and child named Martly three hundred and fifty Dollars I the said Edmund Sanderson for my self my heirs Executors and Administrators do warrant and defend unto the said Caleb Sanderson his heirs assigns for ever from the legal claims of all persons whatsoever given under my hand and Seal this the thirteenth day of March 1832.
Signed Sealed and delivered in the presence of Willis White**[?]**.
Edmund L. Sanderson (Seal)

State of North Carolina } Court of Pleas & Quarter Sessions
Pasquotank County } June Term 1832

The foregoing Bill of Sale from Edmund Sanderson to Caleb Sanderson was exhibited in open Court and proved by the oath of Willis W. Whyte a Subscribing witness thereto, and ordered to be Registered.
Test, Charles Grice, Clk.
Registered in Register's Office of Pasquotank County June 26th 1832 in Book AA Page 245 by John C Ehringhaus, P Regrs.

****

Robert M. Knox A Bill of Sale to John Williams

Rec'd of John Williams One Hundred and Twenty Six Dollars in full for negro Boy Butler, negro Child Ammaretta **[Annetta]** and negro Child Mary which I sold at Public Auction, as Trustee to Saml. Williams, as witness my hand & Seal this Decr. 1833
John Crawford
Robert M. Knox (Seal)

State of North Carolina } Court of Pleas & Quarter Sessions
Pasquotank County } June Term 1835

Pasquotank County
Bills of Sale

Bill of Sale from Robert M. Knox Trustee of Saml. Williams to John Williams was exhibited in open Court and the Execution thereof acknowledged By said Robert M Knox, Ordered Registered.
Registered in the Register's Office of Pasquotank County June 18th 1835 in Book B **[?]** page 371 by John C Ehringhaus, P Regrs.

****

State of North Carolina }
Pasquotank County }

Know all men by these presents that I Shadrack R. Williams of Pasquotank County for and in consideration of the Sum of fifteen hundred dollars to me in hand paid by Thomas B. Williams, of the afore sd. place the receipt whereof I do hereby acknowledge have granted bargained and Sold and by these presents do grant bargained and sell unto the Sd. Thos. B Williams his Exrs., Admrs & Assigns my negro woman Jenny aged about forty years & her four children Fred aged about fourteen, George aged about eight, Miles aged about three years and Harden aged about ten months to have and to hold the aforesaid negro woman Jenny and her children Fred, George, Miles & Harden to the said Thos. B Williams his Exers, Admrs. and assigns for ever, And I the said Shadrach R. Williams for myself my heirs &c shall & will warrant & defend the Title of the aforesaid negroes unto Thos. B. Williams his heirs &c from the claim of any and all persons whatsoever, Given under my hand and Seal this May 24th 1833
Witness, Edward Williams
Shadrach Williams (Seal)

State of North Carolina }
Pasquotank County } June Term 1833

The foregoing Bill of Sale was Exhibited in open Court & the Register thereof duly acknowledge -- ordered to be Registered.

****

Bill of Sale from Fanny Barren to Israel Lister

Pasquotank County
Bills of Sale

Know all men by these presents that I Fanny Barren of the County of Pasquotank and State of North Carolina of the one part and Isreal Lister of the County and State aforesaid of the other part Witnesseth, whereas I the said Fanny Barren have Bargain'd and Sold unto the said Isreal Lester a negro Boy by the name of Dave for and in Consideration of the sum of One hundred Dollars to me in hand paid or secured to be paid, the Receipt whereof I do hereby Acknowledge my self fully Sattisfied Contented and paid, the rite and Tltle of said negro boy Slave I do warrant and defend in as full and ample a manner as by Law as Witness whereof I have here unto Set my hand and Seal.
Signed & Sealed In Presence of us July 18th 1834, Thos Warner

Her
Fanny X Barren
Mark

State of North Carolina } Probate Court
Pasquotank County } February Term 1835

This Bill of Sale from Fanny Barren to Isreal Lester was exhibited & proved in open Court by the oath of William Warner & he subscribing Witness thereto & ordered Registered.
Test, Stephen Charles, Clk
Registered in the Register's Office of Pasquotank County February 9th 1835 in Book BB page 299 by John C. Ehringhaus, P Regrs.

****

Bill of Sale from John Evans To Jacob Reddick

State of North Carolina }
Pasquotank County }

Know all men by these presents, That I John Evans one of the Constables in and for the said County greeting have in obedience to and Execution Issued by Joseph Stokely, one of the acting Justices of the Peace in & for the said County of Pasquotank at the Instance of Solomon Simpson and against James Carver and Jeremiah Rogerson & Joseph R Billops have proceeded to Levy the same upon two negroes to wit man Abraham and man Steaphen the property of Sd. James Carver and after Duly advertising said Negroes at Sundry Public Plaices in said County Did

Expose James Carver's Rite & Title to said negroes to Publick Sale for ready money to satisfy said Execution at the house of Elias Carver on the 15th Day of May 1835 in the said County and that Jacob Reddick Did appear and bid for negro man Abraham twenty five Dollars and for negro man Stephen twenty Dollars which was the Last & highest bids that was made for Either or all of said negroes, the Receipt where of I the said John Evans Do hereby acknowledge have granted bargained & sold and Do by these presents Grant bargain and Sell unto the said Jacob Reddick all of James Carvers Rite Title ans interest to said negroes to him and his heirs for ever and the said John Evans Do bind my self to warrant & for ever Defend the Rite Title & Interest of said Negroes to the said Jacob Reddick as fully & as firmly as in my power both as Constable, in Witness whereof I have hereunto set my hand & Seal the 15th Day of May 1835.
William Relfe
John Evans (Seal)

State of North Carolina }
Pasquotank County }

This Bill of Sale from John Evans to Jacob Reddick was produced in open Court and Acknowledged to be [?] & deed of John Evans and ordered to be Registered.
Test, W.W. Griffin, Clk
Registered in the Register's Office of Pasquotank County in book FF page 24, 1st Octr 1835.
Wm. Gregory, P Regrs.

****

Bill of Sale of Wm. Symons to Seth Etheridge

Received January 17th 1838 fro Seth Etheridge Nine Hundred Dollars in full payment for negro woman Nan & her child Mary the right and title of the aforesaid negroes, I my heirs executors administrators and assigns do warrant and for ever defend unto him the said Seth Etheridge his heirs and assigns, In Witness whereof I do hereunto affix my hand and Seal In Presence of Benj. P. Pendleton
Wm. Symon (Seal)

Pasquotank County Court } March Term 1838

Pasquotank County
Bills of Sale

The **[?]** of this Bill of Sale from William Symons to Seth Etheridge was proved by the oath of B. P. Pendleton, ordered to be Registered.
Registered in the Register's Office of Pasquotank County in book CC page 362 17th March 1838
Wm Gregory, P Regrs.

****

Bill of Sale of Almand Sanderson to Edmund Sanderson
State of North Carolina - Pasquotank County

Know all men by these Presence that I Almand Sanderson of the County and State Afsd. Of the One Part and Edmund Sanderson of the same County and State of the other Part Witnesseth That for an in Consideration of the Sum of Twenty Three hundred and Twenty five dollars Cash in hand paid before the Ensealing of these Presence the Receipt hereof I do Acknowledge my Self fully and absolutely Contented and paid have This day Bargained Sold Conveyed and Confirm unto the Afsd. Edmund Sanderson five Negroes by the names of Jack, Simon, Obid, Graisey, and Martha **[?]** to have and to hold to the afsd. Edmund Sandersons own use **[Smudged]** behoof and to his heirs for Ever and further I the afsd. Almand Sanderson do agree to and with Afsd. Edm'd Sanderson for to warrant and for Ever defend the Rite and Title of the above Named Negroes To Wit, Jack, Simon, Obid Martha & Gracey and the two horses free and Clear from me my heirs Exors Admrs and Asigns unto the afsd Edmund Sanderson and his heirs for Ever in Witness Whare of I have hear unto Set my Hand and Seal this 26th day January 1835.
Witness **[Smudged]** Barnard
Almand Sanderson (Seal)

State of North Carolina } Court of Pleas & Quarter Sessions
Pasquotank County } March Term 1835

This Bill of Sale from Almand sanderson to Edmund Sanderson was exhibited in open Court & the Execution thereof proved By the oath of Carter Barnard the subscribing witness, Ordered to be Registered.
Test, Stephen Charles, Clk
Registered in the Register's Office of Pasquotank County March 19th 1835 in Book BB page 337 by John C Ehringhaus., P Regrs.

Pasquotank County
Bills of Sale

****

S. Charles, Clk 's Bill of Sale to A.L. Temple, Jacob & Cherry

Whereas Job Carver, Armwell Temple, James Temple Junior, Lucy Temple of full age, and Robin Temple and june Temple infants by their guardian William K. Richardson at the December Term 1839 - of Pasquotank County Court of Pleas and Quarter Sessions did file their certain petition therein setting forth that they are Tenants in Common of several negroes mentioned in said petition and praying for a sale of said negroes so that a fair and equitable division of the said negroes might be made among the said Petitioners - And whereas at the next Term of the said Court, the said Petition coming on to be heard it was ordered, adjudged and decreed that Stephen Charles the Clerk of the said Court with the said negroes mentioned in the Petition - And whereas by virtue of the Power and authority granted mr by the said decree, I the said Stephen Charles Clerk did afterwards to wit on the 20th January 1840 at the Store of J Pritchard in said County of Pasquotank first having duly advertised the time and place of sale - A L Temple appeared and bid for negro man Jacob the sum of Three hundred & thirty Six Dollars - who was the highest bidder and the purchaser of said negro Jacob and Cherry at said sale (the said negroes being two of the negroes mentioned in the petition - and whereas at the March Term 1840 of this said Court the said sale was confirmed -- Now Know all men that I J Stephen Charles, Clerk as aforesaid for and in Consideration of the premises and the further consideration of the sum of Eight hundred and Six Dollars to me secured to be paid the security whereof I do hereby acknowledge here granted, bargained sold and confirmed and by these presents do grant bargain sell and confirm unto the said A.L. Temple negroes Jacob and Cherry being two of the negroes mentioned in the said petition , To have and To hold the said negroes Jacob and Cherry unto him the said A L Temple his heirs executors administrators and assigns forever -- In Witness I have hereunto set my hand and Seal the first day of September 1840.

****

S. Charles, Clk's Bill of Sale To John Taylor
Negro Man Allen

Pasquotank County
Bills of Sale

Whereas Job Carver, Armwell temple, James Temple Junior, Lucy Temple of full age, and Robin Temple and June Temple infants by their guardian William K. Richardson at the December Term 1839 of Pasquotank County of Pleas and Quarter Sessions did file their certain petition therein setting forth that they are Tenants in Common of several negroes mentioned in said petition and praying for a Sale of said negroes so that a fair & equitable division of the said negroes might be made among the said Petitioners -- And whereas at the said Term of the said Court the said Petition coming on to be heard it was ordered, adjudged and decreed that Stephen Charles the Clerk of the said Court sale the said negroes mentioned in the said Petition - and whereas by virtue of the Power and authority granted me by the said decree, I the said Stephen Charles, Clerk did afterwards to wit on the 20th of January 1840 at the store of J Pritchard in said County of Pasquotank, first having duly advertised the time and place of Sale -- I offered the said negroes for sale at public auction when and where John Taylor appeared and bid for negro man Allen (he being one of the negroes mentioned in said Petition) the sum of Five hundred and ninety Dollars - whereas the highest and the purchaser of said negro man Allen at said Sale - And whereas at the March Term 1840 of the said court the said sale was confirmed - Now Know all men that I Stephen Charles Clerk of the said County Court of Pleas and Quarter Sessions for and in Consideration of the premises and the further consideration of the sum of Five hundred and ninety Dollars to me secured to be paid the security whereof I do hereby acknowledge have granted bargained Sold and confirmed and by these presents do grant, bargain Sell and confirm unto the said John Taylor negro man Allen being one of the negroes mentioned in said Petition -- To have and To hold the said negro man Allen unto him the said John Taylor his heirs executors administrators and assigns Forever -- In Witness whereof I have hereunto set my hand and Seal this First day of September 1840

****

Penelope Symon's Bill of Sale To Benjn. S. White

State of North Carolina }
Pasquotank County }

This agreement made and Entered into this 24th day of October In the year of Our Lord One thousand Eight hundred and forty Between

Pasquotank County
Bills of Sale

Penelope Simons of the one part and Benj. S. White of the other witnesseth that for and in Consideration of the sum of Three Hundred Dollars to me in hand paid by the said B.S. White, The Receipt whereof I hereby acknowledge, I the said Penelope Symons do bargain and Sell transfer and deliver unto the said B.S. White his heirs and assigns for Ever a Certain Woman and Child slaves By the name of Plesent and Boy Child Ben the above described negroes, I the said Penelpoe Symons do Warrant and defend free Clear of all Claims of persons what so ever for ever unto the said B.S. White his heirs and assigns for Ever Whereof I Set my hand and Seal - the day and year first written above.
Test, D.H. Kenyon.
Penelope Symons (Seal)

State of North Carolina } Court of Pleas and Quarter Sessions
Pasquotank County } June Term 1841

This Bill of Sale from Penelope Symon to B.S. White was exhibited in open Court and proved by the oath of D. Kenyon, ordered to be Registered.
Test, Stephen Charles Clk.
Registered in the Register's Office of Pasquotank County in Book [?] page 16, 29th July 1841, Wm. Gregory, P Regrs.

****

S. Charles, Clk, Bill of Sale to S. Pendleton, Boy George

Whereas Stephen Pendleton in right of his wife Mary, and George W. Trueblood of full age, and Albert Trueblood, Ann and William Trueblood infants by their guardian Noah Hollowell - at the March Term 1840 of Pasquotank County Court of Pleas and Quarter Sessions did file their certain petition therein setting forth that they are tenants in common of two negroes mentioned in said petition and praying for a Sale of said Negroes for the purpose of a division between them -- And whereas at the same Term of the said Court the said petition coming on to be heard it is ordered, adjudged and decreed that the Clerk of this Court Sell the said negroes on a credit of six months - and whereas by virtue of the Power and Authority granted me by said Decree I Stephen Charles, Clerk did afterwards to wit the 16th April 1840 at Nixonton in the County of Pasquotank first having duly advertised the time and place of Sale - I Offered the said negroes for sale at public auction when and where Stephen Pendleton appeared and bid for negro Boy George the sum of Two hundred and Sixty Dollars who was the highest bidder & the purchaser of said negro George at said Sale (he being one of the negroes mentioned in said petition) and whereas in the June Term 1840 of the said Court the said sale was confirmed - Now Know all men that I Stephen Charles, Clerk as aforesaid for and in consideration of the premises and the further consideration of the sum of Two hundred and Sixty Dollars, to me secured to be paid the security whereof I do hereby acknowledge have granted bargained sold and confirmed and by these presents do geant bargain sell and confirm unto the said Stephen Pendleton negro Boy George (being one of the negroes mentioned in said petition) To have and To hold the said negro Boy George unto him the said Stephen Pendleton his heirs executors administrators and assigns for ever - - In witness whereof I have hereunto set my hand and seal the First day of September, 1840.

****

S. Charles, Clk, Bill of Sale To J. Bailey, Girl Harriet

Whereas Stephen Pendleton in right of his wife Mary, and George W. Trueblood of full age, and Albert Trueblood, Ann and William Trueblood infants by their Guardian Noah Hollowell at the March Term 1840 of Pasquotank County Court of Pleas and Quarter Sessions did file their certain petition therein setting forth that they are tenants in common of Two negroes mentioned in said petition and praying for a sale of said negroes for the purpose of a division between them -- And whereas at the said Term of the said Court the said Petition coming on to be heard it was ordered, adjudged and decreed that the Clerk of this Court sell the said negroes on a credit of Six months, and whereas by virtue of the power and authority granted me by said decree I Stephen Charles Clerk did afterwards to wit on the 16th April 1840 at Nixonton said County of Pasquotank first having duly advertised the time and place of Sale I offered the said negroes for sale at public auction when and where John Baily Jr. appeared and bid for negro Girl Harriett the sum of one hundred and seventy two dollars who was the highest bidder & the purchaser of said negro Girl Harriett at said sale (she being one of the negroes mentioned in said petition) and whereas at the June Term 1840 of the said Court the said sale was confirmed -- Now Know all Men that I Stephen Charles Clerk as aforesaid foe and in consideration of the premises and the further consideration of the sum of one hundred and seventy two Dollars to me secured, to be paid the security whereof I do hereby acknowledge have granted bargained sold and confirmed and by these presents do grant, bargain sell and confirm unto the said John Baily Jr. negro Girl Harriett (being one of the negroes mentioned in said Petition) To have and To hold the said negro Girl Harriett unto him the said John Baily Jr. his heirs Executors administrators and assigns forever -- In Witness whereof I have hereunto set my hand and Seal the First day of September 1840.

****

S. Charles, Clk, Bill of Sale To Daniel Sawyer

Whereas Job Carver, Armwell Temple, James Temple Junior , Lucy Temple, James Temple Junior, Lucy Temple of full age, and Robin Temple and June Temple infants by their guardian William K. Richardson at the December Term 1839 of Pasquotank County Court of Pleas and Quarter Sessions did file their certain petition therein setting forth that they are Tenants in common of several negroes mentioned in said petition and praying for a sale of said negroes so that a fair and equitable division of the said negroes might be made among the said Petitioners -- And whereas at the said Term of the said Court the said petition coming on to be heard it was ordered and adjudged and decreed that Stephen Charles the Clerk of the said Court sell the said negroes mentioned in the said Petition -- And whereas by virtue of the Power and authority granted me by the said decree, I the said Stephen Charles Clerk & did afterwards to wit on the 20th January 1840 at the Store of J Pritchard in said County of Pasquotank first having duly advertised the time and place of Sale -- I offered the said negroes for Sale at public auction when and where Daniel Sawyer appeared and bid for negro man Albert the sum of Three hundred and Eighty one Dollars - who was the highest bidder & the purchaser of said negro Albert at said Sale (he being one of the negroes mentioned in said petition) And whereas at the March Term 1840 of the said Court the said sale was confirmed -- Now Know all men, that I Stephen Charles Clerk as aforesaid for and in consideration of the premises & the further consideration of the sum of Three hundred and Eighty one Dollars to me secured to be paid, the security whereof I do hereby acknowledge have granted, bargained Sold and confirmed and by these presents do grant, bargain, sell and confirm unto the said Daniel Sawyer negro man Albert (being one of the negroes mentioned in said Petition) To have and To hold the said negro Albert unto him the said Daniel Sawyer his heirs executors administrators and assigns forever - In Witness whereof I have hereunto set my hand and Seal the First day of September 1840.

****

Gregory to Hinton

Rec'd of Thos. P. Hinton Two hundred and six dollars for negro man Joe the title of whom I warrant and defend against all and every claim Whatever as Witness my hand and Seal this the 19th day of April 1841
J.N. Tillet
R. Gregory (Seal)

State of North Carolina } Court of Pleas and Quarter Sessions
Pasquotank County } June Term 1841

This Bill of sale from Richard J. Gregory to Thos. P. Hinton was exhibited and proved in open Court by the oath of J.N. Tillet, ordered to be Registered.
Test, Stephen Charles, Clk
Registerd in the Register's Office of Pasquotank in Book EE page 10, 20th July 1841.

****

W.F. Banks, Administrator of Thaddeus Freshwater, Bill of Sale To James C. Johnston, B T Palmer

Know all men by these presents that I William F. Banks, Admr. of Thaddeus Freshwater Dec'd have this day exposed to public sale a Certain negro girl slave named Dolly belonging to said Estate by virtue of an order made at the last Term of Pasquotank County Court when James Palmer as agent for James C. Johnston amongst others appeared and bid for the said Girl the sum of four hundred and fifty dollars and being the highest bidder became the purchaser for the sd. James C. Johnston. Now I the said William F. Bank Admrs. as aforesaid do promise and agree to warrant & defend the right and Title of the said Estate [?] to the said James C. Johnston so far as I am Authorized and empowered to do and no farther, Witness my hand & Seal this 3rd Decr. 1841.

Witness, Thos Palmer
K. F. Banks (Seal)

State of North Carolina } Court of Pleas & Quarter Sessions
Pasquotank County } March Term 1842

Bill of Sale from William F Bankes, administrator of Thaddeus Freshwater Deceased; to James C Johnson was Exhibited in open Court and the Execution thereof proved by the oath of Thomas Palmer the Subscribing witness thereto & ordered that the same be Registered.
Test, Stephen Charles, Clk
Registered in the Register's Office Pasquotank, in Book EE page 107, 6th April 1842
Wm. Gregory P Regrs.

****

Peggy Stokely's Bill of Sale To Emily Stokely

Know all Men by Thease presents That I Margaret Stokely of the County of Pasquotank and State of North Carolina for the good will & Love and affection which I have and beare to My Sister Emma Sawyer the Wife of Daniel Sawyer have given granted and Delivered to the Said Emma Sawyer One Certain Negro girl by the Name of Rachal aged about thirteen years and do by thease presents Absolutely give grant and Deliver unto the Said Emma Sawyer her Heirs Executors Admrs and assigns Said girl Rachal as above Described with all Her Increase for ever the right and Title whereof I the Said Margarett do Hereby agree to bind my Self My Heirs Exrs and Admrs to Warrant and forever Defend in Witness Whereof I have hereunto Set My hand and Seal this third Day of August in the year of our Lord One thousand Eight Hundred and forty Two and in the Presents of
Witness, J D Stokely
Margaret Stokely (Seal)

State of North Carolina }
Pasquotank County } December Term 1842

This Bill of sale from Margaret Stokely to Emily Stokely was Exhibited in open Court and proved by the oath of J.D. Stokely the Subscribing witness.

Test, Stephen Charles, Clk
Registered in the Register's Office of Pasquotank County in Book EE page 197, 7th Jany 1843
Wm Gregory P Regrs.

****

Philip Pritchard's Bill of Sale To Margaret Harris & others

State of North Carolina }
Pasquotank County }

Know all men by these presents, that I Philip Pritchard of the County of Pasquotank and State of North Carolina in consideration of the sum of seventy four dollars and eighty eight cents to me in hand paid by Miles Whitehurst of the same place, the receipt whereof is hereby acknowledged in full, have granted, bargained and sold, and by these presents do grant, bargain, sell and convey unto, Margaret Harris and Laurany Harris, a certain Negro Boy slave named Anderson about fourteen years old, to have and to hold the said the said slave, unto them the said Margaret Harris, Isaac Harris & William Harris, their heirs and assigns executors and administrators forever free and discharged of any and all incumbrances whatsoever except what is hereinafter named, And for the better security of the Title hereby conveyed, I for my self my heirs and assigns, to and with the said Margaret, Isaac, and William Harris aforesaid their heirs and assigns, do warrant and defend the title that the said Philip Pritchard purchased at the sale of the slaves of Grandy Harris from the lawful claim or claims of any and all persons whatever.

Nevertheless Miles Whitehurst the payor in this instrument doth except the use of the said boy Anderson for the term of his natural life.
In Testimony whereof I the said Philip Pritchard do hereunto set my hand and Seal this 11th day of November A.D. 1843.
Signed Sealed and delivered in presence of William Pritchard Jr.
Philip Pritchard (Seal)

State of North Carolina } Court of Pleas & Quarter Sessions
Pasquotank County } March Term 1844

This deed was exhibited in open Court and proved by the oath of Wm. D. Pritchard the subscribing witness -- ordered that the deed be Registered
Test, W.W. Griffin, Clk
Registered in the Register's Office of Pasquotank in Book EE page 367, 1st April 1844, Wm Gregory, P Regrs.

****

Bill of Sale From J. M. Jackson To Barney Jackson

February the 28th 1843 Rec'd of Barney Jackson Twenty one hundred Dollars in full Payment on the following Named Negroes and others as follows, Property as follows, one boy Named Alfred Twenty two years old, Five hundred Dollars, one Woman Named Clo thirty Nine Years old Two hundred Dollars, one Girl Named Mary Thirteen years old three hundred Dollars, one Ditto Named Hannah seven years old Two hundred and fifty Dollars, one boy Named Emanuel[?] Six years old Two hundred & fifty, three horses, one yoke of oxen, three cows & yearling, Fourteen hoggs, one [?] , one ox Cart, one ref of Black Smith Tools, allso all of my stock of provision and farming untensils, House hold & Kitchen Furniture, the right and Title of the above named [?] & the property I the said JM Jackson do warrant and defend to him the said B Jackson to him his heirs and assigns forever For my self My heirs & assigns and all lawful Claim or Claims of all and every person or persons Whatsoever, And I the said J M Jackson am to carry on the Crop & pay of the hands as it is to be given and pay of the hands out of the same said other expences For which I the said Barney Jackson do pay him Two hundred & fifty dollars and all family expenses be sides the above named sum Where unto I Set my hand and Seal in presents of Alfred A. Turner
Jos M Jackson (Seal)

State of North Carolina } Court of Pleas & Quarter Sessions
Oasquotank County } March Term 1843

This Bill of was Exhibited in open Court & acknowledged
Test, S. Charles, Clk
W.W. Griffin
Registered in the Register's Office of Pasquotank County in Book EE page 357, 1st, Aprl 1843.

Wm Gregory, P Regrs.

****

William S. Markham's Bill of Sale To John Markham

State of North Carolina }
Pasquotank County }

This indenture made and entered into this 17th day of February 1844 Between William S. Markham of the one part and John Markham of the other part Witnesseth that whereas heretofore Vizt. On the 20th day of July 1836 John Willson executed to said William S. Markham & Spence M. Mead a Deed in Trust for certain real and personal property therein described for the purpose of paying & securing the payment of a certain debt due to John C. Ehringhaus therein mentioned which will fully appear by reference to said Deed in Trust which is registered in Pasquotank County in Book R bb page 122 and whereas in pursuance of the directions of said Deed the said William S. Markham proceeded to Sell the property herein after conveyed at Public Sale at the House of the said William S. Markham after having given due Notice according to the terms thereof on the 17th day of February 1844 when and where John Markham being present bid for the property herein conveyed the Sum of Three Hundred and Five Dollars for negro man Jack, the above price being the highest and best bid. Now therefore for and in Consideration of the aforesaid Sum of Three Hundred and Five Dollars to me paid by the said John Markham the receipt whereof I di hereby acknowledge, I the said William S. Markham have given granted bargained & Sold & by these presents do give grant bargain & Sell unto the said John Markham his heirs & assigns forever all the right title & interest in the said negro Man Jack conveyed in said deed in trust.

To have and to hold the aforesaid negro man Jack unto him the said John Markham his heirs & Assigns forever, In Testimony whereof I have set my hand & Seal the day & year first above written in Presence of HW Skinner.
William S. Markham (Seal)

Court of Pleas & Quarter Sessions }
Sept Term 1844 }

This Bill of Sale was produced in open Court and proved by the oath of H. W. Skinner the subscribing witness, Let the deed be registered.
Test, W.W. Griffin, Clk
Registered in the Register's office of Pasquotank in Book (EE) page 408, 8th Decr. 1844
Wm Gregory, P Regrs.

****

Lemuel Taylor's Bill of Sale to Red Williams

Know all men by these presents that I Lemuel Taylor for and in Consideration of the Sum of Two hundred and fifty Dollars to me in hand paid by Reddick Williams the receipt whereof I hereby Acknowledge Have bargained Sold and conveyed unto him The Said Reddick Williams his heirs and assigns All of my right Title and interest in an undivided Lot of Negroes which I inherited In Common with the heirs of Edward Williams Dec'd to wit -- Lamb, George, David, Jin, Edmond, Nancey, Sam, Frederick & Wilson, It being the sixth part of said negroes and the said Lemuel Taylor do for my self my heirs Executors and Admrs. agree to warrant and forever Defend the right title and Interest of said Negroes unto him the said Reddick Williams his Heirs and assigns against the Claim or Claims of all persons Claiming under us whatsoever in Witness whereof I have hereunto Set my hand and Seal March 3rd 1845.
Witness, JD Stokely
His
Lemuel X Taylor (Seal)
Mark

State of North Carolina } Court of Pleas & Quarter Sessions
Pasquotank Couny } June Term 1845

This Deed was produced in open Court & proved by the oath of J.D. Stokely the subscribing witness & ordered to be Registered.
Test, W.W. Griffin, Clk.
Registered in the Register's office of Pasquotank in (EE) page 506, To term June 1845.
Wm Gregory, P Regrs.

****

Pasquotank County
Bills of Sale

George White's Bill of Sale to Jordan White

State of North Carolina }
Perquimans County }

Know all men by these presents that I George White of the County and State aforesaid for and in consiferation of the Sum of five Dollars to me in hand paid or secured to be paid, the receipt of which is hereby acknowledged and myself therewith fully satisfyd and paid have bargained sold transferred Conveyed and delivered, and by these presents doth fully positively and absolutely bargain sell transfer convey and deliver unto Jordan White of the County of Pasquotank & State aforesaid, A certain negro woman named & called Fillis aged about 42 years and two negro Children one Girl by the name of Fanny aged 2 or 3 years & one boy Child named Rufus aged about 6 months to have and to hold the above named negroes free and clear from the Lawful Claim or demand of me my heirs Exrs. Admrs or any person or persons whatsoever - In Testimony whereunto I the Sd Geo White have hereunto set my hand & Seal this 29th day of August AD 1846.
Test, William Wood
George White (Seal)

North Carolina }
Pasquotank }June Term 1853

The foregoing Bill of Sale was exhibited in open Court & duly acknowledged & ordered to be Registered
J W Hinton, Clk
Registered in Book JJ page 227
WP Mathews, P Regrs.

****

Jno. T. William's Bill of Sale To Lovey S. Pool

For and in consideration of the Sum of four hundred dollars to me in hand paid by Mrs. Lovey S. Pool of the State of N. Carolina and County of Pasquotank I have this day bargained Sold and Conveyed unto her the said Lovey S. Pool her heirs and assigns forever a certain negro woman named

Pleasant and child Catherine, The right and title to the aforesaid negro woman and child I hereby warrant and defend unto her the said Lovey S. Pool her heirs and assigns forever. Given under my hand and Seal this the 2nd day of May A.D. 1846
Signed & Sealed in presence of Job Carver.
Jno T. Williams (Seal)

State of North Carolina } Court of Pleas & Quarter Sessions
Pasquotank Count } Sept Term 1846

This Bill of sale was produced in open Court and the execution duly acknowledged by John T. Williams and ordered to be Registered.
Test, W.W. Griffin, Clk
Registered in Book FF page 240 Sep. 28th 1846
Wm Elliott PR by G Elliott.

****

Bill of Sale for Milley

State of North Carolina }
Pasquotank County } Jan. 2nd 1847

Know all men by these presents for and in consideration of the sum of three Hundred and fifty Dollars to me in hand paid, the receipt whereof is hereby acknowledged, I do hereby grant bargain & Sell to Thomas Lister negro woman Milly aged about nineteen years of age and I do hereto for my self executors administrators & assigns Warrant & defend the title to said negro to Thos Lister his executors, administrators & assigns forever free from all incumbrances whatsoever.
Witness Edm: H. Perkins jurat
Nancy Blount

State of North Carolina } Court of Pleas & Quarter Sessions
Pasquotank County } March Term 1847

This Bill of Sale was produced in open Court and the execution proved by the oath of Edmd. H. Perkins the subscribing witness & ordered Registered.
Test, W.W. Griffin, Clk

Pasquotank County
Bills of Sale

Registered April 12 1847 in Book FF Page 361.
Wm. Elliott, PR

****

Grandy Richardson's Bill of Sale To James T. Banks

State of North Carolina }
Pasquotank County }

Know all men by these presents that we John J. Grandy and Daniel Richardson for and in Consideration of the sum of one dollar to us paid by James T. Banks, and also in consideration of the terms being performed by said Banks, upon which the property herein after named was conveyed to us - we have bargained, Sold, Released and reconveyed & do by these presents, bargain, Sell, Release and Reconvey unto the Said James T. Banks his heirs and assigns, all our Right Title and interest in negro woman Milly and her three Children, Harriett, Billy and Margaret the said negroes said Banks to have possessed of them after the expiration of the present year for which Term they are hired to Joseph A Turner, or sooner if by Consent of the hirer.

Witness our hands & Seals this 16th August 1849.
Gilbert Elliott, jurat
Jno J Grandy (Seal)
Danl. Richardson (Seal)

State of North Carolina } Court of Pleas & Quarter Sessions
Pasquotank County } Decr. Term 1849

This deed was Exhibited in open Court and proved by the oath of G. Elliott, subscribing witness and ordered to be registered.
Test, W.W. Griffin, Clk
Registered in Book 99 page 221
W P Mathews, P R

****

Thos. R. Spence's Bill of Sale To Jonathan Edney

Know all men by these presents that I Thomas R. Spence of the County of Camden and State of North Carolina of the one part Jonathan Edney of the same place of the other part Witnesseth that for and in consideration of the sum of Eight Hundred & sixty dollars to me Thos R Spence in hand paid by the said Jonathan Edney the receipt whereof is hereby acknowledged have bargained sold & conveyed unto the said Jonathan Edny His Heirs Executors Admrs & Assigns forever two certain negroes Known by the names of George & Mahala To have and to hold the above negroes which (I heired from my fathers Estate) and I the said Thos R Spence for my self my Heirs Exers Admrs & Assigns do covenant & agree with the said Jonathan Edney His Heirs Exrs Admrs & Assigns that we will warrant & forever defend the above named negroes against the claim or claims of each & every person or persons whatsoever, In Testimony whereof I have hereunto set my hand & affix my seal this 1st day of December 1851.
Jno T. Williams
Thos R Spence (Seal)

State of North Carolina } Court of Pleas & Quarter Sessions
Pasquotank County } Decr. Term 1851

This deed was Exhibited in open Court & the execution duly acknowledged & ordered to be Registered.
Test, W.W. Griffin, Clk, Page 63 JJ

****

State of North Carolina }
Pasquotank County }

Know all men by these presents that I James Harris for and in Consideration of the sum of Seven Hundred Dollars to me in hand paid by Wilson W. Williams, the receipt whereof is hereby acknowledged, and the further consideration of one Half of the nett proceeds of sales of [?] negroes hereby conveyed, over and above the sum of Seven hundred Dollars aforesaid, I the said James Harris have bargained and Sold and by these presents do bargain and sell unto him the said Wilson W. Williams Two Certain Slaves to wit, man Jesse and woman Susan - To have and to hold the said negro slaves Jesse & Susan to him the said W.W. Williams his executors & administrators & Assigns in fee simple, forever, and the said Williams doth covenant & agree to with the said Harris that he will send said slaves away and obtain the best price that can be obtained & hereby account to him the said Harris for the half of nett proceeds of said slaves over & above the aforesaid Seven Hundred Dollars - In Witness whereof we the said James Harris & W.W. Williams have hereunto set our hands & Seals this the 11th day of Sept. 1852.

Witness, W.W. Griffin
His
James X Harris (Seal)
Mark
Wilson W. Williams (Seal)

It is further agreed by these parties that if the said negroes shall not nett Seven Hundred Dollars advanced by W.W. Williams afsd the said Harris binds himself and his heirs to pay to said Williams his Exers & Admrs, the difference between the nett and the seven Hundred dollars, afd.

Witness, W.W. Griffin (Seal)
His
James X Harris
Mark
W.W. Williams (Seal)

****

A.W. Morgan's Bill of Sale To Eliza Pritchard

State of North Carolina }
Pasquotank County }

Know all men by these presents that I, Anthony W. Morgan of the State & County aforesaid for and in consideration of the sum of ninety dollars to me in hand paid by Eliza Pritchard, of the same State & County the receipt whereof is hereby acknowledged, have given, granted, bargained, sold & delivered and by these presents do give, grant, bargain, sell and deliver unto the said Eliza Pritchard, her Executors, administrators & assigns all my right and interest in and to Negro woman Lovey & her son Enoch & her increase, being one eighth of said negros.

To have & to hold my right & interest in & to said negroes Lovy & her son Enoch & her increase unto the said Eliza Pritchard her executors, Administrators and Assigns forever free & Clear of all claim of my self my executors & Administrators or any person or persons claiming under me or them.

Witness my hand and Seal this the **[Blank]** day of November A.D. 1853
In Presence of Griffin - Pritchard
Anthony Morgan (Seal)

****

Kennedy To M. White
Elizabeth City N.C. March 15th 1855

Know all men by these presents that I William W. Kennedy have this day sold unto Milly White a free Woman of Color, a negro man named Allen known as Allen Dogier, for the sum of Eight hundred dollars, the receipt Whereof is hereby acknowledge, and I the Sd. Kennedy do hereby Warrant and defend the Title to sd. negro man to her the sd. Melly White forever. Witness my hand & Seal this day & date above written.
Test, John O Kelley, J
W W Kennedy (Seal)

State of North Carolina }
Pasquotank County } May 21st 1855

The forgoing Bill of Sale was this day Exhibited before me & the execution thereof proved by the oath of Jno O'Kelly the Subscribing witness, let it be Registered
J W Hinton, Clk
Page 472, Book LL, Registered
W G Lamb, PR

****

July the 6th 1857 from John C. Ehringhaus, Clerk & Master of the Court of Equity Three hundred Sixteen Dollars 44/100 being one third of this **[?]** of Negro Jerry belonging to Richard H l**[?]**, Morris Snowden **[?]** Skinner, the latter now dead upon whose Estate I have administrated.
J. W. Hinton, Clk

****

Know all men by these present, That I[?] B. Elliott of the County of Norfolk and State of Virginia for & in consideration of the sum of Eight hundred & fifty Dollars, to me in hand paid by John C. Ehringhaus, Clerk & Master of the Court of Equity of this County of Pasquotank and State of North Carolina, The receipt whereof I hereby fully admit and acknowledge, have bargained, sold & delivered & by the presents do bargain, sell and unto the said John C. Ehringhaus, Clerk & Master as aforesaid, his Executors, Admrs Assigns & Successors in Office, a certain Negro Girl Slave Liddy to have & to hold the said Negro Girl Liddey, unto him the said John C. Ehringhaus the said John C. Ehringhaus, Clerk & Master, his Executors, Admrs assigns & Successors in Office and I the said Albert R. Elliott, for my self, my heirs assigns, hereby warrant & will forever defend the right Title to the said Negro Girl Liddy, free & clear from all claims demands whatsoever, Witness my hand & Seal this 19th day of November 1857
Witness, Wm. C. Bu[?]
A.R. Elliott, Clk

****

Powers to Pool

For value received in the sum of two hundred dollars, I have this day bargained, Sold, Sell & Convey, & deliver to William G. Pool, his heirs and Assigns, a certain negro slave named Henrietta, aged about four Years.

To have and to hold the said slave Henrietta, to the said Pool & his heirs forever, moreover, I Warrant said slave sound & the Title good.

In Witness whereof I have hereunto set my hand & Seal This 8th of Decr. 1858. Signed, Sealed & Delivered in the Presence of Geo. D. Pool.
Millicent Powers (Seal)

North Carolina } December 18th 1858
Pasquotank }

The within Bill of Sale was this day exhibited before me and the execution thereof was duly proved by the oath of Geo. D. Pool the Subscribing Witness thereto - Let it be registered
Jas. W. Hinton, Clk

Registered in Book M. M. Page 452 by Timothy Gilbert, PR

****

W.H. Jones & D.P. A. Cartright's Bill of Sale to Robert Simpson
2/5 of 1/2 of Stephen

North Carolina }
Pasquotank County }

Know all men by these presents that we Walton H Jones and D.P.A. Cartright of the State of Tennessee for and in Consideration of the sum of Fifteen follars fifty Cents to Each of us in hand paid the receipt of which is hereby acknowledged have bargained, sold, and conveyed and do by these presents bargain sell and convey unto Robert Simpson all our undivided interest and share in and to an old Negro Man Named Stephen the same formerly belonging to James Cartright Dec'd our share and interest in the said slave being one fifth of one half to Each of us To have and to hold all our said shares and interest in said slave to him said Robert Simpson his executors, Admrs. and assigns forever.

In Testimony whereof We the said Walton H. Jones & D. P. A. Cartright have thereto set our hands and Seals - this the 19th February 1859.
Signed Sealed & Delivered in the presence of Thomas Pritchard
Walton H. Jones By GW Brooks his Atty in fact (Seal)
D.P.A. Cartright (Seal)

North Carolina }
Pasquotank County } Court September Term 1859

This Bill of Sale was exhibited in open Court and the execution thereof proved by the oath of Thomas Pritchard the subscribing Witness thereto, Let it be Registered.
JW Hinton, Clk by C G Elliott, DClk
Registered in Book M. M. Page 584 the 16th of September 1859 by Timothy Gilbert, Public Register

****

Wm. Shannon's Bill of Sale to J Woodard

Pasquotank County
Bills of Sale

State of North Carolina }
Pasquotank County }

Know all men by these presents that I Wm. Shannon for the Sum of three hundred & fifty dollars have this day Bargained & Sold unto JA Woodard a negro woman by the name of Harriett age about forty years to have & to hold unto him the said Woodard his heirs Executors & Admrs. in fee Simple & I furthermore Warrant & Defend the Right from all claim or claims whatsoever.
In Testimony whereof I have set my hand & Seal, May 1st 1858.
Wm Shannon (Seal)

North Carolina } February 11th 1859
Pasquotank County }

The within Bill of Sale was this day exhibited before me and the execution thereof was duly acknowledged by Chas G. Elliott, D.C.
Registered in Book M. M. Page 488 by Timothy Gilbert, PR.

Chapter Nine

Pasquotank County

Miscellaneous

North Carolina State Archives
Pasquotank County Records
Records of Slaves and Free Persons of Color
C.R.075.928.9

Hiring of Slaves

Mr. Nathan Overman
Please to pay Devotion White the Sum of Fifteen Pounds Currency which shall be good for so much in our Settlement on the Accts of Pomp's Hire
June 6th 1796
Thomas Jordan
C Cartright

Caleb Trueblood
May 1st 1788 to William Overman.
To the Hier of a Negro woman 8 Mo. For five Pounds

[?] from the Commissioners of the Town of Eliz. City Thirty five dollars for one month, hire of my self a Negro Man Daniel.
Witness Will Shannon
His
John X Morris
Mark
Augst 31st 1829

Mr. Denis Dozier you can have Jesse one month at the rate of fifty dollars per year, I shall endeavour to see you in the course of one month, you can give him passes when needed and see to him for me, I am yours &c.
January 18th 1828
Peter Dozier.

State of North Carolina.

This is to certify that Nathaniel [?] Resident, Resident of Camden County State of N. Carolina has employed in the Dismal Swamp a negro man by name of Jack Miller of the following description: 5 feet 10 & 1/2 inches high, of black complexion, aged about 32 years, has a scar on the right great toe, left cheak larger than the right. Given under my hand and seal of Office, at Elizabeth City, on the 5th day of February. 1851.
W.W. Griffin, Clk.

This is to Certify that the within named Man Sam Miller is now in my employment in my Swamp.
Jany 28th 1851
Arch Riddick.

State of North Carolina
Pasquotank County
This is to certify John & Nathaniel Ga[?] Resident of Camden County & State of N. Carolina has employed in the Dismal Swamp a negro name of Sam Miller of the following description: 5 feet 7 inches high, of Dark complexion, aged about 37 years, with a small naked spot on the top of the head.

Given under my hand and seal of office, at elizabeth City, on the 30th day of Jany. 1851
W.W. Griffin, Clk

25th Sept 1771
This will be Delivered by negro Pashence who I hired of Mr. Ellgood a bout a month ago and she seems to be Big With Child and I have no Place nor house for her to have it in-- Thought Proper to send her home and shall Be glad you'd Take her and I must loos her Time -- for it is impossible for her to have it here for I have no Body to Take any care of her from Sr Your Humble Servant
Abner Harrison.

Article of ageement made between Fisher Trueblood & Willis Case both of the County of Pasquotank that the said Fisher Trueblood for the Consideration of the sum of twenty two pounds to him in hand paid by the sd. Willis Case agrees to Let his negro Sam work with the or for the sd. Willis Case two year and three months from the date of the articles which Daniel Trueblood hath for sd. Sam and to work for sd. Cases his heirs & assigns but if the Sd. Sam should die in that time the said Trueblood is to pay the same [?] of pay to the said Case in proportion to the time he had to work My hand this 6th day of April 1789
Fisher Trueblood.

Negro Ben of AC & PC Huffins for the year 1857

An Account of the negro Ben of the negroes belonging to Augustus C. Huggins & Pauline C. Huggins bind out
1 day January 1857 to 1 day January 1858.

Daniel	Jesse Sanderlin	100.00
Ben	Jasper Etheridge	180.00
Rit	Owen Holms	190.00
Nathan	Jasper Etheridge	180.00
Ciler	do do	180.00
Brooks	Lott Williams	90.00
Polly, Alick, William		

& Nat George Ward towit
bid $10

Prince	Jasper Etheridge	180.00
Minter & Rose	Jesse Sanderlin	23.00
Hepsey	do do	35.00
Vicy	Denis Aman	20.00
Sam	George Ward	15.00
Cloy	do do	60.00
Emiley	Robert Dorson	67.00
Caty & Edward	George Ward	50.00
Allen	Ezekiel T. Phillips	66.00
Elias	do do	45.00
		1421.00

****

Travel Passes

The Negro Charls hath leave to pass and behalf on his Good behaviour for three Days this 26th Day of the %th Mo. 1798
Zachariah Nixon.

****

Quaker Manumission Dispute

Presentment, Grand Jury of Pasquotank County

North Carolina } Sessions
Pasquotank County }

The Jurors for the State and County aforesaid, do present, that the County of Pasquotank, is reduced to a Situation, of great perrel and danger, in consequence of the proceedings, of the Society of people, called Quakers. That the idea of emancipation, among their Slaves is publicly held out to them, and incouraged by the conduct of the Quakers; that the minds of the Slaves, are not only Greatly corrupted and allianated from the Services of their Masters in condequence of such conduct but always are protected, harbored, and encouraged by them -- Arsons, are even committed, without a possibility of discovery.

Pasquotank County
Miscellaneous

The Grand Jury, are so perfectly Sensible, the infatuate enthusiasm of the Quakers as to partial & general emancipation, that they see a present alarm amongst the minds of the people, and for[?] prospect of imminent to impend, by the influence and designing attempts of the Quakers to this purpose, which unless prevented must burst with destruction, around the Citizens of the State.

The Grand Jury reflecting upon the Miserable havock and masscres which have lately taken place in the West Indies, in consequence of emancipation; Knowing the opinion of the Northern States;of the many hundred thousand Slaves around them; and of the infatuated enthusiasm of Men Calling themselves religious, who are amongst them; Conceive it a duty which they owe to themselves, their families, and their Country to present this existing, and alarming evil and to present the people called Quakers and their abettors, as the Authors of the Common Mischief in this Quarter of the World; Where independent of foreign opinion, emancipation is publicly held out by the Quakers, to the Negroes, and private funds established in support of it.

The Grand Jurry present that speedy resolute Measures ought to be adopted, by the good since and Spirit of the people, in order to prevent, that common appeal to Arms in their own defence which at present appears to be almost, if alltogether Necessary.
True Bill, Henry Lankester, Foreman.

Edenton District
October Term 1793

The Grand Jurors for the aforesaid District present as a Grievaance, the Destressing Inconvenience, the good people of the district lay under from the Inefficiency of the Laws intended to restrict the Emancipation of Slaves. That the people called Quakers in other respect good Citizens, have by their Conduct, made that Species of property not only of small Value, but have Rendered it dangerous to the person at Safety of the proprietors of Negroes, and those who live in the Vicinity of them, by enfranchising their own Slaves and sowing discontent and disobedience in the minds of their Neighbors Slaves. That it is now become Necessary for the preservation of good Order and the Security of the Citizens of this District that Measures should be Taken to put a Stop to this Evil

Pasquotank County
Miscellaneous

It is not for the grand Jury to point out the remedial Laws, but to declare a necessity for them; They therefore require their representatives in the next general Assembly; to lay this their presentment before the Legislature -- In whose Wisdom they Confide - and whose Protection as Citizens they Demand trusting that Measures will be taken so to modify the religious Enthusiasam which pervades their Quaker Neighbours: that the Citizens of this District may Enjoy a full participation of a Constitution which they have assisted to raise Vizt. A protection of their Personal Liberties and Properties.

1. Woolsey Hathaway, Foreman, 2. William Saterfield, 3. Thomas E. Hare, 4. J.H. Ward, 5. Thomas Simons, 6. Enoch Dauge, 7. Thomas Davis, 8. John Burn, 9. Saml. W. Johnston, 10. Enoch Darley, 11. Jos. Banks, 12. Willis Roberts, 13. Joseph Tarkenton, 14. Spencer Thach, 15. James Temple, 16. John Campbell.

[The top part of this document has been torn away]

of Consequence which we believe to be and Duty to prefer to Every temperal Consideration And Eclipsing that Testemony which we Humbly Conceive God hath given us to bear, that under this Glorious Gospel Dispensation, he will in his own time bring his whole Creation under that, Peaceable & happy Disposition, That Nation Shall not lift up sword Against Nation, Neither Shall they Learn War any More.

We have refuted the Payment of no Taxes for the Suport of Government. We keep our own poor from being Chargable to the Public: And shall think ourselves in Duty bound to detect any Hipocritical Pretenders who might be Desirous to search themselves under our Profession, if, if we can have any favour allow'd to us, and so hoping you may be pleased in tenderness, to take our Case under your Consideration.

We Conclude in behalf & by Appointment of our Society with Sincear Respects your Friends.

Thos: Newby }Joseph White
Thos: Nicholson } Joseph Robinson.

Returns of the the Sale of Negro Girl Tamer

Pasquotank County
Miscellaneous

In obedience to the annexed order of the Court of Pleas and Quarter Sessions, I proceeded to offer said Negro girl at publick Sale at the Store of Joseph Pritchard after giving Twenty days Notice and the last bid being three Hundred and eight Dollars said Negro girl was Sold to Wilson Spence for the same as will appear in an Inventory return by June Term 1842.

His
Reddin X Sawyer, Admrs.
Mark

To the Sale of Negro girl Tamer by order of Court $308 Dollars Sold on the 30th of April 1842.

Court Appearance

Pasquotank }
County }

Coll. Thomas Hunter Mr Henry Acknowledges themselves Indebted to our Soverign Lord the King in the Sum of five hundred pounds Proclamation money for the good behavior & appearance of a Negro fellow Called Ben the Property of Mr. Palin of the said County, to appear at the Court House of the County Afsd. On the first Tuesday in December anno Domini 1742.

Petition of Ruth Tillett

Pasquotank County,

To the Worshipfull the Justices of the Inferior Court of Pleas & Quarter Sessions of the County of Pasquotank County now in Court Setting. The Humble Petition of Ruth Tillett a free Born coloured Woman. Humbly sheweth unto your Worships, That she was Born of a Free Woman named Ann Tillett, the Daughter of the wife of one Tillet of Powls Point, in Currituck County supposed by a Black Man; That Your Petitioner's Mother moved from Currituck to a Neighborhood on Little River; and was delivered of your Petitioner at the house of one Timothy Mead, where she remained until the death of her Mother and the said Timothy , at whose Vendue she was Sold to one Blackstock who she verily believes was not ignorant of her Condition and Rights to Liberty, and Sold her to a distant

Merchant called Barny Coff of Newbern, At which Place she had eight several Masters each getting rid of her, as soon as they could, on hearing of her story and resolution to regain her Liberty. That **[Faded]** Last Master John Bishop, she made her Escape and came to her Native County, to which place the said Bishop followed her and sold her to one Zachariah Jordan (and he as she has been informed gave no Purchase Money for her, and that the said Bishop injoined the said Zachariah Jordan to inquire into her rights and if true, to let her enjoy them, and if Otherwise to send him payment, which was like the Common honest Behaviour of his Life) who she believes, no ways ignorant of the Premises, Still detains her in Slavery and Distress. Your Petitioner humbly begs to inform your Worships, that she has been so happy as to find reputable and honest Evidence akive, altho at the Distance of Forty Years, of her Birth and of her Civil and Social Rights, Whereupon your poor and Distressed Petitioner humbly prays (Altho her complection which is an Act of the Almighty God, Not her Crime) Your Worships will of your Mercy, take her case under your Guidance and Consideration, and to render her such Redress as to your Worships in Your Great Wisdom and Justice you shall deem Meet.

Depositions Concerning former Slaves of Jesse Rogerson 1892

Services Accepted, Grandy Adalett, Attys for Defts. We agree that the depositions shall be taken on the 24th instead of 25th of Feby 1892. Grandy Adlett, Attys for Defts.
J.W. Albertson Attys for Pltffs

North Carolina }
Pasquotank }

To Robert Harvey
Take Notice that on the 24th day of Feby A.D. 1892 at the Store house of Josiah Nicholos at Belvidere Perquimans County between the hours of 10 AM and 4 PM the deposition of Daniel Lilly **[Silly?]** will be taken to be read in an action now pending in the Superior Court of Pasquotank County wherein Henry Jordan & Wife Penny and others are Plaintiffs and you are Defendant. The deposition is taken on behalf of the Plaintiffs.
Henry Jordan & Wife Penny
By J. W. Albertson Atty

Pasquotank County Miscellaneous

Pasquotank County --- In the Superior Court
State of North Carolina,

To Josiah Nicholson of Belvidere Perquimans Co.

We, having confidence in your prudence and fidelity, do hereby authorize and empower you to cause Daniel Lilly as witness in behalf of the Plaintiffs to come before you at such time and place as you shall appoint, and him to examine on oath, concerning all such matters and things as he may know, respecting a controversy now pending in our Superior Court of Pasquotank County wherein Henry Jordan & Wife Penny and others are Plaintiffs, and Robert Harvey is Defendant, as well on the part of the said Plttfs as the said Defendant and said depositions to take in writing under your hand and seal up and send the same to our Court at the Court House in Elizabeth City, on the third Monsay in March 1892.

Witness Jno. P. Overman, Clerk of said Court at my office in Elizabeth City this 16th day of Feby 1892
J.P. Overman, Clerk of Pasquotank County, NC.

State of North Carolina }
County of Perquimans }

I, Josiah Nicholson of Belvidere Perquimans County N.C. to whom the Commission herewith returned, was directed, do hereby Certify That in obedience thereto, I Caused to appear before me, at my Store house at Belvidere Perquimans County, on February 24th 1892, Daniel Lilly, the Witness therein named, and between the hours of 10 AM and 4 PM of said day did take his testimony as Commanded, he having been duly sworn according to law, which deposition is as follows Viz.

Quest 1 - What is your name? And your age
Answr - My name is Daniel Lilly: and I am Seventy Eight Years of age.

Quest. 2 - Where you born, & where have you Lived?
Answr. 2 - I was born in Perquimans County N.C., I have always lived in Perquimans County as my home, though for about three years I worked over in Pasquotank County.

Quest. 3rd - Did you know Jesse Rogerson, if so where did he live?
Answr. 3rd - I did know him - and he lived in the upper part of Perquimans County N.C. at the place now occupied by Richard Hurdle - about two miles from my home.

Quest. 4th - Did you know any of this children, and if so give their names.?
Answr. 4th - I knew three of his children, and their names were Abel Rogerson, Jeremiah Rogerson and Betsy Rogerson - afterwards Betsy Stallings & wife of Daniel Stallings.

Quest 5th - Did you know any of the Slaves of Jesse Rogerson & if so State their names?
Answr. 5th I did know them or the most of them and their names were Rose, Celia (an old woman) Sam, Charles & Amos

Quest 6th - Do you know whether there was a woman named Rose, who belonged to the Estate of Jesse Rogerson?
Answr. 6th - Yes - there was a woman by the name of Rose belonging to said Estate.

Quest. 7th - Did the said Rose have any Children, and if so State their names
Answr 7th - Rose's Children were Sam, Charles, Amy and Harriet - the two former went by the name of Sam Rogerson and Charles Rogerson - and the two daughters were Amy Stallings & Harriet Stallings.

Quest 8th - Did ahe (Rose) have any other children except the ones you named?
Answr 8th - Not that I knew of.

Quest 9th - What opportunity did you have for knowing Rose's family? Did you live with her owner, or near them? Did you see them often, did you see her children often? How long did you acquaintance with her and her children continue?
Answr 9th - I lived near them - and I frequently worked in the Rogerson family - on the farm in the time og Jeremiah Rogerson after his father's death - and the lifetime of Hannah Rogerson - the widow of Jesse and said Jeremiah Rogerson managed the farm for himself and mother and employed me as a laborer on the farm and I worked with and in the Company with the slaves and at that time the aforementioned Slaves - Viz Rose - and her children Sam and Charles were small boys - large enough to do some work - and my knowledge of them Continued for several years - at least until they went away or were taken away - as I frequently saw them and was frequently with them - I also Continued to know Rose up to the

time she left that neighborhood - and afterwards I frequently saw her as she then lived down near the place now Called Belvidere.

Quest 10th If you knew Sam Rogerson, how long did you know him; Where did you first know him, and when did he leave your neighborhood.
Answr. 10th - I knew Sam Rogerson up to the time he went away from a little boy - and I think he was between the age of fifteen and twenty when he went away bit I do not know precisely about his age, I had personally known him for fifteen or more years before he went away - I do not remember the date of his leaving my neighborhood - I know that I worked with Jeremiah Rogerson & his Mother in 1832 - and that Sam was then a small boy

Quest 11th **[Creased, Unreadable]**
Answr 11th - He lived with Hannah Rogerson, Jesse Rogerson's widow - and with Jeremiah Rogerson - her Son said Jeremiah Rogerson and his mother lived as one family and it was then that I lived and worked for Jeremiah Rogerson - and Sam was then there as one of the undivided family of Slaves.

Quest 12th Did you ever live with the owner, or at the house where Sam lived, if so state the name
Answr 12th - I do not know that there was any division made of the Slaves of Jesse Rogerson Dec'd between or among his Widow and Children - I always understood it that Abel Rogerson sold Sam Rogerson but whether as his individual property or for a Division of his fathers Estate, I know not - I believed Sam to belong to the Rogerson Family when I lived with them.

Quest 13th How long did you live at **[Creased]**, with the said Sam in the family of Jeremiah Rogerson & Mother at least one month & worked on the farm in company with him

Quest 14th What become of Sam, Did he go away from your Neighborhood, if so - where did he go?
Answr. 14th - Sam was sold as a Slave to a man in Elizabeth City - I think by the name of Glover - and I think Sam was a Servant in a Hotel in Elizabeth City for several years - I remember to have seen Sam in Elizabeth City after he was sold away from my neighborhood

Quest 15th Who was Sam's Mother?

Answr. 15th - Sam's Mother was Rose - a Slave woman belonging to Jesse Rogerson and his heirs.

Quest 16th Is Rose living or dead?
Answr 16th - Rose is dead - I do not know how many years - for she had moved out of my immediate neighborhood and lived with a man as her husband, near Belvidere for many years previous to her death.

Quest 17th If you know, State what become of her other Children - the Children of - are any of them living - and what are their names?
Answr. 17th - Rose's Son Charles went to Gatesville N.C. or in the County of Gates - and never returned to Perquimans - That I know of - Rose's daughter Amy and Harriet are still living and near Belvidere N.C.

Quest 18th Did Rose have any other Children besides those you Mentioned?
Answr. 18th - She did not that I know of.

Quest 19th Did you see or know Sam after he went to Eliz. City?
Answr. 19th - I did see and know Sam as many times as two or three times in Eliz. City

Quest 20th What is the Consideration of your health? Are you able to travel without risk to health?
Answr 20th - My Health is very poor - am old & infirm nearly blind - and am not able to travel without great risk to my health. I further declare that I have no interest in said Case and am not Concerned in its prosecution,

His
Daniel X Lilly
Mark

Witnesses, J Nicholson & [?] Copeland

Affirmed to and subscribed before me this day by the above named Affiant, and I Certify that I read the said Affidavit to said Affiant, and acquainted him with its Contents before he executed the same - and that said Affiant is personally known to me, and that he is a credible person - and so respected in the Community in which he resides.

Witnes my hand and Official Seal This the 24th day of February 1892.

Josiah Nicholson
Commissioner (Seal)

Appendix A
Glossary of Legal Terms

Appendix A

Glossary of Legal Terms

[Definitions of legal terms appearing in transcriptions within this book are derived from *Black's Law Dictionary*. See footnote below.]

A & B (Assault & Battery): The unlawful touching of another individual without excuse or justification.

Action of Trover: A remedy to recover the value of personal property wrongfully converted by another person or persons to his own use.

Affiant: An individual who creates and subscribes an affidavit. Interchangeable with deponent.

Agent: An individual authorized by another to act in place of another person.

Alias Capias: The issuance of a second writ.

Assignee: An individual who receives an assignment. An individual whom the law vests the right; Executor or Administrator.

Attachment: The legal seizing of someones property to comply with a writ or judicial order to satisfy a judgment not yet rendered.

Atrix: Female Plaintiff.

Bailiwick: A given area over which a bailiff or sheriff has authority or jurisdiction.

Appendix A
Glossary of Legal Terms

Calaboose: An old term for jail or prison. From the Spanish word, "*calabozo*."

Capias: A general name for different types of writs requiring an officer to detain someone in custody.

Certiori: A writ issued by a superior court to an inferior court for the purpose of an investigation into irregularities.

Commission: A warrant issued by a government empowering an individual to do certain acts.

Commissioner: An individual to whom a commission is directed by a government or a court.

Decree: In equity, a sentence or order of the court after considering the case.

Deposition: A pretrial discovery method by which one party, through their attorney asks oral questions of the other party.

Dimunition of the Record: A phrase stating that the record delivered from an inferior court to a superior court for review is incomplete.

Determination: A decision given by a court implying an ending of a controversy or suit.

Enfeoff: A gift of hereditaments to another.

Equity Courts: Courts that deliver justice according to the system of equity. Equity courts are sometimes called, "Courts of Chancery."

Esquire: A title given to sheriffs, justices of the peace, and barristers at law.

Et als: Latin term meaning "and others."

Ex Parte: Done for, or on the application of, one party only.

Appendix A
Glossary of Legal Terms

Execution: The carrying out of an act to its completion.

Exemplifications: An official transcript or certified copy of a document retrieved from public records to be used as evidence.

False Imprisonment: An individual who is placed in detention without his consent, and without lawful authority.

Fi Fa (Fieri Facias): A writ requiring a sheriff to satisfy a judgment levied from a debtors property.

Forma Execution: The prescribed form of execution..

Forma Pauperis: A provision made for a poor person to have their day in court without liability for fees or costs.

Free Persons of Color: Term applied to all persons not part of the white race, including Indians.

F.W.C.: Free woman of color: Term applied to all persons not part of the white race, including Indians. The term was not used much after the Civil War.

Goal (Gaol): An obsolete English term for prison or Jail.

Guardian: An individual invested with power for caring for someone who is incapable of handling their own affairs.

Guardian ad litem: A special guardian appointed by the Court to represent an infant or unborn person.

Gaurnished: A furnishing or garnishment.

Hue & Cry: A loud outcry to pursue felons (robbers and murderers), and all who heard it were bound to join in the pursuit.

Habeas Corpus: A writ commonly directed to a sheriff ordering him to deliver a prisoner, or an individual who is to be detained. The purpose is to test the legality of the detention, and not whether the individual is guilty or innocent

Appendix A
Glossary of Legal Terms

Inops Consilli: Without legal counsel.

Injunction: A court order prohibiting an individual from committing a certain act, or ordering an individual to undo an injury.

Indenture: A contract by which bonds and debentures are issued stating the form of bond, maturity date, amount of issue, descriptions of assets, interest rates and various other terms.

Inquest: An inquisition by a coroner, sometimes accompanied by a jury to investigate the death of someone who has been killed, or died under suspicious circumstances.

Next Friend: An individual who acts for the benefit of an infant; or a person who is not able to look after his own business or interests. It is similar to guardian ad litem.

Ne Exeat: A writ that forbids an individual to flee the country, state or jurisdiction of the court.

Nol Pros (Nolle Prosequi): The prosecuting attorney will no longer prosecute the case.

Non Compus Mentes: Incompetent, or not of sound mind.

Non Suit: A judgment against the plaintiff when he is unable to prove his case.

Outlaw: In English law, an individual who has been banned from the protection of the law.

Partition: The dividing of lands owned by joint tenants or tenants in common.

Prima Facie: A fact supposedly to be true unless disproved by evidence to the contrary.

Recognizance: An obligation of an individual, before a magistrate, that he will perform some act required by law.

Appendix A
Glossary of Legal Terms

Referee: An individual who is referred by the court in a cause pending to listen to the testimony and parties involved and return a report to the court.

Replevin: A legal action giving the owner or person entitled the right to repossession of property from someone who has wrongfully taken or detains his property.

Subpoena: An order to appear at a specific time to testify upon a matter.

Solicitor: The chief law officer in a government body.

Special Venire: To appear in court, or citizens from whom a jury is selected. A Special Venire is usually called for a protracted case.

Surety: An individual who is primarily liable for payment of debt, or for the performance of obligation of another.

Statute of Limitations: Statutes of the Federal Government and States that set a given amount of time for which certain actions can be brought forth.

Severalty: Individuals who own real or personal property without other persons sharing in the ownership.

Struck Off: In the language of an auctioneer, by the fall of his hammer, property is to be "Struck Off," which signifies the bidder is entitled to property after paying for it.

Scifa: Abbreviation for "Scire Facias."

Scire Facias: A judicial writ requiring a debtor to appear and show cause why judgment against him should not be revived. An order to show cause why mortgaged property should not be sold to satisfy a debt.

Slave: An individual who has no freedom and is subject to another in whole. His person and services are completely under the control of another. He belongs to his Master, and his industry and labor are not his own. His Master may sell or dispose of his person.

Appendix A
Glossary of Legal Terms

True Bill of Indictment: An endorsement issued by a grand jury upon finding sufficient evidence for a criminal charge.

Trespass: The unlawful interference with another's rights or property.

Tenants in Common: Tenants who hold the same property (including Slaves) together by several and distinct titles.

Trustee: An individual who is chosen or appointed by law to execute a Trust.

Testamentary Trustee: An individual chosen or appointed to fulfill or carry out a trust created by a Will.

Tax District: A district to which a tax is ratably apportioned, and levied upon its population.

Venditioni Exponas: In Latin - You expose to sale. The sale is usually directed by the sheriff.

Venire Facias: A writ directed to the sheriff to command that he cause twelve good and lawful men to come to court on a given day to serve as jurors.

Vi et Armis: The use of Force and Arms.

Writ: A judicial order that is written for a specific act, or giving power to another to have it done.

Writ of Detinue: An order to recover, in specie, the property or chattels from an individual who acquired them lawfully, but retains the property without lawful right.

Writ of Venire: A command to appear in court, or citizens from whom a jury is selected.

Appendix A
Glossary of Legal Terms

Writ of Replevin: An order giving the owner or person entitled the right to repossession of property from someone who has wrongfully taken or detains his property.[3]

[3] Henry Campbell, M.A., ***Black's Law Dictionary***, 6th ed. (St. Paul, Minn.: West Publishing Company, 1990.)

Table of Cases

Civil and Criminal Actions

CASES

Table Of Cases
Civil and Criminal Cases

Table Of Cases
Civil and Criminal Cases

Table Of Cases
Civil and Criminal Cases

Table Of Cases
Civil and Criminal Cases

Table Of Cases
Civil and Criminal Cases

Table Of Cases
Civil and Criminal Cases

Table Of Cases
Civil and Criminal Cases

Index

Index

C

Index

D

E

F

G

Index

I

J

N

O

S

Index

Index

Index

Index

Index

Index

W

Index

Y

ABOUT THE AUTHOR

WILLIAM L. BYRD, III has been involved in genealogical and historical research for more than thirty years. His primary areas of interest are Native Americans, African Americans, West Indians, East Indians and Moors in Virginia, North Carolina, and South Carolina.

He has been published by the *North Carolina Genealogical Society Journal*, the *Magazine of Virginia Genealogy*, *The Rowan County Register*, and *The South Carolina Magazine of Ancestral Research.* He has also co-authored articles with Sheila Stover in the *North Carolina Genealogical Society Journal*, *The Augustan Society Omnibus*, the *Pan-American Indian Association News*, and the *Eagle: New England's American Indian Journal.* He has received an "Award of Special Recognition" from The North Carolina Society of Historians in the category of "The History Article Award" for preserving North Carolina history.

He is a U.S. Army Veteran from the Vietnam era, and served with the U.S. Armed Forces Overseas. He is currently retired, and resides with his family in Hickory, North Carolina.

Other Heritage Books by William L. Byrd, III:

Against the Peace and Dignity of the State: North Carolina Laws Regarding Slaves, Free Persons of Color, and Indians

Bladen County, North Carolina Tax Lists: 1768 through 1774, Volume I

Bladen County, North Carolina Tax Lists: 1775 through 1789, Volume II

For So Long as the Sun and Moon Endure: Indian Records from the North Carolina General Assembly Sessions, & Other Sources

In Full Force and Virtue: North Carolina Emancipation Records, 1713-1860

North Carolina General Assembly Sessions Records: Slaves and Free Persons of Color, 1709-1789

North Carolina Slaves and Free Persons of Color: Chowan County, Volume One

North Carolina Slaves and Free Persons of Color: Chowan County, Volume Two

North Carolina Slaves and Free Persons of Color: Pasquotank County

North Carolina Slaves and Free Persons of Color: Perquimans County

Villainy Often Goes Unpunished: Indian Records from the North Carolina General Assembly Sessions, 1675-1789

Other Heritage Books by William L. Byrd, III and John H. Smith:

North Carolina Slaves and Free Persons of Color: Burke, Lincoln, and Rowan Counties

North Carolina Slaves and Free Persons of Color: Hyde and Beaufort Counties

North Carolina Slaves and Free Persons of Color: Iredell County

North Carolina Slaves and Free Persons of Color: Mecklenburg, Gaston, and Union Counties

North Carolina Slaves and Free Persons of Color: McDowell County

North Carolina Slaves and Free Persons of Color: Stokes and Yadkin Counties

www.ingramcontent.com/pod-product-compliance
Lightning Source LLC
LaVergne TN
LVHW011104300926
849160LV00008B/272
* 9 7 8 0 7 8 8 4 3 2 8 4 2 *